MODERN HISTORY OF JAMMU AND KASHMIR

CONCEPTS IN COMMUNICATION
INFORMATICS & LIBRARIANSHIP
(CICIL)

For a list of titles in this series,
see pp. 808 at the end of the book

About the Authors

J.C. Aggarwal (*b.* 1928), fromer Deputy Director of Education/Executive Director of Delhi Bureau of Textbooks, Delhi Administration has had a varied experience in the field of education. He had singly/jointly authored about 150 books on Education, Social Sciences and Current Problems. In collaboration with S.P. Agrawal, he had written *Modern History of Punjab, Documentation Encyclopaedia of UNESCO and Education* (in two Parts); *Women's Education in India; National Policy on Education: Agenda for India 2001; Indian Writings on Education, 1979 to 1986,* and *Vocational Education in India.* His other recent publications include: *Yearbook of Indian Education, 1991: World Overview; Ramamurti Report 1990 on National Policy on Education in India;* and *Survey of Educational Documents in the World since 1983,* etc.

S.P. Agrawal (*b.* 1929) was Director, National Social Science Documentation Centre, ICSSR, Government of India and thereafter Member Secretary, Indian Association of Social Science Institutions. He was also the Vice-Chairman of the Asia and Pacific Information Network in Social Sciences (APINESS). In 1988 he was awarded the degree of Doctor of Philosophy in Education (*Honoris Causa)* by International University Foundation. Presently, he is Member, Round Table on Research in Reading, IFLA, and Member, International Committee for Social Science Information and Documentation. He is also Member of Board of Studies of National Archives of India and Hindi Advisory Committee, Ministry of Coal, Government of India. Born and brought up in the cradle of freedom movement which he joined at the tender age of twelve, he gained an insight into political problems and developed a sense of responsibility which bore fruit as an information scientist committed to Gandhiji's philosophy and action-plan in the field and its social concept. He has written extensively on various aspects of education, Indian polity and library and information science.

Concepts in Communication
Informatics & Librarianship—64

General Editor : **S.P. Agrawal**

MODERN HISTORY OF JAMMU AND KASHMIR

A look back into ancient glorious Kashmir
focusing confrontation and failures leading to present
turbulent Kashmir and a peep ahead.

(Including Select Documents and Comprehensive Reference Bibliography covering all aspects of Jammu and Kashmir, 1844-1994)

Volume II
1975 Kashmir Accord to 1994
Appendices and Comprehensive Reference Bibliography

J.C. AGGARWAL
former Executive Director
Delhi Bureau of Textbooks, Delhi Administration

S.P. AGRAWAL
former Member Secretary
Indian Association of Social Science Institutions, New Delhi

Specific contribution on 'Sources of the History of Kashmir',
by **Dr (Mrs) Madhvi Yasin**

CONCEPT PUBLISHING COMPANY, NEW DELHI - 110059

ISBN 81-7022-556-6 (Set)
ISBN 81-7022-558-2 (Volume II)

First Published 1995

J.C. **Aggarwal** (*b.* 1928)
S.P. **Agrawal** (*b.* 1929)

Published and Printed by
Ashok Kumar Mittal
Concept Publishing Company
A/15-16, Commercial Block, Mohan Garden
NEW DELHI-110059 (India)

CONTENTS

VOLUME I

Appendices

Volume II
1975 Kashmir Accord to 1994
Appendices & Comprehensive References Bibliography

17

Kashmir Accord between Smt. Indira Gandhi, Prime Minister of India and Sheikh Abdullah, February 1975

(Agreed conclusions which led to Sheikh Mohammad Abdullah's accord with Mrs. Indira Gandhi, Prime Minister, and his subsequent assumption of office as Chief Minister in February 1975)

1. The State of Jammu and Kashmir which is a constituent unit of the Union of India, shall, in its relation with the Union, continue to be governed by Article 370 of the Constitution of India.

2. The residuary powers of legislation shall remain with the State; however, Parliament will continue to have power to make laws relating to the prevention of activities directed towards disclaiming, questioning or disrupting the sovereignty and territorial integrity of India or bringing about cession of a part of the territory of India or cession of a part of the territory of India from the Union or causing insult to the Indian National Flag, the Indian national Anthem and the Constitution.

3. Where any provision of the Constitution of India had been applied to the State of Jammu and Kashmir with adaptations and modifications, such adaptations and modifications can be altered or repealed by an order of the President under Article 370, each individual proposal in this behalf being considered on its merits; but provisions of the Constitution of India already applied to the State of Jammu and Kashmir without adaptation or modification are unalterable.

4. With a view to assuring freedom to the State of Jammu and Kashmir to have its own legislation on matters like welfare measures,

cultural matters, social security, personal law and procedural laws, in a manner suited to the special conditions in the State, it is agreed that the State Government can review the laws made by Parliament or extended to the State after 1953 on any matter relatable to the Concurrent List and may decide which of them, in its opinion, needs amendment or repeal. Thereafter, appropriate steps may be taken under Article 254 of the Constitution of India. The grant of President's assent to such legislation would be sympathetically considered. The same approach would be adopted in regard to laws to be made by Parliament in future under the Proviso to clause 2 of the Article. The State Government shall be consulted regarding the application of any such law to the State and the views of the State Government shall receive the fullest consideration.

5. As an arrangement reciprocal to what has been provided under Article 368, a suitable modification of that Article as applied to the State should be made by Presidential order to the effect that no law made by the legislature of the State of Jammu and Kashmir, seeking to make any change in or in the effect of any provision of Constitution of the State of Jammu and Kashmir relating to any of the under-mentioned matters, shall take effect unless the Bill, having been reserved for the consideration of the President, receives his assent; the matters are –

(a) the appointments, powers, functions, duties, privileges and immunities of the Governor; and
(b) the following matters relating to Elections namely, the superintendence, direction and control of Elections by the Election Commission of India, eligibility for inclusion in the electoral rolls without discrimination, adult suffrage and composition of the Legislative Council, being matters specified in Sections 138, 139, 140 and 50 of the Constitution of the State of Jammu and Kashmir.

6. No agreement was possible on the question of nomenclature of the Governor and the Chief Minister and the matter is therefore remitted to the Principals.

Mirza Mohammad Afzal Beg

G. Parthasarathi

New Delhi, November 13, 1974

18

Jammu and Kashmir Issue in Election Manifestoes of Indian Political Parties, 1989 and 1991

18.1. Bharatiya Janata Party (BJP)

1989 Manifesto

The BJP will delete the temporary Article 370 of the Constitution of India and scrap the 59th Amendment of the Constitution.

The BJP views with concern the recent developments in the State of Jammu and Kashmir and the continued discrimination against the people of Jammu. The rabid communal and pro-Pakistan elements are spearheading a massive hate-India campaign in Kashmir valley and the entire region is engulfed by widespread terrorism. The unabated infiltration and smuggling all along the western border needs to be effectively curbed. The BJP suggests that:

1. Effective and immediate measures to weed out the foreigners from Jammu and Kashmir, Rajasthan and Gujarat to be taken.

2. Border with Pakistan should be effectively guarded by creating a security belt to stop infiltration of trained terrorists and smuggling of arms and ammunitions, narcotics and other contraband commodities, and

3. A regional council for Jammu to be formed so that regional imbalances in development be removed.

1991 Manifesto

1. Weed out Pakistan elements from the valley.
2. Hold free and fair elections in the State as soon as conditions stabilise there.
3. Have separate Regional Development Council for Jammu and Ladakhi.
4. Make relief and rehabilitation facilities available to Kashmir refugees, settling them particularly in the hills of Pir Panjal Range.
5. End all uncertainty about the future status of the State by deleting Article 370 of the Constitution.

18.2. Communist Party of India (CPI)

1989 Manifesto

The situation in Kashmir is getting increasingly serious. The pro-Pak elements and secessionists are on the rampage. Over the years the Congress rulers have been complicating the Kashmir situation. The communal elements in the country like the BJP have added fuel to the fire by launching attacks on Article 370.

The Congress rulers have always wanted yesmen to rule Kashmir. Installation of G.M. Shah after dismissing the elected Government of Dr. Farooq Abdullah in 1984 is one such example.

The electoral process in the State has almost always been eroded through rigging, undermining the confidence of the people in elections and hurting the Kashmir sentiment. The pro-Pak elements have taken advantage of it and misled the young generation. There is need to look at the problem with sympathy and to make a determined effort to wean away the Kashmiri youth. A series of measures—political, administrative and economic—will have to be taken.

1991 Manifesto

Immediate multi-pronged political initiatives at all levels—economic, administrative, psychological, political and mass levels—to solve the Punjab, Jammu and Kashmir and Assam problems.

18.3. Communist Party of India-(Marxist) (CPI-M)

1989 Manifesto

No mention of Kashmir Problem

1991 Manifesto

Immediate solution of Punjab, Kashmir and Assam problems by conceding the genuine demands of the people of these States for protection of their identity within the framework of Indian unity.

18.4. Indian National Congress (Cong-I)

1989 Manifesto

No mention of Kashmir Problem

1991 Manifesto

The Congress will turn to the people of Jammu and Kashmir to seek their cooperation and participation in the search for solutions to the problems in that troubled State. To this end people's committees will be constituted at different levels and will function till such time as the State Assembly is constituted through free and fair elections. Stern action will be taken against secessionist forces. Our borders with Pakistan and along the line of control in Jammu & Kashmir will be sealed. Special attention will be paid to facilitating and augmenting employment for the unemployed youth of Jammu and Kashmir, both in the State and in other parts of the country.

18.5. Janata Dal-Socialist (JD-S)

1991 Manifesto

We emphasize the value of dialogue, mutual understanding and other persuasive methods in resolving social conflicts. It is hoped that the unrest in Punjab, Assam and Jammu and Kashmir will be resolved amicably in the near future.

18.6. National Front (NF)

1989 Manifesto

No mention of Kashmir Problem

1991 Manifesto

The National Front is convinced that the ultimate solution for violent militancy in parts of the country is restoration of faith in democratic political process within the federal Constitution. The National Front would want the agony of Punjab and Jammu and Kashmir to end.

The National Front reiterates its commitment for preserving the sanctity of Article 370 in consonance with its approach to problem of national unit.

The National Front is committed to economic development of Punjab and Jammu and Kashmir and to finding early solution for the problem of unemployment in these states along with the rest of the country.

19

Jammu and Kashmir Governor Jagmohan's Proclamations and Letters to Government of India 1989 to 1991 (Including other Communications)

19.1. Letter to Prime Minister Rajiv Gandhi, April 8, 1989

Dear Prime Minister,

The situation is fast deteriorating. It has almost reached a point of no return. For the last five days, there have been large-scale violence, arson, firing, hartals, casualties and what not. Things have truly fallen apart. Talking of the irsih crisis, British Prime Minister Disraeli had said: 'It is potatoes one day and the Pope next.' Similar is the present position in Kashmir. Yesterday it was 'Maqbool Butt"; today it is *Satanic Verses;* tomorrow it will be 'repression day' and the day after it will be something else. The Chief Minister stands isolated. He has already fallen – politically as well as administratively; perhaps, only constitutional rites remain to be performed. His clutches are too soiled and rickety to support him. Personal aberrations have also eroded his public standing. The situation calls for effective intervention. Today may be timely, tomorrow may be too late.

Yours sincerely

(Sd.)

Jagmohan

19.2. Letter to Prime Minister Rajiv Gandhi, May 14, 1989

Dear Prime Minister,

From May 8 to 13, there have been 14 bomb blasts and six cases of firing and cross-firing. Four persons died and about 20 were injured. A tourist bus proceeding from Gulmarg to Srinagar was fired upon, and four tourists were injured. The current administrative and political structure has once again proved unequal to the task. During the *hartal* period, no worthwhile activity has been visible at the political front to counter the move of the subversionists. What is still more worrying is that every 'victory' of the subversionists is swelling their ranks, and the animosity is being diverted against the Central authorities. I have indicated my anxiety to the Chief Minister.

Your sincerely,
(Sd,)
Jagmohan

19.3. Governor's Rule : Proclamation*, January 19, 1990

P-1/90 of 1990: Whereas I, Jagmohan, Governor of the State of Jammu and Kashmir, am satisfied that a situation has arisen in which the Government of the State cannot be carried on in accordance with the provisions of the Constitution of Jammu and Kashmir (hereinafter referred to as the State Constitution);

Now, therefore, in exercise of the powers conferred by Section 92 of the State Constitution and of all other powers enabling me in that behalf, and with the concurrence of the President of India, I hareby proclaim that I –

(a) assume to myself all the functions of the Government of the State and all powers vested in or exercisable by any body or authority (other than the powers vested in or exercisable by the High Court) in the State; and

(b) make the following incidental and consequential provisions which appear to me to be necessary or desirable for giving effect to the objects of this Proclamation, namely,

* The Proclamation was issued under Section 92 of the Jammu and Kashmir Constitution.

(i) the operation of the following provisions of the State Constitution is hereby suspended, namely, Sections 35 to 41 (both inclusive), so much of Section 43 as relates to the allocation among the ministers of the business of the Government of the State, Section 44, so much of Section 53 as relates to the stipulation of a maximum interventing period of six months between the last sitting in one session of the legislature and the date appointed for its first sitting in the next session, Sections 51 to 57 (both inclusive), clauses (b) and (c) of Section 58 and the first proviso thereto, Sections 59 and 60, sub-section (2) of Section 61 so far as it relates to clause (c) of and the first proviso to Section 58 and to Section, 60, Sections 65, 66, 67, 71 and 72, 74, 75 and 76, sub-sections (3), (4) and (5) of Section 79, Sections 80, 81 and 82, sub-section (2) of Section 83, Section 84 to 88 (both inclusive) and so much of Section 187 as relates to the laying of the report with a memorandum before the Legislature of the State;

(ii) in the exercise of the powers of the Legislature to make laws under or by virtue of this Proclamation, I shall prepare such bills as I deem necessary and declare in respect of any bill so prepared that I assent thereto;

(iii) in the exercise of the powers of the Legislative Assembly to make grants under sub-section (1) of Section 83 of the State Constitution, I shall, as often as I may deem it necessary and pending due appropriation of law,

(a) make, by notification in the official Gazette, grants in advance in respect of the estimated expenditure or grants in respect of supplementary or additional expenditure for the period during which this Proclamation may be or is in force,

(b) make, by notification in the official Gazette, grants for meeting any expected demands, and

(c) make, by notification in the official Gazette, exceptional grants which form no part of the current service of the financial year, and

(iv) any reference in the State Constitution to Acts or Laws of or made by the Legislature of the State shall be construed as including a reference to Acts or Laws made in exercise of the powers of the Legislature of the State by me under this Proclamation and the Jammu and Kashmir General Clauses Act, 1977, as in force in the State shall have effect in relation to any such Act or Law as if it were an Act of the Legislature of the State.

(Sd.)
Jagmohan,
Governor, Jammu & Kashmir

Place: Jammu
January 19, 1990

19.3.1. Section 92 of the Jammu and Kashmir Constitution

92 *Provisions in case of failure of constitutional machinery in the State*: (1) If at any time the Governor is satisfied that a situation has arisen in which the Government of State cannot be carried on in accordance with the provisions of this Constitution, the Governor may by Proclamation—

(a) assume to himself all or any of the functions of the Government of the State and all or any of the powers vested in or exercisable by any body or authority in the State;
(b) make such incidental and consequential provisions as appear to the Governor to be necessary or desirable for giving effect to the objects of the Proclamation, including provisions for suspending in whole or in part the operation of any provision of this Constitution relating to any body or authority in the State;

Provided that nothing in this section shall authorise the Governor to assume to himself any of the powers vested in or exercisable by the High Court or to suspend in whole or in part of the operation of any provision of this Constitution relating to the High Court.

(2) Any such Proclamation may be revoked or varied by a subsequent Proclamation.

(3) Any such Proclamation whether varied under sub-Section (2)

or not, shall, except where it is a Proclamation revoking a previous Proclamation, cease to operate on the expiration of six months from the date of which it was first issued.

(4) If the Governor by a Proclamation under this section assumes to himself any of the powers of the Legislature to make laws, any law made by him in the exercise of that power shall, subject to the terms thereof, continue to have effect until two years have elapsed from the date on which the Proclamation ceases to have effect, unless sooner repealed or re-enacted by an Act of the Legislature, and any reference in this Constitution to any Acts of or laws made by the Legislature shall be construed as including a reference to such law.

(5) No Proclamation under sub-section (1) shall be issued except with the concurrence of the President of India.

(6) Every Proclamation under this section shall, except where it is a Proclamation revoking a previous Proclamation, be laid before each House of the Legislature as soon as it is convenced."

19.4. Dissolution of the Assembly: Proclamation, February 19, 1990

In exercise of the powers conferred upon me by Clause (b) of Sub-section (2) of Section 53 of the Constitution of Jammu and Kashmir, I hereby dissolve the Legislative Assembly.

(Sd.)
Jagmohan

19.4.1 Sub-Section(2) of Section 53 of J & K Constitution

Sub-section (2) of Section 53 reads as under:
"The Governor may from time to time –
(a) prorogue the Houses or either House,
(b) dissolve the Legislative Assembly."

19.5. Letter* to the President of India, January 30, 1990

Respected Rashtrapatiji,

It is exactly 10 days ago that I took over. I could not snatch even

* Copy to the Prime Minister, the Home Minister and the Vice President.

a single minute to write even a brief report. The situation was so grim and critical.

Due to total inaction, unbelievable incompetence, widespread corruption and passive connivance, the administrative machinery and all other levels of power structure had been taken over by the subversionists and their collaborators. Majority of the officials are active or passive supporters of these elements. The remaining are mortally afraid.

Unfortunately, in our country, the people go over to the winning side. Since subversionists have been scoring one victory after another in the last six months or so, the public has gone over to their side. Listed terrorists are openly harboured, given money, food and vehicles. Quite a number of officers even salute them. Senior officers turn their face the other way. Jailors and doctors help detenus in escaping. Some of the pistols issued to the political workers are being used for the commission of the crimes. When I took over, Kashmir stood almost on the point of no return.

It was, indeed, a miracle – may be providential – that Kashmir was saved on January 26, and the nation spared of acute national and international embarrassment. The story of this day is a long one and need to be told in depth at a later stage.

Using my past contacts with the officers and the people, I am re-asserting the authority of the State. Some of the branches of power structure have started leaning towards me. But my mission in this respect has been seriously undermined by the impression that is being created by Dr. Farooq Abdullah that he is returning to power. Neither bureaucracy nor other organs of the State polity would cooperate with me if such an impression persists.

I think the gravity of the situation in Kashmir has not dawned upon the nation. The fundamental issue today is whether the nation wants to keep Kashmir or hand it over to Pakistan or accept an independent theocratic State. I would beg of you to send our critics to Kashmir. Reality may dawn upon them. They may find that they were unwittingly playing an unpatriotic role. It would be a grave tragedy to hand over power at this stage to those very elements who have brought the State to the brink of disaster.

I have invited eminent journalists of the country to see things for themselves. They include Nikhil Chakravarty, Arun Shourie, Inder Malhotra, R.K. Mishra, Kuldip Nayar, Pran Chopra, H.K. Dua, etc.

I have accepted the assignment solely with the motivation of lending a helping hand in overcoming a national crisis. I have exposed myself and my family to grave personal risk. I am not even drawing any pay. My approach has been spelt out in my policy statement which I made immediately after I took over.

I have done my bit in regard to the events of January 26 and I am proud of it. But it may be difficult for me to continue if the current impression persists and I am not fully supported in public. I have already a broken and shattered Administration at my disposal. If the Commander, too, is everyday sniped at, the chances of success could well be imagined.

In my view, the way to solving the Kashmir crisis is:

(i) Assert vigorously the authority of the State and create an impression in the public that, no matter what the cost be, the subversionists and their collaborators would be firmly dealt with and eliminated;
(ii) Create solid, sound and healthy institutional framework;
(iii) Adopt an absolutely just and fair approach to people in regard to day-to-day administration and speedily redress the backlog of grievances;
(iv) Reorient the development pattern in the State to stop big wastage; and
(v) implement vigorously economic packages such as recruitment of 7,000 BSF personnel and 3,000 teachers, etc.;
(vi) Dissolve the State Assembly immediately and hold elections after six months or so. By that time some of the subversive elements would be eliminated and some would prefer to participate in the elections. And various groups would balance each other out. A new leadership may; emerge which, besides looking to the Union, would enjoy real support of the people, particularly the youth, and would not be so corrupt and callous as the previous State Government.

It would be wrong, if not suicidal, to resort to short cuts or temporary solutions. Infection has gone deep into the vital organs. Unless this infection is first exterminated, we would stumble from one critical situation to another.

Yours sincerely,
Sd/-
Jagmohan

19.6. Letter* to the Home Minister, Government of India Mufti Mohammad Sayeed, February 20, 1990

Dear Home Minister

I am writing to you with reference to our telephonic talk regarding my decision to dissolve the State Assembly. I do not think there is anything to be unhappy about. In this connection, I wish to make the following points clear:

(i) The Jammu and Kashmir Constitution empowers the Governor, and no one else, to dissolve the State Assembly;
(ii) Under the Constitution, the Governor is required to act in his own good conscience and exercise his judgement and take the decision independently;
(iii) Without dissolution, there was no moral legitimacy for the use of force on an extensive scale. Nor was it possible for me and the Advisers to secure the obedience of our orders from the local officials who were constantly being fed with the impression that Dr. Farooq Abdullah and his colleagues were coming back after the role of 'butcher' has been played by the Governor;
(iv) The statements issued by Dr. Farooq Abdullah, asking for inquiry at the international level and comparing Kashmir with a Nazi camp, were inciting the people to create more and more violence. A verbatim copy in Urdu (with English translation) of one such statement issued by him is enclosed. A note setting out that implications of this statement is also enclosed; and
(v) As far back as January 30, I had clearly indicated my views in regard to the dissolution. If there were any reservations in this regard, I could have been clearly told so beforehand.

The other points in regard to the justification of my decision are contained in the press note on the subject. A copy of the said press note is enclosed.

I have no doubt that my decision is administratively, morally and constitutionally correct and would considerably help in removing

---

*Copy to the Secretary to the President.

misgivings of the people and restoring peace and normalcy in the State. Some relaxation of tension in the atmosphere is visible even today. The Constitution, to the faithful allegiance of which I have taken oath, precludes me from taking into consideration any extraneous factor.

Shri Mufti Mohammad Sayeed
Home Minister
Government of India
New Delhi

Yours sincerely
Sd.
Jagmohan

19.7. Open Letter to the Kashmiris, May 26, 1990

Dear Kashmiri brothers and sisters,

I do not know why I feel like writing to you when I am leaving the State. Today, you may not understand my motivation. But one day you would.

You would recall that on the very first day of my arrival for the second term, I advised you to remember that new routes are discovered only from points at which the caravans lose their way. Unfortunately, even before the new pathway could be charted by me, made safe and shown to you as a way to happy future, it was submerged by a flood of intentional falsehood. There were persons at work, who were hell bent to misrepresent the facts and subvert my efforts.

At the oath-taking ceremony itself, I declared that I would function like a surgeon to stitch the bleeding wound and also work as 'nursing orderly' to serve the patient with care and compassion and put him on the way to full recovery. But they made the surgeon look like a butcher and the nursing orderly a heartless sweeper of the blood-splattered floors of a slaughter house.

I appealed to all to remember that one basic principle of all religions was to relieve human pain and to consider service to the needy as service to God. On the day of Id-ul-Fitr, I specially pleaded, 'Let us honour the spirit of this auspicious day and work as saints of service'. They propagated that I was a communalist.

Time and again I warned that we should not ignore the real India – the India of synthesis and assimilation. And yet they called me a Hindu chauvinist.

On the death of a young man, I wrote to his father, Dr. Mohammad Yousaf Khan: "Let no more Shabirs die, and let us create a situation in which no policeman is seen on the streets and they remain full of tourists". They shrieked that I had the outlook of 'Hallaqu' and Hitler.

I dissolved the State Assembly to give everybody a fresh opportunity to secure power through ballot. Instead of acknowledging that this was the fairest and the healthiest initiation of the political process, they went on adumbrating that I was advocating only a law and order approach.

I proceeded in right earnest to analyses the nature and pattern of terrorism and snap its chains and links, and also eliminate its by-products. They were bent upon hiding the maladies and preventing me from treating these maladies from their roots and dealing with the various infections that had invaded the body.

They knew that I had nothing to do with the searches conducted on January 20 or with the firing on the so-called funeral procession of Moulvi Farooq. Yet they went on with their calculated campaign of spreading lies.

You would, sooner or later, understand the machinations of these persons and regret having fallen prey to them.

You see your own history, both recent and distant. In the recent past, who were the custodians of your political destiny? Were they not your own people? It were they who turned out to be fake guides and inadequate leaders in whom the malady of political degeneration made quick inroads. In their search for uninterrupted power and glory and establishment of personal rule in the guise of democracy, they manipulated your minds and never allowed you to adjust to the reality as long as they remained at the helm of affairs. Accession was final and India was a haven of secularism, but as soon as power slipped out of their hands, they brought out green handkerchiefs from their pockets, with the salt of Pakistani brothers wrapped in between, and India became an imperial power out to destroy the identity of Kashmir. They extended their legs to both boats and kept you in the disturbed water in between. As was bound to happen, you got hurt frequently. But that did not matter much to them. They continued with their power game.

How much service did they render to you and how much to themselves? You know the answer. Most of you have read the 'Red

Book' and the 'Black Book'. Was it not one of the dissatisfied youth amongst you who wrote: 'What to speak of others, it is our own people who are treating us like sheep and plucking our wool mercilessly.'

For all the ills of unemployment and deprivation, they found the Central Government a convenient whipping boy. They misused Article 370 to misappropriate the resource-base of the State and built a self-serving nest of power. They got more than average share of the Union funds. But they misapplied them. Did you not notice that in 1986, with the same scale of funds, roads were laid, lakes and streams cleaned, cities made beautiful, environment improved and rural development works executed with such speed and effectiveness that the State's rating in this regard jumped from the 25th position to the tenth? I request you to consider dispassionately who is your real well-wisher and who is not.

You need to learn from your long history as well. Today some of you are leaning towards Pakistan and inclined to accept its hug. It would turn out to be the bear's hug, I am sure. Remember that in the mid-eighteenth century some of you felt the same way towards Afghanistan and invited Ahmed Shah Abdali. You never had it so bad. Once you place yourself in the fist of Pakistan, you would soon find how strongly it clenches on you. In fifty years or so, your identity would be diluted, if not lost. In the name of Islamic brotherhood, there would be inter-marriages and large-scale settlement in the Valley. The Punjabi-dominated military junta and landed aristocracy which really rule Pakistan would not show any sensitivity or compunctions in this regard. You would find yourself being swept away. But then it would be too late. Even your voices would be stifled.

Remember that the worst form of tyranny is one which is established through the combination of a narrow interpretation of religion and military might. Everything is thrust upon the people in the name of God. That is what the mediaeval monks did. And this is what cliques in Pakistan are doing.

And where is the viability for an independent entity? Hard facts of geography, history, defence and resources are against it. What to speak of any future development expenditure, the government would not be able to pay salaries to about hall of its existing staff. Would Pakistan leave you alone? And would not dreams soon turn into nightmares?

You are obsessed with the notion of identity without fully understanding what it really means. Do you realise that, at the moment, your identity is collapsing? The cancerous culture of the Kalashnikov is eating into its vitals. No trace of it would be left, unless remedial measures are taken straightway.

Some of you, with incitement from across the border, are trapping the youth by weaving a myth of immortality or presenting a vision of a grand future. There is no such immortality. How can anything good come out of a perverse philosophy of crime? A person is dubbed as a police informer or his style of life is labelled as un-Islami and he is slaughtered. Who decides the issue? It is the accuser himself. I know of a case of a poor young girl who was shot dead for allegedly leading what was called a un-Islamic way of life. The accuser pronounced the judgement. The poor father was made to say in public that the allegations against her were true. What else could he do, unless he himself wanted to meet the same fate as that of his daughter? How many such crimes would you allow to be committed?

When the current phase of fury and frenzy has boiled over, you would find yourself having been tricked. If you think calmly and in depth, you would understand the parameters of the hoax to which you are being subjected. You would realise that you have been imagining an enemy that does not exist, and you have been made to run towards mirages where *kafirs* are supposedly hatching conspiracies against you.

The hour of tiredness would arrive. But by that time the self-inflicted torture would have taken its toll. Exhaustion would linger on; it might even debilitate you.

It is not the artificial affinity brought through a narrow interpretation of religion, but an enlightened polity and inspired spirituality that would provide real scope for amelioration and herald an era of true freedom and true progress. The soiled pages of our past history point to the urgent need for a reformed and rejuvenated Kashmir prospering within a reformed and rejuvenated India. If this does not come about, both will sink into third rate existence.

Against the prejudices of time and malignancy of the past, I tried to create a just situation wherein all of you would have a fair opportunity to evolve new leadership or choose the old one after chastening it, and work for a new pattern of development and a humane and balanced order based upon spiritual secularism – real secularism which derives ethical values from the fundamentals of all religions, fundamentals about which Nud Rishi and Lal Ded had spoken in these words; 'There is one God with a hundred names; there is not a single blade of grass which does not worship Him.'

But the times were 'out of joints'. The poisonous darts of a soulless Indian polity repeatedly attacked me. Wounded and bleeding, I am leaving the State. This may be a minor crime of the forces of disruption and distortion. But what is unpardonable is their crime of prolonging the collective agony of the people – the agony which I was confident of ending within a couple of months.

In this letter, I cannot pen all that has happened, is happening, and might happen in future. One day, I would write all about it. You may read and judge the truth.

Wishing you early peace and recovery from the cure malady,

Yours sincerely
Sd/-
Jagmohan

19.8. Open Letter to Rajiv Gandhi, Former Prime Minister of India, April 21, 1991

Dear Shri Rajiv Gandhi

... For, all along, I have persistently tried to keep myself away from party politics and to use whatever little talent and energy I might have to do some creative and constructive work, as was done recently in regard to the management and improvement of the Mata Vaishno Devi shrine complex and to help in bringing about a sort of culture – a renaissance without which our fast decaying institutions cannot be nursed back to health. At the moment, the nobler purposes of these institutions, be they in the sphere of executive, legislature or judiciary, etc., have been sapped and the soul of justice and truth sucked out of them by the politics of expediency.

. . .

Warning Signals

. . .from the beginning of 1988, I had started sending 'Warning

Signals' to you about the gathering storm in Kashmir? ...

To recapitulate and to serve as illustrations, I would refer to a few of these signals. In August 1988, after analysing the currents and undercurrents, I had summed up the position thus: "The drum-beaters of parochialism and fundamentalism are working overtime. Subversion is on the increase. The shadows of events from across the border are lengthening. Lethal weapons have come in. More may be on the way." In April 1989, I had desperately pleaded for immediate action. I said: "The situation is fast deteriorating. It has almost reached a point of no return. For the last five days, there have been large-scale violence, arson, firing, hartals , casualties and what not. Things have truly fallen apart. Talking of the Irish crisis, British Prime Minister Disraeli had said: 'It is potatoes one day and Pope the next.' Similar is the present position in Kashmir. Yesterday, it was Maqbool Butt; today it is *Satanic Verses*; tomorrow it will be repression day and the day after it will be something else. The Chief Minister stands isolated. He has already fallen – politically as well as administratively; perhaps, only constitutional rites remain to be performed. His clutches are too soiled and rickety to support him. Personal aberrations have also eroded his public standing. The situation calls for effective intervention. Today may be timely, tomorrow may be too late.' Again, in May, I expressed my growing anxiety: "What is still more worrying is that every *victory* of subversionists is swelling their ranks and the animosity is being diverted against the Central authorities."...

... If you had any serious reservation about my accepting the offer of J & K governorship for the second term, you could have adopted the straightforward course and apprised me of your views. I would have thought twice before going into a situation which had virtually reached a point of no return ...

...

Reality

... before the imposition of Governor's Rule on January 19, 1990, there was a total mental surrender. Even prior to the day (December 8, 1989) of Dr. Rubaiya Sayeed's kidnapping, when the eagle of terrorism swooped on the State with full fury, 1,600 violent incidents, including 351 bomb blasts, had taken place in eleven months. Then, between January 1 and January 19, 1990, there were as many as 319 violent acts—21 armed attacks, 114 bomb blasts, 112 arsons, and 72 incidents of mob violence.

. . . all the components of the power structure had been virtually taken over by the subversives. For example, when Shabir Ahmed Shah was arrested in September 1989 on the Intelligence Bureau's tip-off, Srinagar Deputy Commissioner flatly refused to sign the warrant of detention. Anantnag Deputy Commissioner adopted the same attitude. The Advocate-General did not appear before the Court to represent the State case. He tried to pass on the responsibility to the Additional Advocate General and the Government Counsel. They, too, did not appear.

. . . what happened on the day of Lok Sabha poll on November 22, 1989? In a tantalising gesture TV sets were placed near some of the polling booths with placards reading: 'anyone who will cast his vote can take this as a gift'. Near some other booths, coffins were placed with a cryptic note: 'anyone who will cast his vote will get this'. No one in the Administration of Dr. Farooq Abdullah took any step to remove such symbols of defiance of authority.

. . . Sopore is the hometown of Ghulam Rasool Kar, who was at that time a Cabinet Minister in the State Government. It is also the hometown of the Chairman of the Legislative Council, Habibulla, and also of the former National Conference MP and Cabinet Minister, Abdul Ahad Vakil. Yet only five votes were cast in Sopore town. In Pattan, an area supposedly under the influence of Iftikhar Hussain Ansari, the then Congress(I) Minister, not a single vote was cast...

And you still thought that subversion and terrorism could be fought with such political and administrative instruments.

Around that point of time, when the police set-up was getting rapidly demoralised, when intelligence was fast drying up, when infiltration in services was becoming deeper and deeper, when the press was bringing stories of subversive plans like TOPAC,. . . Dr. Farooq Abdullah, was either going abroad or releasing 70 hard-core and highly motivated terrorists who were trained in the handling of dangerous weapons, who had contacts at the highest level in Pakistan-occupied Kashmir, who knew all the devious routes of going to and returning from Pakistan and whose detecting had been approved by the three-member Advisory Board presided over by the Chief Justice. Their simultaneous release enabled them to occupy key positions in the network of subversion and terrorism and to complete the chain which took them again to Pakistan to bring arms to indulge in killings and kidnappings and other acts of terrorism. For example, one of the released persons, Mohammad Daud Khan of Ganderbal, became the Deputy Commander-in-Chief of a terrorist outfit, Al Bakar, and took a leading part in organising a force of 2,500 Kashmiri youth. Who is to be blamed for all the heinous crimes subsequently committed by these released 70 terrorists? I would leave this question to be answered by the people...

The truth, supported by preponderance of evidence, is that before January 19, 1990, the terrorist had become the real ruler. The ground had been yielded to him to such an extent that he dominated the public mind. He could virtually swim like a fish in the sea. Would it matter if the sea was subsequently surrounded?

...

... in the Rajya Sabha on May 25, 1990

Referring to the so-called interview to the Bombay weekly, *The Current*—an interview which I never gave—Salve* chose wholly unjustified expressions: "There was a patent and, palpable attitude of a very disconcerting communal bias and therefore, he (Governor) was happy under the garb of eliminating the terrorists, the saboteurs and the culprits, in eliminating the whole community as it were; now the Governor has himself given profuse and unabashed vent to his malicious malignity, hate and extreme dislike, branding every number of a particular community as a militant."

I know Salve. I do not think, if left to himself, he would have done what he did. Clearly, he was goaded to say something which was against his training and background. But the elementary precaution which any jurist, at least a jurist of Salve's eminence, would have taken, was to first check up whether any such interview to the *Current Weekly* had been given by me, and, if so, whether the remarks attributed to me were actually made. The unseemly haste was itself revealing. The issue was raised on May 25, while the weekly was dated May 26-June 2, 1990...

... I was left with no other option but to file a Rs.20 lakh damages suit against the *Current Weekly* in the Delhi High Court. The case may take a long time and I may donate the damages, if and

---

* N.K.P. Salve M.P.

when awarded, to charity, but I intend sparing no effort to expose all those who have played dirty roles in the disinformation-drama.

Article 370

. . .

What I had really pointed out in August-September 1986 was: 'Article 370 is nothing but a breeding ground for the parasites at the heart of the paradise. It skins the poor. It deceives them with its mirage. It lines the pockets of the "power elites". It fans the ego of the new sultans. In essence, it creates a land without justice, a land full of crudities and contradictions. It props up politics of deception, duplicity and demagogy. It breeds the microbes of subversion. It keeps alive the unwholesome legacy of the two-nation theory. It suffocates the very idea of India and fogs the very vision of a great social and cultural crucible from Kashmir to Kanyakumari. It could be an epicenter of a violent earthquake in the Valley—an earth quake, the tremors of which would be felt all over the country with unforeseen consequences.'

I had argued, 'The fundamental aspect which has been lost sight of in the controversy for deletion or retention of Article 370 is its misuse. Over the years, it has become an instrument of exploitation in the hands of the ruling political elites and other vested interests in bureaucracy, business, judiciary and bar. Apart from the politicians, the richer classes have found convenient to amass wealth and not allow healthy financial legislation to come to the State. The provisions of the Wealth Tax, the Urban Land Ceiling Act, the Gift Tax, etc., and other beneficial laws of the Union have not been allowed to be operated in the State under the cover of Article 370. The common people are prevented from realising that Article 370 is actually keeping them impoverished and denying them justice and also their due share in the economic advancement.'

My stand was that the poor people of Kashmir had been exploited under the protective wall of Article 370 and that the correct position needed to be explained to them. I had made a number of suggestions in this regard and also in regard to the reform and reorganisation of the institutional framework . . .

Subsequent events have reinforced my view that Article 370 and its by-product, the separate Constitution of Jammu and Kashmir must go, not only because it is legally and conditionally feasible to do so, but also because larger and more basic considerations of our past history and contemporary require it. The Article merely facilitates the growth and continuation of corrupt oligarchies. It puts false notions in the minds of the youth. It gives rise to regional tensions and conflicts, and even the autonomy assumed to be available is not attainable in practice. The distinct personality and cultural density of Kashmir can be safeguarded without this Article. It is socially regressive and causes situations in which women lose their right if they marry non-State subjects and persons staying for over forty-four years in the State are denied elementary human and democratic rights. And, above all, it does not fit into the reality and requirement of India and its vast and varied span. What India needs today is not petty sovereignties that would sap its spirit and aspirations and turn it into small 'banana-republics' in the hands of 'tin-pot dictators' but a new social, political and cultural crucible in which values of truth and rectitude, of fairness and justice, and of compassion and catholicity, are melted, purified and moulded into a vigorous and vibrant set-up which provides real freedom, real democracy, and real resurgence to all.

I must also point out that when other States in the Union ask for greater autonomy, they do not mean separation of identities. They really want decentralisation and devolution of power, so that administrative and developmental work is done speedily and the quality of service to the people improves. In Kashmir, the demand for retaining Article 370 with all its 'pristine purity', that is, without the alleged dilution that has taken place since 1953, stems from a different motivation. It emanates from a clever strategy to remain away from the mainstream, to set up a separate fieldom, to fly a separate flag, to have a Prime Minister rather than a Chief Minister, and Sadar-i-Riyasat instead of a Governor, and to secure greater power and patronage, not for the good of the masses, not for serving the cause of peace and progress or for attaining cultural unity amidst diversity, but for serving the interests of the 'new elites' , the 'new sheikhs'.

All those aspiring to be the custodians of the vote-banks continue to say that Article 370 is a matter of faith. But they do not proceed further. They do not ask themselves: what does this faith mean? What is its rationale? Would not bringing the State within the full framework of Indian Constitution give brighter, luster and sharper teeth to this faith and make more just and meaningful?

In a similar strain, expressions like 'historical necessity' and 'autonomy' are talked about. What do these mean in practice? Does historical necessity mean that you include, on paper, Kashmir in the Indian Union by one hand at a huge cost and give it back, in practice, by another hand on the golden platter? And what does autonomy or so-called pre-1953 or pre-1947 position imply? Would it not amount to the Kashmiri leadership saying: 'You will send and I will spend; you will have no say even if I build a corrupt and callous oligarchy and cause a situation in which Damocles' sword of secession could be kept hanging over your head'?

Kashmiri Pandits

. . . Anyone trying to be fair is dubbed communal. The case of the Kashmiri Pandits bears eloquent testimony to this fact.

Whatever be the vicissitudes of the Kashmiri Pandits' history and whatever unkind quirks their fate might have brought to them in the past, these all pale into insignificance in comparison to what is happening to them at present. The grim tragedy is compounded by the equally grim irony that one of the most intelligent, subtle, versatile, and proud community of the country is being virtually reduced to extinction in free India. It is suffering not under the fanatic zeal of mediaeval Sultans like Sikandar or under the tyrannical regime of Afghan Governors, but under the supposedly secular rule of leaders . . . whose unabashed search for personal and political power is symbolised by calculated disregard of the Kashmiri migrants' current misreable plight and the terrible future that stares in their eyes. And to fill their cup of pain and anguish, there are bodies like 'Committee for Initiative on Kashmir' which are over-anxious and over-active to rub salt into their wounds, and to label anyone who wants to stand by them in their hour of distress as communal.

In a soft, superficial, permissive and, in many ways, cruel India which has the tragic distinction of creating over one lakh refugees from its own flesh and blood and then casting them aside like masterless cattle to fend for themselves on the busy and heartless avenues of soulless cities, chances for Kashmiri Pandits to survive as a distinct community are next to nothing. Split, scattered, and deserted practically by all, they stand today all alone, looking hopelessly at a leaking, rudderless boat at their feet and extremely rough and tumultuous sea to face before they can reach a safe shore across to plant their feet firmly on an assured future.

The deep crisis through which the Kashmiri migrant, or for that matter, the entire Kashmir, is passing is really the crisis of Indian values—the perversion, in practice, of its constitutional, political, social and moral norms. If I visited the camps of the refugees and tried to extend the firm hand of justice to a community in pain, if I instructed that, instead of cash doles, the migrant Government servants should be given leave salary, and if I conceded the demand of a widow of the person brutally killed by a terrorist, for allotment of a house on payment, I became communal, a 'known anti-Muslim', about whom concocted stories were planted in the press, If, on the other hand, someone falsely accused the Indian army and the Governor's Administration, if he assailed 'Jagmohan in particular' of giving inducements through provisions of plots and trucks, without giving particulars either of plots or of trucks, his accusations got published all over the press, his reports were flaunted in national and international forums and were copiously quoted in Parliament. . . and he was labelled as secular and progressive and champion of human rights and what not.

Hard Evidence

. . . I must invite attention to some hard evidence about what the people of the Valley actually thought about me before. . . the smear campaign on my appointment for the second term.

Writing in the *Indian Express's* issue of July 30, 1987, under the caption 'The Alliance in Kashmir', Pran Chopra, reputed political commentator, noted:

> "But there is a recent example from which Farooq Abdullah can learn much; despite the same limited resources and the same administration to work with, but through sheer diligence and application, Governor Jagmohan accomplished so much during the recent spell of Governor's rule that everyone I met was full of praise for it. I had not expected to see so much affection shown for Governor's rule in a State so highly politicised as Kashmir is, especially because the present Governor is also thought wrongly, as I now learn, to have been responsible for foisting G.M. Shah's rule on the State. But

diligence and application are not qualities which people have detected much in the Chief Minister yet."

V.N. Narayanan, Editor-in-Chief of the *Tribune*, after touring the Valley for three days in June 1989, wrote three articles titled 'J&K Today'. In the last article Narayan said: "Out of curiosity I put one question to everybody I met in Srinagar, Anantnag and Pahalgam recently: 'Who do you think would give the best government to the State?' It was not a surprise that without exception the answer was: 'The Governor.' 'Any Governor?' 'No, the present Governor – Jagmohan'."

This is the scene as depicted by the noted journalist Kum Kum Chadha at the time of my departure from the State in the second week of July 1989:

> "Tears, emotion, poetry, sentiment, adjectives and smiles marked the farewell of Jagmohan who relinquished charge as Governor of Jammu and Kashmir last week. Perhaps no other Governor has, in recent times, got the kind of tribute from the people as Jagmohan did. For them, he was a 'messiah', an architect, a crusader, a reformer, a revolutionary and a visionary. The nostalgia of Governor's rule still lingers. Even its bitterest critics admit its achievement." . . .

Earlier, on February 27, 1987, Prem Bhatia, in his editorial comments in the same paper, said:

> "In Jammu & Kashmir itself, many of those who opposed the imposition of Governor's rule following the fall of the G.M. Shah Ministry did not take long to praise Jagmohan who showed a rather uncommon responsiveness to the people's problems."

This is what A.N. Dar, Editor of the *National Herald*, observed in his article, 'What is Wrong in Kashmir', of April 15, 1989:

> "It has to be admitted that the last two years in Kashmir have been administratively sterile. The coalition has not been a shining example of purposeful administration. This is sad indeed, more so because it had the example before it of what

the Governor Jagmohan did during Governor's rule. Jagmohan showed that it was possible to win the goodwill of the people through fair-minded, selfless and effective administration. Even the fundamentalists and the anti-nationals accepted that he was fair and efficient."

The widely circulated Urdu daily of Kashmir, *Srinagar Times*, in its issue of July 8, 1988, editorially observed: "What Governor Jagmohan did during the six months of Governor's Rule, to set right the deteriorating conditions in the Valley and improve its environment, would never be forgotten by the people of Kashmir." The same newspaper, in its issue of February 19, 1987, published an editorial—Memory of Governor's Rule is coming to mind* and stated:

"During Governor's Rule the administration became alert and development and construction work got speedily executed. Whatever work was done was done properly and in a neat and clean manner. The important roads like Maulana Azad Road, Dal Gate Road, Boulevard and many other roads which were earlier being repaired and damaged every year, were made with such solid and sound material that in spite of grave winter and continuous snow-fall, the roads remained in excellent shape. Even when heavy bulldozers were put on the road for removing the snow, they remained as strong and smooth as they were before snow-fall and not even a single rubble or stone came out.

The offices functioned in a disciplined manner and everyone attended office in time. The Governor listened to the grievances of the people personally, high or low, rich or poor, man or woman, urban or village folk. He passed some order or the other on every application. He followed up the matters and ensured that his orders were complied forthwith. Now, no one is attending to the grievances of the people and they are seen waiting for days in the Secretariat."**

Nikhil Chakravarty, the noted political analyst, in his Sunday

* This is a translation of the caption to the editorial written in Urdu.

** Translation from Urdu by the author.

column of October 30, 1988, wrote:

> "One finds common people in many parts of the Valley getting bitterly disenchanted with Chief Minister, and in contrast praising Jagmohan's period of Governor's rule." In its issue of April 6, 1989, *The Hindu* reported:

> "In fact, a large number of youth indicated that they would be more than satisfied if the Governor, Jagmohan, were once again allowed to take over the administration."

On my demitting office on July 12, 1989, the reporting of *The Hindustan Times* from Srinagar was as under:

> "...
>
> Fed up with the prevarication of Chief Minister Farooq Abdullah, the people always had a ray of hope in Jagmohan. During Governor's Rule, the bureaucracy was tamed and developmental work proceeded at a feverish pitch. New roads were constructed and old ones repaired almost in every corner of the State. People were bewildered as they had rarely seen an elected government function at such a furious pace. For the people, it was like a dream come true.
> Even today when people travel along a pot-holed road, they call it a 'Farooq Abdullah Road', but a well-metalled road is known as 'Jagmohan Road'.
>
> ...
>
> Tourists still fondly remember the time they spent in the city forest. On the slopes of Shankaracharya-Zaberwan hills, descending to the shores of the Dal Lake, the city forest was created during Governor's rule. Tourists descended in hordes on the 907 hectares of the city forest to delight in the peace and serenity of its exquisite foliage and lush greenery. It was also given the status of a national park, but with the installation of the Farooq Government, thousands of trees were felled to convert the area into a golf course.

. . ."

A 21-year-old Kashmiri youth, Javed, went to Pakistan for training. While returning in a group of 85 trainees, he was apprehended at the border by the Indian Army. In an interview to the press and television, Javed gave an account of his experience. Describing the conditions in Pak-occupied Kashmir, he said, "They have only outdated suspension bridges. The roads are as bad as these were in Srinagar before Jagmohan came to the State.' Despite turning militant, the Kashmiri youth nursed a latent respect for the welfare and development work done by me in Kashmir.

The purpose of citing these comments and observations is not to draw attention to personal achievements but to expose the treacherous role of those elements in national and State leadership who moved heaven and earth to portray me as anti-Muslim and anti-Kashmiri and in the process scuttled the great effort to rescue the State from the jaws of death and destruction. I could have tapped, for the good of the State and the country, the regards and affections which existed for me in the inner layers of the Kashmiri mind . . .

. . . Dr. Farooq Abdullah, was not to be left behind in the drive launched to create an 'anti-Muslim' image of mine. In his interview published in the *Times of India* of August 3, 1990, he said, "A known anti-Muslim was appointed as Governor of a Muslim majority State". How untrue, how unfair, was the propaganda, should be obvious from the fact that on November 7, 1986, at the time of his swearing-in ceremony, Dr. Farooq Abdullah, in a public speech, for which the records exist, said: "Governor Sahib, we would need you very badly. It is, indeed, amazing that such remarkable work could be done by you in a short time through an imbecile and faction-ridden bureaucracy. If today three ballot boxes are kept—one for the National Conference, one for the Congress and one for you, your ballot box would be full while the other two ballot boxes would be empty."

The misfortune of our country is that we have leaders like Dr Farooq Abdullah who have no regard for facts or truth and whose superficiality is matched only by their unprincipled politics.

Incidentally, did it not strike you that Dr. Farooq was virtually accusing your late mother of being anti-Muslim because she was the Prime Minister when, in April 1984, 'a known anti-Muslim' was appointed, for the first term, as 'Governor of a Muslim majority State?'

. . . Dr. Farooq Abdullah, on February 15, 1990, issued a written statement to the press in Urdu in which he, *inter alia*, said, "The Governor, in the personification of 'Hallaqu' and 'Changez Khan', is bent upon converting the Valley into a vast graveyard. On account of continuous curfew since January 20, it is difficult to say how many hundreds of people have become victims of the bull of the army and para-military forces, and in this general slaughter how many hundreds of houses have been destroyed. At this moment, when Kashmiris are witnessing their beloved country being converted into a vast graveyard, I appeal to the national and international upholders of humanity to intervene in Kashmir and have an international inquiry made into the general slaughter of Kashmiris at the hands of army and para-military forces."

Here is . . . 'patriot' calling Kashmir 'Aziz Wattan', suggesting a separate country. . . . asking for an international inquiry into the general slaughter of the Kashmiris by the Indian Army and para-military forces. . . speaking about the continuous curfew for twenty-five days in the Valley and his consequent inability to find out how many 'hundreds of innocent and unarmed Kashmiris' had been massacred and how many hundreds of Kashmiri houses raised to the ground although he knew perfectly well that there had been a number of days when there was no day-curfew, partially or wholly, and the authorities had brought out the list of casualties, about 40 up to February 16, and were daily asking the public to provide with the additional names, if they had any, so that correction in the official list could be made. Here is an erstwhile Chief Minister who did not care to explain how 'innocent and unarmed people' were ruthlessly shooting down I.A.F. officers, B.S.F. jawans, senior officers of the Television and Telecommunications Department and young men in the streets; and how, while inciting people through lengthy and ferry statements, he did not find a single word to condemn such brutal murders.

Is the nation not entitled to know why you have not disowned such unfortunate behaviour on the part of Dr. Farooq Abdullah? And how do you account for his recent statement as published in the *Times of India* of February 7, 1991: 'I directed my partymen to lie low, go across the border, get training in arms handling; do anything but do not get caught by Jagmohan'?

. . . The politics of unscrupulousness was brought to its lowest depth.

Roots

. . .

. . . Poisonous seeds were persistently planted in the Kashmiri psyche. And these were liberally fertilised. Those of you whose obligation it was to stop these plantation and their fertilisation, were not aware of even the elementary lesson of history: to compromise with the evil was only to rear greater evil; to ignore the inconvenient reality was only to compound it; to bow before the bully was only to invite the butcher the next day.

I could cite scores of cases to support my contention. Here, I would restrict myself to only two examples.

Softness and Surrender

On October 2, 1988, Mahatma Gandhi's birthday, his statue was to be installed in the new High Court complex at Srinagar. The function had been announced. The Chief Justice of India, R.S. Pathak, was to do the formal installation. But a few Muslim lawyers objected. They threatened to cause disturbance at the time of the function. The Chief Minister gave in, almost willingly, to the bullying tactics. The function was cancelled.

What were the implications of what happened? A secular Kashmir, part of a secular India, could not have, even in its highest seat of justice, a statue of the Father of the Nation, of a sage who laid down his life for communal harmony. Who was the person spearheading the move against the installation? It was none other than Mohammad Shafi Bhat, an advocate of the J & K High Court and an active member of the National Conference, who was later on given party ticket for Srinagar Lok Sabha seat in the elections held in November 1989 . . .

At that time there was National Conference(F)-Congress(I) Ministry in office. Such was its lack of adherence to principles, such was the character of Congressmen who formed part of the Ministry and such was its disposition to cling to power that not even a little finger was raised when the function was cancelled.

That bully's appetite could not have been whetted better.

Intimidation could not have secured better results. The trouble-makers could not have perceived a more casual and non-committed adversary. Was it not natural for them to nurture higher ambitions and think that more spectacular results could be achieved by deploying a more aggressive and threatening strategy? Only a naive would believe that in the context of the Kashmir situation, softness and surrender on basic principles would not act as an invitation to terrorism and militancy.

The Union Government enacted the Religious Institutions (Prevention of Misuse) Act, 1988. It was made applicable to all the States of the Union except J&K. Because of Article 370, concurrence of the State Government was needed for extension of this law to the State. But the same was not given. Why? Because J & K is different. What an argument for not having a law which aimed at eradication of misuse of religious premises for political purposes!

Nowhere was this law needed more than in the State of J & K. Nowhere were religious places misused more than here. Nowhere were seeds of fanaticism and fundamentalism sown every Friday more assiduously than from the pulpits of mosques here. Nowhere was it preached more regularly than here that Indian democracy was un-Islamic, and Indian secularism was un-Islamic. And yet, neither the State Government which was ruled by two supposedly secular parties, nor the Union Government took the matter seriously. . . . the law which was considered good for 100 million Muslims in other parts of India, was not considered good for 40 lakh Muslims of Kashmir.

What was the use of the nationalist forces ruling the country when they would not act in national interest at all; when they remained mental slaves of the politics of communalism; when they were inclined to place reliance on words and not on deeds; when they did not lead, but succumbed; when they encouraged, and not defeated separatist elements; when, instead of building a new society, strong in human and spiritual values, they did everything, wittingly or unwittingly, to repair, renovate and strengthen the old, decaying and smelly citadel of obscurantism; and when they invariably gave precedence to expediency over the basic goals and principles of our Constitution? What could be the result of all this? . . .

A Basic Question

. . . the prospects of my success . . . caused worry to Pakistan authorities, including Mrs. Benazir Bhutto and her agencies like ISI. They clearly understood that I could not only set the administrative machinery right, get it rid of internal subversion and secure loyalty and cooperation from a sizable section of the bureaucracy, but also win over public support by speedily redressing the grievances of the people, launching a drive against corruption, and reviving the tenor and tempo of the development of 1986. They, therefore, mounted a special campaign agains me. That also explains Mrs. Benazir Bhutto's hysterical outburst against me personally on Pakistan television and in her public speeches. ...She knew that I was aware of the deeper currents of Kashmir polity and administration and my approach was bound to be effective and fruitful. Mrs. Bhutto also knew that Pakistan had benefited immensely from the shallowness and superficiality of the approach of the earlier regime. How could she and her officers of the ISI allow their years of labour to go waste when they had almost attained their objective?

. . .

There are many other facets of Kashmir's truth which lie buried underneath the heaps of disinformation and also of superficiality and shallowness. . . . One day, I hope, the country will acquire the true perspective of the problem. . . .

. . .

The country's polity and administration have assumed such a character that it has become incapable of solving, from its roots, any serious problem. Elections have virtually lost all meaning. And these would continue to be meaningless until and unless Indian democracy and its constitutional structure acquires a healthy cultural base, a pure soul and soil, from which the seed of justice, truth and selfless service could sprout and blossom into a Great Tree providing shade and shelter from Kanyakumari to Kashmir. Currently, the inner light is gone, and we are being led virtually by blind men with lanterns in their hands. We stumble from one crisis to another. As a poet says:

It has happened
and it goes on happening
and it will happen again.

With best wishes,

Your sincerely,
(Sd.)
Jagmohan

20

President Venkataraman's Observations on Kashmir Issue, 1994

Kashmir figures at many places in Shri R.Venkataraman's account of *My Presidential Years*. Here are few excerpts from his version of the developments in Kashmir during V.P. Singh's Prime Ministership, December 2, 1989 to November 1990

On January 19, Prime Minister V.P. Singh and the Home Minister called on me and explained that law and order had practically collapsed in Kashmir and that the situation was worsening day by day. They proposed to appoint Jagmohan, who had earlier been an effective Governor of Jammu and Kashmir, again as Governor. I accepted the suggestion and informed General Krishna Rao immediately. . .

The equation between Farooq Abdullah and Jagmohan had been none too good. It was Jagmohan who had recommended the dismissal of the Farooq Ministry during Indira Gandhi's regime in 1983. Farooq feared that this act would be repeated and he tendered his resignation on the night of January 19. When General Krishna Rao accepted the resignation and requested him to continue in office till an alternative government was formed, Dr. Farooq flatly refused. Attempts by his friends Jyoti Basu and Chandra Shekhar to persuade him to continue in office proved futile. This necessitated the promulgation of Governor's Rule under Article 92 of the Jammu and Kashmir Constitution. The Assembly was kept in suspended animation. Papers were hurriedly put up to me and these were immediately approved to avoid a constitutional impasse.

The situation in Srinagar took an ugly turn; people defied the curfew and came out on the streets challenging the government.

There were reports of police mutiny though they were officially denied. But it was a fact that there was cross-firing between the local police and the C.R.P.F. At best, the government's control in Kashmir was only partial. Pakistan started fishing in trouble waters, stepping up insurgency activities with infiltrators and inflammatory statements. The Foreign Minister of Pakistan attending the SAARC meeting blatantly told our side that the Kashmir issue was very much alive...

On January 29, Mufti Mohammad Sayeed met me and talked about the appointment of Governor and about the Kashmir situation. I told him of my suggestion to the Prime Minister that Governor Jagmohan might be advised to constitute a peace committee of all Kashmiri leaders, such as Abdul Ghani Lone, Moulvi Farooq and Farooq Abdullah, irrespective of affiliations, so as to impress on the rest of the world that all responsible people were against terrorist activities and that the disruption of life in Kashmir was the work of anti-social elements. The Home Minister was not impressed with the idea; he felt that the local leaders, being terrorised by the militants, would not respond to the call of the Governor and the move might become infructuous. On the other hand he thought that the Prime Minister's proposal for an all-party meet on Kashmir might prove useful and wanted me to persuade Rajiv Gandhi to cooperate.

After the "Beating Retreat" function, Rajiv Gandhi met me and gave his assessment of the situation in Kashmir. According to him, law and other had broken down completely in Srinagar, there was a mutiny by the local police and the cross-firing between the C.R.P.F. and the local police had resulted in a number of casualties. He was candid enough to admit that Jagmohan could not be recalled within a week of his appointment but suggested that the Governor might contact Farooq Abdullah and other leaders in an effort to ease the tensions. I explained that Kashmir was a national issue and not a party matter and the Kashmir Government's failure in controlling the situation might internationalise the issue. I also reminded him of the Pakistan Foreign Minister's assertion that the issue would be raised in the United Nations. Rajiv Gandhi agreed that the issue should be faced by the nation solidly. He also responded readily to my suggestion for his participation in the all-party consultations . . .

(pages 339-341)

On March 4 . . . Rajiv Gandhi, Narasimha Rao, Farooq

Abdullah and two others met me and gave their assessment of the situation in Kashmir.

They felt that the Kashmir Government had lost control over the Valley, and the strong-arm measures of Jagmohan had been counter-productive and had alienated the entire people. The police were threatening to go on strike and were refusing to obey orders of the administration. Repression had to be stopped and a political solution found. Farooq Abdullah added that Jagmohan should be recalled . . .

On March 5, V.P. Singh called on me at 12 noon and discussed the issue with me for 90 minutes. He frankly admitted that the situation was grave, the people of the Valley had turned hostile and there was no one who could control the situation. When Governor's rule was proclaimed, the Assembly was kept in suspended animation. Jagmohan without consulting the Prime Minister or the President, exercised his authority under the Kashmir Constitution and dissolved the Legislative Assembly and further queered the pitch. V.P. Singh was greatly annoyed with Jagmohan, but did not want to recall him as that would further embolden the terrorists . . .

On March 7, the Prime Minister discussed the issue with political parties and it was resolved that an all-party group should visit Kashmir the next day to study the situation. Rajiv Gandhi reported his impressions to me on March 9. According to him, the people he met and saw talked about *azadi* (independence) and the lower grade government employees were hostile to the Governor and thus indirectly to India. His suggestions were:

(1) Mufti Mohammad Sayeed, the Home Minister, might replace Jagmohan as Governor, or a Cabinet Minister might be appointed as Minister in Charge of Kashmir Affairs, with instructions to start a dialogue with the political leaders of Kashmir.
(2) The dissolved Assembly might be revived if legally feasible or an advisory council appointed.

I told Rajiv Gandhi that the ideas he had put forward were not mutually exclusive and that we could work out a solution by permutation and combination of these proposals . . .

On March 15, George Fernandes came for breakfast. Our talk turned to Kashmir and he gave his perception of the problem.

According to his assessment, the government was not effective in the Valley; the present leaders of Kashmir, including the Governor, were not popular with the people and could not move in the Valley without police protection; and the cry for independence (*azadi*) was gaining momentum.

He suggested a dialogue with the people of the Valley, for some kind of autonomy for them. I recalled to him that as Defence Minister, I had suggested in 1983 to Indira Gandhi that Ladakh may be made a Union Territory as demanded by the local people, Jammu given the status of a State, and that the Valley dealt with as a separate entity, but it did not find any response. I wondered whether the idea proposed by George Fernandes would receive any consideration at all in the country. I also pointed out the possible repercussions of such a proposal in Punjab where a demand for similar status might come up and create more violence and tensions. We had a meaningful chat but found no solution. So we agreed to continue the search . . .

(pages 347-350)

In a bid to suppress the militant activity, Governor Jagmohan resorted to very harsh measures using para-military forces in Kashmir. Despite official reports giving details of militants captured or shot dead and cache of weapons recovered from them, the militants struck again and again killing a large number of innocents. Hence curfew had to be clamped for eight days continuously in Srinagar in May 1990. This caused untold misery to the people. Since wage-earners could not go out and earn a living and the well-to-do also could not go out to buy anything, there was total alienation of the entire population of Srinagar from both the Kashmir and Central governments. This caused a furore in Parliament and attracted criticism not only from the Kashmir, but from other States as well.

George Fernandes, as Minister in charge of Kashmir Affairs, was pursuing a policy of reconciliation with the militants and was meeting some of them clandestinely. Jagmohan on the other hand was resorting to a policy of suppression and therefore was annoyed with Fernandes.

In this atmosphere of bitterness and rancour, the militants assassinated, on May 21, one of the respected leaders of Kashmir, Moulvi Farook. It was said that Moulvi Farook was in touch with George Fernandes and was responding to the reconciliation approach propounded by the latter and therefore the militants removed him from the scene. Since Moulvi Farook was a popular leader, there was great resentment against his assassination and the people's anger reached uncontrollable levels over the dastardly crime.

A fitting funeral procession was organised for the Moulvi. It was said that some militants had infiltrated the ranks of mourners and started creating trouble during the procession. The CRPF, which was in great strength, immediately opened fire killing a large number of people. This violent incident touched off more criticism from the CPI and other political parties and an acrimonious debate followed in Parliament. While the BJP members defended the firm measures against the militants and terrorists by Jagmohan, other parties condemned the Governor for unleashing "a reign of terror" and repression in the Valley. They said that the Governor had turned "a paradise on earth into a valley of hell".

There was a strong plea for withdrawing Jagmohan from Kashmir. The Congress, headed by Rajiv Gandhi, launched a virulent attack on Prime Minister V.P. Singh in Parliament.

I was in Shimla on my usual sojourn when the Parliament debates were going on. The Prime Minister rang me up saying that he was withdrawing Jagmohan from Kashmir and appointing Girish Saxena, former chief of RAW, as Governor in his place . . .

The next day, only one proposal regarding Kashmir reached me. I learnt that Yashwant Sinha (whose name had been mentioned by V.P) had declined the office of Punjab Governor. The Kashmir proposal consisted of three parts:

(1) acceptance of the resignation of Governor Jagmohan;
(2) appointment of Saxena as Governor, and
(3) nomination of Jagmohan by the President as Member of the Rajya Sabha.

The last part of the proposal was not even mentioned to me by V.P. Singh. I accepted the first two parts and minuted that the third may wait for sometime. I wanted to discuss this matter with the Prime Minister as I felt that such a nomination would be criticised from several angles. When this was reported to the Prime Minister, he called me again at Shimla and said Jagmohan's nomination to the Rajya Sabha was part of the arrangement and that he would like the proposal to be accepted immediately. I explained to V.P. Singh my regard for the competence, efficiency and ability of Jagmohan but nominating him in the present context would be incongruous and asked the Prime Minister to reconsider the matter.

Next morning, the Prime Minister sent a message that the Cabinet had already considered the matter and had approved this proposal. Having performed my constitutional function of advising the Prime Minister, I assented to the nomination. As I expected, there was a lot of criticism of the nomination from all quarters . . .

(pages 381-384)

21

Overview of Kashmir Issue

21.1. Introduction

The State of Jammu and Kashmir is situated in the extreme north in the Indian sub-continent covering an area of 84,471 square miles, and is the largest of the Indian States. To the north-east it is bordered by Tibet, to the north by Chinese Turkestan (Sinkiang) and to the north-west by the Soviet Republic of Turkestan and Afghanistan. To the West it borders Pakistan.

The State is almost entirely mountainous, and it may be geographically divided into three areas: tracts in the north, containing the districts of Ladakh and Gilgit; the middle region of the "Happy Valley" of Kashmir; and the large level areas of Jammu in the south. These three regions are divided from each other by the snow-bound outer Himalayan ranges.

Srinagar is the summer, and Jammu, the winter capital of the State. The Jhelum Valley road connects Srinagar with Pakistan *via* Rawalpindi and Abbottabad. The Banihal Road provides a link between Srinagar and Jammu over the Banihal Pass. From Jammu one road leads to Sialkot in the Pakistan Province of the West Punjab, and another to Pathankot in Punjab.

According to the census of 1941, the total population of the State was 4,021,616. This was made up of Muslims 77.11 per cent; Hindus 20.12 per cent.; Sikhs, Buddhists and others 2.77 per cent. The majority of the Hindus are found in Jammu district, and Srinagar city also has a fairly large Hindu population.

The Dogra dynasty, represented by Maharaja Hari Singh, ruled the Jammu and Kashmir State, for just over a hundred years, by virtue of the Treaty of Amritsar of 1846, concluded by Raja Gulab

Singh with the British. At that time Gulab Singh held Jammu, Ladakh and Baluchistan; while Kashmir and Gilgit were under the Sikh rulers of Lahore. With the defeat of the Sikhs in the Punjab by British forces, the Kashmir and Gilgit territories held by them were transferred to the Dogra dynasty. According to the Imperial Gazetteer: "The general and practical result therefore, of the Treaty of Amritsar was to confirm Gulab Singh in what he already possessed, and to transfer to him the Province of Kashmir with its newly acquired authority over Gilgit."

21.2 PART I – Events Leading up to the Accession of Jammu and Kashmir to India

Jammu and Kashmir, until August 15, 1947, was an autonomous State in treaty relations with, and subject to the Paramountcy of, the Crown of England. Like other Indian States, it had, however, no international existence. On that date, the Indian Independence Act came into force, and the new Dominions of India and Pakistan came into being. The Indian States became free to decide whether they would accede to one or the other of the two Dominions. The position of the Indian States on the transfer of power was made clear in His Majesty's Government's Declaration of June 3, 1947, supplemented by the Statement issued by the British Cabinet Mission on May 11th, 1946. A large number of States acceded to the Dominion of India. The State of Jammu and Kashmir announced its intention of negotiating Standstill Agreements with both India and Pakistan. In fact, however, the State signed a Standstill Agreement only with Pakistan and entered into no agreement with the Government of India, prior to its accession on October 26th, 1947.

The object of the Standstill Agreement was to provide for the continuance of economic and administrative relations between the State and Pakistan on the same basis as had existed before the creation of the new Dominions. Nevertheless, in an effort to coerce the State into accession to Pakistan, the Pakistan authorities cut off supplies to Kashmir of food, petrol and other essential commodities, and hindered the free transit of travellers between Kashmir and Pakistan. Economic pressure was thus applied simultaneously with military pressure in the form of border raids. Conditions in the State were made more difficult by the communal disturbances which broke out in the two Punjabs after the announcement of the partition.

There was a large influx of refugees into the Southern districts of the State, and the State became a channel for the passage of Muslim refugees moving from East Punjab to West Punjab and for non-Muslims moving in the opposite direction.

Preliminaries to the invasion of Kashmir and Jammu, which finally decided the Maharaja and his people to accede to the Indian Dominion, began soon after the partition on August 15th. On the 29th of August, 1947, the Maharaja of Kashmir received a telegram from one Raja Yaqub Khan on behalf of the public of Hazara, alleging attacks on Muslims in Poonch, and informing him that the Hazara Muslims were "much perturbed". The telegram continued "We are ready to enter the State fully equipped to fight with your Forces. You are requested to ease the situation soon, otherwise be ready to bear the consequences". Throughout the month of September, reports of infiltration into the State territory from the border districts of Pakistan continued to come in. The State Government made representations to the authorities of those districts. The representations brought denials, but no action. On the 31st of August 1947, Major-General Scott, General Officer Commanding, Jammu and Kashmir State Forces, submitted a report regarding the situation in the State. About Poonch he said "Damaged communications. Telegraph and wireless under repair. Hostile casualties 20 to 50". He continued "Army action to be confined to maintaining order and arresting persons known or suspected of rioting, looting, murder or inciting. No reason to think that troops had acted otherwise". He also reported "situation in Hazara and Rawalpindi areas very unsatisfactory. There is little doubt that the recent disturbances in Bagh Tehsil were led by armed gangs from Pakistan. Exaggerated reports of events in Poonch circulated in these Pakistan districts in which State troops are cited as the aggressors. Possibility, even probability, of further intervention in much greater force must be provided against". On the 4th of September, Major-General Scott reported that "500 hostile tribesmen wearing green and *Khaki* uniform, and leather and web equipment" were seen. A protest in the following terms was made direct to the Pakistan Army and to General O. de T. Lovett, Officer Commanding 7th Infantry Division. "Gangs sattis armed estimated 200 to 300 from Tehsils Kahuta and Murree (both in Pakistan) raiding State territory for loot, murder, and rousing Jhelum river in area Panjar and seven miles north and south of Owen Ferry. Please take immediate action to prevent and recall". On the 12th of September, Major-General Scott reported that "Quiet and confidence was being restored in Poonch Jagir". However, early in October, activities by armed men in uniform in various districts of Poonch were again reported. On the 4th of October, raiders armed with Tommy-guns were reported in the Chirala area, and more raiders were seen passing to the Jhelum river. Fighting was also reported between the raiders and States Forces from Bagh in the Rawalkot area.

Similar activity was observed in Mirpur. Fort Owen was besieged and was evacuated by State troops on the 15th of October. Four to five thousand raiders in green uniforms were observed. On the 18th October, the Kotli-Poonch road was breached and heavy fighting took place. From Bhimbhar, large scale offensive preparation across the border in Pakistan including movement of lorries was seen. On the 20th of October, the Wazir of Mirpur sent a message that armed men were earthing opposite Chechiam and Mangla. On the 22nd, he reported that raids on Owen were being methodically carried out. On the 23rd of October, heavy fighting was reported from Kotli which had, by now, been completely cut off from Poonch by road blocks put up by the "raiders".

On the 24th of October, 1947, the Government of India received the first request for military aid from the Government of the Jammu and Kashmir State. At that time the Government of India had no agreement, military or political, with the State. A document signed by the British Chiefs of Staff of the Indian Armed Forces states that on the 24th of October information of the capture of Muzaffarabad was received by the Commander-in-Chief in India. No plans for sending troops to Kashmir had up to that time been considered by the Indian Army. On the 25th the Government of India directed the preparation of plans for sending troops to Kashmir by air and road. Indian troops were sent to Kashmir by air on the 27th, following the signing of the Instrument of Accession on the previous night.

The accession was legally made by the Maharaja of Kashmir, and this step was taken on the advice of Sheikh Abdullab, leader of the All-Jammu and Kashmir National Conference, the political party commanding the widest popular support in the State. Nevertheless, in accepting the accession, the Government of India made it clear that they would regard it as purely provisional until such time as the will of the people of the State could be ascertained.

21.3 PART II – The Invasion

The main attack on State territory began in the third week of October. Major Khurshid Anver, who led the frontier tribes-men in the attack on Srinagar, describes the strategy of this attack. In an interview to the *Dawn* newspaper (Karachi) reported on December 7th, he said that the attack on Kashmir was originally planned from two sides – one from the regions adjoining Kashmir State and the tribal belt that is on the West, and the other from the border districts to the Southern Pakistan. 'D' day was actually fixed for October 21st, but the attack could not be launched till the next day. Major Anver then describes the progress towards Srinagar along the Kohala-Baramula road. The main column made considerable progress on the Kohala-Baramula road, fanning out and devastating the villages and towns on either side. Uri fell to the raiders, and on October 27th or 28th they captured Baramula, and indulged in an orgy of rape, arson and looting. Women were abducted, and a large number held in a concentration camp at Alibeg in terrible conditions. Alibeg is in Kashmir State territory and is run by the "Azad Kashmir Government". Originally it had over a thousand Kashmiri women of all religions. Of these only a couple of hundred have survived. The road to Srinagar now lay open before the raiders.

Faced with this threat, the Maharaja of Kashmir approached the Government of India for assistance on the 24th of October. On the 26th, the State formally acceded to India. On October 27th, the first contingent of Indian airborne troops landed in Srinagar in the morning. However, it is not until reinforcements had arrived that the Indian troops could attack the raiders who had advanced to Pattan, only 17 miles from Srinagar. On November 8th, assisted by armoured vehicles and planes of the Royal Indian Air Force, Indian troops recaptured Baramula. They found the town completely ruined. . . Continuing their advance along the difficult road from Baramula to Uri, Indian troops found the Mahoora Power House, which supplied the whole of the Srinagar valley with electricity, efficiently wrecked by the raiders. Indian troops captured Uri on November 15th, and removed the serious threat to Srinagar and the surrounding valley. This can be regarded as the end of the first stage of the Kashmir operations.

The second task of the Indian troops was to free large areas in Jammu Province which had been overrun by the tribesmen. The latter had surrounded the towns of Mirpur, Kotli, Poonch, Jhanger. Nowshehra and Bhimbhar. Within the towns small State garrison were holding out. Winter having set in, Indian troops could advance only slowly on the narrow, fair-weather roads connecting Jammu City with these areas. Nowshehra, Jhanger and Kotli were relieved but the Mirpur garrison could not be helped, and finally part of the garrison managed to fight its way out with some of the civilian refugees. In the third week of December, over 5,000 raiders stormed Jhanger which was held by about 200 Indian troops. Encouraged by this local success, the raiders attacked Nowshehra in force, but were beaten back. Since then, Indian troops have been clearing the surrounding area of the raiders. They have succeeded in widening their perimeter of operations and are carrying out offensive patrols to clear the countryside of raiders and protect their own lines of communication. Recent operations around Nowshehra have shown that the composition of the attacking force is approximately as follows:

70 per cent Pathans and Muslims from Dir and Swat States;
20 per cent deserters from State Forces;
5 per cent from Poonch and 5 per cent Sundas.

These figures have been calculated from dead bodies counted by the Indian Army. At present some 86,000 to 88,000 Pathans are engaged in the "Jehad". Of these 73,000 to 75,000 are concentrated in various centres in Pakistan and approximately 13,000 are engaged in Kashmir.

Concentrations of Pathans in Pakistan are reliably understood to be as follows.

Abbottabad	6,000-8,000
Kohat Pass	10,000
Rawalpindi	5,000
Sargodha	7,500
Gujjarkhana	4,000
Jhelum	5,000
Gujarat	10,000
Wazirabad	8,000
Chak Avnru	2,200
Sialkot	3,500
Nirala Head	2,000

Shakergarh	700
Chak Sukho	200
Wagah	200
Lahore	3,000
Chak Pundara-Sahoti	8,000
Approximate Total	73,000-75,000

Indian troops in Kashmir are not, as is believed in some quarters, composed only or mainly of Sikh troops. There are a certain number of them, as the Indian Army includes men from all religions and castes, including Muslims. Among the Indian troops operating in Kashmir are men drawn from the Mahratta, Madrasi, Kumaoni, Mahar, Rajput, Garhwali, Dogra, Jat, Ahir and other regiments. One of our most successful officers in the campaign has been a Moslem, Brigadier Osman. Since Indian troops arrived in Kashmir and Jammu, they have carried out their instructions of promoting and maintaining communal harmony. The Indian Air Force has played a notable part in reconnaissance, the supply and transport and in offensive support of our troops.

As has been stated by the Prime Minister of India on numerous occasions, the task of Indian troops is to clear the raiders from, and restore peace to, Kashmir, as this is necessary to the holding of a plebiscite or a referendum by the people of Kashmir to decide finally as to which dominion they will accede. Indian troops are continuing to fulfil this task.

21.4. PART III – Complicity of Pakistan in the Invasion of Kashmir

There is abundant circumstantial evidence to show that Pakistan has aided and abetted the "Tribal invasion of Kashmir and Jammu. Both official and unofficial organisations are implicated, though the Pakistan Government has officially disowned the invaders operating from bases in its territory. Pakistan's Foreign Minister, Sir Mohd. Zaffrullah Khan, has expressed before the Security Council the inability of his Government to prevent attacks on Kashmir and Jammu, legally part of the Indian Union.

2. This evidence of complicity is based on moral and material aid, on assistance both active and passive given to raiders, in Pakistan.

3. There are some 13,000 Pathans operating in Kashmir today, and they include Waziris, Mahsuds and Mohmands. In Pakistan there are approximately 75,000 tribesmen, concentrated in Punjab districts, many of them bordering on Kashmir or Jammu.

4. Many of the invading tribesmen were recruited by officials of the North-West Frontier Province Government and incited to "Jehad" by the Premier of the Province, ably assisted by the Pirs of Manki Sharif and of Wana, and various Maliks. Tribesmen are collected and harangued with tales of Dogra atrocities on the Muslim inhabitants of Kashmir. The Pir of Wana, for example, one of the most successful recruiting agents, after addressing tribesmen feasts them, and then sends them to meet the Deputy Commissioner of Dera Ismail Khan. Having been addressed by the Deputy Commissioner, the tribesman visit the Superintendent of Police, Dera Ismail Khan and pick up rifles and ammunition. Thus armed they return to the Pir who again speaks to them. Next day, incited to war and tempted by promises of loot in Kashmir, they leave in lorries for their bases.

5. In addition to these acts of official connivance, leaders of the Muslim League party openly canvass aid for the raiders. Meetings are held in the main towns, and, addressed by the local leaders as well as members of the "Provincial Government" of Kashmir and Jammu. These facts are based on information gathered from independent news reports by British and American correspondents as well as from other reliable sources. . .

6. At a press conference at Peshawar on the lst of November, the Premier of the N.W.F.P., Khan Abdul Qayum Khan, appealed to the Arab League to call a Pan-Islamic Conference to meet the common danger to Islam which had arisen with the Indian Dominion's "Invasion of Kashmir". He continued that Muslims did not recognise that there was any difference between the Muslims of Pakistan and those of Afghanistan, Iran or any other Muslim country of the world. He added that the time had come when they should rise or fall together. Referring to Kashmir, he said that the Muslim nation had been outraged by the action taken by the Maharaja of Kashmir in acceding to the Indian Dominion. He urged the Pakistan Government to recognise the Provincial Azad Government. In a press statement issued two days earlier, the Premier of the N.W.F.P. had declared that the Pathans were determined to die to the last man for Kashmir, which was a Muslim majority State and "belonged to

Pakistan as a matter of right". He appealed to every Muslim in Pakistan "to get ready to face the situation". He said that the Pathans would not allow that "invasion" of Kashmir by India. "I can give this assurance with confidence because I have got my hands on the pulse of the Pathans of the tribal areas and the N. W.F.P."

7: Communiques of the "Provisional Kashmir Government" are broadcast by the Pakistan radio, which is a Government organisation and inflammatory statements designed to assist the raiders are also used. The Pakistan Press publishes communiques of the Indian Government under the headline "Enemy Version".

8. A large proportion of the raiders comes from the Frontier Province and tribal areas. They do not come in driblets but travel hundreds of miles through Pakistan in large groups along the main roads, and over bridges guarded by Pakistan troops.

9. The daily attacks on Kashmir and Jammu are launched from bases which are without question in Pakistan. Rawalpindi is one of the main centres and the head of the Azad Provisional Government has offices there. Many of these raiders are concentrated in various towns in Pakistan: Sargodha with about 7,500, Abbottabad with 6,000 to 8,000, Wazirabad with 8,000 and Jhelum with 5,000. These serve as supply depots and training centres. Here the raiders rest and recuperate, replenish their supplies and sell women and other loot captured in the raids. Wounded raiders are also treated in hospital and dispensaries in these towns. It is not without significance that some of these towns are important Cantonments of the Pakistan Army.

10. In transit through Pakistan the raiders are assisted with the supply of transport and petrol. Neither the lorries nor the fuel could possibly be available to the tribesmen except through the knowledge and assistance of officials of the Pakistan Government. Petrol is a rationed commodity, and has to be supplied against coupons issued by district officials. While civilians in Pakistan find it difficult to obtain petrol, there is no difficulty so far as the tribesmen are concerned. In the N.W.F.P., the export and movement of motor vehicle is regulated under Section 3 of the N.W.F.P. Essential Articles Control (Temporary Powers) Act of 1947. Transportation of motor vehicles, other than those used by the Military, is not allowed except on permits issued by the Director of Civil Supplies. Vehicles belonging to the raiders have been found to have Pakistan number plates; those damaged in action have been observed under repair in

workshops in Rawalpindi.

11. Much of the modern equipment used by the raiders cannot be of tribal manufacture and must come from Military stores of the Pakistan Government. The raiders' armoury includes light machine-guns, mortars, mines, signal equipment and wireless sets with batteries. These have been used in quantities far exceeding those lost by the Indian and Kashmir State Forces. As the fighting in Kashmir has progressed, the numbers of raider has increased and the quality of their equipment has improved. Radio messages from the raiders' advanced bases asking for supplies of food and ammunition have been intercepted. The codes employed in these messages are among those used by the Indian Army before partition. These codes are in the possession of the Pakistan Army and were never published. Furthermore, tribesmen and peasants would not have the necessary technical skill to operate wireless transmitters.

12. From the tactics employed in the fighting it is evident that the raiders have received training in modern methods of warfare. Soldiers of the Indian Army have identified former comrades, now serving in the Pakistan Forces, among the raiders. It is known that Pakistan Army personnel, ostensibly on leave, are fighting with the raiders.

21.5. PART IV – India's Objectives

In Kashmir, as in other similar cases, the view of the Government of India has been that in the matter of disputed accession the will of the people must prevail. It was for this reason that they accepted only on a provisional basis the offer of the Ruler to accede to India, backed though it was by the most important political organization in the State.

2. The question of accession is to be decided finally in a free plebiscite; on this point there is no dispute. It is, however, impossible to hold a plebiscite so long as the State is infested by freebooters from outside. The only purpose for which Indian troops are operating in Kashmir is to ensure that the vote of the people will not be subject to coercion by tribesmen and others from across the border who have no right to be in Kashmir. Since the State is now part of India, these troops have a legal and a moral obligation to defend it. Nevertheless they will be progressively reduced after the raiders have left State territory, normal conditions have been

restored and the risk of recurrence of aggression from outside ha ceased. As the Government of India have repeatedly made clea there is to be no victimization of any native of the State, whatever hi political views or affiliations may be, and no Kashmiri will b deprived of the right to vote.

3. The Government of India have been concerned to emphasi these objectives, and it was to this end that they repeatedly invite representatives of Pakistan to discuss the matter with them. Whe efforts to secure a satisfactory settlement by direct negotiation wit Pakistan had failed and the activities of large numbers of tribesme in Pakistan, aided and abetted by Pakistan, intensified the milita pressure on Jammu and Kashmir State and became a threat to Indi itself, the Government of India, as a last resort, appealed to th Security Council of the United Nations to call upon Pakistan to ceas its unnatural action in the interests of peace between the tw countries.

*Extracts from "White Paper on India"**

India took the Kashmir case to the United Nations on January 1948. The matter was admitted to the Security Council at its 226 meeting on January 6, 1948.

The Security Council has passed seventeen Resolutions to sol the Kashmir Issue which is still threatening the world peace.

Tashkent Declaration (1966) and Shimla Agreement (1972) a the landmarks agreements between India and Pakistan.

Since 1990-91, about 2-1/2 million Kashmiri Pandits have bee forced to leave the Kashmir Valley.

---

* White Paper issued by the Government of India on Jammu and Kashmir, 1948

22

Chronology of Significant Events of Jammu and Kashmir State, 3000 BC to AD 1994

Chronology of significant events regarding the State of Jammu and Kashmir is divided as under :

A. Ancient Kashmir	–	From about 3000 BC to 13th century AD
B. Medieval Kashmir	–	Muslim Rule in Kashmir – 14th century to 18th century AD
C. Sikh Rule	–	AD 1819-1846
D. Dogra Rule	–	AD 1846-1947
E. Modern Period	–	Independence to 1994

A. Ancient Kashmir (3000 BC to 13th century AD)

About 3000 BC	–	Sage Kashyap creates the Valley of Kashmir
Mahabharata Period (2500 BC)	–	Gonanda (2448 BC) the first known King of Kashmir. Contemporary of the King Jarasandh of Magadha
273-232 BC	–	King Ashoka extends his control over Kashmir. Founding of Shrinagari (near today's Srinagar) by Ashoka
First and Second century AD	–	Kashmir under Kushans
AD 515-550	–	Rule of Mihira-Kula, a Hun Chief
About AD 600	–	Kashmir under King Vikramaditya of Ujjain

AD 631	–	Hiuen Tsang, the celebrated Chinese scholar visits Kashmir
AD 724-761	–	King Lalitaditya
AD 855-883	–	King Avantivaram builds the town of Avantipur and the Sun Temple
AD 883-902	–	King Shankaravarman builds Shankara-pura-pattan (now known as Pattan)
AD 939-949	–	King Yasaskaradeva, a Brahmin King
AD 949 to 1003	–	Gupta Dynasty founded by Parva Gupta
AD 950-958	–	Ksema Gupta
AD 950-1003	–	Queen Dida dominates the scene
AD 1003-1101	–	First Lohara Dynasty of the Kshatriyas
AD 1003-1028	–	King Samgramaraja. Invasion by Sultan Mahmud of Ghazni
AD 1028-1063	–	King Ananta. Kashmir comes under the influence of Sahi Princes of Punjab.
AD 1063-1089	–	King Kalsa
AD 1089-1101	–	King Harsa
AD 1101-1155	–	Second Lohara Dynasty
AD 1101-1111	–	King Uccale
AD 1128-1155	–	King Jaya Simha. Period of Aryan Renaissance in Kashmir
AD 1147-1149	–	Kalhan writes *Rajtarangani*
AD 1171-1286	–	Bopadeva Dynasty
AD 1286-1320	–	Damra Dynasty
AD 1320	–	Invasion by Dulacha, a Mongol warrior. Loot and destruction
AD 1320-1323	–	Rule of Rinchana, a Ladakhi Buddhist who embraced Islam.
AD 1323-1328	–	King Udyanadeva. Invasion by Achala, a Turko-Mongol Invader

B. Muslim Rule in Kashmir (14th to 18th century AD)

AD 1339-1342	–	Commencement of Muslim Rule in Kashmir. Shah Mir's Regime
AD 1354-1373	–	Sultan Shihab-ud-Din. Devastating flood in Kashmir
AD 1373-1389	–	Sultan Hindal assuming the title of Qutub-ud-Din

AD 1389-1413	–	Sultan Sikandar, known as 'But-Shikan'
AD 1420-1470	–	Sultan Zain-ul Abidin, A liberal ruler. In the field of construction, he is called 'Shah Jahan of Kashmir'
AD 1515-1516	–	Epidemic sweeps the Valley. Countless deaths
AD 1540-1551	–	On November 1540, Mirza Haider Dughlat, a Mugal General establishes control over Kashmir with only 400 soldiers
AD 1561	–	Founding of Chak Dyansty by local people
AD 1576-78	–	Severe famine in Kashmir. About half of the population of the Valley said to have died
AD 1589	–	Mughal Rule in Kashmir.
AD 1589, 1598 and 1601	–	Akbar visits Kashmir
AD 1605-1627	–	Jahaṇgir visits Kashmir 6 times
AD 1627-1658	–	Shah Jahan makes several trips to Kashmir.
AD 1658-1707	–	During Aurangzeb's long reign of 59 years, Kashmir had 14 Governors
AD1671-57	–	Persecution of Brahmans during the Governorship of Iftikar Khan
AD 1675 November 11	–	Martyrdom of the ninth Sikh Guru Teg Bahadur at Delhi
AD 1746-1747	–	Devastating flood followed by horrible famine
AD 1753	–	Ahmad Shah Abdali of Persia conquers Kashmir through one of his Generals and establishes Afghan Rule
AD 1755	–	A severe famine in Kashmir
AD 1783	–	George Forster, an Officer of the East India Company visits Kashmir

C. Sikh Rule in Kashmir (1819-1846)

AD 1819 July 15	–	After two unsuccessful attempts, in 1812 and 1814, Maharaja Ranjit Singh's Forces under Misser Dewan Chand capture Kashmir
AD 1819-1846	–	Sikh Rule in Kashmir under ten Governors.
AD 1832	–	Severe famine in Kashmir

D. Dogra Rule (1846-1947)

AD 1846	–	The last Governor, Imam-ud-Din surrenders possession of Kashmir to Raja Gulab Singh in pursuance of the Treaty of Amritsar
AD 1878-1879	–	Devastating famine
AD 1924-1927	–	Constitutional Reforms through Constitutional Acts of 1924 and 1927
AD 1931, July 13	–	Serious riots outside the Srinagar Jail
1932	–	Founding of the Jammu and Kashmir Muslim Conference with Sheikh Mohammed Abdullah as President
1934	–	Introduction of a dyarchical form of Government in the light of Glancy Committee Report
1938-1939	–	Muslim Conference renamed All Jammu and Kashmir National Conference, with the initiative of Sheikh Abdullah
1944	–	National Conference adopts a programme called 'Naya Kashmir' and demands Parliamentary democracy in the State. M.A. Jinnah visits Kashmir and receives reception from the National Conference
1946	–	Maharaja of Kashmir bans the entry of Jawaharlal Nehru to Kashmir. Nehru defies the prohibition order and is arrested and released
1946, May 10	–	National Conference launches the 'Quit Kashmir' movement against the Dogra rule
1947, May 20	–	Arrest of Sheikh Abdullah along with other prominent leaders of National Conference
June 1947	–	Lord Mountbatten pays a four-day visit to Kashmir.

E. Modern Period (Independence to 1994)

1947

July-August	–	Mahatma Gandhi visits Srinagar and meets the Maharaja on August 1

August 10	–	Dismissal of R.C. Kak from the office of the Prime Minister of Kashmir
August 12	–	In response to a telegram of August 12 from the Prime Minister of Jammu and Kashmir, Pakistan agrees into a Standstill Agreement with effect from August 15, 1947
September 29	–	Release of Sheikh Abdullah after his 'unqualified apology'
October 22	–	Full scale tribal invasion of Jammu and Kashmir backed by Pakistan regulars on Kashmir
October 23	–	Tribesmen seize Muzaffarabad
October 24	–	Maharaja Hari Singh approaches the Government of India for assistance. Capture of Mohara Power Station by Tribesmen. Srinagar plunged into darkness
October 24-26	–	Baramulla falls into the hands of raiders
October 25	–	V.P. Menon, Secretary in the Ministry of States Government of India flies to Srinagar
October 26	–	Maharaja Hari Singh sends the Instrument of Accession for acceptance by the Government of India
October 27	–	Lord Mountbatten accepts the Instrument of Accession.
October 27	–	Indian Air Force planes carry the first batch of Indian troops to Srinagar, under the command of Lt. Col. Ranjit Rai. Ranjit Rai loses his life near Baramulla
November 3	–	Major Som Nath Sharma engages the raiders at Badgam, near the airport. He is outnumbered 1 to 7. He is killed and awarded Padam Vir Chakra posthumously. He was the first Indian to receive the highest gallantry award. Brigadier Rajinder Singh loses his life
November 7	–	Battle of Shaltang proves decisive. No danger to Srinagar

1948

January 1	–	India takes the Kashmir case to the Security Council*
January 20	–	UN Security Council establishes United Nations Commission for India and Pakistan (UNCIP)

1949

March 21	–	Admiral Nimitz designated as Plebiscite Administrator
June 20	–	Maharaja Hari Singh leaves the State and vests all powers in Yuvraj Karan Singh
July 27	–	Karachi Agreement and Cease-Fire

1950

January 26	–	With the adoption of the Indian Constitution, Jammu and Kashmir comes under the territorial and Constitutional jurisdiction of India

1951

May 1	–	Proclamation issued instituting the Constituent Assembly
September-October	–	National Conference gets all the 75 seats (73 in unopposed). Boycott of elections by Jammu Praja Parishad
October 31	–	Constitutent Assembly starts its deliberations

1952

July 24	–	Delhi Agreement giving special powers to State of Jammu and Kashmir

---

* All the Resolutions of the Security Council are given separately in chapters 5, 8, 11, and 15

August 19 – J&K Constitutent Assembly accords approval to the Delhi Agreement. Agitation by Jammu Praja Parishad against Delhi Agreement. Their slogan was : one constitution, one symbol.

1953

May 11 – Arrest of Dr Shyama Prasad Mookerjee, President of Bharatiya Jana Sangh

June 23 – Death of Dr Mookerjee in Kashmir jail

August 7 – Dismissal of Sheikh Abdullah on account of his anti-Indian views and his arrest

August 9 – Bakshi Ghulam Mohammad sworn in as Prime Minister

1954

February – J&K Contituent Assembly ratifies State's Accession to India

May 14 – President of India issues the first Constitution (Application to J&K) Order extending certain provisions of Constitution of India to the State of Jammu and Kashmir

1955

August 9 – Plebiscite Front formed by Mirza Afzal Beg

1956

Constitution (Seventh Amendment Act 1956) abolishes the category of Part B State. Jammu and Kashmiris included as one of the States of India under Article 1

1957

January – After the formal inauguration of its

		Constitution, J&K Constitution Assembly dissolves itself

1958

January 8	–	Release of Sheikh Abdullah
April 29	–	Rearrest of Sheikh Abdullah. He is charged with conspiracy to cause forcible Annexation of the State by Pakistan

1959

April 1	–	Abolition of the permit system for entry into the State of Jammu and Kashmir

1962

January 25	–	Magistrate commits Sheikh Abdullah and his companions to the Sessions Court

1963

October 4	–	Resignation of Bakshi Ghulam Mohammad as Prime Minister of the State of J&K. Shamsuddin becomes the Prime Minister
December 27	–	'Holi Relic' reported missing from Hazratbal Shrine. Violent agitation

1964

January 4	–	'Holi Relic' located and located and placed back in the Shrine
February 3	–	Identification of the 'Holi Relic' and stoppage of agitation
February 29	–	Ghulam Mohammad Sadiq becomes the Prime Minister
April 8	–	Withdrawal of the Conspiracy Case against and release of Sheikh Abdullah
May	–	Sheikh Abdullah visits Pakistan and Azad Kashmir capital Muzaffarabad

1965

February	–	Sheikh Abdullah goes abroad
March 28	–	Sheikh Abdullah meets Chou En-Lai, Prime Minister of China
May 9	–	Arrest of Sheikh Abdullah in New Delhi
May 30	–	Amendment of Jammu and Kashmir Constitution. Denominations of 'Prime Minister and Sadar-i-Riyasat' changed to 'Chief Minister' and 'Governor' respectively
August 5	–	Thousands of 'Mujahids' and 'Razakars' enter the Valley
September 1	–	Pakistan Army launches a massive attack in the Chamb Jurian sector
September 22	–	Cease-fire on the initiative of the Security Council

1966

January 10	–	Tashkent Declaration signed by the Indian Prime Minister Lal Bahadur Shastri and Pakistan President Ayub Khan. Both the parties agree to withdraw their troops to the position held by them on August 5, 1965

1967

December 8	–	Release of Sheikh Abdullah

1968

January 8	–	Expulsion of Sheikh Abdullah, Mirza Afzal Beg and G.M. Shah from the State of Jammu and Kashmir
January 12	–	Plebiscite Front banned

1971

		Liberation movement of Bangladesh. Indian Army moves into Bangladesh

December 3	–	Pakistan attacks J & K.
December 13	–	Syed Mir Qasim becomes the Chief Minister after the death of G.M. Sadiq.
December 16	–	Pakistani forces surrender in Bangladesh
December 17	–	Pakistan accepts Cease-fire

1972

July 3	–	Shimla Agreement. Kashmir issue becomes a bilateral issue

1975

February 24	–	Indira Gandhi-Sheikh Abdullah Kashmir Accord
February 25	–	Sheikh Abdullah sworn in as Chief Minister
April 13	–	Revival of National Conference by Sheikh Abdullah
July 5	–	Sheikh Abdullah dissolves Plebiscite Front and merges it with National Conference

1977

March 25	–	Congress Party withdraws its support to Sheikh Abdullah in the Legislative Assembly. Sheikh Abdullah secures dissolution of the Assembly
June 30	–	In the State Assembly elections, National Conference wins 39 seats (out of 42) in the Valley, 7 seats (out of 32) in the Jammu region and both the seats from Ladakh. Congress (I) practically wiped out in the Valley
July 9	–	Sheikh Abdullah sworn in as Chief Minister

1982

September 8	–	Passing away of Sheikh Abdullah. Dr Farooq Abdullah (son of Sheikh Abdullah) sworn in as Chief Minister

983

ıne 5	–	During State Assembly Elections, conflict develops between Congress (I) and National Conference

984

anuary 3	–	Kidnapping of Ravinder Mhatre, an Indian diplomat posted at Birmingham and his alleged murder by the members of Kashmir Leberation Army
pril 26	–	Jagmohan assumes the office of State Governor
uly 2	–	Dismissal of the Ministry of Farooq Abdullah. G.M. Shah becomes the Chief Minister

986

ebruary 11	–	Execution of Maqbool Bhatt (founder President of the J&K Liberation Front) at Tihar Jail, Delhi
Iarch 7	–	Dismissal of the Ministry of G.M. Shah. Imposition of Governor's Rule in the State
eptember	–	President's rule in the State
Iovember 7	–	Rajiv-Farooq Accord and Coalition Ministry of National Conference and Congress (I) with Dr. Farooq Abdullah as Chief Minister

987

Iarch		Coalition parties sweep the polls

989

anuary 13	–	15 persons killed in Jammu on the eve of Guru Gobind Singh birthday.

July 12	–	Jagmohan demits office of Governor of J K State. General (Retd.) K.V. Krishna R appointed Governor of J&K State
August 14	–	Pakistan Independence Day celebrated J&K
August 15	–	Black out and *hartal* observed on Indi Independence Day.
November	–	Vice President BJP Tikkalal Taploo, gunn down in Srinagar. Justice Ganjoo murder in Hari Singh Street. P.N. Bhat, well-known journalist killed in Anantnag
December 8	–	Kidnapping of Dr Rubaiya Sayeed daugh of the Home Minister of India, Mu Muhammad Sayeed and her subseque release on December 14 in exchange terrorists
December 20	–	United Bank of India looted
December 21-28	–	Several Bomb blasts in the Valley

1990

January 3	–	Inspector of Intelligence Bureau shot dea
January 5	–	'Self-determination Day' observed
January 19	–	General (Retd.) K.V. Krishna R relinquishes charge of Governor of J& State
January 19	–	Jagmohan takes oath of the office Governor of J&K State
January 24	–	Akali Leader Simranjit Singh Mann, vis Srinagar
January 25	–	Meeting between Mann and Jagmoh Four IAF officers including Squadr Leader Ravi Khanna shot dead Rawalpura bus stand. Curfew imposed check the terrorist activities on the eve Indian Independence Day
January 26	–	Illumination at Government buildings Srinagar.
January 30	–	Dr. Farooq Abdullah's press statem accusing the Governor's administration.

February 19 – Dismissal of Dr. Farooq's Ministry. Imposition of Governor's Rule

March 11 – One Central Cabinet Minister designated as Minister of J&K. George Fernades, Railway Minister acquires this designation

April 6 – Kidnapping of Professor Mushir-ul-Haq, Vice-Chancellor of Kashmir University and his murder thereafter

1991

January 21 – Kidnapping of Deputy Inspector General, Security

February 27 – Kidnapping of the daughter of the National Conference Member of Parliament Saifuddin Soz in Srinagar

March 23 – 'Pakistan Day' celebrated, Pakistani flags hoisted at various places

August 27 – Rajya Sabha approves the extension of President's rule in Jammu and Kashmir State

September 22 – Kidnapping of Tassaduq Deva, brother-in-law of Gulam Nabi Azad, Union Minister, Government of India

October 27 – Indian forces repulse a major attack by Pakistani forces on an Indian outpost in the Kargil sector of Kashmir

November 7 – Kidnapping of M.S. Khan, brother of Hamid Ullah Khan, Advisor to the Governor of J&K State

December 11 – Ekta Yatra of BJP from Kanyakumari to Kashmir. About 3 lakh Kashmiri Pandits leave Kashmir during 1990-91.

1992

January 26 – BJP 'Ekta Yatra' ends at Srinagar. National Flag hoisted at Lal Chowk, Srinagar by BJP President Murli Manohar Joshi

March – Release of Tassaduq Deva and M.S. Khan,

		presumably in exchange of three detenus

1993

March 12	–	Resignation of Governor G.C. Sexana and appointment of General K.V. Krishna Rao as Governor of J&K State
April 22	–	Police Strike
October 15	–	Cordon around the Hazratbal shrine for 32 days to flush out the terrorists

1994

May-June	–	'Save Doda District' and 'Jail Bharo Andolan' by BJP
August	–	Successful completion of Amar Nath Yatra by about 45,000 devotees
August 15	–	Indian Prime Minister P.V. Narasimha Rao's declaration about Kashmir as an integral part of India.
September 14	–	Rocket attack on J&K Secretariat

APPENDICES

GEOGRAPHY AND TOPOGRAPHY OF KASHMIR AND LADAK*

Political Geography

The territories of the Kashmir State comprise two provinces, Jammu and Kashmir, each of which is administered by a Chief Officer, or Governor, Styled *Hakim-i-ila*. The districts of Baltistan or Skardu and Ladak are included in the province of Jammu ; and the district of Gilgit, including Astor, in Kashmir. The territory of Punch is administered by Raja Moti Singh, who holds it under a grant from the Maharaja.

Boundaries

When the treaties of 1846 were made, Gulab Singh held, as Raja of Jammu, the hill chiefship around Jammu in a more or less complete state of subjection, and Ladak and Baltistan by right of conquest, and Gilgit had become an appendage of the Sikh governorship of Kashmir. The general and practical result therefore of the Treaty of Amritsar was to confirm Gulab Singh in what he already possessed, and to transfer to him the province of Kashmir with its newly-acquired authority over Gilgit.

Treaty Provisions

The clauses in the treaties of 1846, which relate to the boundaries of the Kashmir State, are as follow:

(I) By the 4th Article of the Treaty of Lahore, dated the 9th March 1846, the Maharaja of Lahore ceded to the East India Company "in perpetual sovereignty, as equivalent for one crore of rupees, all his forts, territories, rights, and interests in the hill

* As recorded in 1890

countries which are situated between the rivers Beas and Indus, including the provices of Kashmir and Hazara."

(II) By the first Article of the Treaty of Amritsar, dated the 16th March 1846, the British Government transferred and made over "for ever, in independent possession to Maharaja Gulab Singh, and the heirs male of his body, all the hilly or mountainous country, with its dependencies, situated to the eastward of the River Indus and westward of the River Ravi, including Chamba and excluding Lahoul, being part of the territories ceded to the British Government by the Lahore State, according to the provisions of Article IV of the Treaty of Lahore, dated the 9th March 1846."

(III) The 2nd Article of the Treaty of Amritsar provided that the eastern boundary of the tract transferred by the Article just quoted should be "laid down by Commissioners appointed by the British Government and the Maharaja Gulab Singh respectively for that purpose," and should be "defined in a separate engagement after survey."

(IV). The 4th Article of the Treaty of Amritsar stipulates that "the limits of the territories of Maharaja Gulab Singh shall not be at any time changed without the concurrence of the British Government."

The Eastern Boundary

From the valley of the Chandra Bhaga to the Gya peak (lat 32° 31', long. 78° 28') the boundary line has been defined by Commissioners, as it here divides the territories of the British and the Kashmir Maharaja. From the Gya peak northwards the Chinese territories adjoin the Kashmir State. The following is an extract from the Commissioner's Report:—

> "In 1830, when Captian A. Cunningham surveyed the Lahoul districts, the boundary between the States of Kulu and Chamba was formed by the Nalda and Chugam nalas, two tributaries of the Chandra Bhaga, the one on its left and the other on its right bank. Form the head of the Chugamnala the Commissioners determined that all the country to the eastward, which is drained by the Bhaga, the Chandra Bhaga, and their tributaries, belonged to the British district of Lahoul; and that the boundary between Lahoul and the Zauskar district was the

Snowy Range (called Paralassa by Dr. Gerard) dividing the drainage of the Bhaga and Chandra Bhaga from that of the Zauskar river.

"Beyond the Bara Lacha pass to the eastward, the Commissioners found that there was an old well-known boundary stone, called Phalang Danda, which marked the limit between Lahoul and Ladak. This stone is noticed by Moorcroft (I., p. 220). It stands in the midst of an open plain on the right bank of the Yunam river. As there was no known or recognised boundary mark on the other side of the stream, the Commissioners selected a remarkable cream-coloured peak, called Turam, as the northern limit of the British territory on the left bank of the river. As this peak is situated at the end of one of the spurs of the great snowy chain, already determined as the northern limit of the Lahoul district, it forms a natural continuation of the boundary line from the westward. The bearing of the Turam peak from the Phalang Danda is 9° to the northward of west.

"As it appeared that the country to the eastward of the Phalang Danda belong to Spiti, the Commissioners determined that the boundary between Spiti and Ladak on the westward should be the Yunam river. A straight line was accordingly drawn from the Phalang Danda to the junction of the first *nala* on the right bank of the Yunam, from which point the Yunam river forms the boundary as far as the junction of the Ts-arap river.

"Almost due north-east form this junction there is a remarkable square rock on the top of the hill, which from its resemblance to a fort, has received the name of Lanka. This curious and well-known peak was selected as another fixed point in the boundary, to which a straight line should be drawn from the junction of the Ts-arap river."

The following passages from Captain Cunningham's journal* also describe a portion of the boundary :

"*Monday, 7th Septemeber*—To mouth of Ts-arap river, $6\frac{1}{4}$ miles. Road good, over a long level, alluvial plain, in the midst

* *Consultation*, 30th December 1848, No. 704.

> of which was a square block of micas late thickly imbedded with large crystals of quartz. This stone, which is 8 feet square and 12 feet high above the ground, is called Lingti by the people of Kulu according to Moorcroft, and *Phalang Danda* by the Ladakis. The only name that we could learn was *Phalang Danda*, which means the boundary stone, the stone being a well-known boundary mark between the States of Kulu and Ladak. Almost due east from the junction of the Ts-arap and Yunam rivers there is, on the top of the hill, a remarkable square rock, which has so much resemblance to a fort that it had received the name of *Lanka* from the shepherds and traders who frequent these parts. It is a well-known point, and it can be seen from the Bara Lacha pass as well as from the neighbourhood of the Gunam lake."

From the Lanka peak to the eastward, the Commissioners, adhering to the principle which they had first laid down, determined that the whole of the Ts-arap valley and its tributaries belonged to the British Government; and that the snowy range on its right bank, which feeds all the northern affluents of the Ts-arap river, should be the boundary between Ladak and the British districts of Spiti. This same range extends towards the east, past the southern end of the Tsomoriri lake, where it forms the well-knowm boundary between Ladak and the Chinese territory. The Commissioners, therefore, determined that the boundary between Ladak and Spiri should continue from the head of the Ts-arap along this same range to the Chinese boundary, thus including within Spiti all the streams which water that district, and giving to Ladak all the streams which water it south-eastern district of Rupshu.

In 1872 the boundary line was drawn from the village of Narbu Sumdo (lat. 32° 41', long. 78° 26') along a ridge to the Gya peak. At this point the boundary line of the Kashmir State adjoins Tibet.

Writing in 1875, Mr. Drew, who was for some time the Maharaja's governor of Ladak, stated that[2] :

> "from the Kuenlun mountains southwards to the head of the Changehenmo valley, the boundary between Ladak and Tibet is quite doubtful. From the head of the Changchenmo valley to

---

2 *Jammu and Kashmir Territories*, page 496..

> the south and south-west till Gya peak is reached, the boundary appeared to be fairly well understood as representing actual occupation,"

so far that it divides pasture lands occupied by the subjects of the Maharaja from those occupied by subjects of Lhasa.

"In the neighbourhood of the Pangong lake,"Mr. Drew observes, "there have been boundary disputes, which may now be said to be latent."

Northern Boundary

At present it extends from the small State of Nagat on the west to the frontier of Tibet on the east. It had not yet been definitely determined. It includes the northern boundaries of Baltistan and Ladak.

Mr. Elias's account–Writing in 1878 about the trade routes to Central Asia, Mr. Elias, the British Joint Commissioner at Leh, said[2]:

> "In the above description the various loops of the road are followed up to the Yarkand frontier at Shahidula, but it would appear from the latest maps that the Maharaja's territory hardly extends so far as that post, but is limited by the Kuenlun water-parting, i.e., the Karakoram."

Mr. Drew's account–Beginning from the north-western end of the line, Mr. Drew describes the boundary thus :–

"(a) From Nagar for the most part, and from the upper part of the Hunza valley, the separation is effected by a great and alomst impassable ridge of mountains.

"(b) As to the boundary with Yarkand territory, from the Mustgh pass to the Karakoram pass, there is no doubt whatever; a great watershed divides the two territories.

"(c) From the Karakoram pass eastwards to past the meridian of 80° there has been no authoritative demarcation, and as the country is quite uninhabited for more than 100 miles in every direction, the actual state of occupation is no guide."

---

2 *Political A.*, July 1878, No. 408.

North-Western Boundary

Commissioners were sent to demarcate this boundary, but do not appear to have arrived at definite results.

Colonel Tanner's account—Colonel Tanner of the Survey of India, who was for a time on duty at Gilgit, has described* the boundary thus :

> "From the Kaghan boundary the frontier line follows the watershed of the Indus, the Kishan Ganga, and the Astor streams, till it dips into the Indus valley at a point nearly opposite Thalicha. It then follows the Indus for a short distance (say 2miles), after which it strikes up-hill to the watershed of the Gilgit river on one side, with Darel, Tangir, and Hndar on the other. This ridge is followed to a point where the Batras stream rises. It then leads down the Batras and Gakuch watersheds to Hupar on the Gilgit river, ascends the range opposite Hupar so as to take in the slopes above Hatun, circles round that place, descends, crosses the Ishkuman stream, and then strikes up the range, following the ridge to a point north of Bar. From this point ice-fields and glaciers occur, and the boundary is undefined; it eventually strikes a spur which leads south, down to the Hunza river midway between Budlas and Moyun, crosses the river and ascends the slope on the opposite side, after which it is taken along the east of the Himalayas over Rakaposhi to the Mustagh pass".

Western Boundary

Writing in August 1850, Major Abbott stated the western boundary to be complete, and described* it in these words[3] :

> "The Jhelum being here full of cultivated islands, boundary pillars are set up in the same, as the boundary ascends the river nearly to Manghuk, where the islands cease, and the deep, rapid, clearly-defined current of the Jhelum requires no

---

* In an un-official note to Mr Crawford

3. Letter No. 215, dated 2nd August 1850, to the Secretary to Board of Administration., Foreign Department Consultation, 27th September 1850, No. 31.

columns to aid in exhibiting the boundary. At the confluence of the Nainsuk or Kunhar river with the Jhelum, the boundary quits the latter river and climbs the current of the Nainsuk to Berarkót British and Berarkót of Jammú where, leaving the river, it strikes to the summit of the Dhab mountain, about 6 miles, and then follows the ridge of that very elevated mountain until lost in the snow, the water falling into the River Kishan Ganga belonging to Jammú, that received by the Nainsuk being British.

"Here also no boundary pillars are required, the mountain ridge being the best possible boundary. In the snow aforesaid terminates the boundary common to British India and Jammú – the British boundary afterwards meeting with lands inhabited by independent tribes."

The Hazára settlement report says that Kághán, part of the Hazára district, is separated from these independent countries by the Kághán range, and from Kashmír by the mountain range bordering the left bank of the Kunhar river. So, too, Mr. Drew (Jammu and Kashmir Territories, page 496) states that from the confluence of the Jhelum and Kaghan (or Kunhar) rivers "the boundary line, still fixed and undisputed,follows the ridge which divides the drainage of Kaghan from that of Kishan Ganga."

Southern Boundary

(1) *From the Jhelum to the Ravi* – The only portion of the British Kashmir boundary which has been demarcated with boundaries is that which lies between the rivers Jhelum and Ravi from a point above Dulial to Madhopur, i.e., from lat. 32° 58',long. 73° 45', to lat. 32° 22', long 75 39'.

(2) *From the Ravi to the Lahoul border* – The southward curve of the River Ravi is the boundary for most of the border between Madhopur and a point about 14 miles west-north-west of the town of Chamba. In regard to this portion* the Boundary Commissioner explained the principles which he had followed thus :

---

* Political A., August 1870, No. 359

> "It was impossible in some cases to avoid the river boundaries.
>
> "When the river was a single clear stream, without cultivated islands, the main current was laid down as the boundary, and one boundary pillar of masonry was planted where the boundary from the east first entered the river, and another where it left the river, though the interval should be of many miles.
>
> "When the boundary ran through the inhabited islands of a river, as in the Jhalum above the town so named, pillars were built all along the line dividing lands, and on either side of the subordinate arms of the river where these formed the boundary.
>
> "Where the boundary line entered a river and ran up the main stream for miles, the boundary pillars were generally of greater size and stability than the ordinary pillars.
>
> "As rivers in India are constantly encroaching upon the land at their salient curves, and receding from it at their re-entering curves, and village lands become thus transferred from one State to the other, it was ruled that the proprietor of such village should remain, not withstanding, still proprietor, paying his dues to each State according to the extent and value of his lands in either."

The Chamba border was apparently[4] demarcated with pillars by Captain Abbott in 1848-49. It reaches the westward limit of the Lahoul boundary defined[5] by Captain Cunningham's Commission at a point 29 miles due north of the confluence of the Chandra Bhaga tributaries of the Chenab, and about the same distance west-north-west of the Bara Lacha pass. There is apparently[6] no doubt about the boundary on the Chamba border.

Physical Geography

Natural Features

The form of the gound of the Maharaja's territories is thus generally

---

4. Letter from Captain Abbott, to the Resident at Lahore, No. 259, dated 23rd March 1848. Foreign Department Consultation, 30th December 1848, No. 161.
5. Foreign Department Consultation, 30th December 1847, Nos. 701 and 702.
6. Drew's "Jamú and Kashmír Territories," page 497.

described by Drew :

The lowest part is the strip of plain on the sounth-west, which is continuous with the great level plain of the Panjab; it is 900 to 1,000 feet above the sea. The mountains begin along a very definite line; the first ridge is a line of hills from 2,000 to 3,000 feet above the sea. Next comes a tract of rugged country which includes various ridges (3,000 to 4,000 feet) running nearly parallel to the first one, with long narrow valleys (2,000 feet) between them.

The foregoing is on the whole a rugged space, partly covered by a low forest or scrub, partly of bare sandstone rock.

Next within is a tract occupied by hills, commonly of 8,000 to 10,000 feet, covered with pasture, or else with forest. These hills are not like the last, in parallel lines, but in ramifications, divided by equally remifying valleys, some of the latter being as low as 2,500 feet.

More lofty mountains are then met with, which rise first to rocky heights, and then to the region of perpetual snow. A great chain of snowy mountains running south-east and north-west divides the drainage of the Chenab and Jhelum rivers form that of the higher branches of the Indus. The summits vary from 27,000 to 15,000 feet. Branches from this enclose the valley of Kashmir (5,000 to 6,000 feet) with hills, many of which are 14,000 to 15,000 feet high.

All beyond is a wide tract of mountainous country, the whole of which is at a high level with peaks from 17,000 to 22,000 feet and more; it is the north-west part of Tibet; and Ladak, Baltistan, and Gilgit are divisions of it. The valleys of this region vary very much in character: in the south-east part are high, level, flat valleys from 1 to 5 miles in width, at elevations of 14,000 and 15,000 feet; from that in a north-west direction their height descends (the space at the same time narrowing, lofty mountains always bounding them) ultimately to as low as 5,000 feet; at the lower levels also are sometimes widenings of the valley bottom.

In a few places are table-lands (too wide to be called valleys) surrounded by mountains. The most remarkable are the Deosai plateau (12,000 to 13,000 feet) and the Lingzithang and Kuenlun plains (16,000 to 17,000 feet).

Vigne remarks that the general character of the southern slopes of the Himalaya is, that they are comparatively bare of trees, although covered with long grass, and that the northern side of Kashmir, although so far from the plains and divided from them by four or five intervening ranges, is, in accordance with this rule, nearly free from jungle, although covered with long grass and verdure, whilst the southern side on the contrary is nearly one mass of forest. He adds :

> "The reasons for this given to me by the Kashmiris were , in the first place, that no trees would grow where the bank was open to the hot winds from India, and further that no jungle will grow where the ground is not exposed to the rays of the morning sun."

It is certainly true that the fruits of the southern side of the valley are always the best. The reasons thus given are more plausible than satisfactory, but the fact of there being in many places so little forest on the southern abutments of the lower Himalaya, and still less on those of Kashmir, is simply owing to their receiving the rays of the sun more vertically than the long slopes on the opposite side of the valley.

Shaw gives the following graphic description of the difference in the aspect of the country on the two sides of the main Himalayan ridge :

> "The Bara Lacha pass is the boundary between two separtae regions distinguished by their physical characters. On the southern side is what may be called the true Himalayan region. Here the gigantic ranges are covered with perpetual snow, furrowed by glaciers, and they rise from amidst dense forests which clothe their flanks up to a certain elevation.
>
> "They are separated by deep gorges, whose sides are precipices, and through which large rivers flow. In fact the scenery is alpine.
>
> "Once across the Bara Lacha pass, however (or any other pass on the same range), you enter a region where all gorges or valleys appear to have been filled up by an encroaching sea of gravel, which has risen to within a few hundred yards of the summits of the ranges. The space between the mountains no longer plunges down in a seemingly bottomless ravine whose sides narrow down till they barely leave room for the stream. Instead of that it is occupied by a broad, high level plain, out of which the summit ranges merely rise like undulations. We

noticed the prevalence of the *horizontal* after the *vertical* lines to which the Himalaya has accustomed us. It is like leavig a *Gothic cathedral* and approaching the *Parthenon*. At the same time, a kind of drought seems to have fallen over the face of the country.

"There are no vast fields of snow to supply streams of water, and no frequent showers to maintain verdure. It seems as if we had here a rough block from which nature intended hereafter to carve out the usual features of a mountain country by some change of climate which would bring snow and ice and water to sweep out the masses of earth or gravel by which the mountain ranges are now glued together. Crossing the Bara Lacha pass we are in barren or Tibetan region, where green spots are about as rare as islands in the ocean, and universal gravel is the rule.

"But there is one deep broad trench, which divides the region into two, lengthwise, that is (roughly) from south-east to north-west. This is the valley of the upper Indus or Ladak. This trench, however, does not descend below 10,000 or 11,000 feet of elevation.

"The round barren hills resemble nothing so much as a gigantic gravel-pit, unless it be a series of heaps of cinders, and have not a blade of verdure on them. There is hardly any snow even on the highest mountains around, for the outer ranges intercept every particle of moisture almost which could fall in the shape of snow.

"So that here at 15,000 feet they have no more snow in winter than on the Kangra range at 5,000 feet. But the dry cold and the bitter wind are in the inverse proportion."

Extent—The dominions of the Kashmir Maharaja extend approximately—

From south-east to north-west	400 miles
From south-west to north-east	350 miles
From south to north	240 miles
From east to west	350 to 400 miles

The area is estimated at 68,000 square miles

Plains and Valley

Vigne estimates the plains in the valley of Kashmir, including th *wudars*, to contain, at a rough calculation, about 650 square miles, and that on the neighbouring mountains there is an extent of at least 150 square miles of pasturage. Mr. Vigne's estimate, however, is too low. Mr. Drew considers the area of the valley to be more probably between 1,800 and 1,900 square miles, and a calculation for the purposes of the land settlement in progress, based upon partial measurement compared with the total revenue, shows that the area within which culturable land lies cannot be less than 1,500 to 1,600 square miles, omitting the lakes. The pasture lands are very extensive and valuable; the Kashmir cattle grazing during the summer up to the confines of Ladak, while the higher altitudes are covered with thousands of sheep. But 150 square miles does not even adequately represent the grazing area of the valley itself. About one third of the valley may be said to afford grass, and the swamps and edges of the lakes produce very nourishing food for cows, besides which the slopes of the mountains, properly belonging to the villages below, can hardly be reckoned at less than a rim of two square miles along an edge of, say, 180 miles. – (*Wingate*).

The *margs* or mountain-downs, which are numerous on the tops of the range of hills immediately below the Pir Panjal, and also upon the northern slopes of those mountains which enclose the north-eastern side of the valley, are a peculiar feature of the country; covered with rich pasturage, they afford sustenance during the summer months to large herds of ponies, cattle, sheep, and goats. The principal of these *margs* frequented by Europeans are Gulmarg, above Baramula, to the eastward of Srinagar; Killan, about 1,000 feet above Gulmarg, Sonamarg in the Sind valley, and Tosha Maidan a few miles south of Gulmarg.

The most considerable of the minor valleys are the Lolab to the north, the Sind valley and Tilail to the north-east, the Nowbug and Maru Wardwan valleys to the south-east, and the Lidar valley also south-east.

Ladak is one of the most elevated regions of the earth, and very barren.

The lowest valleys have an elevation of about 9,000 or 10,000 feet.

The principal plains are the Deosai on the north-eastern

boundary of Kashmir, the Dipsang, south of the Karakoram pass; the Hanle, the Kiang, the Lingti and the Linzithang or Aksai Chin. These plains are for the most part bare and unproductive, affording few means of subsistence to man or beast. The Hanle plain is vary green during the summer months, and gives good feeding to large flocks of sheep.

Mountains

The great Himalaya, which bounds India on the north, in one continuous chain of gigantic peaks, from the southward bend of the Brahmaputra to the holy lake of Manasarowar, is extended to the westward from the sources of the Sutlej to the magnificent peaks of Nanga Parbat at the great bend of the Indus.

This western half forms the watershed parting between the Indus and its five affluents, and also divides the great Hindu family of India from the Bhots of Tibet; lastly, it divides the cold and dry climate of Tibet, with its dearth of trees, from the warm and humid climate of India, with its luxuriance of vegetable productions.

There is one marked differnce between the eastern and western Himalayas: the inferior ranges of the eastern chain generally run at right angles to its axis, whereas those of the western chain are mostly disposed in subordinate parallel ranges. Thus we find no less than two distinct and independent ranges to the south of the western Himalaya, both stretching in the same general direction from south-east to north-west. These ranges may be called the middle Himalaya and the outer Himalaya.

Beyond the Himalaya the same system of parallel chains will be observed in at least three distinct ranges of mountains, which may be called the trans-Himalaya, the Kailas or Gangri range, and the Karakoram, beyond which latter is the Kuenlun range, forming the northern slope of the Great Tibetan plateau as the Himalaya form the southern.

The Himalaya divides the headwaters of the Sutlej from those of the Indus, and extends to the western limits of Astor and Rondu. The Kailas or Gangri range runs through the midst of western Tibet along the right bank of the Indus to the junction of the Shyok.

The main range (the western Himalaya) has already been noticed.

The mid-Himalaya divides the valleys of Spiti, Lahoul, Kishtwar, and Kashmir on the north, form those of Kulu, Chamba, and Punch on the south.

The outer Himalaya are those hills which occur between the mid-Himalaya and Siwaliks, or low hills which rise immediately out of the great plain of the Panjab.

These different ranges form the principal features, and conseqently the natural boundaries of the Hill States. The whole mass of mountains from the Kuenlun range to the plains of the Panjab had an average breadth of nearly 300 miles. (*Cunningham.*)

Lakes

The lakes of the Kashmir valley are numerous, and may be divided into those in the valley itself, and those upon the mountains surrounding it; of the former the following are the principal :—the Dal or "city lake," which is situated on the north-east of Srinagar, and connected with the Jhelum by a canal called the Tsont-i-kul, or "apple-tree canal," which enters it opposite the palace.

The Anchar is situated to the north of Srinagar; it is connected with the Dal by means of the Nali Mar, and it flows into the Sind river near Shadipur. It stretches as far south as the Idgah, where it is called the Kashal Sar; the portion midway near the village of Atsan is known as the Atsan Nambal; the Mar canal passes through it.

The Anchar can scarcely be called a lake; it is caused by the waters of the Sind overflowing the low ground to the north of the city.

The Manas Bal is situated near the right bank of the Jhelum, with which it is connected by a canal which enters it about 400 yeards below the village of Sumbal.

The Wular is the largest of all the lakes, and is situated to the east of Sopur; the Jhelum flows through it.

Among the mountain lakes the following are the most important:—the Konsa Nag, situated on the top of the Pir Panjal range, above the village of Sedau; the Shisha Nag, situated above the head of the Lidar valley, on the raod to the cave of Amrnath; and Gangarbal Nag and Sarbal Nag, situated on the top of Haramuk, which overlooks the north-eastern shore of the Wular.

The city of Srinagar may be said to be surrounded with lakes and morasses, but only those to the north approach the actual limits of the city.

On the south, close ot the left bank of the Jhelum, with which it communicates by a canal, the Vetnar stretches for some miles parallel with the belt of dry land which is traversed by the high road to Shupion; near to it is the Nagat Nambal, and, to the west of the road, on the left bank of the Dudh Ganga, lies the head of the Bimman, one of the series of morasses lying between the slopes on the south-west side of the valley and the Jhelum, which extend the entire distance to the Wular lake.

This lake extends from 5 to 6 miles from north to south, and is 2 to 3 miles from east to west at its broadest point. The mountains rise abruptly along its eastern edge.

The average depth of this lake is not more than 7 to 10 feet, though in one place it reaches 26 feet; the water being very clear, the bottom covered with weeds is almost constantly visible.

With a single exception, all the lakes in Ladak are land-locked, and, consequently, more or less salt. The principal are the Pangong lake, the Pangur Tso, the Tsomoriri lake, and the Tso-kar. There are besides some extensive salt lakes scattered about the Kuenlun plains.

The lakes in Ladak are all at a great height; they are moreover gradually drying up, as becomes apparent by the unmistakeable marks of larger surfaces remaining from former times. There are two small mountain lakes in the range of hills east of Jammu, Surninsar, and Mausar, situated respectively 14 and 20 miles distant form Jammu.

One of the principal rivers of Kashmir is the Jhelum, which in its course nearly intersects the valley. Formed by the junction of three streams, the Arpat, the Bring, and the Sandran, which rise at the south-east end of the valley, it receives in its course numerous tributaries; among those which join it by the right bank are the Lidar from the north-east near Islamabad, and the Sind from the east opposite Shadipur, and after emerging from the Wualr lake, the Pohru, which flows into it in the neighbourhood of Sopur. By its left bank it is joined by the combined waters of the Veshau and Rembiara near Murhama, by the Ramchu at Karkarpur, by the Dudh Ganga at Srinagar, and by the Suknag near Shadipur.

The Kishan Ganga, or river of Krishna, which has its sources on the edges of the Deosai plains and in the Tilail valley, is a very considerable stream; it flows in a north-north-westerly direction, and skirts the north-western extremity of Kashmir, joining the Jhelum just below the town of Mozafarabad, opposite the Domel dak bungalow.

The Maru Wardwan river drains the valley of that name; it takes its rise from the Saga glacier on the pass leading into Suru at the north-eastern extremity of the valley, and flows southward, joining the Chenab or Chandra Bhaga above Kishtwar. This latter river traverses Kishtwar, Badrawar, and Riasi, flowing into the plains at Aknur some miles to the west of Jammu.

Of these rivers the Jhelum is navigable from the neighbourhood of Islamabad to Baramula, a distance of about 60 miles. The boats used in Kashmir are of various kinds, *viz.*, the *bahats, dunga, shikara, khuch, tsatawar, larinao, chakwari, parinda,* and *dinbahnao*.

The *bahats* is the largest description of boat, and is employed exclusively in the transport of grain and merchandise: some of these barges are of great size, and their draught is considerable, so much so that for about four months in winter there is not sufficient water in the river to float them. They have sloping mat-roofs running down the centre. For these boats a deep channel is maintained in the bed of the river, which enables them to traffic much longer than they otherwise could. The family live on board throughout the year. The smaller *bahats* is called *wahat.*

The *dunga* is the ordinary passenger boat of Kashmir; it is a long flat-bottomed craft, usually about 56 feet in length and 6 feet in width, drawing about 2 feet. It has a reed-mat roof, and similar mats are rolled up along the sides; when they are dropped a fairly confortable room is made. The boat people live in a compartment at the back. In winter the *dungas* engage in carrying *shali* (paddy) to Srinagar.

The *shikara* is of the same shape as the *dunga*, but much smaller, being usually only about 36 feet long, $3\frac{1}{2}$ feet wide, and 1 foot deep. It is chiefly used in and about Srinagar, and answers the purpose of a carriage.

The *khuch* is a very large boat without a roof or awning, and is used for the carriage of goods. It is also called *khachu*.

The *tsatawar* is the smallest, lightest, and swiftest of all the boats used on the Kashmir lakes.

The *larinao* is a State barge, in which the boatmen are seated both before and behind the canopied portion occupied by the passenger. It is a sort of house-boat.

There are two other State boats, the *parinda* (a very light, long craft, with a small canopied space towards the fore part, propelled by

30 to 40 men, and possessing great speed) and the *chikwari*, a more substantial boat with a heavier canopy. All the boats on the Jhelum are propelled by heart-shaped paddles.

The *bahats,* or large grain-boats, are generally worked by poles, men on either side descending an inclined plane from the roof of the boat and chanting as they push.

The crew of the *dunga* are most useful, and on shore will act in almost any capacity. Lastly, there is the *dinbahnao* (or *dhemnao*), a little "dug-out", used for the cultivation of the melon-beds of the Dal lake, and for carrying vegetables, &c., to market. It is worked by a man or woman, squatted in the bow, with one paddle.

The Jhelum is spanned by thirteen bridges in its course through the valley of Kashmir; they are of peculiar construction and are called *kadals*.

In Ladak and Baltistan the principal river is the Indus, which flows in a general north-west direction through the whole length of these two provinces in a deep trough between the trans-Himalayan range on its left bank and the Kailas and Karakoram ranges on its right bank. Its chief tributaries on the left bank are the Hanle, Zanskar river, the Dras and Astor rivers, while on the right bank it receives the Shyok, the Shigar, and the Gilgit rivers. The Shyok receives the Nubra and the Changchenmo rivers; while the Shigar is formed by the junction of the Basha and Braldu rivers.

Both the Jhelum and the Chenab also join the Indus after it has entered the plains of the Panjab. The most remarkable feature about the Indus and its tributaries is the general parallelism of their courses, which has been determined by the direction of the principal mountain chains, and the same similarity may be observed in the peculiar knee-bends which are common to all the rivers of the Panjab. For the curious sweep southward, which occurs in the Sutlej below Bilaspur, is also found in all the other river; in the Beas below Hajipur; in the Ravi near Basaoli; in the Chenab below Kishtwar; in the Jhelum below Mozafarabad; and in the Indus at the junction of the Gilgit river.

Cunningham gives the following account of the passage of rivers in Ladak :

Passage of Rivers

The rivers are generally crossed by fording. *Gal* is the Tibetan term for a ford. In summer, the morning is the best time for fording, for after 10 or 11 a.m. the waters are much increased by the melting snows.

Ferry (grukha)

The common people are usually ferried over on a single inflated skin, but influential men are usually taken over on a raft, formed by placing a *charpai* on two inflated skins. The Shyok, opposite Satti, is crossed by boat in summer.

Bridges

There are two kinds of bridges met with in Ladak–

(1) The *zampa* or wooden bridge, made usually of large beams of poplars. Good specimens are to be seen at Lah and Khalsi.

(2) The *chug-zam,* or suspension bridge, is common on the Indus and Shyok, above their junction. It is formed of two stout ropes of twisted birch twigs, about the thickness of a man's arm.

The *chug-zam* is a very cheap and easy mode of bridging a stream, and is, when new and well constructed, quite safe. The passage of old bridges is, however, often both difficult and dangerous. In them the suspension ropes form a great curve; the sides are frequently unwattled and completely open, and the roadway sometimes reduced to a single rope. (*Cunningham.*)

Climate

Owing to the great variations of level, the climate must necessarily be different for every region.

The temperature ranges from more than the tropical heat of the Panjab summer, to such an intensity of cold as keeps perpetual snow on the mountains. In inhabited places even, the variation is such, that in the lower parts the people go about nearly unclad; in the higher, sheepskins are worn, and in some places the people are confined to their houses for seven months in the year by snow. The element of moisture also causes much variety in climate, and consequently in aspect of country.

Regions of four different degrees may be roughly distinguished as follow :–

(1) Where the periodical rains prevail, as in the southern portions of British territory, including the outer hills and middle mountains.

(2) where the rains do not reach, but there is rainfall enough for all crops, but rice, without irrigation. This area embraces Kashmir.

(3) Where irrigation is necessary for crops, and the hillsides are bare, with the exception of a little forest. This is a semi-Tibetan climate, and includes Astor, part of Gilgit and of Baltistan.

(4) A nearly rainless tract, where irrigation is necessary for crops, and the whole country is entirely bare. This has a Tibetan climate and includes the rest of Gilgit, the greater part of Baltistan, and all Ladak.

Communications

Roads

The cart-road now under construction up the Jhelum valley from Mari to Srinagar is the only road practicable for wheeled traffic. The remainder are only practicable for pack animals. Mr. Girdlestone says of the roads :

> "On land the means of communication in the towns are narrow, tortuous streets, whose uneven pavemnet is excruciating to the feet, and in the country the tracks worn by passengens and cattle, and following the inequalities of the ground. In the side valleys, the footpath soon becomes difficult as the upper gorges are reached."

Mr. Wynne reported in 1873 that the Maharaja intended henceforth to devote to the improvement of roads an annual sum of half a lakh of *chilki* (ten-anna) rupees. Up to date little or nothing has been done towards the repairs of the roads.

To Srinagar the principal roads from India are :

(a) The Mari road, nearly finished, suitable for wheeled traffic, and with little alteration for a narrow-gauge line.

(b) The Pir Panjal route, which is very bad and much less used than formerly. Ponies go along it with difficulty.

(c) The Sialkot-Jammu-Srinagar route, a good deal used by natives, suitable for baggage animals.

From Srinagar the principal roads are :

(a) To Gilgit *via* the Kamri or Dorikun passes, Astor and Bunji. This road is continued to Chitral and then by the Dorah pass into Zebak. It is passable for baggage animals, but difficult in places.

(b) To Lah *via* the Zoji La and and thence on to Yarkand. A certain amount of money is being yearly spent by the Joint Commissioners on this road, and consequently it is generally very good going for baggage animals.

(c) To Skardu *via* the Zoji La and Indus valley. From where it leaves the Leh road, this road is extremely bad and barely passable for baggage animals.

In the valley the best road is perhaps that leading from Srinagar to Shupion, and thence to the Pir Panjal pass. Other well-marked tracks are the roads from Baramula to Srinagar on the one side, and to Islamabad and Vernag and thence to the Banihal pass on the other side; the road to Leh up the Sind valley and thence over the Zoji La, and the road to Gilgit following the course of the Jhelum, and then skirting the east side of the Wular lake. All the roads appear to date from the time of the Delhi Emperors. Of the village paths, it may be said that from any large village there is usually a decent track leading to Srinagar. But communication between villages is very difficult owing to rivers, canals, unbridged irrigation cuttings, rice-lands, and swamps. On all main tracks the villagers maintain little crossings of logs covered with mud over irrigation canals and streams. Near Srinagar the roads generally begin with a mile or two of poplar avenue. The traffic is by ponies, mules, and coolies. (*Wingate*)

Bellew gives the following interesting account of the mode of tracking out a pass by the aid of yaks on the high passes of Ladak :

"Before essaying the passage of the glacier, it is customary to

> drive a herd of ten or twelve yaks across to ascertain the route. These, in their way, sagacious animals, when urged up the side of the glacier, crowd together for a consultation on its edges, and after a good deal of grunting one of them takes the lead, the others following in single file. The leader, with his nose down on the snow, sniffs and grunts his way cautiously, and when tired, falls back for the next to take up the lead till land is reached on the other side. The Bhots follow the track of their brutes and erect little pillars of snow here and there along the route by way of guide in case of mists or snow obscuring the track."

Not unfrequently in the valley of the Indus, blocks of rocks are set in motion by the step of the wild sheep. These stone avalanches are of constant occurrence in these hills after rain and during the period the winter snows are melting away; and they are one of the most dreaded dangers, the traveller had to face. And, hence, it is that the Bhot never thinks of camping in the open in these valleys, but always takes shelter in the cavern of some secure bank, or scoops out, or walls in, some ready hollow under the lee of any firm rock.

Sandals

In the Kashmir valley the better class of people wear *chaplis*, which consist of a soft-leather sock, laced, and over it a strong, think leather sole, bound to the foot by thngs, terminating in one buckle. Coolies, both in the valley and in the mountains, wear sandals made of rice-straw. *Chaplis* are useless in wet weathere, but the straw-shoe is good and safe, and worn over the European boot is comfortable, and safe for mountain climbling. (*Wingate.*)

The Tibetan sandals, or mocassins, will wear for a surprisingly long time, provided they do not get wet. They are made of ibex-skin, and on account of their roughness and pliability they are admirably adapted to walking over steep or dangerous paths.

Communications

Water

In the valley of Kashmir the Jhelum and the canals connected with it are much used as a means of communication, and have hitherto served all the purposes of traffic.

To avoid the necessity of crossing the dangerous Wular lake, through which flows the main stream of the Jhelum, a navigable canal was constructed in very early times to connect Sopur with Srinagar.

This canal, which is called the Naru, leaves the left bank of the river immediately below Shadipur and runs southward, dividing into two branches, the smaller of which continues straight on through the marshes to Patan and Palhallan, while the other turns to the right and finally enters the southern portion of the Wular lake.

When the water is high enough, this, which is the shorter route, is always selected by the boatmen when passing between Srinagar and Baramula.

Irrigation channels are numerous; of these the Shahkul canal in the Khourpara *pargana*, the Naindi and Ninnar canals, near Islamabad, are among the most important.

The construction of a canal connecting Aknur with Jammu was commenced, but proving a failure was abandoned; it is called the Shahnahar canal. Rafts and small boats are floated down the Chenab, but is cannot be called navigable above Aknur. There are falls and rapids, near where the river makes the knee-bend, which are dangerous. The Indus is too rapid to be navigated in any part of its course through the Kashmir State.

Postal

The earliest rules regarding postal communication with Kashmir were contained in Panjab Notification No. 673, dated 16th March 1867, and provided for the conveyance of a sealed bag to and from the British Officer on duty at Srinagar, by the Maharaja's agency. A fee equal to half the British postage was levied, on behalf of the Maharaja, on all letters to and from visitors in the valley, who used what was termed "the Resident's dak."

Changes in 1870-71

In 1870 the direct eonnection of the Srinagar post office with the office of the Officer on Special Duty was severed; but the Srinager post office has always since been maintained by the Imperial post office during the Kashmir season of each year. At first sanction was experimentally given[7] in 1870; but it was continued[8] permanently in 1871. The establishment was as follows :

1 Deputy Postmaster ...	100 per mensem.
1 Clerk	30 per mensem.
1 Munshif	10 per mensem.
2 Peons	14 per mensem.
Stationery	6 per mensem.

From 1st January 1886 Srinagar was constituted a permanent head office, which is now open throuhout the year. The time of transit between Sialkot and Srinagar averages about 63 hours. The present establishment consists of–

1 Postmaster	150 per mensem.
2 Clerks	30 per mensem.
1 clerk	20 per mensem.
2 Postmen	14 per mensem.
Stationery allowance	6 per mensem.

Source: *Gazetteer of Kashmir and Ladak*, Superintendent of Government Printing Press, Calcutta, 1890.

7. Letter from Financial Department to Director General of the Post Office, dated 19th May 1870.
8. Letter from Financial Department to Director General of the Post Office, No. 1477, dated 16th March 1871.

APPENDIX–2

INTRODUCTION TO THE VALLEY OF KASHMIR*

This report, which is written on the lines of the Punjab Gazetteers, deals with Kashmir proper. Though our Settlement operations have extended to Gilgit and to Jammu territory, it has been necessary to exclude information gathered in those countries, even though connected with Kashmir. It has been difficult to decide what facts should be recorded and what discarded, but so far as it has been possible, I have avoided the repetition of information already presented to the State in the fifteen Assessment Reports of Kashmir which have been written by me. In them will be found the rates of assessment, the mode of classfying and valuing soils, and many facts bearing on the past revenue administration of Kashmir. In this report I shall deal with subjects of general interest. It has been written at odd hours, in the midst of much interruption, and I regret that I have not the leisure to use one half of the notes made by me during the six seasons I have worked in Kashmir. In this opening chapter I allude to matters which may help to elucidate points incidentally mentioned in other parts of the report, and I offer suggestions which may help the future administration of the country. Kashmir, as possessing a distinct nationality, character, language, dress, and body of customs, affords much that is interesting, while its unique history and curious administration are worth careful study. The beautiful valley has been for many years a pleasure resort of Europeans, and many books have been written on the subject of Kashmir. But even the best of these, Drew's *Jammu and Kashmir*, says little about the valley or its people, and most works which I have read do not add much to the information gathered by Vigne. Strange and hazy ideas have prevailed regarding the wealth of the country, the character of the people, and the system of administration – ideas which can only be confirmed or refuted by one whose life and work have brought him into close contact with the villagers and officials. From the first I

---

* Recorded by Walter Roper Lawrence during 1889-1895

have found the villagers communicative as they sat by the camp fire, while the officials are often well informed, and excellent talkers, by no means reticent.

Kashmir in 1887, when the Settlement commenced, may be described as an absolute monarchy. If an aristocracy of power ever existed, the tall poppies were cut down year ago, and the people looked to the Maharaja as their direct lord and master. They yearn for personal rule centred in one man, and they are bewildered and disgusted when rule and power filter into many channels. In Kashmir the Maharaja is represented by a Governor (Hakim-i-Ala), and it is of the highest importance that this official be a man of energy and experience, and that all departments, whether revenue, police, forests, &c., should be absolutely under his control. If this be borne in mind, the administration of Kashmir will be very easy. It is a small country, and an energetic Governor could visit any village in the valley in a day's ride.

Much has been written of the abuses which have prevailed in the administration of Kashmir. They were numerous and deplorable, and when I first came to Kashmir in 1889, I found the people sullen suspicious. They had been taught for many years that they were serfs without any right but with many disabilities. They were called *Zulm parast*, or worshippers of tyranny, and every facility was affored to their cult. They were forced by soldiers to plough and sow, and the same soldiers attended at harvest time. They were dragged away from their houses to carry loads to Gilgit, and every official had a right to their labour and their property. Their simple proposition *yus Karih gonglu sui Karih Krao** was ignored, and their position was infinitely worse than that of the Tiers Etat before the French Revolution. While the villagers were thus degraded, the people of the city were pampered and humoured, and the following passage from Hazlitt's *Life of Napoleon Bonaparte* gives a fair idea of Kashmir before the Settlement commenced :

> 'The peasants were overworked, half-starved, treated with hard words and hard blows, subjected to unceasing exactions and every species of petty tyranny. . . while in the cities a number of unwholesome and useless professions, and a crowd of lazy menials, pampered the vices or administered to the pride and

---

* He who ploughs shall reap.

luxury of the great.'

It was no wonder that cultivation was bad, that the revenue was not paid, and that the peasants were roving from one village to another in the hope of finding some rest and freedom from oppression. The Kashmiri is made up of contradictions. He is timid yet persistent, degraded yet intellectual. Village life meant little to him. His one object was to escape the press-gang when carriage was wanted for Gilgit, and to secure some share of the autumn's grain when the tax collectors appeared. He would not hesitate to throw his burden on to his neighbour's shoulders, and if he failed he would depart to some other village under the aegis of a privileged person who would protect him from the *corvée*, and would allow no one but himself to oppress the wanderer. Pages might be written . . . on facts but it will suffice to say that the system of administration had degraded the people and taken all heart out of them. The country was in confusion, the revenue was falling off, and those in authority were making hay while the sun shone. Strong personal government is, I believe, the only form of government possible in Kashmir for many years to come, but it is difficult for the Maharajas to supervise the administration of the valley when they are away in their winter Capital Jammu. The peasants, one and all, attributed their miseries to the deputies through whom the Maharajas ruled, and they have always recognized that their rulers were sympathetic and anxious to secure their prosperity. But the officials of Kashmir would never allow their master to know the real condition of the people, or to find out that the revenue of the country was diminishing. If the Governor of Kashmir were not active and honest, dishonesty ran rampant through every grade of officialdom.

'There's not a crime
But takes its proper change out still in crime
If once rung on the counter of this world,'

and the slightest weakness or corruption on the part of the Governor had its echo in every corner of the valley. Not only were the officials corrupt but the peasants and their headmen were also dishonest, all joining to rob their master's treasury.

His Highness the Maharaja Pratap Singh, G.C.S.I., recognizing that it was impossible to check these abuses without records and statistics, resolved on effecting a land Revenue Settlement of his country. At first it was extremely difficult to persuade the people that the Settlement would be a reality, or to inspire them with a belief that there would be some continuity in the administration. Little by little, confidence has sprung up. Land which had no value in 1889 is now eagerly sought after by all classes. Cultivation has extended and improved. Houses have been rebuilt and repaired, fields fenced in, orchards planted, vegetable gardens well stocked, and new mills constructed. Women no longer are seen toiling in the fields, for their husbands are now at home to do the work, and the long journeys to Gilgit are a thing of the past. When the harvest is ripe the peasant reaps it at his own good time, and not a soldier ever enters the villages. The old saying-

> *'Batta, batta,*
> *Tah piyada patta,'*

which meant 'we are asking for food and the tax collector is after us,' is no longer heard, for the people are left with ample grain to feed their families. Before 1887 the peasants rarely tasted their beloved food rice. Now all eat rice, and enjoy salt, and the luxury of tea. Little shops are springing up in the villages, and whereas I never saw a metal vessel in any peasant's house three years ago, now a brass cooking-pot is by no means rare.

There has been a great change, but it is important that the State should remember that the change has been sudden, and every effort should be made to keep faith with the villagers. A few breaches of the promises made at Settlement would again plunge the country into confusion, and it is well to bear in mind that many hungry middlemen (*the fermiers*) driven out by the Settlement are waiting and watching. It is well to remember that a people so broken and degraded as the Kashmiris do not in a few years harden into a resolute and self-respecting community. They are a soft, timid people, only too ready to avoid a citizen's responsibilities and to shelter themselves behind the plausible and fraudulent middleman. There is not a single middleman left in the villages at the present time, but if the State withdrew its vigilant watch some 40 per cent of the peasants might again become the serfs of middlemen and officials.

Security of tenure has a magical effect, but I think immunity from forced labour has been as efficacious in promoting confidence among the villages. The construction of the Gilgit road, and the organization of a transport service have done much to abolish the worst incidents of the *corvee*, but if the Maharaja himself had not set the example of limiting the demands made by his camp-followers, 'Purveyance' would have lingered on for years. It was no uncommon thing for 300 sheep to be collected at one stage. Nothing would be paid for them. Now all supplies are paid for. If honest dealing continues for another ten years I believe that the Kashmiris, so hardly spoken of, will become honest. It should be remembered that from the point of view of the peasant, honesty has not hitherto been the best policy.

Kashmir is a very old country, and its people are very old-fashioned. Those who have studied the history of Kashmir say that the people have not changed much since the times of ancient Hindu kings. This is quite possible, but I think that many of the hard things said about the Kashmiris are due to the fact that the official interpreters of their character have been foreigners, often grasping and corrupt, always unsympathetic. Mughal Subahs, Pathan Sirdars, Sikh and Dogra Governors dismissed all difficulties of administration, and all humane suggestions emanating from their masters, with the remark that the Kashmiris were dishonest, treacherous and *zulm parast.* It is the old tale of giving a dog a bad name, and I must confess that during my first year's work in the valley I shared these views. But I soon grew to understand that the Kashmiri, like other orientals, has two sides to his character as distinct as light and darkness. His great yearning is to be left alone – to till his fields and weave his wollen cloth. The official visit, which to us officials seems so pleasant to all concerned, sends the pulse of the village up many degrees, and those are happy who dwell far away from the beaten tracks. The dark side of the Kashmiri is revealed when he is in the presence of officials. He has had good reason to hate and distrust them, and his only weapon against them is deceit. His light side is seen when he is in his field or with his family in the house. Take as an instance the relations of a Kashmiri cultivator with the village shopkeepers. The shopkeeper (*wani*) is a Musalman and must not take *interest*. He lends money to the peasants on a system known as *wad*. A man borrows 50 rupees, and promises to pay this within the year in blankets, ghi, apples, grain, &c. The rate fixed by the *wani* for blankets will be 3 rupees, whereas the market price at which the *wani* will sell is 3 rupees 8 annas, or 4 rupees. No bond (*hujat*) is signed by the borrower, and the only record of the transaction is an entry in the daily ledger of the *wani*. I have always made a point of talking with the *wanis* whenever I see a village shop, and they are unanimous in saying that they never make a bad debt and that they are never obliged to sue a debtor. This state of things does not argue that the Kashmiri peasants are dishonest.

... crime is almost non-existent in Kashmir. Crimes of dishonesty may be said to be absolutely non-existent among the peasants. Property is entirely safe, and during the six years which I have spent in the villages, I have never heard of crimes of theft, or burglary being committed by agriculturists. This surely points to the fact that the Kashmiris are not the dishonest people they are represented to be.

Since 1890 all suits connected with land, saving land situated within Srinagar and a few adjoining villages, have been removed from the ordinary courts and have been made over to me for decision. My procedure has been to hear and decide such suits in the village where the claim has arisen. Under a chenar tree in the presence of the assembled villagers the claimant prefers his suit and the defendant makes his reply. Then the old men of the village and the headmen of the neighbourhood give their opinion on the case, and a brief entry is made by me which finally settles the claim. This may seem a very rough and ready way of disposing of land suits, but so far no man has ever appealed against my decision. If a claimant went to the Courts in Srinagar, the dark side of his character would appear. Pleaders and Court attendants would adulterate his simple claim, and in the same way the defendant would throw off the candour and truthfulness inspired by the presence of his neighbours in the village, and would lie in the most ingenious and surprising manner. For five years this procedure of enquiry on the spot has gone on, and I attribute much of the quiet prosperity which is now growing in the villages, to the fact that money is not spent and bad blood is not engendered by litigation. My system is the old system of the village *panchayat*. The commonest intellect can tell from the faces of the villagers whether the claim is just, and the *genius loci* seems to keep both claimant and defendant to the point and to the truth. This system is easy and possible in Kashmir, for as I have already remarked, one can reach any village in the valley in a day's ride.

My object in alluding to this procedure is to add further testimony to the fact that the Kashmiri peasants are not dishonest. If they had been the hopeless liars they are reputed to be, I could never have disposed of the many suits which have arisen. A Kashmiri will rarely lie when he is confronted in his village by his fellow villagers; he will invariably lie when he enters the murky atmosphere of the Law Courts.

Perhaps this summary procedure would have been impossible if I had not in 1889 induced the State to withhold from the Kashmiris the power to alienate their land by sale or mortgage. If hereafter, when population increases and communications are improved, the State should unfortunately see fit to give the fatal gift of alienation to their Musalman tenants, I trust that some portion of the holding (which should be two acres of irrigated and four acres of dry land) will be rendered absolutely inalienable. I hope too that the suggestion that pleaders should be allowed to intervene in suits connected with land will never be made again, or that if it is made that it will meet with the wise veto which was accorded to it in 1892. If litigation is fostered in Kashmir prosperity in the villages will be checked.

The work of Settlement has been anxious and difficult. Powerful interests were at work against us, and if it had not been for the loyal and consistent support rendered to me by His Highness The Maharaja and his advisers, these interests would have made a Settlement impossible. These adverse interests were :

(1) The official classes and the Pandits who held land on privileged terms.
(2) The headmen of the villages.
(3) The city of Srinagar.

As regards the officials it is pleasant to be able to say that from active opposition they have now passed to friendly co-operation. The Tahsildars, on whom the Revenue Administration chiefly depends, have been reduced from fifteen to eleven. With one exception they are all men of the old officialdom of Kashmir, and at the present time only one of the eleven is a Pandit. It would have been easy to carry out *temporary* reforms in Kashmir, if trained Tahsildars had been imported from the Panjab as was at one time suggested. But apart from the unfairness and unpopularity of such a measure, I am not sure that reforms effected through so foreign an agency would have been permanent. By selecting the best of the Kashmiri officials as

Tahsildars, by raising their pay and by treating them with the respect due to their office, I believe that the most important agents of the revenue administration have grown to look on the Settlement with favour. Of course numbers of superflous officials who hovered round the carcass of the revenue have disappeared from the scene, and the *fermiers* and the solidiers have been obliged to seek other occupations. Happily, owing to the large influx of silver into the country, and to the briskness of internal trade, most of the drones have found a livelihood. As regards the privileged holders of land every effort has been made to treat them with indulgence, and for another ten years they will continue to be privileged, though their revenue will be somewhat higher than it used to be. The headmen of villages have on the whole accepted the change brought by the Settlement without any prolonged opposition. They have now to pay revenue for their land like other cultivators, but thier social position is better, and they are paid five per cent on Revenue Collections, whereas formerly they received nothing.

The interests of the city have from the earliest times been opposed to the interests of the villages. The city people want grain and other village produce at rates far below the cost of production. 'What the eye does not see the heart does not grieve'—and the authorities saw and heard the city, but the villagers were out of sight and out of mind.

Low prices of the chief staple rice (lower this year, 1894; than they have been for years) coupled with difficulty in selling the State grain brought into Srinagar at the end of 1893, the opening of a cart road from Baramula to Srinagar, the extraordinary increase in the amount of silver now in circulation in the city, and last, but not least, the growing desire of shawl-weavers and even Pandits to obtain labour, all point to the conclusion that a new era has dawned for Srinagar, and that before long honest industry will be the rule, and helpless and ignorable dependence on the State and its charities will be the exception.

I have urged on the authorities for the establishment of Technical Schools; and the State which has unwittingly done so much to pauperize and emasculate the population of its summer capital, has splendid work now before it in raising the *Shahr-bash** to the position of self-helping and industrious citizens.

* City people.

. . . A feeling of impatience may be aroused when the reformer sees that the Kashmiris are opposed to changes which are obviously for their good. It should, however, be remembered that if it had not been for their essentially conservation nature the Kashmiris would have succumbed to the stern rules of social evolution, and would have been blotted out as a distinct nationality by their strong superiors the Mughals, Pathans, Sikhs, and Dogras. It is no exaggeration to say that these successive dynasties have left no impress on the national character – that there has been no progress in the ordinary sense of the word, and that the Kashmiris are now, in spite of many experiments in administration, very much what they were in the times before the Mughal conquest linked the valley with India. It is therefore necessary to be patient, and it is wrong to condemn the Kashmiri if he is sceptical regarding the advantages of progress. The people have a keen intellect, and this joined to their steady aversion to change makes them very difficult subjects for administrative experiments. Many changes have been introduced by the Settlement, but they have been made after a careful study of the character and ideas of the people. Old institutions have been adapted to new wants, and in the future reform will be futile unless it proceeds on these lines. But in order to understand old institutions it is essential to learn the customs of the people, and the shortcomings of past administrations are chiefly due to the fact that the authorities considered the Kashmiris and their usages unworthy of study. My experience is that in dealing with so peculiar a people nothing, however small, is unimportant if it gives a clue to the working of their minds. Take as instances the old practice of espionage, or the blind credence which the village people place in any news coming from Srinagar. The Kashmiris are well styled *Hawabin**, and it would save much trouble and disquietude if the State would endeavour to suppress the evil system which still lingers on of disseminating false rumours. The *Zaina-kadal*, or fourth bridge of the city, used to be the place where false rumours were hatched, but now the news makers have moved to the first bridge, the *Amiran-kadal*. Though the wise knew that *Khabar-i-Zaina-kadal*** was false, the majority are not wise, and mush misery is caused to the villagers by the reports which emanate from the city. The Kashmiris are very unstable and very

* Watchers of the wind.

** News from the *Zina-kadal.*

prone to give undue weight to rumours. They are emotional and ruled by sentiment. They will do excellent work on water-courses and embankments if coaxed, and praised, and encouraged with small presents of snuff. They will do little if paid a full daily wage. They like and admire stern determination in their ruler. All they ask is that they may have access and hearing on certain occasions. They are accomplished talkers, but have an instinctive dread of their words being committed to paper. Writing in their opinion is a trap and a fraud. While on the whole they like certainty in the revenue administration, and are not as some suppose enamoured of the elastic properties of a fluctuating assessment, they would hate our western ideas of justice and judicial procedure. I have done my utmost to leave the system of Kashmir alone where it was possible, and should deplore the introduction of elaborate rules and procedure. These Sibylline books, with officials as interpreters, would do no good to Kashmir. All that the State need now do for its agricultural population is to leave the villagers alone. Cholera and small-pox should be grappled with so that the population – at present inadequate – should increase and multiply. Kashmir is generations behind the Punjab, and what is good and necessary in the Punjab is dangerous and premature in this country. A wise Kashmiri with whom I was conversing on the subject of the alleged oppression of the police, said, in answer to a question of mine, 'Of course the police annoy us, and I presume that this is the purpose for which they are employed. There is no crime in the country, and the police must have something to do.' There is no doubt work for the police in the city and towns and on the road, but I doubt whether their presence is necessary in the villages. But police are necessary in the Panjab districts, and it has perhaps been argued that human nature being the same in all countries police are required in the districts of Kashmir. I merely mention the police as an instance to show that Kashmir is a peculiar country, which need not necessarily be administered at present by the strict pattern adopted in British India. While the object of administration should be to leave the people alone to recover from the atrophy which has been caused by over-government, much can be done by example and advice.

Source: *The Valley of Kashmir,* by Walter Roper Lawrence, H. Frowde, London, 1895; reprint by Kesar Publications, Srinagar, 1967.

CONSTITUTIONAL PROVISIONS REGARDING STATES AND UNION TERRITORIES IN INDIA

PART I
THE UNION AND ITS TERRITORY

1. Name and territory of the Union – (1) India, that is Bharat, shall be a Union of States.

[1][(2) The States and the territories thereof shall be as specified in the First Schedule.]

(3) The territory of India shall comprise –

(a) the territories of the States;

[2][(b) the Union territories specified in the First Schedule; and]

(c) such other territories as may be acquired.

2. Admission or establishment of new States – Parliament may by law admit into the Union, or establish, new States on such terms and conditions as it thinks fit.

[3]**2A.** [*Sikkim to be associated with the Union*] – *Rep. by the Constitution (Thirty-sixth Amendment)* Act. 1975, s. 5 (w.e.f. 26-4-1975)

3. Formation of new States and alteration of areas, boundaries or names of existing States – Parliament may by law –

(a) form a new State by separation of territory from any State or by uniting two or more States or parts of States or by uniting any territory to a part of any State;

(b) increase the area of any State;

(c) diminish the area of any State;

(d) alter the name of any State:

[4][Provided that no Bill for the purpose shall be introduced in either House of Parliament except on the recommendation of the

President and unlesss, where the proposal contained in the Bill affects the area, boundaries or name of any of the State[5] ***, the Bill has been referred by the President to the Legislature of that State for expressing its views thereon within such period as may be specified in the reference or within such further period as the President may allow and the period so specified or allowed has expired.]

[6][*Explanation I*—In this article, in clauses (a) to (e), "State" includes a Union territory, but in the proviso, "State" does not include a Union territory.

Explanation II—The power conferred on Parliament by clause (a) includes the power to form a new State or Union territory to any other State or Union territory.]

4. Laws made under articles 2 and 3 to provide for the amendment of the First and the Fourth Schedules and supplemental, incidental and consequential matters—(1) Any law referred to in Article 2 or Article 3 shall contain such provisions for the amendment of the First Schedule and the Fourth Schedule as may be necessary to give effect to the provisions of the law and may also contain such supplemental, incidental and consequential provisions (including provisions as to representation in Parliament and in the Legislature or Legislatures of the State or States affected by such law) as Parliament may deem necessary.

(2) No such law as aforesaid shall be deemed to be an amendment of this Constitution for the purpose of Article 368.

FIRST SCHEDULE[7]

(Articles 1 and 4)

1. THE STATES

Name	Territories
1. Andhra Pradesh	[8][The territories specified in sub-sectioin (1) of Section 3 of the Andhra State Act, 1953, sub-section (1) of Section 3 of the States Reorganisation Act, 1956, the First Schedule to the Andhra Pradesh and Madras (Alteration of Boundaries) Act, 1959, and the Schedule to the Andhra Pradesh and Mysore (Transfer of Territory) Act, 1968, but excluding the

	territories specified in the Second Schedule to the Andhra Pradesh and Madras (Alteration of Boundaries) Act, 1959.]
2. Assam	The territories which immediately before the commencement of this Constitution were comprised in the Province of Assam, the Khasi States and the Assam Tribal Areas, but excluding the territories specified in the Schedule to the Assam (Alteration of Boundaries) Act, 1951 [9][and the territories specified in sub-section (i) of Secion 3 of the State of Nagaland Act, 1962] [10][and the territories specified in Sections 5, 6 and 7 of the North-Eastern Areas (Reorganisation) Act, 1971].
3. Bihar	[11][The territories whcih immediately before the commencement of this Constitution were either comprised in the Province of Bihar or were being administered as if they formed part of that Province and the territories specified in clause (a) of sub-section (1) of Section 3 of the Bihar and Uttar Pradesh (Alteration of Boundaries) Act, 1968, but excluding the territories specified in sub-section (1) of Section 3 of the Bihar and West Bengal (Transfer of Territories) Act, 1956, and the territories specified in clause (b) of sub-section (1) of Section 3 of the first mentioned Act.]
[12][4. Gujarat	The territories to in sub-section (1) of Section 3 of the Bombay Reorganisation Act, 1960.]
5. Kerala	The territories specified in sub-section (1) of Section 5 of the Reorganisation Act, 1956.
6. Madhya Pradesh	The territories specified in sub-section (1) of Section 9 of the States Reorganisation Act, 1956 [13][and the First Schedule to the Rajasthan and Madhya Pradesh (Transfer of Territories) Act 1959].
[14][7. Tamil Nadu]	The territories which immediately before the commencement of this Constitution were either comprised in the Province of Madras or were

being administered as if they formed part of that Province and the territories specified in Section 4 of the States Reorganisation Act, 1956, [15][and the Second Schedule to the Andhra Pradesh and Madras (Alteration of Boundaries) Act, 1959,] but excluding the territories specified in sub-section (1) of Section 3 and sub-section (1) of Section 4 of the Andhra State Act, 1953 and [16][the territories specified in clause (b) of sub-section (1) of Section 5, Section 6 and clause (d) of sub-section (1) of Section 7 of the State Reorganisation Act, 1956 and the territories specified in the First Schedule to the Andhra Pradesh and Madras (Alteration of Boundaries) Act, 1959].

[17][8. Maharashtra	The territories specified in sub-section (1) of Section 8 of the State Reorganisation Act, 1956, but excluding the territories referred to in sub-section (1) of Section 3 of the Bombay Reorganisation Act, 1960.]
[18][9. Karnataka	The territories specified in sub-section (1) of Section 7 of the State Reorganisation Act, 1956 [19][but excluding the territory specified in the Schedule to the Andhra Pradesh and Mysore (Transfer of Territory) Act, 1968]
[20][10. Orissa	Ther territories which immediately before the commencement of this Constitution were either comprised in the Province of Orissa or were being administered as if they formed part of that Province.
20[11. Punjab	The territories specified in Section 11 of the States Reorganisation Act, 1956 [21][and the territories referred to in Part II of the First Schedule to the Acquired Territories (Merger) Act, 1960] [22][but excluding the territories referred to in Part II of the First Schedule to the Constitution (Ninth Amendment) Act, 1960] [23][and the territories specified in sub-section (1) of Section 3, Section 4 and

	sub-section (1) of Section 5 of the Punjab Reorganisation Act, 1966].
[20][12. Rajasthan	The territories specified in Section 10 of the States Reorganisation Act, 1956 [24][but excluding the territories specified in the First Schedule to the Rajasthan and Madhya Pradesh (Transfer of Territories) Act, 1959].
[20][13. Uttar Pradesh	[25][The territories which immediately before the commencement of this Constitution were either comprised in the Province known as the United Provinces or were being administered as if they formed part of that Province, the territories specified in clause (b) of sub-section (1) of Section 3 of the Bihar and Uttar Pradesh (Alteration of Boundaries) Act, 1968 and the territories specified in clause (b) of sub-section (1) of Section 4 of the Haryana and Uttar Pradesh (Alteration of Boundaries) Act, 1979, but excluding the territories specified in clause (a) of sub-section (1) of Section 3 of the Bihar and Uttar Pradesh (Alteration of Boundaries) Act, 1968, and territories specified in clause (a) of sub-section (1) of Section 4 of the Haryana and Uttar Pradesh (Alteration of Boundaries) Act, 1979.]
20[14. West Bengal	The territories which immediately before the commencement of this Constitution were either comprised in the Province of West Bengal or were being administered ad if they formed part of that Province and the territory of Chandernagore as defined in clause (c) of Section 2 of the Chandernagore (Merger) Act, 1954 and also the territories specified in sub-section (1) of Section 3 of the Bihar and West Bengal (Transfer of Territories) Act, 1956.
[20][15. Jammu and Kashmir	The territory which immediately before the commencement of this Constitution was comprised in the Indian State of Jammu and Kashmir

[26][16. Nagaland	The territories specified in sub-section (1) of Section 3 of the State of Nagaland Act, 1962.]
[27][17. Haryana	[28][The territories specified in sub-section (1) of Section 3 of the Punjab Reorganisation Act, 1966 and the territories specified in clause (a) of sub-section (1) of Section 4 of the Haryana and Uttar Pradesh (Alteration of Boundaries) Act, 1979, but excluding the territories specified in clause (b) of sub-section (1) of Section 4 of that Act].
[29][18. Himachal Pradesh	The territories which immediately before commencement of this Constitution were being administered as if they were Chief Commissioners' Provinces under the names of Himachal Pradesh and Bilaspur and the territories specified in sub-section (1) of Section 5 of the Punjab Reorganisation Act, 1966.]
[30][19. Manipur	The territory which immediately before the commencement of this Constitution was being administered as if it were a Chief Commissioner's Province under the name of Manipur.
20. Tripura	The territory which immediately before the commencement of this Constitution was being administered as if it were a Chief Commissioner's Province under the name of Tripura.
21. Meghalaya	The territories specified in Section 5 of the North-Eastern Areas (Reorganisation) Act, 1971.]
[31][22. Sikkim	The territories which immediately before the commencement of the Constitution (Thrity-sixth Amendment) Act. 1975, were comprised in Sikkim.]
[32][23. Mizoram	The territories specified in Section 6 of the North-Eastern Areas (Reorganisation) Act, 1971.]
[33][24. Arunachal Pradesh	The territories specified in Section 7 of the North-Eastern Areas (Reorganisation) Act, 1971.]

[34][25. Goa	The territories specified in Section 3 of the Goa, Daman and Diu Reorganisation Act, 1987.]

II. THE UNION TERRITORIES

Name	Extent
1. Delhi	The territory which immediately before the commencement of this Constitution was comprised in the Chief Commissioner's Province of Delhi
[35]*	*
[36]*	*
[37][2.] The Andaman and Nicobar Islands	The territory which immediately before the commencement of this Constitution was comprised in the Chief Commissioner's Province of the Andaman and Nicobar Islands.
[38][3.] [39][Lakshadweep]	The territory specified in Section 6 of the State Reorganisation Act, 1956.
[40][[38][4.] Dadra and Nagar Haveli	The territory which immediately before the eleventh day of August, 1961 was comprised in Free Dadra and Nagar Haveli.]
[41][[42][[38][5.] Daman and Diu	The territories specified in Section 4 of the Goa, Daman and Diu Reorganisation Act, 1987]
[43][[38][6.] Pondicherry	The territories which immediately before the sixteenth day of August, 1962, were comprised in the French Establishments in India known as Pondicherry, Karikal, Mahe and Yanam.]
[44][[38][7.] Chandigarh	The territories specified in Section 4 of the Punjab Reorganisation Act, 1966]
[45][*	* *]
[46][*	* *]

[FOURTH SCHEDULE][47]

[*Articles* 4(1) *and* 80(2)]

Allocation of Seats in the Council of States

To each State or Union Territory specified in the first column of the following table, there shall be allotted the number of seats specified in the second column thereof opposite to that State or that Union Territory, as the case may be.

1. Andhra Pradesh	18
2. Assam	7
3. Bihar	22
[48][4. Goa	1]
[49][[50][5.] Gujarat	11]
[51][[50][6.] Haryana	5]
[50][7.] Kerala	9
[50][8.] Madhya Pradesh	16
[52][[50][9.] Tamil Nadu	[53][18]
[54][[50][10.] Maharashtra	19]
[55][[50][11.] Karnataka	12
[50][12.] Orissa	10
[50][13.] Punjab	*[7]
[50][14.] Rajasthan	10
[50][15.] Uttar Pradesh	34
[50][16.] West Bengal	16
[50][17.] Jammu and Kashmir	4
[56][[49][18.] Nagaland	1]
[57][[49][19.] Himachal Pradesh	3]
[50][20.] Manipur	1
[50][21.] Tripura	1
[50][22.] Meghalaya	1
[58][[49][23.] Sikkim	1]
[59][[49][24.] Mizoram	1]
[60][[60][25.] Arunachal Pradesh	1]
[60][[60][26.] Delhi	3]
[61][27.] Pondicherry	1
[62][	
[63][	
TOTAL	*[233]]

NOTES

1. Subs. by the Constitution (Seventh Amendment) Act. 1956, s.2, for cl (2)
2. Subs. by s 2, *ibid.*, for sub-clause (b)
3. Ins. by the Constitution (Thirty-fifth Amendment) Act. 1974, s. 2 (w. e. f. 4-3-1975)
4. Subs by the Constitution (Fifth Amendment) Act, 1955, s. 2, for the provio
5. The words and letters "specified in Part A or Part B of the first Schedule" Omitted by the Constitution (Seventh Amendment) Act. 1956. s 29 and Sch.
6. Ins by the Constitution (Eighteenth Amendment) Act. 1966. s.2
7. Subs. by the Constitution (Seventh Amendment) Act, 1956, s 2, for the First Sch.
8. Subs. by the Andhra Pradesh and Mysore (Transfer of Territory) Act, 1968 (36 of 1968), s. 4. for the former entry (w.e.f. 1-10-1968)
9. Added by the State of Nagaland Act, 1962 (27 of 1962), s. 4 (w.e.f. 1-12-1963)
10. Added by the North-eastern Areas (Reorganisation) Act, 1971 (81 of 1971), s.9 (w.e.f. 21-1-1972)
11. Subs.. by the Bihar and Uttar Pradesh (Alteration of Boundaries) Act, 1968 (24 of 1968), s 4. for the former entry (w.e.f. 10-6-1970)
12. Sub. by the Bombay Reorganisation Act, 1960 (11 of 1960), s 4. for entry 4 (w.e.f. 1-5-1960)
13. Ins. by the Rajasthan and Madhya Pradesh (Transfer of Territories) Act. 1959 (47 of 1959). s 4 (w.e.f. 1-10-1959)
14. Subs. by the Madras State (Alteration of name) Act. 1968 (53 of 1968), s 5. for "7 Madras" (w.e.f. 14-1-1969)
15. Ins. by the Andhra Pradesh and Madras (Alteration of Boundaries) Act. 1959 (56 of 1959) s 6 (w.e.f. 14-1-1969)
16. Subs. by s. 6, *ibid.*, for certain words (w.e.f. 1-4-1960)
17. Ins. by the Bombay Reorganisation Act, 1960 (11 of 1960), s. 4 (w.e.f. 1-5-1960)
18. Subs. by the Mysore State (Alteration of name) Act, 1973 (31 of 1973), s 5. for "9 Mysore" (w.e.f. 1-11-1973)
19. Ins. by the Andhra Pradesh and Mysore (Transfer of Territory) Act, 1968 (36 of 1968), s 4. (w.e.f. 1-10-1968)
20. Entries 8 to 14 renumbered as entries 9 to 15 by the Bombay Reorganisation Act, 1960 (11 of 1960), s 4 (w.e.f. 1-5-1960)
21. Ins. by the Acquired Territories (Merger) Act. 1960 (64 of 1960), s 4 (w.e.f. 17-1-1961)
22. Added by the Constitution (Ninth Amendment) Act, 1960, s 3 (w.e.f. 17-1-1961)
23. Ins. by the Punjab Reorganisation Act, 1966 (31 of 1966), s. 7 (w.e.f. 1-11-1966)
24. Ins. by the Rajasthan and Madhya Pradesh (Transfer of Territories) Act, 1959 (47 of 1959), s 4 (w.e.f. 1-10-1959)
25. Subs. by the Haryana and Uttar Pradesh (Alteration of Boundaries) Act, 1979 (31 of 1979), s. 5. for the former entry (w.e.f. 15-9-1983)
26. Ins. by the State of Nagaland Act, 1962, (27 of 1962), s. 4 (w.e.f. 1-12-1963)
27. Ins. by the Punjab Reorganisation Act, 1966 (31 of 1966), s. 7 (w.e.f. 1-11-1966)
28. Subs. By the Haryana and Uttar Pradesh (Alteration of Boundaries) Act, 1979 (31 of 1979), s. 5 for the former entry (w.e.f. 15-9-1983)
29. Ins. by the State of Himachal Pradesh Act. 1970 (53 of 1970), s. 4 (w.e.f. 25-1-1971)

30. Ins. by the North-Eastern Areas (Reorganisation) Act, 1971 (81 of 1971), s. 9 (w.e.f. 21-1-1972)
31. Ins. by the Constitution (Thirty-sixty Amendment) Act, 1975, s. 2 (w.e.f. 26-4-1975)
32. Ins. by the State of Mizoram Act, 1986 (34 of 1986), s. 4 (w.e.f. 20-2-1987)
33. Ins. by the State of Arunachal Pradesh Act, 1986, (69 of 1986), s. 4 (w.e.f. 20-2-1987)
34. Ins. by the Goa, Daman and Diu Reorganisation Act, 1987 (18 of 1987), s. 5 (w.e.f. 30-5-1987)
35. Entry 2 relating to "Himachal Pradesh" omitted by the State of Himachal Pradesh Act, 1970 (53 of 1970), s. 4 (w.e.f. 25-1-1971)
36. Entries relating to Manipur and Tripura omitted by the north-Eastern Areas (Reorganisation) Act, 1971 (81 of 1971), s. 9(w.e.f. 21-1-1972)
37. Entries 4 to 9 renumbered as entries 2 to 7 by s. 9, *ibid* (w.e.f. 21-1-1972)
38. Subs. by the Laccadive, Minicoy and Amindivi Islands (Alteration of Name) Act, 1973 (34 of 1973), s. 5, for "The Laccadive, Minicoy and Amindivi Islands." (w.e.f. 1-11-1973)
39. Ins. by the Constitution (Tenth Amendment) Act, 1961, s. 2.
40. Subs. by the Goa, Daman and Diu Reoraganisation Act, 1987 (18 of 1987), s. 5, for entry 5 (w.e.f. 30-5-1987)
41. Ins. by the Constitution (Twelfth Amendment) Act, 1962, s. 2.
42. Ins. by the Constitution (Fourteenth Amendment) Act, 1962, ss 3 and 7 (w.e.f. 16-8-1962)
43. Ins. by the Punjab Reorganisation Act, 1966 (31 of 1966), s. 7 (w.e.f. 1-11-1966)
44. Entry 8 omitted and entry 9 renumbered as entry 8 by the State of Mizoram Act, 1986 (34 of 1986), s 4 (w.e.f. 20-2-1987)
45. Omitted by the State of Arunachal Pradesh Act, 1986 (69 of 1986), s. 4 (w.e.f. 20-2-1987)
46. Subs. by the Constitution (Seventh Amendment) Act. 1956, s. 3, for the Fourth Sch.
47. Entry 4 Ins. by Goa, Daman and Diu Reorganisation Act, 1987, (18 of 1987), s. 6 (w.e.f. 30-5-1987).
48. Subs by the Bomaby Reorganisation Act, 1960 (11 or 1960), s. 6, for entry 4 (w.e.f. 1-5-1960).
49. Entries 4 to 26 renumbered as entries 5 to 27 by the Goa, Daman and Diu Reorganisation Act, 1987 (18 of 1987), s. 6 (w.e.f. 30-5-1987).
50. Ins. by the Punjab Reorganisation Act, 1966 (31 of 1966), s. 9 (w.e.f. 1-11-1966).
51. Subs. by the Madras State (Alteration of Name) Act, 1968 (53 of 1968), s. 5, for "8, Madras"·(w.e.f. 14-1-1969).
52. Subs. by the Andhra Pradesh and Madras (Alteration of Boundaries) Act, 1959 (56 of 1959), s. 8 for "17" (w.e.f. 1-4-1960).
53. Ins. by the Bombay Reorganisation Act, 1960 (11 of 1960), s. 6 (w.e.f. 1-5-1960).
54. Subs. by the Mysore State (Alternation of Name) Act, 1973 (31 of 1973), s. 5, for "10 Mysore (w.e.f. 1-11-1973)
55. Subs. by the Punjab Reorganisation Act, 1966 (31 of 1966), s. 9 for "11" (w.e.f. 1-11-1966)
56. Ins. by the State of Nagaland Act, 1962 (27 of 1962), s. 6 (w.e.f. 1-12-1971).

57. Ins. by the State of Himachal Pradesh Act, 1970 (53 of 1970), s. 5 (w.e.f. 25-1-1971).
58. Ins. by the Constitution (Thirty-sixth Amendment) Act, 1975, s. 4 (w.e.f. 26-4-1975).
59. Entries 23 and 24 renumbered as entries 24 and 25 respectively and before entry 24 as so renumbered new entry 23 ins. and entry 25 omitted by the State of Mizoram Act, 1986 (34 of 1986), s. 5 (w.e.f. 20-2-1987)
60. Entries 24 and 25 renumbered as entries 25 and 26 respectively and new before entry 24 ins. and entry 26 omitted by the State of Arunachal Pradesh Act, 1986 (69 of 1986), s. 5 (w.e.f. 20-2-1987)
61. Entries 4 to 26 renumbered as entries 5 to 27 by the Goa, Daman and Diu Reorganisation Act, 1987 (18 of 1987), s. 6 (w.e.f. 30-5-1987)
62. Entries 23 and 24 renumbered as entries 24 and 25 respectively and before entry 24 as so renumbered new entry 23 ins. and entry 25 omitted by the Sate of Mizoram Act, 1986 (34 of 1986), s. 5 (w.e.f. 20-2-1987)
63. Subs. by the Goa, Daman and Diu Reorganisation Act, 1987, s. 6, for "232' (w.e.f. 30-5-1987)

APPENDIX–4

CONSTITUTION OF JAMMU AND KASHMIR ,1956-57 : ARTICLE 3

The State of Jammu and Kashmir is an integral part of India and shall remain permanently its integral part.

Note : The State Constituent Assembly passed the Constitution for Jammu and Kashmir on November 17, 1956 and it came into force on January 26, 1957.

APPENDIX–5

SOURCES OF THE HISTORY OF KASHMIR (TENTH-TWELFTH CENTURY)

Dr (Mrs) Madhvi Yasin

The Indians, before the advent of the Muslims into India, did not maintain historical records almost as a rule. There was no system of maintaining archives and repositories. This scarcity in historical literature is aptly expressed by Dr. R.C. Majumdar: "We have to admit that the literary genius of India, so active and fertile in almost all conceivable branches of study, was not applied to chronicling the records of kings and fall of states and nations".[1] Again, "It is a well-known fact that with the single exception of *Rajatarangini* (History of Kashmir), there is no historical text in Sanskrit dealing with the whole or even parts of India".[2] But it should never mean that the sources for the study of the history and culture of Kashmir are very few and far between, though it is very unfortunate that scholars do not take the trouble of going beyond *Rajatarangini*.

The Greek, Chinese and indigenous records and accounts form a very important source of information for the period preceding tenth century AD. For the period between tenth century to twelfth centruy, the sources may be divided into two broad categories: (1) Muslim chronicles or Arabic literature, and (2) Kashmir chronicles.

Muslim Chronicles

Among the Muslim sources Al-Beruni's India is a mine of information. It is trustworthy and most reliable on topography, routes, sacred places and customs and manners of the people. Stein is all praise for Al-Beruni's critical acumen and laborious research and says the "he could look through the mountain".[3] Al-Beruni utilized his long stay at Ghazna and in the Punjab (AD 1017-30) to collect information on Kashmir. In the first chapter of his book,

Kitab-ul-Hind, he writes that Mahmud of Ghazna "utterly ruined the prosperity of the country (of India), and performed those wonderful exploits by which the Hindus became like atoms of dust scattered in all directions".[4] That was the reason, according to Al-Beruni, that Hindu sciences fled to places like Kashmir and Benares.[5] He refers to Kashmir as the high school of Hindu learning and repeatedly mentions Kashmiri authors. It appears that among his informants, if not among his actual teachers, there were Kashmiri scholars.[6] He makes a particular mention of his Kashmiri informants with whom he conversed regarding the miracles of Kudaishahr, i.e., the Kaptesvara Tirtha. The same holds good about his note on the pilgrimage to the temple of Sarada.[7] The details regarding a local Kashmiri festival and the anecdote about the propagation of the Sisyahitavritti in Kashmir could not have reached him but by verbal communications.[8] Al-Beruni also refers to Kashmiri almanac, which, in the opinion of Stein, could only be secured through Kashmiri Pandits.[9]

Abu Raihan Muhammad Ibn Ahmad Al-Beruni composed certain Sanskrit treatises and circulated them among the people of Kashmir. This speaks of special relations which he had with Kashmir. He graphically narrates the rigid isolation of the Valley. Such a statement could only be possible when he had direct contacts with the people of the Valley.[10] There is much strength in Sir Mark Aurel Stein's opinion that Al-Beruni accompanied Mahmud of Ghazna in his unsuccessful invasion of Kashmir, which probably took place in AD 1021. It afforded him ample opportunities to acquaint himself with the topography of the region with local assistance.[11]

Al-Beruni's account of Kashmir is mainly contained in Chapter XVIII, which gives "various notes on the countries of the Hindus, their rivers and ocean".[12] Fortunately, it is more detailed with regard to Kashmir.

Al-Beruni gives in broad outlines the political division of the mountain region which lies between the great Central Asian watershed and the Punjab plain. He refers to the pedestrian habits of the people and the use of *Palkis* by the nobles. The description is very precise and is corroborated by Kalhana. He further observes :

> "They are particularly anxious about the natural strength of their country, and therefore take always much care to keep a strong-hold upon the entrances and roads leading into it. In consequence it is very difficult to have any commerce with

them. In former times they used to allow one or two foreigners to enter their country, particularly Jews, but at present they do not allow any Hindu whom they do not know personally to enter, much less other people".[13]

Al-Beruni gives a vivid picture of the Kashmir Valley. The capital is correctly described as "being built along both banks of the river Jhelam, which are connected with each other by bridges and ferry-boats". The climate of Kashmir, as described by Al-Beruni, is far more exect than any other account available to us previous to the second quarter of the nineteenth century.[14]

Al-Beruni's account is not only scientific but the only detailed account available in regard to Kashmir for the first quarter of the eleventh century A.D. His historical perspective, penetrating insight and deep understanding could not be over-estimated. "He does not blindly accept", says Professor Sachau, "The traditions of former ages; he wants to understand and criticise them. He wants to sift the wheat from the chaff, and he will discard everything that militates against the laws of nature and of reason".[15]

Muru' Fu-L Zahab of Al-Masudi is another Arabic work on India with a passing reference about Kashmir. He was a great traveller and an acute observer. He deservedly continues to be one of the most admired writers in Arabic. His book, which was translated into English by Dr. Sprenger with the name *Meadows of Gold*,[16] gives only that Kashmir is a kingdom with many towns and villages enclosed by very high and inaccessible mountains, through which leads a single passage closed by a gate. The number of towns and villages is estimated at from sixty to seventy thousand.[17] This scanty detail by this well-travelled observer is due to habitual and physical seclusion of the people and the country in those days. He died in Egypt in 345 A.H. (AD 956).

Muzhatu-L Mushtak of Al-Idrisi gives a brief reference about Kashmir. He was born at Centa, in Morocco, towards the close of the eleventh century.[18]

Kashmir Chronicles

The Kashmiri Saiva philosopher, literary critic and intellectual giant, Abhinavagupta, was born between AD 950 and 960 in a Brahmin family, which had migrated from Kanauj to Kashmir during the reign of King Lalitaditya. He was a prolific writer whose works cover a wide range of subjects – Dramaturgy, Rhetoric, Philosophy and the Philosophy of Poetry. His main contribution is to Saiva philosophy and his expositions are simply superb.

Kshemaraja, who flourished in the reign of Samgramaraja (AD 1003-1028), wrote many treatises, such as *Shiva-Sutra-Vritti, Spandasandoha* and many commentaries on Tantras. *Shiva-Sutra-Vritti* is important with regard to Saivism in Kashmir.

Kshemendra, rightly regarded as the doyen among the Sanskrit poets of Kashmir and among the Kashmiri chronlcers, is the most useful authority. He was born on the Dal in the locality where the Nishat Bagh now stands in the days of Ananta. Kshemendra's father, Prakashachandra, was a rich man, very learned and of generous temperament. The exact date of Kshemendra's birth is unknown but his literary career runs from AD 1037 to 1066. Kshemendra studied at the feet of several teachers but notable among them is Gangaka. His studies covered Hindu Law, Sanskrit Grammar, Politics, Medicine, Music and Painting. He is said to be the author of many books, of which thirty-four are believed to be available.

Kalhana has criticised his *Nripavali* for many errors and accuses him of "consistent carelessness".[19] Keith in his *History of Sanskrit Literature*, has discussed Kshemendra's *Brihatkathamanjari* and other works at some length.

In 'Samayamatrika', one of Kshemendra's best poems, an attempt has been made to describe the snares of courtesans. It is a collection of stories, in which there is an interesting account of the wanderings of his heroine Kankali through the length and breadth of the Valley. Numerous places of her wandering are traceable on the map. These places have been described with local variations and colour, which make the rendering extremely interesting. In this poem we, for the first time, find mention of the Pir Panjal Pass (Pancaladhara) and its hospice (matha). We also get a glimpse of the ancient salt trade routes. It also mentions a Budhist convent, the Krityasrama Vihar, where Kankali's conduct as a nun is the cause of no small scandal.

Stein remarks "His works, composed in the second and third quarter of the eleventh century, form important landmarks in several field of Indian literature. Kshemendra seems to have had a genuine interest, rare enough among Indian scholars, for the realities of his country and the life around him".[20]

Mankha, the fourth son of Veshovrata and grandson of Pandit Mammata, was a great poet of independent mind. Ruyyaka, the celebrated author of *Alankarasarvasva,* was the teacher of Mankha. Mankha rose to the post of the Director of Dharmarth and also became the Foreign Minister. Raja Sussala looked upon him as a great philosopher. Mankha was the contemporary of Kalhana. He wrote his first book *Shrikanthacharita* at the age of twenty-five, probably in AD 1039. The book, though brief, is similar in character to Bilhana's *Vikramankadevacharita* in its description of Kashmir and Pravarapura. Jonaraja has written a commentary on this book which is very useful in explaining the points of local interest.

Bilhana, the poet, was senior to Kalhana in age. He was born in Khunamush or Khonamusa, six miles from Srinagar. His father, Jyashtha Kalasha, was a learned Brahmin and a specialist in Sanskrit grammar.[21] Finding no scope for his talents, he bade good bye to his native land at the tender age of sixteen in the reign of King Kalasha (AD 1063-1089). [22] He visited important places in Northern India and travelled to the Deccan. He became famous as the court-poet of the Chalukya King Tribhuvanmalla Parmardi of the South. Bilhana is the author of *Vikramankadevacharita, Karna-Sundari Mala* and *Chaurapanchasika*.

In the last Canto of his historical poem, the *Vikramankadevacharita*, Bilhana vividly describes the beauties of the Kashmir Valley and its capital. The main importance of the poem consists in the exactitude of the topography. Professor Buhler, during his tour of Kashmir in 1875, had the satisfaction of visiting the poet's birth place, the present village of Khunamoh, and verifying on the spot every point of the description which Bilhana gives of that "coquettish embellishment of the bosom of Mount Himalaya".[23] As a poet his style and language is very lucid and enchanting.

The *Lokaprakasha* is a very useful dictionary (*kosh*) compiled through the efforts of many scholars including Kshemendra. It is particularly useful for the study of the social life and administrative structure. In Book II the name of Shahjahan finds mention, which suggests that some portion of the work was compiled as late as the seventeenth century AD. The work represents a strange mixture of the usual dictionary and a practical handbook dealing with the various topics of administration and private life in Kashmir.[24] Stein praises its secular character and is grateful for the topographical details which it gives.[25]

The *Lokaprakasha* consists of four parts. The first part deals with the four principal casts and sixty sub-castes. It also gives the titles of the ministers and officers of the State. The second part, which seems to have been written during the Muslim period in Kashmir and up to the seventeenth centruy AD, gives details about bills of exchange, bonds, commercial contracts, official orders and so forth. This part is the biggest and most important of all. The third part supplies us with a list of synonyms of different varieties of fish, birds and mice, and of salt, gold ornaments and gold coins. The fourth part begins with a satire on the Kayasthas (i.e., writers and physicians) and on Brahmins who had become Muslims. It also gives a list of the districts of Kashmir.

The *Lokaprakasha* supplies the earliest list of Kashmir Parganas. The Pargana list contains local names of ancient date, side by side with comparatively modern ones. The only drawback of the work is that is is difficult to know exactly when the different sections were compiled.

Mammata and Other Poets of the Period

The beginning of the twelfth century AD saw three celebrated scholars decorating the literary firmament of Kashmir. They are Mammata and his two brothers. Mammata was the second son of the scholar Jaiyata Bhatta, the eldest was Jaiyata and Uvvata was the youngest. All the three brothers were noted litterateurs, but Mammata was the most distinguished of them all. His book *Kavya-Prakasha* on prosody is very valuable and is prescribed for higher examinations in Sanskrit language. Eighty-seven commentaries are known to have been written on the *Kavya-Prakasha* of which twenty-five are available. Mammata is said to be the maternal uncle of Harsha, the great poet-king of Kanauj. The *Shabda-Vyapar-Vichara* is another well-known work of Mammata on grammar in which the usage of words has been discussed.

The period under review has the rare distinction of having Kalhana's *Rajatarangini*, "The River of kings" – the most important source of the history of Kashmir. But the whole ancestry and the life of the author is hidden in oblivion. Kalhana shares the common fate of the Indian authors of note whose memory lives solely in their works. The *Rajatarangini* gives the name of the author as 'Kalhana', the son of the great Kashmiri minister, "the illustrious Lord

Canipaka". Historical deductions reveal that he was a Brahmin by caste. The Sanskrit style of *Rajatarangini* is similar to that of the accepted style of the Pandits of Brahmin descent. The introduction to each book of his chronicle is begun by prayers to Shiva in his form of *Ardhanarishwar* representing the God in union with Parvati. Besides, Jonaraja, the continuator author of *Rajatarangini*, has referred to Kalhana with the epithed "dvija". A study of his chronicle displays his friendly attitude towards Buddhism. His faith may be epitomised in one word "eclecticism".

The name Kalhana was derived through the Prakrit "Kalhan" from the Sanskrit word "Kalyana", meaning "blessed".

Kalhana wrote his work during the years AD 1148-1149. The style and the spirit of the work show that the author must have attained a mature age. The elaborate description of the unsteady conditions of Sussal's reign (AD 1112-20) makes it clear that he must have been of age at that time. Hence, his probable date of birth might have been the beginning of the twelfth century.

The century of the birth of Kalhana was marked, in the history of Kashmir, by a dynastic upheaval resulting in many important political changes. King Harsha (AD 1089-1101) seemed at first to give Kashmir a period of good government but he fell victim to his own lavishness and extravagance. After his murder, Kashmir, for seven years more, witnessed civil wars which brought death and destruction in their train.

Kalhana was gifted with a scientific approach and a critical temperament. His portrayal of the various classes of Kashmiri people is very graphic and true to life. The reaction of the common folk to the disturbed political conditions of the time is full of realistic touches. He says that the people were "callously prepared to welcome any change". His description of the idle and indifferent city crowds and their feelings shows that he thoroughly understood the nature of his countrymen.

The unsettled political conditions of the time negatived all chances of patronage to the creative works of art; hence *Rajatarangini* was not written under the patronage of any king. Kalhana had a high sense of his responsibilities. He considers only historians "worthy of praise, whose word, like that of a judge, keeps free from love or hatred in relating the facts of the past". . . "and surpasses even the stream of nectar,... and can place the past times before the eyes of men".

It is interesting to note that Kalhana prepared himself for the role of a poet. The Sanskrit classical poetry cultivated by Kalhana reveals that he had an intensive training in the Indian rhetoric, the *Alankarshastra*, and had equal mastery of Sanskrit grammatical lore. His literary studies were deep and comprehensive. All the known literature of his time, beginning from Epics to Kalidas's work *Raghuvansha* and *Meghaduta* and Bilhana's *Vikramankadevacharita* and *Harshacharita*, were read by him. Stein says: "His literary training, indeed, had been of the strictly traditional type and the manner in which he employed it shows no conscious departure from the conventional norm. Yet it is clear that Kalhana was not a man of schools, absorbed in his Shastras."

Kalhana scrupulously studied the original sources including inscriptions of various kinds before he started writing the *Rajatarangini*. He also studied coins and inspected buildings.

Kalhana found all possible avenues to his hereditary of the country. So the best way to employ his talents, he thought, was to write down the history of his country from the ancient down to his own time. He was also inspired by regional patriotism. By painting a glorious picture of the past he wished that his countrymen should shed the inferiority complex, feel proud and try to emulate their past traditions. Therefore, the Great Asoka, he shows, was the kind of the King whose examples were to be followed. It is Kalhana's sheer patriotism when he says: "Kashmir may be conquered by the force of spiritual merits, but not by the force of soldiers."

Kalhana has honestly and impartially related the events. While recording the contemporary happenings Kalhana has presented the principal figures in their individual characters and not as types. Here he represents a contrast to Bana and Bilhana in treating historical personages, who have painted their heroes all white and enemies all black.

The *Rajatarangini* is a class by itself in Indian literature. It is very much different from *Charitas*, which were composed under royal patronage. The scholar-poets of *Charitas* had the rare gift of inventing fables and myths and applying thier talent in glorifying the achievements of their patrons. Their works are masterpieces of literature dabbling in subtle poetic art, rhetorical embellishment and alamkarshastra. The *Rajatarangini*, on the other hand, is the work of a detached and impartial mind, viewing the past and present with historical acumen and not in a spirit of hero worship or pleasing the patron. The *Rajatarangini* not only forms a class by itself in Sanskrit compositions but has a striking resemblance in character to the chronicles of medieval Europe and of the Islamic East.

While writing the first three books (chapters) of the *Rajatarangini*, Kalhana made full use of tradition whether written or oral, and the chronicles which were evidently based on such traditions. In writing down these traditions, at times, the critic in Kalhana comes out. For instance, he mentions three traditions of the death of King Lalitaditya, without stating what is true, and comments: "When the great meet their end, there arise stories indicative of their uncommon grandeur". King Meghavahan's exploits have been described in such a fanciful manner that Kalhana himself is apprehensive that they might not be believed, but for them were eyewitness accounts.

For the last two chapters of his book, the main sources were his contemporaries, his father, fellow-countryment and his own memory. Thus many incidents of the treachery of Bhiksacara's troops, he categorically writes, were witnessed by him. It is no surprise that much of the history of the previous two generations, he got from his father and father's friends, who held key-posts in the politics of their times.

To give the details, *Rajatarangini* consists of eight books (chapters) of unequal size, written in Sanskrit in nearly 8,000 verses of rare literary merit. The text may roughly be divided into three sections:

1. Book I-III, are based on traditions.
2. In Books IV-VI, dealing with Karakota and Utpala dynasties he has made use of the works of earlier chroniclers who were contemporaries or near contemporaries of the events they described.
3. For Books VII-VIII, dealing with the two Lohara dynasties, he made use of personal knowlege and eyewitness accounts, the latter often perhaps received at second or third hand.

The style of the *Rajatarangini* is not crude or difficult. These are scattered verses adorned in flowery language, or donned in fanciful imagery, of country Sanskrit. Kalhana's idea was that even a historical text must be a work of art and he tried to make his work attractive to readers. His accounts are graphic and vivid except in his last two books, where so many characters are introduced without proper introduction. Kalhana, who had maintained strict adherence to chronology from the beginning of the book, had in the second and third sections not followed it to the letter. Evidently he was writing his book for those, who were familiar with the events of the period.

Kalhana in writing the *Rajatarangini* sets a tradition for history writing. His book, after him, was continued by four successive historians from the point where he left, to some years after Kashmir's annexation by the Mughal Emperor, Akbar.

The mission of a historian, according to Kalhana, is to make vivid before one's eyes pictures of a bygone age. History has a unique gift of immortalizing personages and events, and in this it even surpasses the mythical ambrosia, 'while the latter immortalizes only the man who drinks it, the former all those whom it touches'. Kalhana was aware that his work would not only achieve permanence, but would enliven all the actors as well as himself. He had another object also in view. He says: "This saga, which is properly made up, should be useful for Kings as a stimulant or a sedative, like a physic, according to time and place." Kalhana expected that both good and bad kings would derive profit from his work. He was a staunch advocate of historical impartiality.

Kalhana's assessment of more recent happenings is fair. He paints no character wholly black or white. He had deep insight into man's nature and his psychology. He says: "As in heaven the little clouds change shape, and take on the form of elephants, leopards, monsters, serpents, horses and other beasts–so do the waves of feeling change in the hearts of mortals, from kindness to harshness as the moments vary."

The didactic feature of *Rajatarangini* may be traced to the selection of Sauta rasa in a sentiment of resignation. Here Kalhana's avowed motive is to show that material property and royal possessions are objects of transitory glory. The evil acts of man recoil on him by the strange hands of destiny. In the same way, acts of policy, statecraft and individual conduct are again and again praised and analysed in the light of Dharma or Nitishastra.

The *Rajatarangini* appears to wage a war in favour of benevolent despotism and deprecates feudalism. Believing in orthodox *Rajniti* (Statecraft), Kalhana had his own conception of good government. Explicitly or implicitly the *Rajatarangini* carries the idea that a strong king is the ideal king, who has firm control over unruly elements, but is benevolent towards his people and sympathetic to their wishes. He chooses his ministers with discretion, and listens to their counsel with respect. Kalhana has shown his unflinching disapproval of the Damars, the petty feudal chiefs, who were the cause of anarchy and confusion in Kashmir since the death of Harsha. Another motive, perhaps, in writing the *Rajatarangini* was that of inspiring the kings of Kashmir with their ancient glory and prowess, and to curb the unruly elements, who aimed at making the king weak. He says: "The crab kills its father, and the white ant destroys its mother, but the ungrateful Kayasthas, when they become powerful, destroy everything." At times Kalhana becomes pessimistic. The words put in the mouth of Harsha symbolises it: "This land, after having been a virtuous woman, has fallen like a prostitute into the arms of the insolent. Henceforth, whoever knows how to succeed by mere intrigue will aspire to that kingdom, whose power has gone." Here the historian shows his prophetic vision. He is no more simply a poet or a scholar.

The *Rajatarangini* is a saga showing the force of *Karma*. Whatever good or bad a man does in this life, Kalhana believes, he reaps the harvest for that in the life to come. Often the force of *Karma* shapes events and provides the basic moral sanction.

Fate, according to Kalhana, is the second force influencing the human destiny. Fate is sometimes used as a synonym for God. God or the Gods often influence human affairs. Sometimes adverse fate is overcome by those who trust in their arms. Here also the *Rajatarangini* gives another hopeful message to his countrymen that whatever fate or the Creator might have in store for them, only a strong king confident of his powers could save Kashmir.

The *Rajatarangini* interlinks the *Karma* of the kings with that of their subjects. Good kings arise through the merits of their subjects. A king and his subjects could mould the orders of nature.

This great work has also some shortcomings. The sources used by Kalhana were not critically analysed and discussed. His narrative becomes more legendary and anecdotal in the middle of the ninth century, when one seems to reach contemporary records. "Of the defects of the records and the conflicting opinions which according to Kalhana's introduction rendered his task difficult, we nowhere receive a distinct indication." Fabulous stories, manifest impossibilities, exaggerations and superstitious beliefs have been described as historical truths, which betray his credulity. He has not separated historical legends from history. Similarly, Kalhana's chronology is also not based on scientific data. Of course, one cannot expect critical judgement in matters of chronology from an author who had started dating history from a legendary date of the coronation of Yudhisthira from the epics, and attributes three hundred years to a single ruler, Ranaditya. Kalhana could not and should not be blamed for this, as it was a general trend among Indians, so precisely described by A1-Beruni. "Unfortunately the Hindus do not pay much attention to the historical order of things, they are very careless in relating to chronological succession of their kings, and when they are pressed for information, and are at a loss, not knowing what to say they invaribly take to tale-telling."

The *Rajatarangini* also presents a contrast within itself—its earlier part is more of a fiction, and the later part, that is early medieval part, is real history. It vividly describes the falling glory of Kashmir,—palace intrigues, murders, seditions, civil wars and treachery. The life of the ordinary common folk has not been touched. It is the history of kings, royal families and nobility, justifying the title "River of the Kings".

Kalhana's work was continued by Jonaraja, Srivara, Prajabatta and Suka. The *Rajatarangini* has made Kalhana immortal; but Kalhana himself was sure about the worth of his work.

Even the gods must die:
But sovereign poetry remains,
Stronger than death.

REFERENCES

1. R.C. Majumdar, ed., The *Vedic Age*, 47.
2. C.H. Philips, Ed., *Historians of India, Pakistan and Ceylon,* p. 13.
3. M.A. Stein, *Rajatarangini*, p. 359(II).
4. Edward Sachau, *Al-Beruni's India*, i, p.22.
5. *Ibid.*, i, p.173
6. *Ibid.,* ii, p.181.
7. *Ibid.,* see note B, i, p. 37.13.
8. *Ibid.,* i, p.135.
9. *Ibid.,* i, p.391
10. *Ibid.,* Preface, p. xxiv ; Professor Sachau's Introduction, p.xx
11. Stein, p. 360 (ii).
12. *Al-Beruni's India*.
13. *Ibid.,* p.206
14. *Ibid.,* p.211.

15. *Ibid.,* Preface, p.xxv.
16. The first part of the *Meadows of Gold* was translated into English by Dr. Sprenger, London, 1841; French translation by Barbier de Meynard and Pavet de Courteille, Paris, 1851.
17. Sprenger, I, 382
18. A full translation of the whole work into French was published at Paris in 1836 and 1840 by M. Jaubert and from this, Elliot translated some extracts into English.
19. U.N. Ghoshal, 'The Dynastic Chronicles of Kashmir', *Indian Historical Quarterly*, September 1942, p.198
20. Stein, II, 375
21. Professor Buhler, to whom we own the discovery of Bilhana's chief work, has given in his Introduction an admirable analysis of the Sarga XVIII, as illustrating the poet's biography. For his description of contemporary Srinagar see pp.7ff.
22. *The Hamdard*, Srinagar, 14th and 21st September, 1941; Keith, *History* of *Sanskrit Literature,* 1928, p.153-158
23. See Report, p. 4ff
24. Professor A. Weber has published the extracts of the work in Indische Studien, p. 289-412; XVIII, 298, 300
25. Stein, II, 376

APPENDIX–6

BAHIS OF KASHMIR (MATAN) AS SOURCE OF THE HISTORY OF KASHMIR

Madhavi Yasin

Recently with emphasis on socio-economic history the importance of *Bahis* maintained in different regions of India by different castes and categories have come to limelight. In this context also comes the *Bahis* maintained by the *Pandas* (priestly class) at Matan[1], which is also called Bhavan *Bavan* in Kashmiri.[2] This *Tirtha* is one of the most sacred pilgrimage centres in Kashmir on the way to the Amarnath cave. *Vishnu Surya*[3], under the form of *Martand* is worshipped here. On account of its sacred origin, Hindus every year visit this place to perform *Shradh* to their dead so that their souls rest in peace and attain salvation. In this respect the place has the same significance as that of Gaya, Hardwar, and Sangam. The rush of the pilgrims is more during the *Malmas* and *Bhanumas* or *Adityamas*, which in the cyclic order falls around after two and a half years. Traditionally it is held that *Shradh* performed during this period has more religious merit and excellence. Another reason for attraction to this place is its being on the way to the holy cave of Amarnath, where thousands of pilgrims from India and abroad throng in the month of *Shravan* to see ice *lingam*, which waxes and wanes with the appearance of the moon. The holy mace of Lord Shiva, which is carried from the city of Srinagar to Amarnath, has its first important camp at Matan, which adds to the socio-religious importance of Matan.

These circumstances helped in the emergence of a set of professional priests called *Pandas*. Quite ingeniously they have maintained the records of the pilgrims and visitors. They charm the pilgrims and visitors with their tact, poise, and submission. They make adequate arrangements for the stay and comfort of their clientele (*yajman*). They say that in their *Bahis* they have records of more than thousand years on the birch bark (*Bhoj-Patra*). But they do not show them. On reliable information gathered from these, they do not have records more than three hundred years, as during the upheaval of Sikandar's time when many priests ran away for fear of life, the records might have perished. It is said that all had fled except eleven families. Now it has become a proverb in Kashmiri language to indicate scarcity.[4] Those who suffered but stayed in Kashmir are called as *Malmasis*, and those who returned in Zain-ul-Abidin's time, when peace and order was restored[5], are known as *Bhanumasis* (pronounced in Kashmiri dialect as *Banamasis*). Malmasis take *Bhanumasis* as aliens. Even their calendar registers variations.[6]

Bahis

Older *Bahis* or record books are stated to have been maintained on birch bark. Old *Bahis* are of hand made, Kashmiri paper and mounted with leather binding. Modern *Bahis* are of mill made paper mounted with leather or rexine binding. The length and breadth of *Bahis* generally is 30" by 9 to 12". *Pandas* keep it folded so as to reduce it to half of its size. They note down the details about the visitors and pilgrims on the *Bahis*. The language written on the *Bahis* is in *Sharda* script. Sometimes they persuade the prominent and influential visitors/pilgrims to write in their own languages. Therefore, following scripts and languages find place in the *Bahis* : Sharda, Modi, Lhanda, Sanskrit, Persian, Gurmukhi, English, Gujarati, Marathi, Dogri, Pahari, Devnagari, Bengali and Sindhi. This indicates that people mostly came from Northern India. When the recording of the pilgrims began hardly fifteen to twenty families were in the profession, gradually their number increased to one hundred and fifty. Therefore, the families branched off and also shared the *Bahis* in terms of families, sur names, or habitat. In early times the *Pandas* used to generally record the *Saptarsi Samvat* or *Laukika Samvat* which was current in Kashmir. Later on they switched to the *Bikrama Samvat* and occasionally recorded the Saka, Hijra, and Christian era too. The dates when recorded by the pilgrims/visitors are written according to their choice. *Pandas* have divided between themselves areas and specific families, which is going on undisturbed from generation to generation. Broadly speaking an entry would record a detailed bio-data of their clientele. The *Pandas* record the bio-data of each Yajman in three to five or seven lines utmost.

List of Prominent Families Covered by the Bahis

A: Royal Family Outside India

Nepal – Baskar Nath has the *Bahi* of the Maharaja of Nepal.

B. Pilgrims Outside India

Chinese pilgrims – Sham Lal Lamba has the *Bahi* of the Chinese pilgrims.

C. Royal Families from erstwhile Princely States of India

(i) Badari State – Pandit Dinanath has the *Bahi*.
(ii) Bikaner State – Sham Lal has the Bahi of Rathors.[7]
(iii) Chamba State – Lakshmi Nathji Gora has the *Bahi*.
(iv) Chinani State – Shivaji Madhusudan has the *Bahi*.
(v) Darbhanga State – Baskar Nath has the *Bahi*.[8]
(vi) Himachal State – Lakshmi Nathji Gora has the *Bahi*.
(vii) Kapurthala State – Lakshmi Nathji Gora has the *Bahi*.[9]
(viii) Jaipur State – Sham Lal and Badri Nath Tikku have the *Bahi* of Kachwahas.[10]
(ix) Jammu and Kashmir State – Dina Nath Kachru has the *Bahi* of the Dogra family.[11]
(x) Jodhpur State – Balkeshwar has the *Bahi* of Rathors.[12]
(xi) Khurva State – Dinanath Kachroo has the *Bahi*.
(xii) Patiala State – Lakshmi Nathji Gora has the *Bahi*.[13]

The Royal families after their signatures also affixed their seals.

D. Prominent Dignitaries

(i) Birlas – Som Nath Musa has the *Bahi*.
(ii) Nehrus – Balkeshwar Sher has the *Bahi*.
(iii) Tagore – Jailal Khan has the *Bahi* bearing the signature of Rabindra Nath Tagore and details about his visit.

E. Pilgrims from Hyderabad State

S.N. Musa had the Bahi of the pilgrims coming from Hyderabad

State

A Few Peeps into the Contents

A. Nepal Royal Family

(i) Maharaja Veer Jang Bahadur Shah—He came to Bavan in the month of *Baisakh* 1985 Bikrimi.
He was on a tour of Kashmir. Details about him are in the Nepali (Gorkhali) language on the *Bahi*.

(ii) Hem Shamsher Jang Bahadur Rana—He visited Bavan on August 4, 1936.

(iii) Jagat Shamsher Jang Bagadur Rana—He visited this place in August 3, 1938. Details about him are in Sharda script. He signed in English.

(iv) Daman Shamsher Jang Bahadur Rana—He was the Counsellor General for Nepal in India. He visited Bavan on June 13, 1945.

(v) Veer Vikram Shah Mahendra—He visited Bavan in AD 1963. He was on his way to the holy pilgrimage of Amarnath cave.

(vi) Gajendra Bahadur Raj Bahadur—He was the Minister for Foreign Affairs, Nepal. He visited the place on May 3, 1969. He was accompanied by B.P. Pande, Nepalese Ambassador in India (New Delhi).

(vii) Kirti Nidhi Bisht—He visited Bavan in May 1, 1972.

B. Royal Family from the Princely State of Jammu and Kashmir

Dogra Period

(i) Main Surat Singh—He was grandfather of Maharaja Gulab Singh. He came here in 1876 Bikrimi. He performed *Shradha* to his dead father and grandfather. He stayed in a camp (tent) near the sacred *Tirtha*.

(ii) Maharaja Gulab Singh—visited Bavan on 26, *Sawan*, 1899 Bikrimi. Details about his visit and stay are in Persian. He signed in *Dogri*.

(iii) Maharaja Ranbir Singh—visited the place on 29, *Haar*, 1907. Details about him are written in Persian. He signed in Dogri.

(iv) Maharaja Pratap Singh – visited the place on 17 *Jeth*, 1961, Bikrimi. He performed *Shradha* to Ranbir Singh and Gulab Singh. He signed on the *Bahi* in English and Dogri. Details about him are written in Urdu.

(v) Raja Amar Singh – He was the son of Ranbir Singh. He stayed at Matan for three days from 26 *Haar* to 20 *Haar*, 1956. He accompained his brother Raja Ram Singh and performed *Narayan* Bali.

(vi) Sikh Dev Singh – He was the son of Raja Baldev Singh of Poonch. He performed *Shradha* to his father and grandfather on 2, *Jeth*, 1976 Bikrimi.

(vii) Wazir Lakhpat – Resident of Kishtwar. He was the son of Shobha Ram.

(viii) Gopal Swami Ayangar – He was the Prime Minister of Jammu and Kashmir State. Visited the place on April 6, 1937.

C. Royal Families from the Princely States of India other than Jammu and Kashmir

(i) Maharaja Babu Ram Narayan Singh – He was from Badri State, U.P. He visited Bavan in 1943 Bikrimi while on his way to visit the holy cave of Amarnath.

(ii) Raja Baldev Singh – He was from Kamaka State, Jaipur. He came in 1943 Bikrimi. He signed both in Hindi and English.

(iii) Maharaja Gopal Singh – He was from Khurva State, Ajmer. He visited Bavan on 10 *Asuj*, 1957 Bikrimi. He signed in Hindi.

(iv) Maharaja Bhawani Singh – He was from the Jahahlawar State, Rajputana. Visited Bavan on May 17, 1900. Details about him are in English.

(v) Maharaja Jiwan Singh – He was from Kishen Garh State, Ajmer. He was the son of Prithvi Singh. He visited Bavan in 1959 Bikrimi. Maharaja Raghu Nath of Ajmer was also with him. Signatures are both in Hindi and English.

(vi) Maharaja Rameshwar Singh – He belonged to Darbhanga State, Bengal. He visited *Bavan* in Shaka, 1842.

(vii) Rani Girija Devi – Rajkumari of Ajar Garh, Bundekhand. She came here in 1926 with her two brothers.

(viii) Maharaja Bajrang Bahadur Singh – He was from Badri

State, U.P. He was the son of Maharaja Krishna Prasad Singh. He visited the place in *Jeth* 1987 Bikrimi. He signed in English.

(ix) Maharaja Visheshwar Singh—He was from Darbhanga State, Bengal. He was the son of Maharaja Rameshwar Singh. He visited the place in February 7, 1939.

(x) Kunwar Devendra Narayan Singh—He was from the Kerva State, U.P. He was the son of Durga Narayan Singh. He visited the place on August 17, 1962.

D. Visitors from Punjab and North West Frontier Province of British India

(i) Hari Chand Mehra—He came to Bavan in Bikrimi 1965 from Peshawar, accompanied by his mother Lajwanti.

(ii) Rai Bahadur Kidar Nath Khanna—He also came to this place from Peshawar during Pratap Singh's time.

(iii) Sardar Hari Singh—He was the Chief of Wehali, District Jehlum. He visited Bavan in *Haar*, 1969, Bikrimi.

(iv) Rai Bahadur Tirth Ram Shah—He was the resident of Nawa Shahar, District Hazara. He visited Bavan on 16th *Sawan*, 1971.

(v) Diwan Kishen Kishore—He was the son of Diwan Bhagwan Dass of Dadiwalia, Lahore. He visited Bavan in 1974 Bikrimi. He signed both in English and Urdu.

(vi) Mukund Lal Sahani—He was to visit Bavan in July 27, 1917 from Sialkot.

(vii) Fateh Chand Sahani—He was the resident of Jalal Pura Jeta, Gujarat and visited Bavan on September 17, 1932.

(viii) Roshan Lal Mehra—He came from Peshawar in 1996 Bikrimi, with his wife Satya.

E. Nehru Family

(i) Bansi Dhar (Koul)—He visited the place in 1945 Bikrimi. He came alongwith Narayan Koul.

(ii) Bishambar Nath—He visited the place in 1945 Bikrimi.

(iii) Nana Lal—He was the brother of Moti Lal Nehru, and son of Gangadhar Nehru. He visited Bavan in *Ashvin* (Kashmiri *Asuj*) 1960, Bikrimi, and performed *Shradha*.

(iv) Moti Lal Nehru – He came to Bavan thrice. He signed in Urdu on the *Bahi*.

(v) Kunwar Bahadur – He was Judge, Chief Court, Punjab. He was the son of Bansidhar Nehru, and came to Bavan in *Ashvin* (Kashmiri *Asuj*) 1961 Bikrimi. He signed in English.

(vi) Shanti Dhar – She was the daughter of Rattan Narayan Nehru. She visited Bavan in 1983, 1987, 1988, 1989, 1991 and 2001 Bikrimi.

(vii) Radha Mohan Nehru – He visited Bavan in *Shravan* 1988 Bikrimi.

(viii) S.R. Pandit – He was the son-in-Law of Moti Lal, and visited Bavan in *Jeth* 1991 Bikrimil. He signed in Hindi.

(ix) Brij Lal Nehru – Son of Nand Lal Nehru. He visited Bavan on January 20, 1935 and August 11, 1940. In 1940, he came along with Shobha Nehru, his daughter-in-law, to see only the place.

(x) Jawahar Lal Nehru – He visited Bavan on February 23, 1940, then on June 15, 1942 alongwith Feroze Gandhi and Indira Gandhi. Feroze signed in Urdu on the *Bahi*. He came again on July 11, 1962, alongwith Indira Gandhi, Sanjay and Rajiv. Bakshi Ghulam Mohammad, the Prime Minister of Jammu and Kashmir accompanied them. From Bavan they went to see the ruins at Martand. They were on a tour to Pahalgam.

(xi) Kamala Nehru – She visited Bavan on June 8, 1940 on her way to Pahalgam.

(xii) Sarojvati Nehru – She visited Bhavan on June 15, 1941.

(xiii) Rameshwari Nehru – Wife of Brijlal Nehru and mother of B.K. Nehru, visited Bavan in 1943.

(xiv) Krishna Nehru (Hatti Singh) – Daughter of Moti Lal Nehru. She visited the Bavan on *Jeth*, 2002 Bikrimi.

(xv) Indira Gandhi – She visited Bavan in 1945 (earlier she had accompanied her father on June 15, 1942 and again on July 11, 1962).

F. President of India

Rajendra Prasad – He accompanied by his wife Raj Bansi Devi visited Bavan on October 10, 1955. He performed *Puja*. He signed in Hindi.

Bahis at Koti Tirth

Professor P.N. Pushp, ex-Director, State Archives, Jammu and Kashmir told me that the *Bahis* are not only kept at Matan, but also at some other *Tirthas* of Kashmir like the Koti Tirtha.[14] He salvaged some loose sheets of the Koti Tirtha *Bahis* from some apothecary (in Kashmiri called as *Buhur*), who was selling medicines wrapped in the *Bahi* paper. He purchased them. The Bahis entered the bio-data of their *Yajman* in the order given in the Table A6.1 :

The entries in the Bahi show that the Pandas wrote the bio-data in *Sharada*, but the pilgrims signed in the script of their choice. Photostat sheets, which were shown to the author, depict that Karam Chand, son of Kishen Chand of Bira records in his own hand in Urdu the fact that he has appointed Ishar Dass as his *Purohit* at the Koti Tirtha. On the same sheet Kan Chand, an official in the Court of Gulab Singh, records in his own hand in the Persian language the fact that he appoints Budhram, son of Sadram for purposes of *Puja* and *Shradha*, etc., at the *Tirtha*, dated *Bhadon* 15, 1907 Bikrimi (in Persian). The document also bears three signatures in *Sharda* and five seals of which as many as four are in Persian languages. Sometimes they performed *Shradh* of four or five deceased relatives.

Conclusion

Bahis, if properly scrutinized, could provide missing links in tracing out the genealogical tables of the families listed in them. Badri Nath Kachroo, a Panda, who also works as the manager of the Broca Press, Srinagar, told me that the records in the *Bahis* are accepted by the Law Courts in the Kashmir Valley. Many a times the litigants have produced these *Bahis* to stake claim to ancestral parentage. He has also got genealogical records of most of the prosperous Punjabi Hindu families, e.g., Sahanees, Chopras, Khannas, Aroras, etc., who had migrated from Pakistan and settled in Kashmir. He was asking prohibitive price for selling the *Bahis* in his custody. The *Pandas* in Kashmiri are called as *Pand*; they are well to do. Now-a-days they have diversified their professional activities to other fields as well. They are at present occupying responsible positions in government establishments and are even engaged in trade. The *Pandas* are generally endogamous, i.e., marrying within the circle of their

	Name	Surname Caste	Gotra	Residence	Father's Name	Grand-father's name	Grand father's Sur-name	Mot-her's name	Brother's Name	Some-times Sis. name	Uncle's Name	Son		Date
15	Shiv Charan	Kanya Kubja Bra-hmin	Up-manya	Bhesuna	Tilak Nath	Khusalasi	Iswari Prasad	..	..	..	Chande Dib	..	..	..
16	Shiv Charan	..	Kashap	..	Durga Prasad	Adomal	Dac-hyant	..	MadwarLal Gaya Din	..	Ram Din Oganu Prasad	Ayodya Prasad, Bhagwan Din	Father's Pind Dan	..
17	Ram Sevak	..	Bhardwah	Fatheh-pur	Bhasa-wan	Jaya Ram	..	..	Ganga Din, Ram Gulam	..	..	..	..	..
18	Ram Kumar Brahma-chari	..	..	Amank-athe Lamal Dal Bengal	Nand Kumar	..	..	..	..	..	..	..	...	..
19	Shri Nath	..	Bhardwaj	Village Sripur Bengal	Bhula Nath	..	..	..	..	..	..	..	..	..

20	Thakur Das Brahma-chari	..	Kashap	Sakle Amapur Hyala Bhara-satha	Thakur Chetam	Bhairav Chandra Hor	..	..	Isar Chandra hora, Mit Ram Chandra hore, Sam Chandra hora	..	..	..	Samvat 2145 Bikrami	..
21	Radhika Prasad	Brahmin Ray	..	Calcutta	Ishwar Chandra Roy	..	..	..	..	..	..	..	..	..
22	Manomali Bando-padyaya	Kanya-Kubja	Shandilya	Calcutta Village — Sukhthyar	Ganga Naray-anam	Ram Prasad	Ram Ram	..	Madhu Sudan	..	..	..	Pilgrimage to Amar-nath (Samvat 1920 Bikrami)	..
23	Chandra Mohan	..	..	Calcutta Village — swakha-chyar	Narve Kante	Atma Nandan	..	..	..	..	..	..	Pilgrimage to Amar-nath (Samvat 1920)	..
24	Kanchand	..	Kashap	Bira	Sohan Lal	Roshan Rai	..	..	..	..	..	..	Shradh	..

professional connections. The Kashmiri Pandits generally do not enter into matrimonial alliance with them in view of the fact that they accept alms (*dakshina*) in lieu of religious services. The younger generation is feeling restless and has given up the profession due to the stigma attached to it and also their inclination for Government jobs. They want to open a new chapter for themselves. The *Bahis* are now lying uncared for.

Prof. Pushp, who lent me the sheets to get photostat, told me that he had once talked to the *Pandas* of Matan about the desirability of getting a few selections from the *Bahis* microfilmed. They had point blank refused to oblige. Secrecy appears to be trick of their trade. They think that if the contents of their profession are publicised they would lose their clientele. Their almost computerised efficiency in tracing out the ancestry of the pilgrims from their *Bahis* is simply breathtaking.

The *Bahis* under a close research would provide valuable clues to social, economic and cultural ethos of the society covered. They also provide evidence to social mobility of the Indians for religious purposes, when otherwise they were generally immobile. The women who were kept within four walls of the house, were taken out for sacred pilgrimage to Bavan and Amarnath cave by their male folks. In this context it would not be amiss to cast a glance at the spectrum of geographical variety covered by these *Bahis*.

The records are, no doubt, scratchy and disjointed, still their historical value could not be discounted. There is an apprehension that with indifference to this profession among the younger generation, the *Bahis* may fall into the hands of scrap dealers. Institutions like the National Archives could take timely steps even now to salvage whatever is still lying in dark corners.

REFERENCES

1. Vishva Bandu, ed., *Rajatarangini of Kalhan,* Hoshiarpur, 1963, p.136.
2. M.A. Stein, ed., *Kalhan's Rajatarangini on Chronicle of the Kings of Kashmir*, Bombay, Education Society's Press, 1892, Vol. I, p. 141; Fazl Allami, *Ain-i-Akbari*, Asiatic Society of Bengal, Calcutta, Vol. II, p.358.
3. M.A. Stein, *op. cit.*, The Tirth of Martanda is also mentioned in the Nilmata Purana Stanza 1036, among places sacred Surya.
4. *Kasheeri ruda Kahal Ghari.*
5. Jonaraja, *Rajatarangini*, Bombay edition, 1896, 1948; N.K. Zutshi, *Sultan-Zainu'l-Abidin of Kashmir*, Jullundur, 1975, p.69.

6. Pandit Anand Koul, *The Kashmiri Pandit*, Calcutta, 1924, Appendix IV and V, p. 86-88.
7. *Imperial Gazetteer of India*, Oxford, 1908, XIII, p.382-99.
8. *Ibid.*, XI, 163, An State in Bengal, which traces its origin to Mahes Thakur.
9. *Ibid.*, XIV, p.408-416. Sardar Jassa Singh was the founder of the State.
10. *Ibid.*, XII, p.382-99.
11. Ibid., XIV, pp.49-50.
12. *Ibid.*, XIV, p.182
13. *Ibid.*, XX, p.31-50.
14. In Varamul (old Varahmula) now called Baramulla.

APPENDIX–7

STATEMENT OF MUSLIM LEADERS IN JAMMU AND KASHMIR, 1946-47

Mirwaiz Moulvi Yusaf Shah, Muslim Conference, September 25, 1946

The Hindu capitalists want to get the State into their grip, but I warn that if the Government of Jammu and Kashmir gets terrified at the might of the Congress and strikes an unholy alliance with the National Conference fascists, it will have to face the terrific opposition of the Muslims. And this sinister alliance will be smashed to pieces. The Muslims of Kashmir have warded off Pt. Nehru's invasion in 1940, 1945 and 1946. Now he is again out to make a fresh attempt and it is the duty of the Kashmiri Muslims particularly and all the well-wishers of the country to smash up this onslaught.

2. Chowdhry Hamidullah Khan, President, Muslim Conference, May 10, 1947

If Kashmir has to keep itself aloof from carnage and bloodshed, it should lose no time in adopting a strong and bold policy. His Highness the Maharaja Bahadur should declare Kashmir independent immediately. A separate Constituent Assembly to frame the Constitution for the State, according to the wishes of the people, should be established at once. His Highness the Maharaja Bahadur will receive the cooperation of Muslims in carryiny out this policy. The Muslims from 80 per cent of the population. They are represented by the Muslim Conference. The Muslims will welcome the Maharaja Bahadur as the first constitutional ruler of independent and democratic Kashmir.

APPENDIX–8

MEMORANDUM SUBMITTED BY MUSLIM LEADERS IN INDIA TO UN REPRESENTATIVE DR FRANK P. GRAHAM, AUGUST 14, 1951

It is a remarkable fact that, while the Security Council and its various agencies have devoted so much time to the study of Kashmir dispute and made various suggestions for its resolution, none of them has tried to ascertain the views of the Indian Muslims nor the possible effects of any hasty step in Kashmir, however well-intentioned, on the interests and well-being of the Indian Muslims. We are convinced that no lasting solution for the problem can be found unless the position of Muslims in Indian society is clearly understood.

Supporters of the idea of Pakistan, before this subcontinent was partitioned, discouraged any attempt to define Pakistan clearly and did little to anticipate the conflicting problems which were bound to arise as a result of the advocacy of the two nation theory. The concept of Pakistan, therefore, became an emotional slogan with little rationale content. It never occurred to the Muslims League or its leaders that if a minority was not prepared to live with a majority on the subcontinent, how could the majority by expected to tolerate the minority.

It is, therefore, small wonder that the result of partition has been disastrous to Muslims. In undivided India, their strenght lay about 100 million. Partition split up the Muslim people, confining them to the three isolated regions. Thus, Muslims number 25 million in Wastern Pakistan, 35 million to 40 million in India, and the rest in Eastern Pakistan. A single undivided community has been broken into three fragments, each faced with its own problems.

Pakistan was not created on a religious basis. If it had been, our fate as well as the fate of other minorities would have been settled at that time. Nor would the division of the subcontinent for reasons of religion have left large minorities in India or Pakistan.

This merely illustrates what we have said above, that the concept of Pakistan was vague, obscure, and never clearly defined, nor its likely consequences foreseen by the Muslim League, even when some of these should have been obvious.

When the partition took place, Muslims in India were left in the lurch by the Muslim League and its leaders. Most of them departed to Pakistan and a few who stayed behind stayed long enough to wind up their affairs and dispose of their property. Those who went over to Pakistan left a large number of relation and friends behind.

Having brought about a division of the country, Pakistani leaders proclaimed that they would convert Pakistan into a land where people would live a life according to the tenets of Islam. This created nervousness and alarm among the minorities living in Pakistan. Not satisfied with this, Pakistan went further and announced again and again their determination to protect and safeguard the interests of Muslims in India. This naturally aroused suspicion amongst the Hindus against us and our loyalty to India was questioned.

Pakistan had made our position weaker by driving out Hindus from Western Pakistan in utter disregard of the consequences of such a policy to us and our welfare. A similar process is in question in Eastern Pakistan from which Hindus are coming over to India in a large and large number.

If the Hindus are not welcome in Pakistan, how can we, in all fairness, expect Muslims to be welcomed in India? Such a policy must inevitably, as the past has already shown, result in the uprooting of Muslims in this country and their migration to Pakistan, where, as it became clear last year, they are no longer welcome, lest their influx should destroy Pakistan's economy.

Neither some of the Muslims who did migrate to Pakistan after partition, and following the widespread bloodshed and conflict on both sides of the Indo-Pakistan border in the north-west, have been able to find a happy asylum in what they had been told would be their homeland. Consequently some of them have had to return to India, e.g., Meos who are now being rehabilitated in their former areas.

If we are living honourably in India today, it is certainly not due to Pakistan which, if anything, has by her policy and action weakened our position.

The credit goes to the broadminded leadership of India, to Mahatma Gandhi and Pandit Jawaharlal Nehru, to the traditions of tolerance in this country and to the Constitution which ensures equal rights to all citizens of India, irrespective of their religion caste, colour or sex.

We, therefore, feel that, tragically as Muslims were misled by the Muslim League and subsquently by Pakistan and the unnecessary suffering which we and our Hindu brethren have to go through in Pakistan and in India since partition, we must be given an opportunity to settle down to a life of tolerance and understanding to the mutual benefit of Hindus and Muslims in our country—if only Pakistan would let us do it. To us it is a matter of no small consequence.

Despite continuous provocations, first from the Muslim League and since then from Pakistan, the Hindu Majority in India has not thrown us or members of other minorities out of Civil Services, Armed Forces, the judiciary, trade, commerce, business and industry. There are Muslim Ministers in the Union and State cabinets, Muslim Governors, Muslim Ambassadors, representing India in foreign countries, fully enjoying the confidence of the Indian nation, Muslim members in Parliament and State legislatures, Muslim judges serving on the Supreme Courts, high-ranking officers in the Armed Forces and the Civil services, including the police. Muslims have large landed estates, run big business and commercial houses in various parts of the country, notably in Bombay and Calcutta, have their shares in industrial production and enterprise in export and import trade. Our famous sacred shrines and places of cultural interest are mostly in India.

Not that our lot is certainly happy. We wish some of the State Governments showed a little greater sympathy to us in the field of education and employment. Nevertheless, we feel we have an honourable place in India. Under the law of the land, our religious and cultural life is protected and we shall share in the opportunities open to all citizens to ensure progress for the people of this country.

It is, therefore, clear that our interest and welfare do not coincide with Pakistan's conception of the welfare and interests of Muslims in Pakistan.

This is clear from Pakistan's attitude towards Kashmir. Pakistan claims Kashmir, first, on the ground of the majority of the State's people being Muslims and, secondly on the ground, of the State being essential to its economy and defence. To achieve its objective it has been threatening to launch "Jehad" against Kashmir in India.

It is a strange commentary on political beliefs that the same Muslims of Pakistan, who like the Muslims of Kashmir to join them, invaded the State, in October 1947, killing and plundering Muslims in the State and dishonouring Muslim women, all in the interest of what they described as the liberation of Muslims of the State. In its oft-proclaimed anxiety to rescue the 3 million Muslims from what it describes as the tyranny of handful of Hindus in the State, Pakistan evidently is prepared to sacrifice the interests of 40 million Muslims in India – a strange exhibition of concern for the welfare of fellow-Muslims. Our misguided brothers in Pakistan do not realise that if Muslims in Pakistan can wage a war against Hindus in Kashmir why should not Hindus, sooner or later, retaliate against Muslims in India.

Does Pakistan seriously think that it could give us any help if such an emergency arose or that we would deserve any help thanks to its own follies? It is incapable of providiing room and livelihood to the 40 million Muslims of India, should they migrate to Pakistan. Yet its policy and action, if not changed soon, may well produce the result which it dreads.

We are convinced that India will never attack our interests. First of all, it would be contrary to the spirit animating the political movement in this country. Secondly, it would be opposed to the Constitution and to the sincere leadership of the Prime Minister. Thirdly, India by committing such a folly would be playing straight into the hands of Pakistan.

We wish we were equally convinced of the soundness of Pakistan's policy. So completely oblivious is it of our present problems and of our future that it is willing to sell us into slavery – if only it can secure Kashmir.

It ignores the fact that Muslims in Kashmir may also have a point of view of their own, that there is a democratic movement with a democratic leadership in the State, both inspired by the progress of a broad minded, secular, democratic movement in India and both naturally being in sympathy with India. Otherwise, the Muslims raiders should have been welcomed with open arms by the Muslims of the State when the invasion took place in 1947.

Persistent propaganda about "Jahad" is intended, among other things, to inflame religious passions in this country. For it would, of course, be in Pakistan's interests to promote communal rioting in India to show the Kashmiri Muslims how they can find security only in Pakistan. Such a policy, however, can only bring untold misery and suffering to India and Pakistan generally and to Indian Muslims particularly.

Pakistan never tires of asserting that it is determined to protect the interests of Muslims in Kashmir and India. Why does not Pakistan express the same concern for Pathans who are fighting for Pakhtoonistan, an independent homeland of their own? The freedom-loving Pathans under the leadership of Khan Abdul Gaffar Khan and Dr. Khan Sahib, both nurtured in the democratic traditions of Indian National Congress are being subjected to political repression of the worst possible kind by their Muslim brethren in power in Pakistan and in the NWFP. Contradictory as Pakistan's policy generally is, it is no surprise to us that while it insists on a fair and impartial plebiscite in Kashmir, it denies a fair and impartial plebiscite to Pathans.

Pakistan's policy in general and her attitude towards Kashmir in particular thus tend to create conditions in this country which in the long run can only bring to us Muslims widespread suffering and destruction. Its policy prevents us from settling down, from being honourabal citizens of a State, free from suspicion of our fellow-countrymen and adapting ourselves to changing conditions to promote the interests and welfare of India. Its sabre-rattling interferes with its own economy and ours. It expects us to be loyal to it despite its impotence to give us any protection, believing at the same time that we can still claim all the rights of citizenship in a secular democracy.

In the event of a war, it is extremely doubtful whether it will be able to protect the Muslims of East Bengal who are completely cut off from Western Pakistan. Are the Muslims of India and Eastern Pakistan to sacrifice themselves completely to enable the 25 million Muslims in Western Pakistan to embark upon mad, self-destructive adventures?

We should, therefore, like to impress upon you with all the emphasis at our command that Pakistan's policy towards Kashmir is fraught with the gravest peril to the 40 million Muslims of India. If the Security Council is really interested in peace, human brotherhood, and international understanding, it should heed this warning while there is still time.

Dr Zakir Hussain
(Vice Chancellor Aligarh University)
Sir Sultan Ahmed
(Former Member of Governor General's Executive Council)
Sir Mohd. Ahmed Syed Khan
(Nawab of Chhatari, former acting Governor of United Provinces and Prime Minister of Hyderabad)
Sir Mohd. Usman
(Former Member of Governor General's Executive Council and acting Governor of Madras)
Sir Iqbal Ahmed
(Former Chief Justice of Allahabad High Court)
Sir Fazal Rahimtoola
(Former Sheriff of Bombay)
Maulana Hafz-ur-Rehman M.P.
Col. B.H. Zaidi M.P.
Nawab Zain Yar Jung
(Minister Government of Hyderabad)
A.K. Kawaja
(Former President of Muslim Majlis)
T.M. Zarif
(General Secretary West Bengal Bohra Community)

APPENDIX–9

STATEMENT OF DEENDAYAL UPADHAYAYA (BJS), JULY 10, 1964

Shri T.T. Krishnamachari, while asserting in London that the whole of Jammu and Kashmir State legally belonged to India, had expressed the Government's desire to talk to Pakistan on the Kashmir issue. So long as Pakistan is not prepared to accept our legal title to the State, there is no common ground for talks between India and Pakistan on this question. From time to time the Government of India has succumbed to international pressures and talked to Pakistan on Kashmir. It has only led to confusion with regard to our basic stand and has encouraged forces that are conspiring for a further vivisection of India. It has also hampered development of the State. Once for all the Government of India should declare that it would not talk to anybody on the Kashmir question, who refuses to accept the finality and irrevocability of the instrument of accession. It is also necessary that Article 370 of the Constitution is abrogated so that the State may attain an equal status within the Indian Union and citizens of India living in Kashmir are assured of all the guarantees and privileges of our Constitution. It will also put an end to all speculation and kite-flying about the future of the State.

There are people in the country who are advocating various solutions of the problem envisioning secession of the State from India. In the interest of maintenance of the unity and integrity of India it has become imperative that this sort of propaganda is stopped forthwith. Shri Rajaji's suggestion of placing Kashmir under UN is dangerous. We do not want to turn that beautiful Valley and a strategic region of ours into a hot bed of international conflicts. Kashmir, under no circumstances, can be allowed to become another Congo or Laos.

Note: BJS, now BJP, is for the abrogation of Article 370 of the Constitution of India.

Source : *Organiser*, July 24, 1994

APPENDIX–10

MOTION IN THE LOK SABHA FOR REPEALING ARTICLE 370, AUGUST 30, 1968

This House is of the opinion that the present incompatible situation must be brought to an end, in which despite the State of Jammu and Kashmir being an integral part of India, it has a separate Constitution, a separate Head of the State and a separate flag. The State must be brought to the level equal to that of other States of India. To achieve this objective, the House recommends that all necessary actions including the repeal of Article 370 should immediately be carried out.

Note: The motion moved by Atal Behari Vajpayee was discussed for two days and rejected.

APPENDIX–11

MESSAGE OF INDIAN PRIME MINISTER P.V. NARASIMHA RAO ON KASHMIR, AUGUST 15, 1994

With you, without you, in spite of you, Kashmir will remain with India.

Note: Excerpt from the Broadcast to the Nation on Independence Day

APPENDIX–12

UN SECRETARY GENERAL DR BOUTROS BOUTROS-GHALI ON JAMMU AND KASHMIR, SEPTEMBER 10, 1994*

Dr Boutros Boutros-Ghali said though the United Nations Resolutions on Kashmir had "value", their implementation depended on the "political will" of the protagonists or the decision of different UN organs – the Security Council or the General Assembly.

The UN Secretary General made the observation at a Press Conference following discussions with Indian leaders including Prime Minister P.V. Narasimha Rao. His views were solicited by questioners on the relevance of the UN Resolutions for a plebiscite in Kashmir and India's "moral obligation" to abide by them.

"The Resolutions have a value. (But) so long as there is no political will on the part of the protagonists or no decision is taken by different organs of the UN, they cannot be implemented," he explained. The emphasis he sought to lay was clearly on resumption of dialogue between Islamabad and New Delhi, to make which possible, he was willing to be an "honest" broker.

Dr Ghali informed that he discussed the problem of Kashmir in Islamabad as well as in New Delhi. "I mentioned to the two Government," he said, "that I am willing to be an honest broker for resumption of direct talks between the two parties.

"I still hope that I will receive positive answer so that I can play this role of a broker. But we will have to wait and see... what happens to this central role of being a broker," the Secretary General observed.

He clarified in response to further queries on the subject that his objective as a broker was confined to encouraging "direct contact" between the two parties: "They (India and Pakistan) will have to decide . . . how they want to negotiate. There is something called

---

*Based on a Press Conference.

pre-negotiations (for having the dialogue initiated). The role of the Secretary General is to encourage the two to talk."

Dr Ghali told the New Delhi based correspondent of the Pakistan Broadcasting Corporation (PBC), who claimed that Islamabad has accepted his proposal, that he had not received any response from either of the two countries. "I have not made any offer," emphasised the Secretary General, adding: "I have just said I am ready to be an honest broker. (There has been) no response (to the proposal) from anywhere..."

As the Pakistani journalist had argued that the Shimla Accord did not negate the UN Charter, Dr Ghali averred: "The Charter is a common document between all States. But a political will to find a solution is more important. What is important is negotiation; continuous negotiation."

On the prospects of resumption of talks between New Delhi and Islamabad, Dr Ghali remarked that he was always "very optimistic" or else he would not be the Secretary General of the UN. However, he felt that "more strong" political will was required from the two sides to start the dialogue and find a solution to the Kashmir question.

Citing an interview of the Indian Army Chief telecast by CNN, a journalist suggested a Pakistani hand behind the killings of Indian Armymen in Somalia. "I used to receive regular reports from Somalia. I have never heard of such rumours," emphasised Dr Ghali. He said his repesentatives on the ground (in Somalia) were "very, very neutral and very objective (in their assessment)."

The Secretary General's attention was also drawn to Pakistan's support of terrorism. "What's your assessment? Why haven't you condemned it", an Indian journalist asked. Dr Ghali replied: "Any condemnation of any State has to emanate from the UN General Assembly or the Security Council. The Secretary General is only asked to implement the decisions of different UN organs."

Mr Ghali refused to comment on India's allegation of Pakistan waging a "proxy war in Kashmir. "I do not want to comment because an honest broker will not comment," he noted. "I will try to find a common denominator and encourage both sides to talk..."

In another context, the Secretary General observed that he will have to negotiate further with the two parties till they accepted that the "honest broker" should commence his job. There was no immediate comment from official circles here to his proposal. India's position against third party intervention on Kashmir was well known.

Earlier in the day, the Secreary-General had a separate meeting with Mr. V.N. Narayanan, Editor of *The Hindustan Times*, Mr. H.K. Dua, Editor-in-Chief of the *Indian Express* and Mr. Shekhar Gupta of *India Today* magazine.

(Source : *Hindustan Times*, September 11, 1994)

APPENDIX–13

JAMAIT-I-ISLAMI LEADER ON JAMMU AND KASHMIR, OCTOBER 2, 1994

Jamait-i-Islami leader Syed Ali Shah Geelani, after his release from prison, has dismissed the politics of ballots in the prevailing situation in Kashmir as "meaningless".

He says the Government should meet the basic issue of resolving the "Kashmir dispute" through "tripartite talks" between India, Pakistan and Kashmiris.

In his first interview soon after his release from a jail in Jammu, Mr Geelani told the *Hindustan Times* that the release of Mr Abdul Ghani Lone, Chairman of the Peoples Conference and himself was effected by the Government under pressure from international fora. This also coincided with the ongoing session of the UN General Assembly, where Pakistan is expected to raise the Kashmir issue.

Mr Geelani said for "us the elections were meaningless and we are not going to participate". During his year-long detention that ended Saturday morning in Jammu, he said he was not approached by anyone from the government to discuss any such issue. He maintained that "our stand remains unchanged as far as the struggle of Kashmiris for their right to self-determination was concerned."

"I am not happy over my release. It is a bigger jail here where I have come from a small prison", he said and explained that Kashmir is a big jail for it suffers "frequent crackdowns, has the presence of bunkers all-round and the midnight knocks are part of the day-to-day life."

Mr Geelani had documented his jail experiences in his book *Rooded-e-Kafas* or *Jail diary*, when he was in jail for two years from April 1990.

About his role in the given situation in Kashmir where All Parties *Hurriyat* (freedom) Conference was increasingly being challenged by various militant outfits, Mr Geelani said he would "work for keeping up the morale of the people engaged in the struggle besides ensuring unity among the ranks of various groups.

Mr Geelani felt that Kashmir situation was different from Northern Ireland, where the Irish Republican Army (IRA) had halted its military operations against the British Government.

(Source: *Hindustan Times*, October 3, 1994

APPENDIX–14

HUMAN RIGHTS ACTIVIST ON HUMAN RIGHTS VIOLATION BY TERRORISTS IN JAMMU AND KASHMIR, OCTOBER 2, 1994

India should move a resolution in the current session of the UN General Assembly to declare Pakistan a terrorist state for aiding and abetting terrorism in the Kashmir Valley and other human rights violations, noted human rights activist and Member of Parliament, K.A. Khan said.

Addressing a Press conference Mr Khan said the Geneva convention of the United Nations human rights conference had passed a resolution declaring State sponsored terrorism a violation of human rights and Pakistan fell in this category for not only instigation and abetting terrorism in Jammu and Kashmir but also trying to spread it to the entire nation.

He said India should persuade the UN Security Council to ask Pakistan for withdrawing its forces from the Pakistan occupied Kashmir (PoK) in accordance with the UN resolution of August 30, 1948.

Referring to the statement of former Pakistan Prime Minister Nawaz Sharief on the possession of a nuclear bomb by Pakistan, Mr Khan demanded that the forces on the borders should be strengthened to face any kind of misadventure from Pakistan's side "we need to put special emphasis on the security aspect on the Jammu and Kashmir border."

He said the installation of a democratically elected Government in the State would send the right signals and ease the pressure in the international fora.

He accused Pakistan of illtreating Mohajirs and grading them as second class citizens. "We in India are the second largest majority population and the Islamic countries should appreciate the sentiments of the millions of Muslims living in India."

(Source: *Hindustan Times*, October 3, 1994)

APPENDIX–15

BHARATIYA JANATA PARTY ON OMISSION AND COMMISSION OF THE CENTRAL GOVERNMENT IN JAMMU AND KASHMIR, OCTOBER 2, 1994

...The insurgency in Jammu and Kashmir has entered altogether a different phase now. Foreign mercenaries have openly entered the fray and have turned a secessionist movement into a false jihad. Having achieved an "ethnic cleansing" of sorts, in the Valley, the militants are now aiming to achieve something similar in the Doda district of Jammu region...

Instead of facing this situation resolutely and using all the available means effectively, the Narasimha Rao Government has been emasculating the efforts of the security forces, particularly the Indian Army, by dithering at crucial times and by not establishing the appropriate hierarchy and organisation to deal with the situation. Instead of revamping the State administration, now riddled with traitors and corrupt elements, the Narasimha Rao Government continues to pour hundreds of crore down the Kashmir Valley as if this will in some way drown the insurgency...

Kashmiri Migrants

This Government is guilty of criminal callousness towards those over three lakh Hindu migrants from Kashmir who were forced to flee their homes because of this very Government's incompetence to protect them from the militants.

Not once did the Prime Minister visit the migrants what to say of providing of proper relief and rehabilitation for these hapless victims of militancy.

(Source: *Organiser*, October 2, 1994)

APPENDIX–16

SEPARATIST LEADER OF KASHMIR SHABIR AHMED SHAH ON JAMMU AND KASHMIR, OCTOBER 3, 1994

Shabir Ahmed Shah, a leading separatist leader of Kashmir, whose arrest five years ago had sparked off widespread violent reaction all over the Valley, believes that "leaders cannot thrust their decision on the people. It would be people who would have the right to make the final decision regarding their future."

Forty-year-old Shabir, who has spent at least half of his life in jail, in an interview to the *Hindustan Times* on the eve of his release after five-year-long detention at a stretch, said, "We leave it to the people whether they opt for India or Pakistan. They would also be free to have the third option of staying independent of the two countries. We cannot thrust our wishes on the people and we cannot take the people with us on gun point."

Hastily adding that "gun is an important part of the ongoing struggle of people of Kashmir against India", Shabir said that it should not be mistaken as if the gun was the sole guide of the movement. "There should be discreet use of gun for furthering the movement and not for harassing the people." He agreed that the few wrong elements have come in possession of the gun and were misusing it." They and the "penetration by the agencies into the militant groups has to be weeded out."

He would work for the unity of the separatist groups for further consolidating the movement for the "right to self-determination". All this would be done in consultation with elderly politicians, he said and asserted that finally the solution to Kashmir crisis has to be found through dialogue.

Shabir alleged that it was after "all the doors of talks were shut on us that Kashmiri youth picked up the guns seeking their right for self-determination".

Recalling his jail experiences after his arrest on the intervening night of September 27 and 28, 1989, at the highway town of Ramban on Jammu-Srinagar National Highway, he said, Syed Ail Shah Geelani, Moulvi Abbas Ansari, Prof. Abdul Ghani and Abdul Ghani Lone agreed during their period of detention at Mehruli, that there should be single direction and goal for the right of self-determination they should fight for. The outcome of these discussions was the formation of All Parties Hurriyat Conference (APHC) later by various Kashmiri separatist groups.

After his arrest, Shabir who has been christened as "Prisoner of Conscience" by the London-based human rights watch group Amnesty International, said he was kept in solitary cells at Hari Niwas in Srinagar, Udhampur, Jodhpur and Tihar Jail. There was "boiled black tea and brinjals and half-cooked dal" which was served to him during all these days. But "I had no complaints", he said. First time, he was served mutton was when they were shifted to Mehruli during the Prime Ministership of Chandra Shekhar.

Reverting back to his theme of seeking solution of the Kashmir crisis through talks, Shabir Shah said that sans Pakistan such dialogue was meaningless. "Pakistan is an essential party to the dispute as are India and Kashmiris". He said the peace on the sub-continent cannot dawn on till the Kashmir crisis is resolved and neither India nor Pakistan can resolve it by their respective military might.

Listing his priorities, he said, the task before him is to bridge the gap between the Kashmir Valley and Jammu region, Kashmir Valley and Ladakh. He admitted that the "misuse" of the guns by wrong elemens has "brought us bad name in the international community. Our fight is not against any community nor against people of India".

Shabir said that because of his thoughts and frequent shifting from one jail to another and bad health, he could not write anything about his experiences in the jail. "My life is an open book, there was actually nothing to be written about", he said.

He asked the organisations like Panun Kashmir, demanding separate homeland for Kashmiri Hindus in the Valley, that they should "stay with us in bigger Valley, why they are asking for a small piece of land. We are incomplete without them and our struggle is incomplete without them".

When asked about J&K elections, he said: "we will welcome UN sponsored elections and that should be taken as a referendum".

(*Source*: Arun Joshi, *Hindustan Times*, October 14, 1994)

APPENDIX–17

TERRORIST ORGANISATIONS OPERATING IN KASHMIR VALLEY

1. Al Bader
2. Al Hazzah
3. Al-Khomeni
4. Al-Mehmoodi Mijahdin
5. Al Qarblaie Group
6. All J&K Soldiers Field Front
7. Allah Tigers
8. Ansor-ul Islam
9. Dukhtram-e-Milat (Women Wing)
10. Free Army Islami
11. Hizbi
12. Hizbullah
13. Hiz-ul-Zaheed
14. Ikhwan-ul-Musalmeen
15. Inqullabi Council
16. Islamic Jamait Tulba
17. Islamic Jamuric Kashmir
18. J&K Inquilabi Front
19. J&K Libaration Front
20. J&K Liberation Organisation
21. J&K Mahaji Azadi
22. Jinah Liberation Front
23. K.V.C.
24. Kashmir Freedom Army Guerilla Commando
25. Kashmir Freedom KLF Wing
26. Kashmir Freedom Movement
27. Kashmir Liberation Front
28. Kashmir Liberation Tiger
29. Kashmir Students Force

30. Muslim Student Front
31. National Muslim United Front
32. Operation Balakote
33. Peoples Front
34. Peoples League
35. Peoples Liberation Organisation
36. Students Liberation Front
37. T.F.
38. Tehrike-Jahad
39. Tehriqe Azadi
40. Victory Commando Force

APPENDIX–18

TERRORISM IN JAMMU AND KASHMIR

Table A18.1 : Terrorist Violence in Jammu and Kashmir

Year	Total Incidents	Attacks on SF	Attacks on others	Explosion & Arson	Other Incidents
1988	390	6	1	142	241
1989	2154	49	73	840	1192
1990	3905	1098	485	1810	512
1991	3122	1999	321	611	191
1992	4971	3413	507	744	307
1993	4176	2388	520	831	437
Total	18718	8953	1907	4978	2880

Table A18.2 : Killings in Terrorist Violence

	1988	1989	1990	1991	1992	1993	Total
SF Personnel	1	13	132	185	177	178	686
Govt. Officials	1	3	62	57	36	28	187
Top Political Leaders	–	–	1	–	–	2	3
Politicians	–	3	24	10	4	8	49
Judiciary	–	3	–	1	–	1	5
Press Men	–	–	1	1	1	1	4
Hindus	–	6	177	45	67	80	375
Muslims	28	64	575	456	706	725	2554
Sikhs	–	–	6	12	10	3	31
Others	–	–	16	12	35	32	95
Militants	1	–	183	614	873	1074	2745
Total Killed	31	92	1177	1393	1909	2132	6734

Table A18.3 : Kidnappings by Militants

	1989	1990	1991	1992	1993	Total
Incidents	2	57	100	124	169	452
Persons Abducted	2	70	159	183	259	673
Foreigners*	—	–	12	—	—	12
Women	—	8	8	13	23	52
Politicians	—	33	53	26	4	116
Govt. Officers	—	21	27	43	33	124
SF Personnel	—	12	44	30	26	112
Killed	1	29	29	38	88	185
Released**	1	32	73	112	127	245

*Israel-7, Swedish-2, Dutch-1, Japanese-1, French-1

**In most cases released after extortion, torture, exchange of PF militants, Rape, others remaining untraced

Table A18.4 : Explosions Caused in Public Places

Year	Incidents	Killed	Injured
1988	24	15	69
1989	506	7	125
1990	1164	16	500
1991	220	24	85
1992	180	89	400
1993	140	38	267
Total	2234	189	1446

Table A18.5 : Criminal Acts, Extortion* and Lootings by Militants

Year	Incidents	Amount Robbed (in Rupees)
1990	23	2,26,91,200
1991	31	62,30,768
1992	39	64,86,563
1993	44	53,31,326
Total	137	4,07,39,857

Note: Only a small fraction of such cases are reported to the authorities due to fear.

Table A18.6 : Recovery of Weapons from Militants

Weapons/ Explosive	1988-90	1991	1992	1993	Total
Rocket Launchers	141	140	174	93	458
Machine Guns	124	176	174	159	633
AK Series Rifles	1474	2602	3775	2327	10178
Snipper Rifles	–	3	13	57	74
Pistols/Revolvers	858	946	808	738	3350
Ammunition	242007	318623	343699	437668	1341997
Grenades	2994	2236	2818	4633	12681
Rockets	370	329	267	171	1137
Rockets Boosters	156	203	144	98	601
Mines	1101	217	307	756	2351
Guns	30	79	81	91	281
Explosives(Kgs)	1966	588	436	3205	6195
Bombs	708	72	228	336	1348
Grenades Launchers	–	–	1	10	11
Mortar	–	–	–	11	11
WT Sets	22	37	68	154	281

Table A18.7 : Attacks on Minorities

	1986	1987	1988	1989	1990	1991	1992	1993	Total
Hindus	118	225	415	878	177	45	67	64	1989
Sikhs	2	4	5	8	7	9	10	2	47

Table A18.8 : Mass Exodus of the Families of Minorities from Valley to Other Parts of the State of Jammu and Kashmir or to Other States of India

Place	Hindus	Sikhs	Others	Total
Jammu	23653	2836	3120	29609
Delhi	11391	50	–	11441
Others	2014	740	17	2771
Total	37058	3626	3137	43821

Note : Authorities are spending rupees 45 millions per month on cash relief in addition to providing logistic support

Table A18.9 : District-wise Details of Displaced Families

	Descritpion	Jammu	Udh-ampur	Kathua	Rajouri	Doda	Poonch	Total
I.	No. of families regd.	46510	6358	478	28	360	1	53,735
II.	Total Strength	211785	27412	2012	94	1460	5	242768
III.	No. of families accomodated							
	in tents	5059	355	0	0	0	0	5394
	in buildings	1043	2243	138	0	0	0	3424
	Total	6082	2598	138	0	0	0	8818
IV.	No. of camps established	19	6	1	0	4	0	30
V.	No. of tents issued							
	Talab Tillo	75		Muthi		2559		
	Trikuta Nagar	3		Jhdi		753		
	Mistriwala	1053		Purkhu		824		
	Nagrota	659		Indira Nagar		225		
	Udhampur	800		Dodda		50		

Note: Barring a handful of Kashmiri Pandits who are either running their business establishment by buying peace with terrorists or some Government servants who are discharging their duties under security cover, the entire Kashmiri Pandit community has been forced to flee the Valley

Source: A report by Jammu and Kashmur National Front International, Denmark as reported in *Organiser*, November 27, 1994

Bibliography

Commprehensive Reference Bibliography* Covering All Aspects of Jammu & Kashmir 1844-1994

AICC Economic Review (Periodical), 1965, They Shall Not Pass, *AICC Economic Review* 17 (6) September 1, p5-6, editorial

Aazim, Muzaffar, 1978, Experiments in Modern Kashmir Poetry, *Indian Literature* 21 (2) March-April, p92-97

Abad, Abdul
see Abdul Abad

Abba, F.A., 1980, *Profiles of Abdullah*, Srinagar

Abdul Abad, 1987, *Kashmir to Frankfurt : A Study of Arts and Crafts with a Chapter on the Freedom Struggle of Kashmir*, Rima Pub House, New Delhi, xiv, 182p

Abdul Aziz, Mir
see Aziz, Mir Abdul

Abdul Majid Khan
see Khan, Abdul Majid

Abdul Qader, 1958, An Estimate of Work in Irrigation, *KT* 2 (8) December-January, p40

Abdullah, Farooq
see also Mishra, R.K., 1984, I Am being Maligned

Abdullah, Farooq, 1983, Kashmir Integral Part of India : Farooq, *Times of India*, November 3, p1, col 2-5

---

* 1. Bibliographical details of some entries compiled from secondary sources including gray literature could not be incorporated in full.

2. By former Director, National Social Science Documentation Centre (ICSSR) Government of India, compiled with the assistance of Smt G. Aruna

Abdullah, Farooq, 1983, Poll Pact with Cong-I Still Possible : Farooq, *Times of India* April 23, p1, col 4-5 +

Abdullah, Farooq, 1984, Accession Final Says Farooq, *Times of India*, February 2, p1, col 5-6 +

Abdullah, Farooq, 1985, A Fourth Ontological Argument in Ibn Sina's Metaphysics, *Islam and Modern Age* 16 (3) August, p175-188

Abdullah, Farooq, 1985, *My Dismissal*, Vikas Pub, New Delhi, 90p

Abdullah, Farooq, 1986, Reminiscences of Sheikh Sahib, *Sunday Statesman* (Misc) August 31, p1

Abdullah, Farooq, 1988, Jammu and Kashmir on Road to Progress, *Co-operators Bulletin* 31 (1) January, pv-vii

Abdullah, Farooq, 1989, I'm Fighting a War for India : Farooq, *Times of India*, April 12, p1, col 2-5 +

Abdulla, Farooq, 1993, The Kashmir Autonomy, *National Herald* March 19

Abdullah, Sheikh Mohammed

see also Anon, 1964, What Sheikh Abdullah Said; Anon, 1965, Sheikh Abdullah Says; Anon, 1968, The Sheikh Answers Our Questions; Anon, 1969, Will to Solve Kashmir Problem Lacking

Abdullah, Sheikh Mohammed, n.d., *Kashmir Calling*, Kashmir Bureau of Information, Delhi, 4p

Abdullah, Sheikh Mohammed, 1961, *Inaugural Address to Constituent Assembly of Kashmir*, November 5, no publisher

Abullah, Sheikh Mohammed, 1964, Cry for Secession : Abdullah, *Link* 6(37) April 26, p9-11

Abdullah, Sheikh Mohammed, 1968, India, Pakistan and Kashmir : Interview, *Mainstream* (Republic Day Special) 6 (22-23), p15-16

Abdullah, Sheikh Mohammed, 1969, Abdullah Assails Sadiq Govt, *Times of India* November 28, p16, col 1

Abdullah, Sheikh Mohammed, 1969, Abdullah Pays Tribute to Ayub, *Times of India* February 28, p9, col 1

Abdullah, Sheikh Mohammed, 1969, Abdullah's Views on Future Kashmir Set-up, *Times of India* October 25, p5, col 2-3

Abdullah, Sheikh Mohammed, 1969, Will to Solve Kashmir Problem Lacking Says Sheikh Abdullah, *Times of India* October 16, p3, col 4-5

Abdullah, Sheikh Mohammed, 1970, India is My Country; Muslims Asked to Change Outlook; Work for Progress : Sheikh, *Times of India*, February 8, p1, col 7-8

Abdullah, Sheikh Mohammed, 1973, Hands off Kashmir : Sheikh Abdullah Tells Pak Premier, *Times of India* December 1, p1, col 7-8 +

Abdullah, Sheikh Mohammed, 1973, Autonomy Inherent in Accession : Sheikh, *Times of India* January 23, p1, col 4-5

Abdullah, Sheikh Mohammed, 1974, Clashes Instigated to Stall Talks: Abdullah, *Times of India* July 19, p1, col 6-7 +

Abdullah, Sheikh Mohammed, 1974, Pak-Held Areas Part of Kashmir : Abdullah, *Times of India* June 19, p1, col 5-6

Abdullah, Sheikh Mohammed, 1974, Revolution Inevitable if Talks Fail : Abdullah, *Times of India* November 3, p1, col 5-6 +

Abdullah, Sheikh Mohammed, 1974, Talks with Pindi Later, *Times of India* August 22, p1, col 2-4 +

Abdullah, Sheikh Mohammed, 1975, Hands off Kashmir: Sheikh Tells Bhutto, *Times of India*, March 3, p5, col 1-2

Abdullah, Sheikh Mohammed, 1975, Kashmir : Prospect and Retrospect, *Mainstream* (Annual Number) 14 (1-5), p19-21

Abdullah, Sheikh Mohammed, 1975, Plebiscite Demand Now Irrelevant, *Times of India* February 25, p1, col 2-3 +

Abdullah, Sheikh Mohammed, 1976, Ethical and Spiritual Values in Education, *Vedanta Kesari* 63 (6) October, p169

Abdullah, Sheikh Mohammed, 1977, Janata Wants to Scrap Article 370, *Times of India* May 17, p5, col 1-2

Abdullah, Sheikh Mohammed, 1977, N.C. Architect of State's Accession, *Times of India* September 14, p5, col 2-3

Abdullah, Sheikh Mohammed, 1977, A New Beginning in Kashmir, *Mainstream* (Annual Number) 16 (1-6), p17-18

Abdullah, Sheikh Mohammed, 1977, No Rigidity on Ordinance Abdullah, *Times of India* November 26, p1, col 8 +

Abdullah, Sheikh Mohammed, 1977, Search for Allies : Sheikh, *Link* 20 (6) September 18, p23-25

Abdullah, Sheikh Mohammed, 1978, Kashmir Must be Consulted on Indo-Pak Talks, *Times of India* January 21, p1, col 1-2 +

Abdullah, Sheikh Mohammed, 1980, Jamaat Getting Funds from West Asia, *Times of India* September 2, p1, col 3-4 +

Abdullah, Sheikh Mohammed, 1992, Kashmir and National Integration, *Mainstream* (Annual) November 14, p119-122

Abdullah, Sheikh Mohammed, 1993, *Flames of the Chinar : An Autobiography*, abridged and tr from Urdu by Khushwant Singh, Viking, New Delhi, 176p

Abdur Rahman, Syed Sahabuddin
see Rahman, Syed Sahabuddin Adur

Abhayavardhan, Hector, *jt author*
see Madhok, Balraj and Adhayavardhan, Hector

Abraham, A.S., 1977, Pursuit of Public Safety : Preventive Detention a Throwback, *Times of India* November 24, p6, col 3-5

Abraham, A.S., 1981, Views from the Vale : Roots of Kashmiri Ambivalence, *Times of India* November 20, p8, col 3-5

Abul Kalam Azad
see Azad, Abul Kalam

Achanthody, R.N., 1960, A Week in Kashmir : Tour Impressions of a South Indian, *DT* October 30; *DT* November 6

Adair, F.E.S., 1899, *A Summer in High Asia : Being a Record of Sport and Travel in Baltistan and Ladakh*, Thacker, London, 287p, map

Adams, Andrew Leith, 1867, *Wanderings of a Naturalist in India : The Western Himalayas and Kashmir*, Edmonton and Douglas, Edinburg, 333p

Advani, T.M., 1966, Education in Kashmir, *Illustrated Weekly of India* 87 (13) March 27, p21

Afsir Karim,
see Karim, Afsir

Afzal, M. Rafique, *editor*
see Jinnah, Mohammed Ali, 1966, *Selected Speeches and Statements*

Afzal, Q., 1958, Kashmir and Our Foreign Policy, *Pakistan Review*, 6, June, p27, 42

Aga, S.M., 1966, Wookcarving in Kashmir, *Foreign Trade of India,* 37, July, p27-29

Agarwal, Hari Om, 1979, *Kashmir Problem : Its Legal Aspects*, Kitab Mahal, Allahabad, vi, 194p

Agrawala, A.P., ed, 1978, *Moonland Ladakh : A Travellers Guide*, Nest and Wings (India), New Delhi, viii, 134, 16p

Agrawala, Ashvini, 1981, Social Picture of Kashmir in 11th and 12th Centuries AD as Depicted in the Rajatarangini of Kalhana, *Vishveshvaranand Indological Journal* 19 (1-2) June-December, p199-210, footnotes

Agrawala, Shriman Narayan
see Shriman Narayan

Ahangar, Altaf Hussain, 1987, Inheritance Rights of Muslim Women under Kashmir Customary Law, *Islamic and Comparative Law Quarterly* 7 (3), p217-239

Ahangar, M.A.H., 1983, Kashmir Customary Law : Evidentiary Value of Dogra's Code and Gonjoo's Digest : A Review Article, *Islamic and Comparative Law Quarterly* 3 (4) December, p267-278, footnotes

Ahluwalia, H.P.S., 1980, *Hermit Kingdom : Ladakh*, Vikas Pub, New Delhi, 186p

Ahmad
 see also Ahmed

Ahmad, G., 1965, *The Indian War*, Embassy of Pakistan, Information Division, Washington, 14p

Ahmad Gurmani, Mushtaq
 see Gurmani, Mushtaq Ahmad

Ahmad, S. Maqbul and Bano, Raja, 1984, *Historical Geography of Kashmir*, Ariana Pub House, 231p

Ahmad, Z.A., 1965, Fifteen Days in Kashmir Valley, *New Age* 13 (48) November 28, p8-9; 13 (49) December 5, p10-11

Ahmed
 see also Ahmad

Ahmed, Gulzar, n.d., *Pakistan Meets Indian Challenge*, Dehradun, Natraj Publishers

Ahmed, Nasim, 1956, Kashmir and the Commonwealth, *Dawn* (Pakistan) June 21

Ahmed, Nasim, 1956, U.K. Still Favours Plebiscite, *Dawn* (Pakistan) April 4

Ahmed, Nasim, 1957, A Second Jarring Mission?, *Dawn* (Pakistan) March 31

Amhed, Raza
 see Raza Ahmed

Ahmed, Shamim
 see Shamim, Shamim Ahmed

Ahmed Khan, Mahmood
 see Khan, Mahmood Ahmed

Aima, Ashok, 1986, Farm Economy of Cold Desert Regions : A Case Study of Leh, Ladakh, *Indian Journal of Economics* 66 (4) April, p523-528

Aima, Mohanlal, 1969, The Music of Kashmir, *Sangeet Natak*, 11, January-March, p69-73

Aitchison, C., 1963, A *Collection of Treaties, Engagements and*

Sanads relating to India and Neighbouring Countries, Vol XII : *Jammu and Kashmir, Sikkim, Assam and Burma*, Calcutta

Aiyar, Swaminathan S., 1981, What Makes Kashmir Sick, *Eastern Economist* 77 (8) August 21, p364-367, tables

Akbar, M.J., 1985, Of Fathers, Sons and Son-in-Law, *Indian Express* (Magazine) January 6, p5, col 1-8

Akbar, M.J., 1985, *The Siege Within* : *Challenges to a Nation's Unity*, Penguin Books, Middlesex

Akbar, M.J. 1991, *Kashmir* : *Behind the Vale*, Penguin Books/Viking, New Delhi, 232p

Akbar Khan,
see Khan, Akbar

Akbar Krishna, 1984, Let Sleeping Dogmas Lie, *Illustrated Weekly of India* 105 (3) January 15, p13

Akhtar, Bashir, 1981, Sindabad and His Eighth Voyage, *Indian Leterature* 24 (5) September-October, p101 +

Akhtar, Bashir, 1987, Where Water is Scare; A Kashmiri Story, *Indian Literature* 30 (4) July-August, p61-70

Akhtar, Rais, 1992, Kangri : Traditional, Personalized Central Heating in the Valley of Kashmir, *Focus*, 42, Summer, p25-27 bibliography, illustrations

Alam, Mohammed, Shahwar, 1983, Numda Industry of Kashmir, *Khadi Gramodyog* 29 (12) September, p430-435

Alexandrowicz, C.H., 1966, India's Himalayan Dependencies, *Year Book of World Affairs*, 10, p128-143

Ali, Begum Zafar, 1979, Welfare Work in Jammu and Kashmir, *Social Welfare* 26 (2) May, p20-22

Ali, Chaudhri Mohammad
see Mohammad Ali, Chaudhri

Ali, Khurshid,
see Khurshid Ali

Ali, M., 1956, Kashmir Surveyed, *Pakistan Quarterly*, 6, Spring, p4-9, 64-66

Ali, Nisar
see Nisar Ali

Ali, S.M., 1965, Kashmir Crucible, *Far Eastern Economic Review* 48 (10) June 3, p466-468

Ali Mohammad Khan
see Khan, Ali Mohammad

Ali Mohammad Mir
see, Mir, Ali Mohammad

All India Congress Committee
see also AICC

Altaf Hussain Ahangar
see Ahangar, Altaf Hussain

Amar Nath, 1931, *An Echo of the Unknown or The Guide to Ladakh, Leh*, Amar Nath, 119p

Anandi Pal, *jt author*
see Basu, Arabinda and Anandi Pal

Anon, n.d., *Descriptive Analysis of the Kashmir Series of Texts and Studies*, Archaeological and Research Department, Government of Jammu and Kashmir, Srinagar, 66p

Anon, n.d., *Glorious Kashmir : Tourist Guide to Kashmir*, Visitor's Bureau, His Highness' Government of Jammu and Kashmir, 434p, illustrations, maps

Anon, n.d., *The Hindu History of Kashmir*, H.H. Wilson

Anon, n.d., *Jammu Glimpses*, Dogra Mandal, Jammu

Anon, n.d., *Kashmir and China*, Ministry of Information and Broadcasting, Government of Jammu and Kashmir, Srinagar, 9p

Anon, n.d., *Kashmir Facts Speak,* Panum Kashmir Publications

Anon, n.d., *Kashmir Invites You*, Ministry of Information and Broadcasting, Government of Jammu and Kashmir, Srinagar, 21p, map

Anon, n.d., *Ladakh Today*, Directorate of Information, Government of Jammu and Kashmir, 14p, illustrations

Anon, n.d., *Now India Speaks : A Report*, by J&K National Front International, London

Anon, n.d., *They Came to Kashmir*, Department of Information, Government of Jammu and Kashmir, Srinagar

Anon, 1844, Kashmir and the Countries around the Indus, *CR* 2, December, p469-535

Anon, 1864, *Collection of Travels through Turkey in Persia and the East-Indies, Giving an Account of the Present State of Those Countries as also a Full Relation of the Five Years' Wars between Aurangzebe and His Brothers in Their Father's Life-Time, about the Succession, and a Voyage Made by the Great Mogul (Aurangzebe) with His Army from Delhi to Lahore, from Lahore to Bember and from Thence to the Kingdom of Kashmir*, Moses Pitt, London, illustrations, maps, 2 vols

Anon, 1874, Abode of Snow, *Blackwoods Magazine*, 116, p127-145, p410-145, p560-582, p702-722

Anon, 1875, Abode of Snow, *Blackwoods Magazine*, 117, p69-87, p219-237, p336-361, p508-528, p600-615; 118, p60-81

Anon, 1890, *Gazetteer of Kashmir and Ladhak*, Government Printing Press, Calcutta

Anon, 1895, Why We Went to Chitral, *Blackwoods Magazine* 5 (158) September, p402-419

Anon, 1896, *Dry-as-Dust : A Gentle Ramble about Kashmir*

Anon, 1917, *Rules for Observance by Visitors and Residents in Jammu and Kashmir*, Foreign Department, Government of India

Anon, 1933, *Notes for Visitors to Kashmir*, Visitors' Bureau, His Highness' Government of Jammu and Kashmir

Anon, 1944, Kashmir : A Bastion in Defence of India, *JKI* 1 (2) May-June, p5-6

Anon, 1944, Places of Tourist Interest in Jammu and Kashmir, *JKI* 1 (2) May-June, p20-23

Anon, 1946, *Kashmir Trade and Tour : Guide and Business Directory* Rinemisary, Srinagar, 512p, illustrations

Anon, 1947, *Handbook of Jammu and Kashmir State*, 3rd edn, Ranbir Government Press, Jammu, 64p

Anon, 1947, Notes : Kashmir and Pakistan, *Modern Review* 82 (6), December

Anon, 1947, Places of Tourist Interest in Jammu and Kashmir, *JKI* 4 (5) May, p24-29

Anon, 1948, *Behind the Iron Curtain in Kashmir : Neutral Opinion*, Ministry of Kashmir Affairs, Government of Pakistan, Karachi, 16p

Anon, 1948, Communal Struggle, *New Statesman and Nation* 35 (894) April 24, p327

Anon, 1948, *Intelligence Reports concerning the Tribal Repercussions to the Events in the Punjab, Kashmir and India*, Superintendent, Government Printing; Ministry of Kashmir Affairs, Government of Pakistan, Lahore, 36p

Anon, 1948, Kashmir and Hyderabad, *Eastern Economist*, 11 (7) August 15, p255-256

Anon, 1948, *Kashmir before Accession*, Superintendent, Government Printing; Ministry of Kashmir Affairs, Government of Pakistan,

Anon = Personal Authorship not established.

Lahore 53, xxxvii 9p

Anon, 1948, *An Outline of Jammu and Kashmir State Politics : An Insight into the Kashmir Problem*, Muslim League (Great Britain Branch), Branch, Southshields, 72p

Anon, 1948, *Rashtriya Swayam Sewak Sangh in the Punjab*, Government Printing; Ministry of Kashmir Affairs, Government of Pakistan Lahore 22, vi p

Anon, 1949 *The Background of the Kashmir Problem*, Ward Lock Ltd; High Commission for Pakistan, London, 26p, map

Anon, 1949, For Unreserved Acceptance, *Eastern Economist* 12 (18) May 6, p729

Anon, 1950, Epilogue to Kashmir, *Economic Weekly* 2 (21) June 3, p533-534

Anon, 1950, Kashmir : The Next Step, *Economic Weekly* 2 (9) March 11, p245-246

Anon, 1950, Showdown in Kashmir, *Economic Weekly*, 2, February 11, p145-147

Anon, 1951, The Kashmir Tangle, *Economic Weekly* 3 (13) March 31, p314-315

Anon, 1952, Drive through the Waterways of Kashmir, *Kashmir* 2 (9) April 1, p185-186

Anon, 1952, *Five Years of Pakistan (August 1947-August 1952)*, Pakistan Publications, Karachi, 301p, illustrations, photos

Anon, 1952, Graham and Geneva, *Economic Weekly* 4 (40) October 4, p1020

Anon, 1952, *The Kashmir Case : Background of Pakistan's Recent Request for a Meeting of the United Nations Security Council*, Government Printer, Karachi, 13p

Anon, 1952, Margs of Kashmir : A Pictorial Survey, *Kashmir* 2 (9) April 16, p181-184, illustrations

Anon, 1952, With a Camera in Kashmir, *Kashmir* 2 (15) July 1; 2 (16) July 16; 2 (17) August 1

Anon, 1953, Heads I Win, Tails You Lose, *Eastern Economist* 20 (13) March 27, p515

Anon, 1953, Kashmir : What Next? *Economic Weekly* 15 (20) May 18, p795-796

Anon, 1953, *Keys to Kashmir*, Lalla Rookh Publications, Srinagar, 199p

Anon, 1953, Khwaja's Protest, *Organiser* 7 (4) September 7, p9

Anon, 1953, *Ladakh and Its Problems*, S.Stodban, Srinagar

Anon, 1953, Snakes in the Grass, *Organiser* 7 (3) August 31, p1
Anon, 1954, Call of the Valley, *Leader*, July 30
Anon, 1954, Country Life in Kashmir, *Leader* September 5
Anon, 1954, *Indian Attitude on Kashmir*, High Commission for Pakistan, London; Department of Films and Publications, Government of Pakistan, Karachi, 6p
Anon, 1954, Lift Irrigation in Kashmir, *Hindustan Standard* October 25
Anon, 1954, Road to Kashmir, *Leader* June 14
Anon, 1955, Kashmir on Krushchev's Hook, *Thought* 7 (51) December 17, p1-2
Anon, 1955, Khrushchev Explains Soviet View on Kashmir Question, *New Age* 3 (18), p6-10
Anon, 1955, *Ladakh*, Publications Division, Ministry of Information and Broadcasting, Government of India, 28p
Anon, 1955, Ladakh : Asia's Most Strategic Area : Its Future Is Still an Issue, *P.T.*, March 22
Anon, 1955, Ladakh of New Strategic Importance to India, *Current* April 22
Anon, 1955, Nehru Must Meet Pakistan Half Way : Sydney Paper's Comments on Kashmir Dispute, *Pakistan Times*, June 1
Anon, 1955, *Pakistan of 1954*, Pakistan Publications, Karachi, 1, 283p, illustrations
Anon, 1955, *Russian Leaders' Visit to Kashmir*, Lalla Rookh Publications, Srinagar
Anon, 1956, India's Favourite Child, *Economist* 181 (5909) November 24, p704
Anon, 1956, Kashmir : A Pakistani View, *Egyptian Economic and Political Review*, 2, January, p15-17
Anon, 1956, Neighbours in Asia : The Rift between India and Pakistan, *Round Table*, 185, December, p18-25
Anon, 1956, Present Day Ladakh, *K.T.*, 1 (1) September, p26-27
Anon, 1956, Speaking in Kashmir, *Economist*, 178, March 17, p608
Anon, 1957, How Indian See Kashmir Today, *Economist* 183 (5932) May 4, p414
Anon, 1957, Nehru's Kashmir Policy Has Saddened Many : Indian Premier Becoming Less Imaginative, *Pakistan Times*, May 31
Anon, 1957, Peace in Kashmir, *Egyptian Gazette*, May 5
Anon, 1957, Plebiscite in Kashmir is Difficult: Swedish Paper Backs India, *Times of India* April 27

Anon, 1957, Sub-Continental Missiles : Kashmir, *Economist*, 184, August 31, p671-672

Anon, 1957, *World Opinion on Kashmir*, Ministry of Imformation and Broadcasting, Government of Pakistan, Karachi

Anon, 1958, *Kashmir*, Ministry of Transport and Communications, Publication Division, Government of India, Delhi, 60p

Anon, 1958, Mr. Goodfriend Replies, *Organiser* 12 (2) September, p5, 12

Anon, 1959, *Delhi and Northern India Directory with Who's Who, 1958-59*, India Business Publications, New Delhi, 402p

Anon, 1959, *The Kashmir Liberation Movement*, Ferozsons, Lahore; Kashmir Publications, Muzaffarabad (Azad Kashmir), 40p, illustrations

Anon, 1960, Iraq and Kashmir, *Pakistan Times* (Lahore), June 3

Anon, 1960, *Kashmir : As Others See It*, Department of Information, Government of Jammu and Kashmir, Srinagar, 31p

Anon, 1960, Pakistan : What Hope in Kashmir, *Round Table*, 201, December, p74-75

Anon, 1961 *Kashmir at a Glance*, Department of Information, Government of Jammu and Kashmir, Srinagar, 44p

Anon, 1961, Northern Frontiers, *Economist* 198 (6126) January 21, p231-232

Anon, 1961, *Report of the Officials of the Government of India and the People's Republic of China on the Boundary Question,* February 1961, Ministry of External Affairs, Government of India, New Delhi, 342-213p, maps, bibliography

Anon, 1962, *Kashmir*, Publications Division, Government of India, New Delhi, 124p

Anon, 1962, Kashmir : A Case Study in Colonial Politics, *United Asia*, 14 (4) April, p233-238

Anon, 1962, *Kashmir : The Indo-Pakistan Question : A Brief Study*, Permanent Mission of Pakistan to the UN, New York, 71p

Anon, 1962, *Kashmir and the United Nations : Background Report*, Pakistan Embassy, Washington, 39p

Anon, 1962, *The Kashmir Issue*, Permanent Mission of Pakistan to the UN, New York, 22p, map

Anon, 1962, *New Kashmir*, Times of India Pub, Bombay, iv, 54p

Anon, 1962, The Principals and Their Proteges, *Organiser* 15 (43) June 11, p1

Anon, 1962, *Self Contradiction Inc : India vs India on Kashmir*, Free

Kashmir Centre, New York, 72p

Anon, 1962, Three in the Himalaya, *Economist* 205 (6224) December 8, p992-993

Anon, 1962, *Time Bomb in Asia*, Permanent Mission of Pakistan to the UN, New York, 24p

Anon, 1962, The Veto on Kashmir, *The Call* 14 (2) July, p5-6

Anon, 1962, *World Opinion on Kashmir*, Ferozsons; Press Information Department, Government of Pakistan, Rawalpindi, 23p

Anon, 1963, American Interest in Kashmir, *Organiser* 16 (26) February 4, p3

Anon, 1963, Whither Kashmir, *Eastern Economist*, 40, May 24, p1077

Anon, 1964, 1000 Indian's Cannot Stop Abdullah, *Organiser* 18 (16) November 30, p1

Anon, 1964, Abdullah is Asking Questions : He Answered Them Long Ago, *Organiser* 17 (38) April 20, p7 +

Anon, 1964, Abdullah Leaves for Srinagar, *Link* 6 (40) May 17, p6

Anon, 1964, Abdullah Removes the Portraits of Gandhi, Nehru, *Organiser* 18 (18) December 14, p1

Anon, 1964, Abdullah's Formula : Plebiscite in a Different Garb, *Organiser* 17 (41) May 11, p1 +

Anon, 1964, Abdullah's Many Voices, *Link* 6 (36) April 19, p21-23

Anon, 1964, Abdullah's Sinister Game, *Link* 6 (39) May 10, p12-14, illustrations

Anon, 1964, Abdullah's Strategy of Love, *Organiser* 17 (40) May 4, p1 +

Anon, 1964, Bakshi is Happy and Healthy, *Organiser* 18 (19) December 21, p1

Anon, 1964, Bakshi will Never Forget Feb 6, *Organiser* 17 (28) February 17, p1 +

Anon, 1964, Bakshi's Arrest and after, *Eastern Economist* 43 (14) October 2, p624

Anon, 1964, Bakshi's Arrest Welcome Surprise, *New Age* 12 (39) September 27, p20

Anon, 1964, Bakshi's Plot : Abdullah as Sadar-i-Riyasat and Himself as Prime-Minister, *Organiser* 18 (7) September 28, p1

Anon, 1964, Between Bakshi's Cup and Sadiq's Lip? *Organiser* 17 (30) March 2, p1

Anon, 1964, Bhutto's Threat, *Link* 6 (28) February 23, p6-7

Anon, 1964, Britain's Betrayal at Security Council : How Press Saw

Kashmir Debade, *New Age* 12 (8) February 23, p8

Anon, 1964, CPI Secretariat Demands : Clean up J&K Administration : Present Ministry Must Resign, *New Age* 12 (5) February 2, p3

Anon, 1964, Dealing with Abdullah, *Economic Weekly* 16 (17-18) May 2, p747-748

Anon, 1964, The Deepening Mystery of the Bakshi Family : Bakshi and Rashid Try to Explain away, *Organiser* 17 (22) January 6, p7

Anon, 1964, Delhi Diary, *Organiser* 17 (35) March 30, p13

Anon, 1964, Division in Abdullah's Camp, *Link* 6 (45) June 21, p17

Anon, 1964, Documentary, *Seminar,* 58, June, p44-53

Anon, 1964, Excerpts from an Editorial in the Dawn of March 8: Delhi Diary, *Organiser* 17 (32) March 16, p13

Anon, 1964, The Family Feud of Abdullah and Farooq, *Organiser* 17 (52) July 27, p6

Anon, 1964, From Jantar Mantar...to Teen Murti, *Organiser* 17 (31) March 9, p2

Anon, 1964, Further Reading, *Seminar,* 58, June, p63-65

Anon, 1964, The Future of Kashmir, *Swarajya* 8 (50) June 13, p22-23, letter to the editor

Anon, 1964, 'Hindu' Criticises J.P's Assessment of Pakistan, *Organiser* 18 (7) September 28, p14

Anon, 1964, Inside Kashmir, *Link* 6 (27) February 16, p6-7

Anon, 1964, J.P.'s Initiative, *Economic Weekly* 16 (38) September 19, p1522

Anon, 1964, Jana Sangh Stages Massive Demonstration, *Organiser* 17 (40) May 4, p1 +

Anon, 1964, Kashmir : Conflicts in Abdullah's Camp, *Link* 6 (41) May 24, p9

Anon, 1964, Kashmir and the West, *Mainstream* 2 (35) May 2, p7-8

Anon, 1964, Kashmir Approaches, *Far Eastern Economic Review* 46 (2) October 8, p9

Anon, 1964, Kashmir Debate, *Eastern Economist* 42 (21) May 22, p1193

Anon, 1964, Kashmir in Security Council, *Eastern Economist* 42 (8) February 21, p317-318

Anon, 1964, Kashmir Marches ahead, *Organiser* 18 (19) December 21, p4

Anon, 1964, Kashmir, Pakistan and Sheikh Abdullah, *Modern Review* 115 (5) May, p309-310

Anon, 1964, Let Abdullah Remember Abdullah, *Organiser* 17 (41) May 11, p12

Anon, 1964, The Kashmir Problem, *Swarajya* 8 (44) May 2, p12; 8(48) May 30, p8

Anon, 1964, The Moving Finger Writes, *Organiser* 17 (38) April 20, p8

Anon, 1964, Muslim-Majority Doda Gives the Lie to Abdullah's Claims, *Organiser* 17 (49) July 6, p16

Anon, 1964, National Conference, *Link* 6 (42) May 31, p18

Anon, 1964, National Council Resolutions on Kashmir, *New Age* 12 (17) April 26, p5

Anon, 1964, New Kashmir Set-up, *Link* 6 (30) March 8, p12-14

Anon, 1964, New Tactics, *Link* 7 (6) September 20, p18-19

Anon, 1964, Not Bakshi, but Sadiq is Hobnobbing with Sheikh, Charge Bakshi-ites : The Other Side of the Bakshi Episode, *Organiser* 18 (8) October 5, p13

Anon, 1964, Pakistan : On the Eve of Abdullah's Arrival, *Link* 6 (42) May 31, p19

Anon, 1964, Pakistan Also Does Not Trust Abdullah, *Organiser* 17 (43) May 25, p1 +

Anon, 1964, Plan or Plot? What Sheikh and Nehru Have Agreed about Kashmir, *Organiser* 17 (42) May 18, p1 +

Anon, 1964, Plebiscite : Historical Origins Not Very Honourable, *Organiser* 17 (43) May 25, p6

Anon, 1964, RSS Resolves... : Resolution (Regarding Full Integration of Kashmir with India) Adopted at the Annual Meeting of the Akhil Bharatiya Pratinidhi Sabha of R.S.S. at Nagpur on March 28-29, 1964, *Organiser* 17 (36) April 6, p5

Anon, 1964, Reaction to Reorganisation, *Link* 7 (4) September 6, p18

Anon, 1964, *Revolt in Kashmir : British Views on Kashmir Dispute : Editorial Comments in the U.K. Press*, Pakistan High Commission, London, 12p

Anon, 1964, Rowdy Politics, *Link* 7(5) September 13, p16-17

Anon, 1964, The Sad Case of Sir Patrick, *Eastern Economist* 42 (8) February 21, p321-322

Anon, 1964, Sadiq and Bakshi Must Jointly Confront Abdullah and Farooq, *Organiser* 18 (19) December 21, p13

Anon, 1964, Sadiq Government Follows in Bakshi's Footsteps, *Organiser* 18 (6) September 21, p5

Anon, 1964, Sadiq Government Will Be Judged by Performance : Bhartiya Jana Sangh Executive's Resolution of March 1 and 2, *Organiser* 17 (31) March 9, p7

Anon, 1964, Sadiq is Wrong about Abdullah, *Organiser* 18 (6) September 21, p13

Anon, 1964, The Security Council Debate, *Link* 6 (26) February 9, p10-12

Anon, 1964, Security Council to Sheikh, *Economic Weekly* 16 (21) May 23, p878

Anon, 1964, Sheikh Abdullah, *Link* 6 (35) April 12, p6

Anon, 1964, Sheikh Abdullah and Jana Sangh, *Organiser* 17 (37) April 13, p28

Anon, 1964, Sheikh at Large, *Eastern Economist* 42 (16) April 17, p882a-882b

Anon, 1964, Sheikh Strategy, *Organiser* 17 (39) April 27, p13

Anon, 1964, The Story of a De Soto Car for Abdullah, *Organiser* 18 (3) August 31, p15

Anon, 1964, Talks with Abdullah, *Link* 6 (38) May 3, p6-7

Anon, 1964, The Task in Kashmir, *Economic Weekly* 16 (9) February 29, p427-428

Anon, 1964, Towards Climax or Anticlimax, *Eastern Economist* 42 (17) April 24, p964

Anon, 1964, Unholy Pak-China Entente on Kashmir : Statement Dated 25 February 1964 by Communist Pary of India, *New Age* 12 (9) March 1, p1 +

Anon, 1964, Unite to Smash the Imperialist Conspiracy on Kashmir: Statement of CPI Central Secretariat, *New Age* 12 (19) May 10, p1

Anon, 1964, What India Can Do about Kashmir, *Economic Weekly* 16 (10) March 7, p491

Anon, 1964, What Labour Must Remember about Nehru's India, *Organiser* 17 (40) May 4, p15

Anon, 1964, What Sheikh Abdullah said : Analysis Based on His Speeches, Statements and Press Conferences between 1947 and 1953, *AICC Economic Review* 15 (22-23) May 10, p44-50

Anon, 1964, Who Stole the Prophet's Hair, and Why ? *Organiser* 17 (22) January 6, p4 +

Anon, 1964, Withdraw Kashmir Issue from the U.N. : Dange Suggests Immediate Steps for Solving the Present Impasse, *New Age* 12 (20) May 17, p1

Anon, 1964, The World, *Modern Review* 115 (3) March, p161-166
Anon, 1965, Abdullah's Internment, *Link* 7 (40) May 16, p7
Anon, 1965, Abdullah's Mission, *Link* 7 (27) February 14, p17-18
Anon, 1965, The Absolute Importance of August 5 . . ., *Organiser* 19 (8) October 3, p6
Anon, 1965, Action against Enemy Agents, *Link* 8 (11) October 24, p16-17
Anon, 1965, Aggression in Kashmir, *Link* 8 (1) August 15, p14
Anon, 1965, Amateur Diplomacy, *Swarajya* 10 (17) October 23, p29-30, letter to the editor
Anon, 1965, Azad Kashmir is Neither Azad nor Kashmiri, *Organiser* 19 (7) September 26, p9
Anon, 1965, Bakshi and Sadiq Coming together, *Organiser* 18 (34) April 5, p1 +
Anon, 1965, Bakshi's Retirement, *Link* 7 (47) July 4, p13
Anon, 1965, Calendar of Aggression, *Link* 8 (5) September 12, p20-22, map, illustrations
Anon, 1965, Closer Contact with Centre, *Link* 7 (43) June 6, p16
Anon, 1965, Dangerous Kite-flying, *Link* 8 (18) December 12, p13
Anon, 1965, Firm Policy on Kashmir, *Link* 7 (48) July 11, p11
Anon, 1965, GOI's - U.P. - Bihar Muslim Officers Inject Communal Poison in Kashmir : Five Serious Cases, *Organiser* 19 (8) October 3, p8-9
Anon, 1965, The Gathering Storm, *Swarajya* 9 (42) April 17, p25
Anon, 1965, Hero Cities : Amritsar and Jammu, *Link* 8 (6) September 19, p12
Anon, 1965, I Cannot Pretend to be Neutral, *Organiser* 19 (6) September 19, p8
Anon, 1965, In Language Thunderous, in Grammar Wonderous : The Sheikh at U.N., *Organiser* 18 (46) June 27, p10
Anon, 1965, In Nasser's Cairo Ghaffar Khan Ignored and Abdullah Lionised, *Organiser* 18 (33) March 29, p10
Anon, 1965, *Indian Aggression against Pakistan : American Reactions*, Empassy of Pakistan, Information Division, Washington
Anon, 1965, *India's Aggression against Pakistan : Defiance of U.N. Sparks Revolt in Kashmir : The Only Solutions*, High Commision for Pakistan, London, 8p
Anon, 1965, India's Stand on Kashmir : Bad Policy More than Bad Publicity Has Damaged Our Cause, *Organiser* 19 (10) October 17, p14

Anon, 1965, Islam and Kashmir, *Illustrated Weekly of India* 86 (45) November 7, p4, letter to the editor

Anon, 1965, Jammu and Kashmir : Highlights of Progress (1947-65), *Asian Economic Review* 7 (4) August, p559-566, tables

Anon, 1965, Jaya Prakash Narayan's Views, *Swarajya* 10 (24) December 11, p35

Anon, 1965, *Kashmir*, Publications Division, Ministry of Information and Broadcasting; Ministry of Education and Social Welfare, Government of India, New Delhi, 124p

Anon, 1965, Kashmir, *Modern Review* 118 (3) September, p190-191; 118 (4) October, p281-284

Anon, 1965, Kashmir : Delhi More Distant, *Economist* 214 (6332) January 2, p26

Anon, 1965, *The Kashmir Dispute : A Survey*, Permanent Mission of Pakistan to the UN, New York, 10p

Anon, 1965, Kashmir Faced the Storm with a Quiet Confidence, *Organiser* 19 (8) October 3, p14

Anon, 1965, Kashmir Government Thy Name is Corruption, *Organiser* 18 (46) June 27, p1 +

Anon, 1965, *The Kashmir Issue and Indian Aggression in News and Views*, Ferozsons; Department of Films and Publications, Government of Pakistan, Karachi, 55p, illustrations

Anon, 1965, Kashmir Wants New Delhi to Write Off Rs 75 Crore Loans, *Organiser* 18 (49) July 18, p2

Anon, 1965, National Conference and Jana Sangh Workers Arrested in Kashmir, *Organiser* 18 (41) May 24, p14

Anon, 1965, No Taxation, *Link* 8 (1) August 15, p53

Anon, 1965, Official Documents of the United Nations Security Council on the Current Situation in Kashmir, *Indian Journal of International Law* 5 (3) July, p364-402, footnotes

Anon, 1965, Pakistan's Game in Kashmir, *Economic Weekly* 17 (35) August 28, p1325-1326

Anon, 1965, The Pindi-Peking Patriot Must Not be Allowed to Re-Enter India, *Organiser* 18 (34) Aprirl 5, p1

Anon, 1965, Rise and Fall of Azad Puppets, *Link* 8 (6) September 19, p22

Anon, 1965, Russia is Shifting Its Position on Kashmir, *Organiser* 19 (19) December 26, p9-10

Anon, 1965, Saga of Kashmir, *New Age* 13 (37) September 12, p8-9, illustrations

Anon, 1965, Sheikh Abdullah, *Modern Review* 117 (4) April 245-247

Anon, 1965, Sheikh Abdullah, *Swarajya* 9 (50) June 12, p29, letter to the editor

Anon, 1965, Sheikh Abdullah Says : All Those Who Love the Prophet Should Non-Cooperate with Muslim Congressmen, *Organiser* 18 (29) March 1, p16

Anon, 1965, The Sheikh Affair, *Eastern Economist* 44 (15) April 9, p889

Anon, 1965, The Sheikh and His Sancho, *Link* 7 (33) March 28, p12

Anon, 1965, Sheikh's New Role, *Link* 7 (35) April 11, p19-22

Anon, 1965, *Story of Kashmir 1947-65*, Department of Films and Publications, Government of Pakistan, Karachi, 32, xvp

Anon, 1965, To Become a Phizo or Not : That is the Question for Sheikh, *Organiser* 18 (36) April 19, p13

Anon, 1965, UK and the Indo-Pak Conflict, *Economic Weekly* 17 (41) October 9, p1544

Anon, 1965, UN's Failure in Kashmir : A Factual Survey, *Economic Weekly* 17 (40) October 2, p1506-1509

Anon, 1965, War Forced on India, *Swarajya* 10 (12) September 18, p67

Anon, 1965, What Are We Defending? *Swarajya* 10 (19) November 6, p3

Anon, 1965, What Is the Real Objective of Pakistan? : Economic Disruption of India, *Commerce* 111 (2838) September 18, p520

Anon, 1965, What Reporter Raymond Saw and Heard in Kashmir, *Organiser* 19 (16) December 5, p12

Anon, 1966, Army's Lifeline in Ladakh, *Hindustan Times*, June 27, p5, illustration

Anon, 1966, Away from Plebiscite Politics? *Economc and Political Weekly* 1 (5) September 17, p182

Anon, 1966, Border Areas after Tashkent; A Hard-earned Peace, *Link* 8 (24) January 26, p33-37

Anon, 1966, Dhar's Demotion Frustrates Qasim's Bid for Chief Ministership : The Meaning of Cabinet Reshuffle in Jammu and Kashmir, *Organiser* 19 (40) May 22, p2

Anon, 1966, *Guide to Kashmir*, Publications Division, Ministry of Transport and Communications, Government of India, New Delhi, 64p

Anon, 1966, Has There Been any Secret Deal with Pakistan about Kashmir? *Organiser* 19 (28) February 27, p7

Anon, 1966, *Irrigation*, Information Department, Government of Jammu and Kashmir, Srinagar, 11p

Anon, 1966, Kashmir : From Feudalism to Freedom, *Illustrated Weekly of India* 87 (12) March 20, p6-11

Anon, 1966, Kashmir : Keystone of Indian Unity, *Indo-Asian Culture* 15 (2) April, p158-164

Anon, 1966, Kashmir Uncertainty, *Link* 8 (46) June 26, p7

Anon, 1966, New Challenges, *Link* 8 (31) March 13, p17

Anon, 1966, Official Document of the United Nations Security Council on the Current Situation in Kashmir, *Indian Journal of International Law* 6 (2) April, p271-297

Anon, 1966, *Tashkent Declaration in Perspective : President Ayub's Address and Two Broadcasts, Foreign Minister's Statement, Press Opinion, etc.*, Department of Films and Publications, Government of Pakistan, Karachi, 43p

Anon, 1966, Tourism in Kashmir, *Eastern Economist* 46 (12) May 27, p1122

Anon, 1966, Two Types of Refugees, *Link* 8 (24) January 26, p37-39

Anon, 1966, Wither Mr Sadiq? *Organiser* 20 (18) December 11, p4

Anon, 1967, 50,000 Pakistanis Allowed to Enter Kashmir to Vote for Congress, *Organiser* 20 (33) April 2, p13

Anon, 1967, Abdullah to be the Nawab of Kashmir? *Organiser* 21 (19) December 17, p1

Anon, 1967, All the Four Kashmir M.P.s and 56 of 73 M.L.A.s Face Election Petitions, *Organiser* 20 (41) May 28, p9

Anon, 1967, Bakshi Enquiry Report, *New Age* 15 (29) July 16, p2

Anon, 1967, (Book Review), *Interdiscipline* 4 (4) Winter, p364-365
Review of the Book : Lamp, Alastair, 1966, *Crisis in Kashmir (1947-1966)*, Routledge and Kegan Paul, London, 163p

Anon, 1967, (Book Review), *International Studies* 9 (2) October, p221-223
Review of the Book : Gupta, Sisir, 1966, *Kashmir : A Study in India-Pakistan Relations*, Asia, Bombay, 511p

Anon, 1967, Democracy Murdered, *Organiser* 20 (25) Janrary 29, p1 +

Anon, 1967, Dismiss Sadiq Government : Order Fresh Election, *Organiser* 20 (30) March 12, p15

Anon, 1967, Elections in Kashmir Are a Crying Shame, *Organiser* 20 (30) March 5, p1 +

Anon, 1967, Fifteen Years of Development Makes the Economy

Vibrant, *Yojana* 11 (23) November 26, p15-19, illustraions

Anon, 1967, From the Ballot Box, *Eastern Economist* 48 (12) March 24, p519 +

Anon, 1967, Government Is Dead : Long Live the Country, *Organiser* 21 (11) October 22, p1-2

Anon, 1967, Jana Sangh Leader Responsible for Kashmir Incidents : CPI General Secretary Condemns President's Rule, *New Age* 15 (43) October 22, p16

Anon, 1967, Kashmir : End of the Agitation, *Economic and Political Weekly* 10 (5) September 10, p14

Anon, 1967, Kashmir Affairs, *Link* 9 (46) June 25, p9

Anon, 1967, Kashmir Budget, *Commerce* 115 (2936) August 19, p369

Anon, 1967, Kashmir Budget, *Eastern Economist* 49 (7) August 18, p312

Anon, 1967, Kashmir Needs President's Rule, *Organiser* 21 (4) September 3, p1 +

Anon, 1967, Kashmir Will Not Contribute Even One Rupee to Its Fourth 5-Year Plan, *Organiser* 21 (19) December 17, p5

Anon, 1967, Ladakh Demands to be Centrally Administered, *Organiser*, 21 (4) September 3, p14

Anon, 1967, Massive Bogus Voting in Karan Singh's Constituency *Organiser* 20 (40) May 21, p2

Anon, 1967, New Attraction in Kashmir, *Enlite* 1 (8) May 6, p16

Anon, 1967, New Cabinet, *Eastern Economist* 48 (12) March 24, p543-544 +

Anon, 1967, 'Organiser' Nails a J&K Govt Lie, *Organiser* 20 (51) August 6, p10

Anon, 1967, Out of Every 3 Congress M.L.A.s, One is a Minister, *Organiser* 20 (32) March 26, p4

Anon, 1967, Parmeshwarai Was Converted to Islam and Married to Ghulam Rasool, *Organiser* 21 (2) August 20, p2

Anon, 1967, Pindi, Moscow Patriots and Lunatics Prominent in Kashmir Congress List, *Organiser* 20 (21) January 1, p5

Anon, 1967, Sadiq Rehabilitates the Traitor Son of Traitor Father, *Organiser* 20 (41) May 28, p12

Anon, 1967, Second Round of Congress Fraud in Jammu and Kashmir, *Organiser* 20 (28) February 19, p7

Anon, 1967, Sheikh Abdullah, *Link* 10 (19) December 17, p6-8

Anon, 1967, Sheikh Abdullah to be Released? *Organiser* 20 (38) May 7, p15

Anon, 1967, Srinagar Ploting to Arrest Bakshi, *Organiser* 20 (22) January 8, p16

Anon, 1967, The State of Agriculture-6 : Kashmir : Miracle after Two Bad Years, *Commerce* (Annual Number) 115(2956) p146-148

Anon, 1967, To Prosecute Bakshi or Nor to Prosecute Him, *Organiser* 20 (51) August 6, p9

Anon, 1967, Trouble in Occupied Kashmir, Link 9 (32) March 19, p26

Anon, 1967, When Sadiq Govt Went Mad to Win Election for Congress, *Organiser* 20 (32) March 26, p6 +

Anon, 1968, Back in the Valley, *Weekend Review* 2 (15) March 16, p15

Anon, 1968, Balancing Regional Interests, *Commerce* 116 (2963) February 17, p404

Anon, 1968, Bid to Demonopolise Silk Industry, *Commerce* 117 (3003) November 23, p1081-1082

Anon, 1968, (Book Review), *Aryan Path* 39 (6) June, p284-285
Review of the Book : Mehta, Krishna, 1966, *This Happened in Kashmir*, Publication Division, Government of India, New Delhi, 171p

Anon, 1968, (Book Review), *Indian Political Science Review* 2 (3-4) April-September, p239-240
Review of the Book : Puri, Balraj, 1966, *Jammu : A Clue to Kashmir Tangle*, Balraj Puri, 105p

Anon, 1968, (Book Review), *International Studies* 9 (3) January, p376-378
Review of the Book : Lamb, Alastair, 1966, *Crisis in Kashmir (1947-1966)*, Routledge and Kegan Paul, London, 163p

Anon, 1968, (Book Review), *International Studies* 9 (3) January, p379-380
Review of the Book : Gururaj Rao, H.S., 1967, *Legal Aspects to the Kashmir Problem*, Asia, Bombay, 379p

Anon, 1968, (Book Review), *Thought* 20 (23) June 8, p17-18
Review of the Book : Bazaz, Prem Nath, 1967, *Kashmir in Crucible*, Ramposh Pub, New Delhi, xiv, 318p

Anon, 1968, (Book Review), *Thought* 20 (33) August 17, p22-23
Review of the Book : Vashisth, Satish, 1969, *Sheikh Abdullah : Then and Now*, Maulik, 234p

Anon, 1968, *Books on Kashmir : A Select List of Publications*,

National Book Trust, New Delhi, 33p

Anon, 1968, Boost to State Economy, *Thought* 20 (25) June 22, p7

Anon, 1968, Burden of Administration, *Commerce* 116 (2962) February 10, p332

Anon, 1968, Chief Minister Takes the Cudgel, *Thought* 20 (14) April 6, p9-10

Anon, 1968, Collective Efforts Lag, *Commerce* 116 (2969) March 30, p852-853

Anon, 1968, Confusion as before, *Thought* 20 (43) October 26, p9-10

Anon, 1968, Crash Farm Plan, *Commerce* 16 (2979) June 8, p1558-1559

Anon, 1968, Disarray in Secessionist Camp, *Link* 11 (10) October 20, p9

Anon, 1968, Embarrassing Forest Dues, *Commerce* 116 (2970) April 6, p923

Anon, 1968, English Press Naivete about Sheikh Abdullah, *Organiser* 22 (12) November, p7

Anon, 1968, Essential Changes, *Link* 11 (19) December 22, p18

Anon, 1968, Exploiting Kashmir's Mineral Wealth, *Commerce* 116 (2974) May 4, p1217-1218

Anon, 1968, Finding Resources for Fourth Plan, *Commerce* 117 (3005) December 7, p1176-1177

Anon, 1968, Fresh Elections in Kashmir, *Thought* 20 (2) January 13, p4

Anon, 1968, Gajendragadkar Recommends Parity for Jammu and Kashmir, *Organiser* 22 (19) December 21, p5 +

Anon, 1968, Home Coming of a Hero, *Thought* 20 (11) March 16, p9

Anon, 1968, Inadequate Resources for Development, *Thought* 20 (41) November 30, p10

Anon, 1968, Institutional Investor is Cold, *Commerce* 117 (2985) July 20, p134-135

Anon, 1968, Is Sheikh the Problem? *Thought* 20 (21) May 25, p3-4

Anon, 1968, J&K : Faith in Sheikh, *Thought* 20 (13) March 30, p7-8

Anon, 1968, *Jammu and Kashmir*, Department of Information, Government of Jammu and Kashmir, Srinagar, 67p

Anon, 1968, Jammu and Kashmir on Way to Prosperity, *Eastern Economist* 51 (4) July 26, p177-178

Anon, 1968, Justice to the People of Kashmir, *People's Democracy* 4 (10) March 10, p1

Anon, 1968, Kashmir : A Call to Statesmanship, *Thought* 20 (14) April 6, p5

Anon, 1968, Kashmir : How Serious Is the Rift? *Commerce* 117(2996) October 5, p716

Anon, 1968, Kashmir : Merry Living on Grants, *Economic and Political Weekly* 3 (22) June 1, p832-833, tables

Anon, 1968, Kashmir : Sheikh at Cross-Roads, *Mainstream* 7 (8) October 26, p7-9 +

Anon, 1968, The Kashmir Issue : Can Sheikh Abdullah Succeed in His Misssion? *Capital 160* (3997) February 8, p265

Anon, 1968, Kashmir State People's Convention, *Call* 20 (6) November, p7-8

Anon, 1968, Kashmir's New Exchange Earner, *Yojana* 12 (25) December 22, p20

Anon, 1968, Let the Sheikh First Meet Badshah Khan, *Organiser* 21(22) January 7, p4

Anon, 1968, The Liberalization Process, *Thought* 20 (38) September 21, p9

Raju, A.A.N., 1968, Library Movement in Jammu and Kashmir, *Herald Library Science* 7 (2) April, p120-123, bibliography

Anon, 1968, Meeting the Wage Burden, *Commerce* 116 (2965) March 2, p547

Anon, 1968, Mutual Bickerings Impede Settlement, *Thought* 20 (30) July 27, p9

Anon, 1968, Nationalist's Last Opportunity, *Commerce* 117 (2993) September 14, p569

Anon, 1968, Naxalbarism in Kashmir? *Commerce* 116 (2973) April 27, p1154

Anon, 1968, Need for More Tourist Amenities, *Thought* 20 (17) April 27, p10

Anon, 1968, New Challenges to Sheikh Abdullah, *Thought* 20 (4) January 27, p5-6

Anon, 1968, Only Organised Industry, *Commerce* 116 (2966) March 9, p618

Anon, 1968, Pakistan's Aggressive Postures, *Thought* 20 (21) May 25, p10

Anon, 1968, Pindi Waits and Sees, *Link* 10 (24) January 21, p23

Anon, 1968, Planning for Power, *Commerce* 116 (2961) September 3, p269-270

Anon, 1968, Politics in Fertilisers, *Commerce* 116 (2976) May 18, p1357-1358

Anon, 1968, Problem and Scope of Tourism, *Thought* 20 (46) November 16, p9

Anon, 1968, Released Sheikh, *Link* 10 (22) January 7, p6-8

Anon, 1968, Return of the Sheikh, *Link* 10 (37) April 21, p67

Anon, 1968, Revolt against Pindi, *Link* 11 (13) November 10, p19

Anon, 1968, Rule of Law in Kashmir, *Thought* 20 (35) August 31, p4

Anon, 1968, Saboteur Gang, *Link* 11 (16) December 1, p17-18

Anon, 1968, A Sharp Controversy, *Thought* 20 (34) August 24, p7

Anon, 1968, Sheikh Abdullah, *Commerce* 116 (2958) January 13, p72

Anon, 1968, The Sheikh Answers Our Questions, *Organiser* 21 (26) February 4, p2 +

Anon, 1968, Sheikh Affairs Elevated Image, *Thought* 20 (24) June 15, p9

Anon, 1968, A Spoiled Man, *Organiser* 21 (23) January 14, p3

Anon, 1968, The State : The Quiet Struggle, *Link* 10 (48) July 7, p16-18

Anon, 1968, *Story of Kashmir 1947-68*, Department of Films and Publications, Government of Pakistan, Karachi, 73p

Anon, 1968, Subversion of Democracy behind Kashmir's Woes, *Janata* 23 (22) June 23, p17-18

Anon, 1968, Tapping Water Sources, *Commerce* 116 (2977) May 25, p1429-1430

Anon, 1968, An Uneasy Wait, *Thought* 20 (41) October 12, p9

Anon, 1968, Unrest in Occupied Kashmir, *Link* 11 (7) September 29, p25-27

Anon, 1968, The Way Out : The Kashmir Bog, *Thought* 20 (3) January 20, p4-5

Anon, 1968, We Can and Must De-Internationalise the Kashmir Issue, *Organiser* 21 (22) January 7, p4

Anon, 1968, Well-Informed, Illuminating, Thought-Provoking : On Kashmir and Nagaland, *Janata* 23 (24) July 7, p10

Anon, 1968, What Is up the Sheikh's Sleeves? *Commerce* 116 (2967) March 16, p690-691

Anon, 1968, Widening the Small Industry Base, *Commerce* 117 (2983) July 6, p15

Anon, 1968-69 (Book Review), *Indian Political Science Review* 3(1-2) October-March, p96-98
Review of the Book : Gupta, Sisir, 1966, *Kashmir : A Study in India-Pakistan Relations*, Asia, Bombay, 511p,

Anon, 1969, Acute Political Crisis in Pak-Held Kashmir, *Times of India* August 28, p1, col 1-2

Anon, 1969, All-Weather Roads : New Plan for Jammu, *Times of India* p3, col 2

Anon, 1969, Amid the Glaciers in Kashmir, *Hindustan Times* November 9, p1

Anon, 1969, Amusing Exercies, *Thought* 20 (1) January 4, p9-10

Anon, 1969, Bargotra Joins Issue with C.R., *Janata* 23 (50) January 15, p12

Anon, 1969, Battle for Panchayats Elections, *Thought* 21 (32) August 9, p7

Anon, 1969, Between Prosperity and Politics, *Enlight*, July 26, p7-8

Anon, 1969, (Book Review), *Indian Journal of Political Science* 30 (2) April-June, p201; *Mainstream* 7 (48) August 2, p32-33; *South Asian Studies* 4 (2) July, p204-207; *Times of India* (Magazine) October 12, pIV, col 4
Review of the Book : Rahmatullah Khan, 1969, *Kashmir and the United Nations*, Vikas Pub, New Delhi, xii, 199p

Anon, 1969, (Book Review), *India Quarterly* 25 (1) January-March p87
Review of the Book : Sharma, B.L., 1967, *The Kashmir Story*, Asia, Bombay, 271p

Anon, 1969, (Book Review), *Political Science Review* 8 (1) January-March, p131-135
Review of the Book : Khan, M. Ibrahim, 1965, *The Kashmir Saga:* Ripon, 228p

Anon, 1969, (Book Review), *Thought* 21 (42) October 18, p15
Review of the Book : Saraf, Mulk Raj, 1969, *Jammu and Kashmir Guide 1969*, Universal Pub

Anon, 1969, (Book Review), *USI Journal* 99 (415) April-June, p184-185
Review of the Book : Gupta, Sisir, 1966, *Kashmir : A Study in India-Pakistan Relations*, Asia, Bombay, 511p

Anon, 1969, Boycott Call Flops, *Thought* 21 (19) May 10, p10

Anon, 1969, Central Loan Mounting, *Commerce* 118 (3017) March 1, p365

Anon, 1969, Centre Keeping Close Watch on Activites of Sheikh Abdullah, *Times of India* March 7, p11, col 1-2

Anon, 1969, A Check on Galloping Food Subsidy, *Commerce* 119 (3047) September 27, p582

Anon, 1969, Chhamb Jaurian Lives again, *States* December 13, p9

Anon, 1969, Claims and Counter-Claims, *Thought* 21 (34) August 23, p9-10

Anon, 1969, Congress MLAs Criticise Sadiq Government, *Times of India*, March 7, p5, col 1-2

Anon, 1969, The Crippling Food Subsidy, *Commerce* 118 (3026) May 3, p853

Anon, 1969, The Doubtful Success, *Thought* 21 (47) November 22, p9 +

Anon, 1969, Early Implementation of Gajendragadkar Body Report Urged, *Times of India* March 3, p5, col 2-3

Anon, 1969, An End to Boycott, *Thought* 21 (23) June 7, p9-10

Anon, 1969, The Enigmatic Silence, *Thought* 21 (7) February 15, p10

Anon, 1969, Failure of Chavan Mission, *Thought* 21 (17) April 26, p9-10

Anon, 1969, Food Supply at the Cost the Development, *Commerce* 119 September 6, p440-441

Anon, 1969, Gajendragadkar Body's Suggestions Opposed, *Times of India* March 5, p2, col 5

Anon, 1969, The Gajendragadkar Commission Report, *Thought* 21(4) January 25, p12, letter to the editor

Anon, 1969, Gajendragadkar's Views on Article 370 Assailed, *Times of India* January 22, p4, col 2-3

Anon, 1969, Gift from Kashmir, *Thought* 21 (48) November 29, p8

Anon, 1969, Government under Cross-Fire, *Thought* 21 (13) March 29, p9

Anon, 1969, Harnessing through Hydraulics, *Eulite* August 23, p26-27

Anon, 1969, Holiday Guide-VII; Kashmir Will be Costlier This Year, *Times of India* April, p5, col 1-4

Anon, 1969, Independent, Congress Bag One Seat Each, *Times of India* April 30, p1, col 5

Anon, 1969, India Needs Strong Leadership, *Times of India* July 8, p5, col 4-5

Anon, 1969, Infrastructure for States-6 : Kashmir : A Feeble Network, *Commerce* (Annual Number) 119 (3061), p145

Anon, 1969, Is Pakistan Itching for War? *Thought* 21 (29) July 19, p9-10

Anon, 1969, J&K Commission for Land Revenue Abolition, *Times of India* March 2, p7, col 1-2

Anon, 1969, *Jammu and Kashmir Guide,* Universal Publication, Srinagar

Anon, 1969, *Jammu-Kashmir : Jammu, Srinagar City, Gulmarg, Pahalgam*, Department of Tourism, Publication Division, Government of India , Delhi, 26p

Anon, 1969, Jana Sangh Opposes Talks with Pindi on Kashmir Issue, *Times of India* July 12, p2, col 5-6

Anon, 1969, Kashmir: Major Changes, *Link* 11(35) April 13, p17-18

Anon, 1969, Kashmir Govt Food Policy Dricriminatony, *Times of India* January 22, p4, col 3

Anon, 1969, Kashmir Liberalisation Policy Assailed, *Times of India* March 6, p5, col 4-5

Anon, 1969, Kashmir May Not Accept Suggestions on Cabinet Set-up, *Times of India* February 1, p7, col 4-5

Anon, 1969, Kashmir's Decisive Role, *Mainstream* 7(42) June 21, p10-11

Anon, 1969, Lion's Share from the Centre, *Commerce* 118(3021) March 29, p581

Anon, 1969, Major Flood Threat to Kashmir Recedes, *Times of India* May 15, p1, col 1-2

Anon, 1969, Mrs Gandhi Meets Sadiq and Qasim, *Times of India* March 15, p1, col 2-4

Anon, 1969, Many Irrigation Plans Taken up in Jammu, *Times of India* June 7, p5, col 2-3

Anon, 1969, Menace of Unemployment, *Thought* 21(30) July 26, p7

Anon, 1969, Milk Supply Schemes for Jammu, *Times of India* May 30, p5, col 5

Anon, 1969, Ministers in Pak Held Kashmir on Strike, *Times of India* December 24, p9, col 2

Anon, 1969, More Power for Development, *Commerce* 119(3046) September 20, p537

Anon, 1969, Need for Positive Efforts in Resource Mobilisation, *Commerce* 119(3059) December 20, p1188

Anon, 1969, New Farming Methods Yield Good Results in Jammu and Kashmir, *Times of India* April 24, p5, col 3-4

Anon, 1969, Occupied Kashmir Party Denounces Pak Move, *Times of India* October 19, p13, col 2-3

Anon, 1969, Pak Manoeuvres at U.N. to Rake up Kashmir Issue, *Times of India* February 5, p7, col 1-2

Anon, 1969, Plan Allocations Affect Vital Sectors, *Commerce*

118(3013) February 1, p166

Anon, 1969, Politics: Conventional and Un-Conventional, *Thought* 21(22) May 31, p9-10

Anon, 1969, President's Dilemma, *Link* 11(23) January 19, p22

Anon, 1969, Rs 145 Crore Plan for J&K : Governor Outlines Programme, *Times of India* March 4, p5, col 1-2

Anon, 1969, Rs 392 Crore Plan for Development of Kashmir Suggested, *Times of India* Augest 25, p4, col 1-2

Anon, 1969, Regional Staff Quota Unconstitutional, Says Gajendragadkar Body, *Times of India* January 20, p9, col 1-2

Anon, 1969, Report on Kashmir Next Week, *Times of India* January 19, p3, col 2-3

Anon, 1969, Sadiq Inching towards Sheikh Abdullah? *Commerce* 118 (3023) April 12, p692

Anon, 1969, Sadiq Supports Move to Requisition AICC, *Times of India* October 23, p1, col 1-2 +

Anon, 1969, Secessionists on the Defensive, *Thought* 21 (8) February 22, p9

Anon, 1969, Secessionists Thwarted, *Link* 11 (40) May 18, p21

Anon, 1969, Secularism in Kashmir, *Times of India* January 15, p6, col 6, letter to the editor

Anon, 1969, Shades of History, Beauty and Utlity, *Statesman* October 27, p8

Anon, 1969, Smooth Sailing now, *Thought* 21 (11) March 15, p9

Anon, 1969, Snowy Heaven where a Ruler Coved with Peasant Girl, *Times of India* March 9, p5, col 2-4

Anon, 1969, Trouble in the Colony, *Link* 12 (20) December 28, p23

Anon, 1969, Uproarious Document, *Thought* 21 (4) January 25, p9

Anon, 1969, What's the Trouble in Kashmir? *Thought* 21 (12) March 22, p5

Anon, 1969, Will to Solve Kashmir Problem Lacking Says Sheikh Abdullah, *Times of India* October 16, p3, col 4-5

Anon, 1970, 32 Kashmir MLAs Seek Permission to Elect New Leader, *Times of India* March 19, p1, col 1-4

Anon, 1970, 35 Congress MLAs Withdraw Support to Kashmir C.M., *Times of India* March 13, p1, col 7-8

Anon, 1970, Abdullah against Continued Accession of Kashmir to India, *Times of India* June 13, p4, col. 4-5

Anon, 1970, Allocation of Kashmir Portfollos, *Times of India* May 30, p4, col 3

Anon, 1970, Anatomy of a State Monopoly, *Commerce* 120 (3066) February 7, p212

Anon, 1970, Bid to Enlarge Work of J&K Financial Corporation, *Times of India* July 2, p5, col 3

Anon, 1970, Big Challenges before Ruling Party,*Thought* 22 (13) March 28, p9

Anon, 1970 (Book Review), *Calcutta Review* 1(4) April-June, p613-617; *Illustrated Weekly of India* 91 (13) March 29, p49; *Organiser* 23 (32) March 21, p12; *Thought* 22 (4) January 24, p11, *Times of India* (Magazine) May 17, p8, col 1-5
Review of the Book : Sen, L.P., 1969, *Slender Was the Sword : Kashmir Confrontation 1947-48*, Longmans, New Delhi

Anon, 1970 (Book Review), *India Quarterly* 26 (2) April-June, 1982; *Indian Journal of International Law* 10 (3) July, p387-388; *Journal of Indian Law Institute* 12 (1) January-March, p196-198
Review of the Book : Khan, Rahmatullah, 1969, *Kashmir and the United Nations*, Vikas Pub, vii, 199p

Anon, 1970, (Book Review), *Times of India* (Magazine) June 14, p8, col 4-6
Review of the Book : Parmu, R.K., 1970, *A History of Muslim Rule in Kashmir (1320-1819)*, People's Publishing House, New Delhi, xiv, 461p

Anon, 1970, Campaign Rocked against Rough Weather, *Thought* 22 (9) February 28, p9-10

Anon, 1970, Chagrin over Convention, *Link* 12 (45) June 21, p26

Anon, 1970, Communal Riots Figure in Kashmir Convention Discussion, *Times of India* June 9, p5, col 1-2

Anon, 1970, Congress MLA Assails Kashmir Budget, *Times of India* March 11, p5, col 4-5

Anon, 1970, Dal Lake Waters for Crop, *Economic Times* August 4, p3

Anon, 1970, Discontent in Occupied Area, *Link* 12 (51) August 2, p30

Anon, 1970, Disidents Agree to Drop Move to Oust C.M. of Kashmir, *Times of India* March 25, p1, col 7-8 +

Anon, 1970, Emergence of New Class of Landlords, *Commerce* 121 (3095) August 29, p441

Anon, 1970, Facing the Secessionists, *Thought* 22 (30) July 25, p7-8

Anon, 1970, Higher Price for Concoons, *Commerce* 120 (3084) June 13, p1233

Anon, 1970, An Honest Effort, *Thought* 22 (26) June 27, p9-10

Anon, 1970, Increasing Panic and Tension, *Thought* 22 (22) May 30, p9-10

Anon, 1970, Jammu and Kashmir : Unexplored Treasures, *Commerce* (Annual Number) 121 (3113), p154-155, map

Anon, 1970, Jammu and Kashmir : Budget, 1970-71 : High Tempo of Development Expenditure, *Commerce* 120 (3082) May 30, p1152-1153, tables

Anon, 1970, *Jammu and Kashmir : Yearbook and Who's Who*, Ranbir Government Press, Jammu

Anon, 1970, Jana Sangh Raises a Row over Kashmir Govt's New Food Policy, *Times of India* January 24, p5, col 4-5

Anon, 1970, Kashmir Dissidents to Elect New Leader, *Times of India* March 22, p1, col 2-5 +

Anon, 1970, Kashmir Dy Minister Resigns : Governor Prorogues Legislature, *Times of India* March 14, p5, col 2-3

Anon, 1970, Kashmir Is Burning, *Organiser* 23 (48) July 11, p1 +

Anon, 1970, Little Irrigation and Less Fertilisers, *Commerce* 120(3064) January 24, p211

Anon, 1970, Little Kashmir, *Economic Times,* November 9, p4

Anon, 1970, Marketing Dilemna of Kashmir Growers, *Commerce* 120(3086) June 27, p1338-1339

Anon, 1970, Midnight Toppling, *Link* 12(32) March 22, p17

Anon, 1970, Mikoyan Danilov Longinov and Laventiev: Russians Invade Kashmir, *Organiser* 23(39) May 9, p1 +

Anon, 1970, Monies for Measures, *Thought* 22(34) August 22, p10

Anon, 1970, New Booklet Exposes Pak Repression in Occupied Kashmir, *Times of India* January 8, p11, col 3-5

Anon, 1970, New Settlements around Chhamb, *Indian Express* January 13, p4

Anon, 1970, No-Confidence Motion against Speaker in Kashmir Assembly, *Times of India* February 27, p9, col 4-5

Anon, 1970, Operation Jhelum, *Economic Times* August 21, p3

Anon, 1970, P.M.'s Visit to Kashmir Focussed Attention on Economic Progress, *Times of India* August 2, p4, col 6-7

Anon, 1970, Pakistan: Revolt in Occupied Area, *Link* 12(40) May 17, p31

Anon, 1970, Pandenonium in J&K Assembly, *Times of India* March 1, p3, col 3-4

Anon, 1970, People to the Fore, *Link* 12(28) February 22, p18

Anon, 1970, Phased Programme for Power Development, *Commerce* 120(3076) April 18, p793-794

Anon, 1970, Plebiscite Front Buys 27 Trucks, *Onganiser* 23(30) March 7, p5

Anon, 1970, Political Parties in Dis-array, *Thought* 22(4) January 24, p9-10

Anon, 1970, Prospects of the People's Convention, *Thought* 22(7) February 14, p9-10

Anon, 1970, Retired General Talks of U.K. Betrayal of India on Kashmir, *Times of India* January 5, p4, col 2-3

Anon, 1970, Sadiq Reconstitutes Cabinet, *Times of India* May 29, p1, col 5-6

Anon, 1970, Sadiq to Test His Strength in Party, *Times of India* March 21, p1, Col 1-2 +

Anon, 1970, Sheikh Abdullah's State People's Convention, *Indian and Foreign Review* 7(19) July 15, p22-23

Anon, 1970, Sheikh's Plea Not to Look at Kashmir Issue from Muslim Angle, *Times of India* June 11, p5, col 2-3

Anon, 1970, Small Scale Industry in J&K Makes Big Strides, *Times of India* July 30, p5, col 1

Anon, 1970, Some Facets of Development, *Kurukshetra* 18(8) May, p26-27

Anon, 1970, The Storm Blows over, *Thought* 22(14) April 4, p9-10

Anon, 1970, Surplus Budget for Kashmir but More Taxes on the Affluent, *Times of India* March 8, p5, col 4-5

Anon, 1970, Three Musketeers, *Thought* 22(48) November 28, p9

Anon, 1970, Transition Period, *Link* 13(16) November 29, p17

Anon, 1970, The Unusual Excitement, *Thought* 22(46) November 14, p9

Anon, 1970, Vale of Rumours, *Thought* (2233) August 15, p9

Anon, 1970, Violence : The Chinese Style, *Thought* 22(29) July 18, p9

Anon, 1971, 3 per cent Increase in J&K Population, *Times of India* April 19, p10, col 3

Anon, 1971, Abdullah at Odds in Jammu and Kashmir, *Link* 14(16) November 28, p19

Anon, 1971, Afzal Beg Prohibited from Entering Jammu and Kashmir, *Times of India* January 9, p1, col 7-8

Anon, 1971, Arrest of Plebiscite Front Men : CPI J&K Council's Statement, *New Age* 19(4) January 24, p4

Anon, 1971, Azad Kashmiris Fleeing to India, *Organiser* 25(12)

October 30, p5

Anon, 1971, Bakshi in, Sheikh out, *Economic and Political Weekly* 6(2)) January 9, p70-71

Anon, 1971, Bakshi Walks out of Counting Station, *Times of India* March 13, p1, col 2-4 +

Anon, 1971, (Book Review), *Brahamvidya* 35(3-4) December, p370 Review of the Book: Mishra, Mandana, 1968, *Kasmiretihasha*, Shri Lal Bahadur Shastri Rashtriya Sanskrit Vidyapeeth, New Delhi, 14, 310p

Anon, 1971, (Book Review), *Economic and Political Weekly* 6(42-43) October 16, p2195-2200; *Link* 13(48) July 11, p39-40; *Organiser* 25(4) September 4, p10; *Swarajya* 16(5) July 31, p25; *Thought* 23(30) July 24, p19; *Thought* 24(32) August 5, p16-18; *Times of India* August 1, p6, col 6-7,
Review of the Book: Mullik, B.N., 1971, *My Years with Nehru-Kashmir*, Allied, New Delhi, 320p

Anon, 1971 (Book Review), *Swarajya* 16(15) October 9, p20
Review of the Book: Sharma, B.L., 1971, *Kashmir Awakes*, Vakas Pub, New Delhi, xiii, 292p

Anon, 1971, (Book Review), *Times of India* August 1, p10, col 6
Review of the Book: Kapur, M.L., 1971, *A History of Medieval Kashmir , 1320-1586 AD., A.R.B. Pub, Jammu, 272p*

Anon, 1971, Centre Bans Plebiscite Front, *Times of India* January 13, p1, col 2-5 +

Anon, 1970, Confrontation, *Link* 13(13) November 8, p20

Anon, 1971, Cong-I Loses at 23 out of 44 Assembly seats, *Organiser* 24(34) April 3, p16

Anon, 1971, Eminent Kashmiri Muslims, *Illustrated Weekly of India* 92(47) November 21, p47-49

Anon, 1971, Enemies Become Bed-Fellows, *Link* 13(23) January 17, p18

Anon, 1971, Enthusiastic Participation, *Link* 13(33) March 28, p17-18

Anon, 1971, Fishing in Troubled Waters, *Link* 14(12) October 31, p29

Anon, 1971, The Forced Accord, *Thought* 23(42) October 16, p9

Anon, 1971, Hectic War Preparations in Pak-Held Kashmir, *Organiser* 24(51) July 31, p16 +

Anon, 1971, J and K : For a Better Future, *Link* 14(20) December 26, p25

Anon, 1971, JP Advises P.M. to Undo Damage, *Times of India* January 10, p11, col 5-6

Anon, 1971, Jamaat-i-Islamir Manned Polling Stations in Srinagar, *Organiser* 24(33) March 27, p1

Anon, 1971, Jammu and Kashmir, *Eastern Economist* 56(13) March 26, p519-520

Anon, 1971, Jammu and Kashmir: Unexplored Treasures, *Commerce* (Annual Number) 121(3113), p154-155, map

Anon, 1971, The Kashmiries: United against a Common Foe, *Link* 14(12) October 31, p31

Anon, 1971, Legislation Soon to Aid Weaker Section, Says Kashmir Governor, *Times of India* March 14, p11, col 4-5

Anon, 1971, Lessons from the Poll, *Thought* 23(14) April 3, p9-10

Anon, 1971, Lok Sabha Poll Round-up: Rigging the Election? *Though* 23(9) February 27, p7-8

Anon, 1971, Mir Qasim Sworn in as New C.M., *Times of India* December 13, p1, col 6+

Anon, 1971, Mischief in Kashmir, *Link* 13(22) January 10, p8

Anon, 1971, P.M. Commissions Power Station, *Times of India* September 7, p7, col 3-4

Anon, 1971, PM's Visit Fails to End Sadiq Qasim Rift, *Times of India* June 22, p1, col 1-2

Anon, 1970, PRA Amendment, *Link* 13(11) October 25, p25

Anon, 1971, Pak Spy Ring in Kashmir Smashed, *Times of India* January 19, p1, col 2-5+

Anon, 1971, Plebiscite Front is a New Factor, *Times of India*, January 6, p1, col 7-8

Anon, 1971, Political Liberalism Hacked? *Though* 23(3) January 16, p9-10

Anon, 1971, Politics behind Skyjack, *Mainstream* 9(24) February 13, p9-11

Anon, 1971, Popular but Unwise, *Thought* 23(3) January 16, p3-4

Anon, 1971, A Push for Farm Mechanisation, *Commerce* 122(3135) June 5, p1045

Anon, 1971, Search for Ground Water, *Economic Times* July 2, p3

Anon, 1971, Season for Flag Waving, *Thought* (10) March 6, p8

Anon, 1971, Secessionist Mischief, *Link* 13(20) December 27, p9

Anon, 1971, The Shock Absorbed, *Thought* 23(4) January 23, p9-10

Anon, 1971, Sikkim-Style Status for Kashmir, *Thought* 23(48) November 27, p9-10

Anon, 1971, A Thrust through Backwardness, *Janata* 26(44) Novembr 14, p7

Anon, 1971, Water Shortage in Land of Snow, *Financial Express* July 26, p4

Anon, 1972, 66 Candidates Selected by CEC for Jand K Poll, *Times of India* January 21, p3, col 3-4

Anon, 1972, Abdullah Rules out Showdown with Govt, *Times of India* September 19, p10, col 2-3

Anon, 1972, Abdullah Stoops to Conquer? *Organiser* 26(20) December 23, p11

Anon, 1972, Abdullah's Outbursts Evoke Sharp Reaction, *Times of India* March 8, p14, col 3

Anon, 1972, Abdullah's Vision still Obscured, *Link* 14(47) July 2, p18-19

Anon, 1972, Biting Cold Fails to Slow Poll Tempo in Kashmir Valley, *Times of India* February 17, p5, col 1-2

Anon, 1972, (Book Review), *Aryan Path* 43(6) August, p275-276; *Commerce* 124(3178) April 1, p818-819
Review of the Book: Patel, Vallabhbhai, 1971, *Sardar Patel's Correspondence, 1945-50: New Light on Kashmir*, ed by Durga Das, Navajivan Publishing House Ahamedabad, xciv, 394p

Anon, 1972, (Book Review), *Economic and Political Weekly* 7(21) May 20, p1019-1022
Review of the Book: Parmu, R.K., 1972, *A History of Muslim Rule in Kashmir (1320-1319)*, People's Publishing House, New Delhi, xiv, 461p

Anon, 1972, (Book Review), *Indica* 4(2) September, p116-117
Review of the Book: Ray, Sunil Chandra, 1970, *Early History and Culture of Kashmir*, 2nd edn, Munshiram Manoharlal, Delhi, xvi, 288p

Anon, 1972, (Book Review), *India Quarterly* 28(2) April-June, p157-158; *U.S.I.Journal* 102(426) January-March, p92
Review of the Book: Sharma, B.L., 1971, *Kashmir Awakes*, Vikas Pub, New Delhi, xiii, 291p

Anon, 1972, (Book Review), *Journal of Asiatic Society (Bengal)* 14(1), p31-32
Review of the Book: Mishra, Mandan, 1968, *Kashmiretihasah* Shri Lal Bahadur Shastri Rastriya Sanskrit Vidyapeeth, 14, 310p

Anon, 1972, (Book Review), *Mainstream* 10(29) March 18, p39
Review of the Book: Chopra, Surendra, 1971, *U.N. Mediation in*

Kashmir: A Study in Power Politics, Vishal Pub, Kurukshetra, viii, 285p

Anon, 1972, Census 1971: Jammu and Kashmir, *Commerce* 124(3172) February 19, p402

Anon, 1972, Cholera Underplayed, *Link* 14(5) September 12, p26

Anon, 1972, Cong May Not Fare Well in Udhampur, *Times of India* March 1, p5, col 1

Anon, 1972, Congress Set for Majority in Kashmir, *Times of India* March 14, p5, col 2

Anon, 1972, Election in Kashmir, *Swarajya* 16(33) February 12, p25

Anon, 1972, Emphasis on Water Management, *Commerce* 124(3181) April 22, p1016

Anon, 1972, Employment Opportunities, *Thought* 24(44) October 28, p9

Anon, 1972, Free and Fair Elections in J&K, *Link* 14(26) February 6, p20-21

Anon, 1972, Freeing the other Sheikh, *Thought* 24(6) February 5, p6

Anon, 1972, The Grinding Poverty, *Commerce* 125 (3210) November 11, p 1215-1216

Anon, 1972, History Has Justified Sardar Patel's Misgivings, *Organiser* 25(32) March 18, p4

Anon, 1972, Hopes to Break the Ice, *Thought* 24(17) April 22, p4

Anon, 1972, Infighting Weakens Congress in Jammu, *Times of India* February 29, p5, col 3-4

Anon, 1972, J&K: Fair Official Conduct of Poll, *Link* 14(30) March 2, p 26

Anon, 1972, J&K: A Host of 'Independents', *Link* 14(29) February 27, p25

Anon, 1972, J and K: Improvement in Congress Fortunes, *Link* 16(33) March 26, p29

Anon, 1972, J and K: Political Liberalism, *Link* 14(44) June 11, p24-25

Anon, 1972, J-K Secessionsits See the Light, *Link* 14(35) April 9, p19

Anon, 1972, Jammu and Kashmir, *Commerce* 124 (3172) February 19, p 369

Anon, 1972, Jammu-Kathua Rail Link Opened : An Engineering Feat of Great Magnitude, *Indian Railways* 17(7) October p29-30

Anon, 1972, Ladakh Is beginning to Catch up, *States* February 5, p37

Anon, 1972, Kashmir: Rail Link with Jammu, *Commerce* 125 (3204) September 30, p 835

Anon, 1972, Kashmir: The Seikh Speaks out, *Link* 14(46) June 25, p12

Anon, 1972, Kashmir : Year of Fulfilment, *Link* 14(21) January 2, p21-22

Anon, 1972, Kashmir Cabinet Expanded, *Times of India* September 15, p1, col 1-2

Anon, 1972, Mr Beg's Old Tune, *Commerce* 124 (3189) June 17, p1575-1576

Anon, 1972, Manoeuvring for Power and Peace, *Thought* 24(8) February 19, p 9-10

Anon, 1972, Masks Jerked off Known Secessionist Faces in Kashmir, *Link* 14(27) February 13, p19-20, illustrations

Anon, 1972, Massive Irrigation Drive, *Economic Times*, August 9, p3

Anon, 1972, Massive Kashmir Mandate for Congress, *Times of India* March 15, p13, col 1

Anon, 1972, No Serious Threat to Congress in Kashmir, *Times of India* February 26, p4, col 4-5

Anon, 1972, A Pauttern in Power Distribution: Jammu and Kashmir, *Commerce* 124 (3178) April 1, p781

Anon, 1972, Phenomenal Growth in Foodgrains, *Commerce* (Annual Number) 125 (3218), p80-87, tables

Anon, 1972, A Reduced Majority, *Thought* 24(14) April 1, p9-10

Anon, 1972, Sangh to Contest 30 Seats from Jammu Area, *Times of India* February 7, p4, col 1-2

Anon, 1972, Sheikh Changed Attitude, *Thought* 24(52) December 23, p9

Anon, 1972, Sheikh Participates in Civic Elections, *Thought* 24(40) September 30, p9-10

Anon, 1972, Tackling Unemployment, *Commerce* 124 (3186) May 27, p 1375

Anon, 1972, Violence in Kashmir, *Link* 14(31) March 12, p 22

Anon, 1972, Whisper Campaign in Kashmir, *Link* 14(36) April 16, p16

Anon, 1973, Abdullah Dscries Plea for Free Kashmir, *Times of India* December 3, p1, col 1-2 +

Anon, 1973, Belligerent Smells, *Thought* 25(47) November 24, p 9-10

Anon, 1973, (Book Review), *India Quarterly* 29(2) April-June, p180-181
Review of the Book : Chopra, Surendra, 1971, *U.N. Meditating in*

Kashmir: A Study in Power Politics, Vishal Pub, Kurukshetra, viii, 285p

Anon, 1973, (Book Review), *Journal of Bihar Research Society* 59 (1-4), p265-268
Review of the Book: Ghose, Dilip Kumar, 1975, *Kashmir in Transition, 1885-1893*, World Press, Calcutta, xiv, 26p

Anon, 1973, (Book Review), *Quest 80*, January-February, p109
Review of the Book: Raina, Triloknath, ed, 1972, *An Anthology of Modern Kashmiri Verse*, N.D.A., 280p

Anon, 1973, (Book Review), *Thought* 25(50) December 15, p19-20.
Review of the Book: Raina, A.N., 1971, *Geography of Jammu and Kashmir*, National Book Trust, New Delhi, 183p

Anon, 1973, Delievering the Goods, *Thought* 25(36) September 8, p9

Anon, 1973, Divisive Campaigns in J.K., *Link* 15(33) March 25, p16

Anon, 1973, Effecting Land Reforms, *Commerce* 126 (3239) June 2, p1106

Anon, 1973, From Prebicite to Autonomy, *Commerce* 126(3224) February 17, p318

Anon, 1973, The Great Challenge, *Thought* 25(51) December 22, p7-8

Anon, 1973, India 1973 : Social Crucial Questions: A Sympositum, *Gandhi Marg* 17(1) January, p7-8

Anon, 1973, The Indian Sheikh, *Quest* 84 September-October, p65-67

Anon, 1973, J&K: Lack of Infrastructure, *Link* 16(14) November 11, p31-32

Anon, 1973, J.K: Subversives Active again, *Link* 15(51) July 29, p15-16

Anon, 1973, Jammu and Kashmir: Bigger Annual Plan, *Commerce* 126 (3228) March 17, p548

Anon, 1973, The Jehad against Bhairo Nath Shrine, *Organiser* 26(40) May 12, p8-9

Anon, 1973, Kashmir: The Verdict of History, *Link* 15(26) February 4, p22-23

Anon, 1973, Kashmir Government's Jehad on Hindu Landowners, *Organiser* 27(9) October 6, p8-9

Anon, 1973, The Kashmir Mischief, *Link* November 18, p31

Anon, 1973, Land Reforms in Kashmir, *Link* 15(39) May 6, p18-19

Anon, 1973, Mountains of Prices, *Thought* 25(21) March 26, p9

Anon, 1973, Oceanic Tears, *Thought* 25(33) August 18, p9

Anon, 1973, Power Jockeying, *Thought* 25(11) May 17, p9

Anon, 1973, Public Sector Shows Efficiency, *Commerce* (Supplement) 127 (3250) August 18, p25-27

Anon, 1973, Rs 2 Crore Deficit Budget for J & K, *Times of India* March 13, p5, col 6-7

Anon, 1973, A School for Every 118 Students, *Commerce* 126 (3229) March 24, p598-599

Anon, 1973, Sweet Uses of the Sheikh, *Economic and Political Weekly*, 8(42-43) October 20, p1892

Anon, 1973, An Unturned Leaf, *Thought* 25(13) March 31, p9-10

Anon, 1973, Up the Tourist Trade, *Thought* 25(17) April 28, p11

Anon, 1973, Abdullah Hopeful of Accord with Centre, *Times of India* September 19, p1, col 6-7 +

Anon, 1973, Abdullah Refuses to Head a Congress Ministry in J&K, *Organiser* 28(9) October 12, p7

Anon, 1974, Accord Gives Abdullah Only Minor Concessions, *Times of India* November 15, p1, col 1-2

Anon, 1974, Accord with the Sheikh, *Times of India* June 26, p4, col 6, letter to the editor

Anon, 1974, Autonomy in the New Set up, *Thought* 26 (34) August 31, p9

Anon, 1974, (Book Review), *Folklore* 15(1) January, p39
Review of the Book: Handoo, Jawaharlal, 1971, *Kashmir aur Hindi ke Lokgit: Ek Tualanatnak Adhyan*, Bishal Pub (Book in Hindi)

Sundar, K.R., 1974, Break through in Kashmir? *Illustrated Weekly of India* 95 (24) 11 August, p16-19

Anon, 1974, Cautious Optimism on Kashmir: Some Advances Made, *Times of India* July 16, p4, col 7-8

Anon, 1974, A Decisive Phase, *Thought* 26(25) June 29, p9

Anon, 1974, Encore the Rough Weather, *Thought* 26(37) September 21, p9-10

Anon, 1974, Eye on Greater Assistance from Centre, *Commerce* 128 (3280) March 23, p374-375

Anon, 1974, Food Subsidy Muddle in J&K, *Organiser* 27(26) February 2, p13

Anon, 1974, Front Ready to Give up Plebiscite Demand, *Times of India* July 6, p1, col 2-3

Anon, 1974, Growing Unrest among People, *Thought* 26(16) April 27, p9

Anon, 1974, J&K: New Dimensions of Progress, *Link* 16(25) January 26, p41-43

Anon, 1974, Kashmir: Abdullah's Reservations, *Link* 16 (45) June 16, p21-22

Anon, 1974, Kashmir Journey to Settlement, *Mainstream* 12(51) August 17, p8-9 +

Anon, 1974, Kashmir Left out in the Cold, *Times of India* February 23, p4, col 7-8

Anon, 1974, Kashmir Problem nearer Solution, *Thought* 26(23) June 15, p7

Anon, 1974, The Kashmir Tangle, *Capital* 173 (4332) September 26, p466

Anon, 1974, Major Concessions to Abdullah Unlikely, *Times of India* September 8, p1, col 7-8

Anon, 1974, Mir Qasim Rules out Plebiscite, *Times of India* July 14, p5, col 1-2

Anon, 1974, National Interests to be Fully Preserved, *Times of India* December 17, p1, col 7-8

Anon, 1974, New Delhi's Sell out to the Sheikh, *Organiser* 27(45) June 22, p1-2

Anon, 1974, New Measures Taken to Check Corruption in Kashmir, *Times of India* July 2, p4, col 7-8

Anon, 1974, No Move for Changes in Constitution, *Times of India* June 11, p1, col 4-5 +

Anon, 1974, Optimism in Kashmir, *Link* 16 (52) August 4, p19

Anon, 1974, Pandorna's Box in Kashmir, *Times of India*, July 22, p4, col 6, letter to the editor

Anon, 1974, Pindi Has Nothing to do with Kashmir, *Times of India* August 12, p1, col 2-4

Anon, 1974, Plainspeaking by Jammu Advocate Infuriates Sheikh Abdullah, *Organiser* 28(5) September 14, p4

Anon, 1974, Possibility of a Mid-term Poll, *Thought* 26 (11) March 23, p9

Anon, 1974, The Ramifications of Abdullah-Farooq Clash in Kashmir, *Organiser* 28(2) August 24, p7 +

Anon, 1974, Return to Pre-1953 Status in Kashmir Ruled out, *Times of India* August 29, p1, col 5-7

Anon, 1974, Sheikh Abdullah Hopeful of Assuming Reins, *Commerce* 129 (3303) August 31, p 364-366

Anon, 1974, Sheikh Abdullah's Tour of Jammu Region after 21

Years, *Organiser* 27 (37) April 20, p 13

Anon, 1974, Sheikh Offers to Consider Alternative Proposals, *Times of India* June 10, p1, col 1-2

Anon, 1974, Sheikh Wants to be Back in Power on August 9, *Organiser* 27 (46) June 29, p 3+

Anon, 1974, Sprinkler Irrigation Catching on, *Economic Times* April 10

Anon, 1973, State of Corruption, *Thought* 25(52) December 29, p 8-9

Anon, 1974, Struggle for being Heard in New Delhi, *Commerce* 129 (3297) July 20, p110

Anon, 1974, Support to Sheikh-Mrs Gandhi Talks, *Thought* 26 (29) July 20, p9

Anon, 1974, Swaran Singh-Abdullah Talks Inconclusive, *Commerce* 128 (3292) June 15, p 876

Anon, 1974, A Tale of Two Conferences: Vajpayee Outlines Agitation Plan against Sell-out to the Sheikh, *Organiser* 27(50) July 27, p7

Anon, 1974, Talks with Abdullah, *Commerce* 128 (3292) June 15, p869

Anon, 1974, Towards Stability and Progress, *Commerce* (Supplement) 129 (3301) August 17, p29

Anon, 1974, Valley of the Jhelum, *Illustrated Weekly of India* 95(8) April 21, p 6-13+

Anon, 1974, The Wall of Years, *Thought* 26(30) August 3, p9

Anon, 1974, Welcoming Talks with Sheikh Abdullah, *New Age* 22(32) August 11, p12

Anon, 1974, Yarn Shortage Hits Kashmir Looms, *Commerce* 128 (3290) June 1, p 787-788

Anon, 1974-75, Epigraphy: Arabic Persian Inscriptions: Jammu and Kashmir, *Indian Archaeology*, p 61-62

Anon, 1975, 11 More Ministers for Sheikh Cabinet, *Times of India* April 23, p1, col 1-2

Anon, 1975, 70 p.c. Polling in Kashmir By-Elections, *Times of India* July 4, p1, col 1

Anon, 1975, Abdullah, 3 Others Sworn in, *Times of India* February 26, p1, col 3-4+

Anon, 1975, Abdullah, Beg Elected to Kashmir Assembly, *Times of India* July 5, p1, col 6-7

Anon, 1975, Abdullah to Head National Conference, *Times of India* July 6, p1, col 7-8

Anon, 1975, Accord on Kashmir Endorsed by PAC, *Times of India* February 11, p1, col 7-8 +

Anon, 1975, Agreement on Kashmir Is an Essay in Harmony: P.M., *Times of India* March 4, p1, col 1-2 +

Anon, 1975, Bakshi Raj in Kashmir, *Thought* 27 (22) May 31, p9-10

Anon, 1975, Ban on Entry into Secretariat Goes, *Times of India* July 16, p1, col 7-8

Anon, 1975, (Book Review), *Herald of Library Science* 14(2-3) April-July, p190; *Indian and Foreign Review* 12(13) April 15, p23; *Indian Librarain* 29(4) March, p188
Review of the Book: Ganhar, J.N. 1974, *Jammu Shrines and Pilgrimages*, Ganhar Pub, 180p

Anon, 1975, (Book Review), *Indian and Foreign Review* 12(11) March 15, p22
Review of the Book: Gundevia, Y.D., 1974, *The Testament of Sheikh Abdullah*, Palit and Palit, New Delhi, 156 p

Anon, 1975, (Book Review), *Indian and Foreign Review* 12(13) April 15, p 23
Review of the Book: Bamzai, P.N.K., 1975, *Jammu and Kashmir*, Publications Division, Government of India, New Delhi, 62p

Anon, 1975, (Book Review), *Indian Journal of Politics* 9(2) December, p 266-268
Review of the Book: Bhagwan Singh, 1975, *Political Conspiracies of Kashmir*, Light and Life Pub, 158p

Anon, 1975, (Book Review), *Journal of Indian History* 53(3) December, p577-578
Review of the Book: Bawa Satinder Singh, 1975, *The Jammu Fox : A Biography of Maharaja Gulab Singh of Kashmir (1972-1857)*, Southern University Press

Anon, 1975, (Book Review), *Khadi Gramodyog* 21(9) June, p440-441; *Yojana* 19(6) April 15, p 35,
Review of the Book: Rehman, Mahfoozur, 1975, *Co-operative Credit and Agricultural Development,* Sultan Chand, Delhi, xv, 216p

Anon, 1975, (Book Review), *Thought* 27 (1) January 4, p20
Review of the Book: Tomar, D.S., 1974, *Rail Race to Jammu,* Metropolitan, New Delhi

Anon, 1975, Continuing Burden of Food Subsidy, *Commerce* 130 (3332) March 29, p 447

Anon, 1975, Cynosure to All, *Thought* 27(4) January 25, p9-10

Anon, 1975, The Growing Burden of Debt Servicing. *Commerce* 130 (3333) April 5, p 477-488

Anon, 1975, Indira-Abdullah Agreement X-rayed, *Organiser* 28 (29) March 1, p 1-2

Anon, 1975, J&K: A Democratic Victory, *Link* 17 (29) March 2, p 20

Anon, 1975, J&K Bid to Promote Handicrafts, *Times of India* October 17, p5, col 2-4

Anon, 1975, J&K Congress Rejects CM's Merger Plea, *Times of India* June 10, p1, col 1-2

Anon, 1975, J.K's New Venture to Manufacture Tyres and Tubes, *Swarajya* 19(45) May 10, p5-6

Anon, 1975, JS Alone Voices Total Opposition, *Times of India* February 25, p5, col 1-2

Anon, 1975, JS to Continue Drive against Article 370, *Times of India* March 2, p1, col 7-8 +

Anon, 1975, JS to Resist Change in J&K Status, *Times of India* March 5, p1, col 1-2 +

Anon, 1974, Kashmir: Journey to Settlement, *Mainstream* 12(51) August 17, p8-9 +

Anon, 1975, Kashmir: Unresolved Issues of State Politics, *Commerce* 131(3362) October 25, p711

Anon, 1975, The Kashmir Accord, *Capital* 175 (4351) February 20, p266

Anon, 1975, Kashmir Accord: Form and Content, *Mainstream* 13(24) February 15, p9-10

Anon, 1975, Kashmir Accord Example of Trust: P.M, *Times of India* March 13, p1, col 1-4 +

Anon, 1975, Kashmir Accord Gets Final Touches, *Times of India* February 23, p1, col 4-5 +

Anon, 1975, Kashmir Accord Not Against Simla Spirit: P.M. *Times of India* March 14, p1, col 1-2 +

Anon, 1975, Kashmir Accord within Framework of Constitution, *Times of India* February 25, p1, col 1-2 +

Anon, 1975, Keys of the Kingdom, *Thought* 27(6) February 8, p10-11

Anon, 1975, Land of Springs, Lakes and Rivers,*Commerce* (Annual Number) 131 (3372) p213-216, tables

Anon, 1975, List of Central Laws Applicable to J&K, *Times of India* February 25, p7, col 2-3

Anon, 1975, National Conference Back in Kashmir, *Link* 17(48) July 13, p26

Anon, 1975, New Initiative for Horticulture Growth, *Commerce* 131 (3361) October 18, p 674-680

Anon, 1975, New J and K Ministers Sworn in, *Times of India* April 25, p1, col 1-2

Anon, 1974, Opposition to Attend Meet under Protest, *Times of India* February 24, p1, col 4-5 +

Anon, 1975, Pak Alibi Knocked Down, *Link* 18(3) August 31, p22

Anon, 1975, Pilgrims Were Almost in Jaws of Death, *Times of India* August 25, p1, col 4-5 +

Anon, 1975, Politics in Kashmir, *People's Democracy* 11(47) November 23, P7

Anon, 1975, Power to the People, *Thought* 27(9) March 1, p7-8

Anon, 1975, Return of Sheikh Abdullah to Power? *Commerce* 130 (3323) January 25, p64

Anon, 1974, Search for Indentity, *Link* 16(49) July 14, p12-13

Anon, 1975, Sheikh's Plan Misfiures, *Link* 17(43) June 8, p 18-20

Anon, 1975, Six-Point Agreement, *Times of India* February 25, p1, col 3 +

Anon, 1975, Stricter Control on Liquor, *Commerce* 130 (3341) May 31, p820

Anon, 1975, Text of Letters Exchanged, *Times of India* February 25, p7, col 5-7

Anon, 1975, Text of Letters Exchanged on J and K, *Times of India* February 25, p7, col 1-3

Anon, 1975, Uneconomic Holdings Make Co-operatives Essential, *Commerce* 130 (3325) February 8, p139

Anon, 1975, Wasted Years, *Economic and Political Weekly* 10(10) March 8, p417-418

Anon, 1975-76, Explorations and Excavations: Jammu and Kashmir, *Indian Archaeology*, p18-19

Anon, 1976, Abdullah Calls for Continued Co-operation with Congress, *Times of India* April 25, p1, col 2-3 +

Anon, 1976, All Sectors under Tax Net, *Commerce* 132 (3383) May 1, p622

Anon, 1976, Bhutto Cooking up New 'Jehad', *Link* 18(31) March 14, p19

Anon, 1976, (Book Review), *India Quarterly* 32(4), October-December, p487-489
Review of the Book: Saxena, H.L., 1975, *The Tragedy of Kashmir*, National Publishing House, xv, 580 p

Anon, 1976, (Book Review), *Indian History Review* 2(2) January, p417
Review of the Book: Saxena, K.S., 1974, *Political History of Kashmir (300 BC- 1200 AD)*, Upper India Pub, xvi, 364p

Anon, 1976, (Book Review), *Journal of the Institute of Economic Research* 11(1-2) January-July, p82-83
Review of the Book: Rahman, Mahfoozur, 1975, *Co-operative Credit and Agricultural Development*, Sultan Chand, Delhi, xv, 216p

Anon, 1976 (Book Review), *Link* 18 (36) April 18, p36
Review of the Book: Dhar, K.N., 1976, *Glimpses of Kashmiri Culture*, Shri Parmananda Research Institute

Anon, 1976, *Bourne and Shepherd's Royal Photographic Album of Scenes and Personages Connected with the Progress of HRH the Prince of Wales through Bengal, the North West Provinces, the Punjab and Nepal, with Some Descriptive Letterpress,* Bourne and Shepherd, Calcutta, 78p, plates

Anon, 1976, Handloom Industry in Cooperative Sector in Jammu and Kashmir, *Indian Cooperative Review* 13 (4) July, p361-365

Anon, 1976, J&K Annual Plan Outlay for 1977-78 Increased, *Times of India* December 30, p1, col 2-37

Anon, 1976, Jammu and Kashmir: New Industrial Projects, *Commerce* (Supplement) 133 (3403) August 14, p35-37

Anon, 1976, Jammu and Kashmir: New Law on Anvil, *Commerce* 133 (3403) August 14, p327-328

Anon, 1976, Jammu and Kashmir: Priority for Power, *Commerce* 132 (3379) February 28, p262

Anon, 1976, Jhelum Floods Many Areas in Anantnag, *Time of India* August 3, p1, col 7-8 +

Anon, 1976, Land Settlement in Kashmir, *Commerce* 133 (3420) December 11, p1003

Anon, 1976, Mainly Soaps and Candles, *Commerce* 133 (3414) October 30, p15

Anon, 1976, Massive Army, Civilian Bid to Tame Swollen J&K Rivers, *Times of India* August 2, p1, col 1-2 +

Anon, 1976, New Industrial Projects, *Commerce* (Supplement) 133 (3403) August 14, p35-37

Anon, 1976, No Respite from Flood Fury for Lasjan Villagers, *Times of India* August 10, p7, col 3-4

Anon, 1976, People Plug a Breach, Save Town, *Times of India*

August 7, p1, col 3-5 +

Anon, 1976, Sheikh Abdullah and His Party, *Link* 18 (37) April 25, p15

Anon, 1976, Some Fine Statues Salvaged at Babor, *Times of India* November 6, p5, col 1-2

Anon, 1976, State Not yet Fully Prepared for Task, *Times of India* July 19, p5, col 1-4; July 20, p7, col 1-3

Anon, 1976-77 (Book Review), *Quarterly Review of Hitorical Studies,* p53-54
Review of the Book: Ghose, Dilip Kumar, 1975, *Kashmir in Transition* , *1885-1893*, World Press, Calcutta, xiv, 26p

Anon, 1976-77, Epigraphy: Arabic and Persian Inscriptions: Jammu and Kashmir, *Indian Archeaology,* p66

Anon, 1976-77, Explorations and Excaxations: Jammu and Kashmir, *Indian Archeaology*, p19-21

Anon, 1977, 16 More Ministers in Kashmir Sworn in, *Times of India* July 14, p7, col 4-5

Anon, 1977, 19 Held for Disturbing Karan Singh's Meeting, *Times of India* March 7, p1, col 2-3 +

Anon, 1977, 60 p.c. Polling in 32 Jammu Constituencies, *Times of India* July 1, p1, col 7-8

Anon, 1977, 170 Candidates for 42 Seats in J&K, *Times of India* June 10, p11 col 2-3

Anon, 1977, Abdullah Govt Likely by Week-End, *Times of India* July 6, p1, col 4-5

Anon, 1977, Abdullah Wave Sweeps the Valley, *Times of India* June 22, p1 col 2-4 +

Anon, 1977, Abdullah's Scathing Attack on Charan, Ram, *Times of India* June 24, p1, col 6-7 +

Anon, 1977, Abdullah's Sick Bed Plea Moves Many Deeply, *Times of India* July 2, p7, col 2-3

Anon, 1977, Agricultural Development in Jammu and Kashmir, *Journal of Industry and Trade* 27 (2) February, p32-37

Anon, 1977, Article 370 Main Poll Issue in J&K, *Times of India* June 1, p5, col 4

Anon, 1977, Battle Royal between Begum and Maulvi, *Times of India* March 15, p7, col 2-4

Anon, 1977 (Book Review), *Times of India* (Magazine) August 21, p10, col 1-5
Review of the Book: Kapur, M.L., 1977, *Studies in History and*

Culture of Kashmir, Trikuta Pub, 229p

Anon, 1977, Budget Lays Stress on Development, *Commerce* 135 (3463) October 15, p703

Anon, 1977, Communication Links Improved, *Commerce* (Supplement) 135 (3454) August 13, p33-34

Anon, 1977, Cong to Contest Only 3 Seats in Kashmir, *Times of India* February 10, p1, col 4-5

Anon, 1977, Congress Faces a Tough Challenge in Anantnag, *Times of India* February 27, p5, col 4-5

Anon, 1977, Congress-NC Clashes in Kashmir Council, *Times of India* March 26, p7, col 1-2

Anon, 1977, Congress Support to Abdullah Govt Ends, *Times of India* March 26, p1, col 7-8 +

Anon, 1977, Detailed Results of the Kashmir Poll, *Times of India* July 5, p9, col 1-4

Anon, 1977, Detention, Curbs on Press: J&K Ordinance, *Economic Times* November 7, p1, col 1-3 +

Anon, 1977, Detention Ordinance to Check Espionage, *Times of India* November 9, p1, col 4-5 +

Anon, 1977, Doubts on Prohibition, *Link* 20 (10) October 16, p17-18

Anon, 1977, Election Scene VII: Sheikh Abdullah May Turn Tide in Kashmir, *Times of India* March 3, p1, col 2-5 +

Anon, 1977, Electoral Malpractices, *Link* 20 (13) November 6, p20

Anon, 1977, Exquisite Equestrian Statues Discovered, *Times of India* July 4, p5, col 1-2

Anon, 1977, Fodder Can be Second Crop in Kashmir, *Economic Times* December 14, p7, col 1-4

Anon, 1977, Ghulam Kara, Abdul Gani in Kashmir Janata Party, *Times of India* June 6, p5, col 4-5

Anon, 1977, Govt Not to Seek J&K Poll Postponement, *Times of India* June 23, p1, col 3-4

Anon, 1977, J&K Janata List Provokes Protests, *Times of India* June 3, p5, col 1-2

Anon, 1977, J&K Parties' Efforts to Win over Dissidents, *Times of India* March 22, p7, col 1-2

Anon, 1977, Janata Rift Emboldens Sheikh's Party, *Times of India* May 16, p1, col 3-4 +

Anon, 1977, Janata Walkout in Kashmir Assembly, *Times of India* October 9, p1, col 5-6 +

Anon, 1977, Janata Woman Nominee Assaulted in Srinagar, *Times of*

India June 9, p1, col 3-4 +
Anon, 1977, Kashmir Assembly Poll within 3 Months, *Times of India* March 30, p1, col 7-8 +
Anon, 1977, Kashmir Election and Its Aftermath, *Radical Humanist* 41 (5) August, p11-12
Anon, 1977, Kashmir Govt Assumes Power to detain Persons, Curb Press, *Times of India* November 7, p1, col 1-3 +
Anon, 1977, 6 Kashmir Ministers Resign: Sheikh Asks Governer to Disolve Assembly, *Times of India* March 27, p1, col 7-8 +
Anon, 1977, Kashmir Poll Scene: No Party Likely to Get Majority, *Times of India* July 2, p7, col 1-2
Anon, 1977, Kashmir Voting Pattern on Expected Lines, *Times of India* March 25, p11, col 2-3
Anon, 1977, Kashmir's Majestic Chinar, *Mainstneam* 15 (45) July 9, p3
Anon, 1977, Masoodi Keeps Janata Door Open to Abdullah, *Times of India* April 29, p5, col 1-2
Anon, 1977, Maulana Masoodi May Head Janata Unit in Kashmir, *Times of India* April 16, p1, col 7-8 +
Anon, 1977, NC Candidates for J & K Assembly Election, *Times of India* May 24, p5, col 4-5
Anon, 1977, NC Sore at Desai's Dinner with Mirwaiz, *Times of India* June 10, p11, col 2-3
Anon, 1977, A New Beginning in Kashmir, *Mainstream* (Annual Number) 16 (1-6), p17-18
Anon, 1977, No Candidate's Chances Imporve in Jammu, *Times of India* March 11, p9, col 1-2
Anon, 1977, No Fresh Taxes in J & K, *Times of India* September 20, p1, col 1
Anon, 1977, No Signs of Janata Wave in Kashmir, *Times of India* March 10, p1, col 2-3 +
Anon, 1977, P.M. Asks Kashmiris to Vote Fearlessly, *Times of India* June 26, p1, col 7-8 +
Anon, 1977, Political Crisis Brewing in Kashmir, *Times of India* March 25, p4, col 4-5
Anon, 1977, Quarrel Leads to 30 Minute Held-up in Srinagar Poll, *Times of India* March 20, p9, col 2-3
Anon, 1977, Quest for Democracy, *Link* (Independence Day Number) 20(1) August 15, p65-67
Anon, 1977, Reddy's Kashmir Sojourn, *Link* 20(11) October 23,

p13-14

Anon, 1977, Renewed Tensions in J & K, *Link* 20(17) December 4, p22-23

Anon, 1977, The Rot in Kashmir, *Link* 20(19) December 18, p14

Anon, 1977, Secession Threat by Abdullah, *Times of India* May 24, p1, col 8

Anon, 1977, Sheikh Accuses Jha of Favouring Janata, *Times of India* May 20, p5, col 4-5

Anon, 1977, Sheikh's Last Gamble, *Commerce* 135 (3448) July 2, p6

Anon, 1977, Six-Member Abdullah Govt Sworn in, *Times of India* July 10, p1, col 1-2 +

Anon, 1977, Stage Set for Trial of Strength in Assembly, *Times of India* March 26, p1, col 7-8 +

Anon, 1977, Surcharged Atmosphere in Kashmir Valley, *Times of India* February 21, p1, col 2-3

Anon, 1977, Tempo of Electioneering in Low Key in J & K, *Times of India* May 9, p9, col 4-5

Anon, 1977, Too Much of Politics, *Commerce* 135 (5475) December 24, p 1205

Anon, 1977, Tuning to New Wave Length, *Commerce* 134 (3434) March 26, p449-450

Anon, 1977, Violence Mars J & K Panchayat Poll, *Times of India* October 31, p1, col 2-3 +

Anon, 1977, Walk-out in J&K Assembly, Council over ex-PM's Arrest, *Times of India* October 5, p5, col 1-3

Anon, 1977, *White Papers on the Jammu and Kashmir Dispute*, Ministry of Foreign Affairs, Government of Pakistan, Islamabad, 137p, maps

Anon, 1977-78, Exploration and Excavation: Jammu and Kashmir, *Indian Archaeology,* p23-24

Anon, 1978, Abdullah Accuses Speaker of Role in Conspiracy, *Times of India* September 28, p1, col 4-6 +

Anon, 1978, Abdullah again on the Frying Trapeze, *Link* 20 (27) February 12, p20-22

Anon, 1978, Abdullah against Trial of Ex-P.M., *Times of India* July 8, p1, col 5-6 +

Anon, 1978, Abdullah Denies He Wanted Independence for Kashmir, *Times of India* September 10, p1, col 1-2 +

Anon, 1978, Abdullah for Dialogue on Centre-State Ties, *Times of India* January 30, p1, col 4-5 +

Anon, 1978, Afzel Beg Quits Kashmir Govt, *Times of India* September 26, p1, Col 1-3 +

Anon, 1978, Afzal Beg to be Arrested, *Organiser* 30 (19) October 1, p1

Anon, 1978, Afzal Beg's Resignation Accepted, *Times of India* September 27, p1, col 1 +

Anon, 1978, Beg, 9 Others Abstain from Legislatures Meet, *Times of India* September 29, p1, col 3-4 +

Anon, 1978, Beg Accuses Sheikh of Double-Talk, *Times of India* October 8, p1, col 6-8 +

Anon, 1978, Beg and Son-in-Law Expelled from Party, *Times of India* September 30, p1, col 6-7 +

Anon, 1978, Beg Divested of Law Portfolio: Sheikh Extorts Loyalty Oath from Ministers, *Times of India* September 23, p1, col 1-3

Anon, 1978, Beg Says He can Topple Sheikh Govt, *Times of India* October 17, p1, col 7-8

Anon, 1978, Beg Unhurt in Heavy Stone-Throwing, *Times of India* October 5, p1, col 4-5 +

Anon, 1978, Beg's Venture, *Link* 21 (10) October 15, p14

Anon, 1978, Bid to Regain Leadership in Sericulture, *Commerce* 136 (3496) June 10, p959

Anon, 1978, (Book Review), *Times of India (Magazine)* April 2, p10, col 6-8

Review of the Book: Kirpa Ram (Diwan) 1978, *The Gulabnana of Diwan Kirpa Ram: A History of Maharaja Gulab Singh of Jammu and Kashmir,* tr by Suchdev Sigh Charak, Light and Life Pub

Anon, 1978, (Book Review), *Times of India* (Magazine) June 4, p10, col 5-8

Review of the Book: Dhar, Somnath, 1978, *Jammu and Kashmir,* National Book Trust, New Delhi

Anon, 1978, (Book Review), *Times of India* (Magazine) June 4, p10, col 5-8

Review of the Book: Drieberg, Trevor and Sahni, Satpal, 1978, *Jammu and Kashmir: A Tourist Guide*, Vikas Pub, New Delhi

Anon, 1978, (Book Review), *Times of India* (Magazine) June 4, p10, col 5-8

Review of the Book: Teng, Mohan Krishan, *et al*, 1977, *Kashmir: Constitutional History and Documents*, Light and Life Pub, New Delhi, 689p

Anon, 1978, CM Blames Politicians for Fanning Mattan Trouble, *Times of India* August 6, p5, col 3-4

Anon, 1978, Cong-I Dilemma in Kashmir, *Link* 20 (31) March 12, p21

Anon, 1978, Cracks in NC-Cong Alliance, *Times of India* May 25, p1, col 8 +

Anon, 1978, Divided Loyalties, *Link* 21 (8) October 1, p19-20

Anon, 1978, Do People of Jammu Want Regional Autonomy? *Economic Times* February 17, p3, col 1-4

Anon, 1978, Economic Profile of J&K-11: Break-through on Agriculture Front, *Economic Times* April 24, p1, col 2-6; April 25, p4, col 6-8; April 26, p8, col 3-6

Anon, 1978, Factional Politics Led to Beg's Exit: CM, *Times of India* October 8, p1, col 6-7

Anon, 1978, Gulmarg: The New Trend-setter, *Times of India* December 27, p7, col 1-3

Anon, 1978, Industrialisation with Private Sector Bias, *Economic Times* July 9, p7, col 1-4

Anon, 1978, J&K Budget: Rs 49 Crore Deficit, *Economic Times* March 10, p1, col 5-7 +

Anon, 1978, J&K Fails to Achieve Major Breakthrough on Farm Front, *Times of India* May 22, p5, col 3-4

Anon, 1978, J&K Has Few Complaints, *Economic Times* April 7, p1, col 2-4 +

Anon, 1978, J&K Probe into Problems of Child Labour in Carpet Units, *Times of India* September 2, p7, col 1-2

Anon, 1978, Jammu and Kashmir: No Significant Change, *Commerce* 137 (3503) July 29, p200

Anon, 1978, Kashmir Sericulture Industry's Future Bright, *Economic Times*, January 10, p8, col 3-6

Anon, 1978, Lack of Finance and Enterprise, *Commerce* (Supplement) 137 (3506) August 19, p35-37

Anon, 1978, Malpracticcs Alleged in Kashmir Civic Polls, *Times of India* October 16, p5, col 2-3

Anon, 1978, Maulana Masoodi Speaks, *Illustrated Weekly of India* 99(43) November 12, p30-31

Anon, 1978, Mir Waiz Seeks Probe into Poll Rigging by NC, *Times of India* October 24, p5, col 1-2

Anon, 1978, Mobs at Srinagar Polling Booths Teargassed, *Times of India* October 18, p1, col 2-5 +

Anon, 1978, New Tensions in Kashmir, *Link* 20 (21) Junuary 1, p13-14

Anon, 1978, Non-Entities and Discredited Men Dominate New Janata Committee in J&K, *Organiser* 29 (54) June 4, p16

Anon, 1978, Record Tourist Rush in Kashmir, *Times of India* June 21, p5, col 2-5

Anon, 1978, Sheikh on Top in J&K, *Link* 20 (47) July 9, p19-20

Anon, 1978, Sheikh Raises New Bogey, *Link* 21 (9) October 8, p8-12

Anon, 1978, Stress on Industry, Agriculture, *Commerce,* 136 (3486) April 1, p498

Anon, 1978, Tourism Development in Kashmir, *Times of India* December 27, p6, col 7-8 +

Anon, 1978, Troubled Congress Waters in J&K, *Link* 20 (23) January 15, p11

Anon, 1978, Unfair Poll, *Link* 21 (12) October 29, p13

Anon, 1978, Water, Country Liquor to Cost More in Kashmir, *Times of India* March 10, p1, col 5-6

Anon, 1978, Will Agrarian Reforms Succeed? *Commerce* 137 (3499), July 1, p18

Anon, 1978, Your Kind of Holiday on Your Kind of Budget, *Vidura* 15(1) January-February, p12-15

Anon, 1978-79, Explorations: Problems Oriented Surveys: Jammu and Kashmir, *Indian Archaeology*, p25-26

Anon, 1978-79, Other Excavations: Jammu and Kashmir, *Indian Archaeology,* p69-70

Anon, 1979, 150 Hurt on Second Day of Violence in Jammu, *Times of India* February 14, p1, col 1-2 +

Anon, 1979, Abdullah's Troubles in Kashmir, *Link* 21 (26) February 4, p18-19

Anon, 1979, Alliance Talks in Jeopardy, *Link* 22 (11) October 21, p30-31

Anon, 1979, Beg, Abdullah Trade Charges, *Times of India* March 23, p5, col 2-4

Anon, 1979, Big Cut in Food Subsidy, *Commerce* 138 (3536) March 24, p 459-460

Anon, 1979, CPI (M) Unit Formed in Jammu and Kashmir: Big Group Breaks away from Naxalites, *People's Democracy* 3 (36) September 9, p6-7

Anon, 1979, Dismal Failure of Vegetable Development Programme, *Economic Times* May 11, p3, col 2-5

Anon, 1979, Indira Gandhi-Abdullah Deal, *Link* 22 (18) December 9, p13-14

Anon, 1979, J&K : Challenge to Sheikh, *Link* 22 (20) December 23, p21

Anon, 1979, J&K : Popular Outburst, Apathy, *Link* 22 (21) December 30, p18

Anon, 1979, J&K First to Pass Anti-Defection Bill, *Times of India* September 27, p1, col 6-7 +

Anon, 1979, JKSFC to Go Rural, *Economic Times* p5, col 7-8

Anon, 1979, Jammu and Kashmir : Limited Availability of Textbooks, *Commerce* 139 (3558) August 25, p360

Anon, 1979, Jammu and Kashmir : Rabi Sowing May Not be Hit, *Commerce* 139 (3562) September 22, p554

Anon, 1979, Karan Singh Keen to Contest from 2 Constituencies, *Times of India* October 8, p5, col 1

Anon, 1979, Karan Singh vs Abdullah, *Link* 22 (17) December 2, p15

Anon, 1979, Kashmir Sericulture Industry Revived, *Economic Times* August 28, p7, col 6-8

Anon, 1979, Keen Contest Likely in Poonch, Udhampur, *Times of India* December 29, p4, col 5-6

Anon, 1979, Local Issues Dominate, *Link* 22 (19) December 10, p13

Anon, 1979, National Parties Lose Hold in Kashmir , *Times of India* December 25, p1, col 1-4 +

Anon, 1979, Plan to Step up Growth Rate Upset, *Economic Times* February 20, p3, col 1-4

Anon, 1979, Poonch Confrontation-1: Agitators in No Mood to Relent, *Times of India* February 13, p1, col 1-3 + ; February 14, p5, col 2-4

Anon, 1979, Poonch Trouble Escalates, *Link* 21 (27) February 11, p19-20

Anon, 1979, Precarious Balance, *Link* 21 (32) March 18, p23

Anon, 1979, Probing for Alliance, *Link* 22 (8) September 30, p25

Anon, 1979, Rs 1.3 Cr Deficits for J&K, *Economic Times* March 16, p1, col 1-4 +

Anon, 1979, Ruling Party's Confidence, *Link* 22 (5) September 9, p20

Anon, 1979, Shah to Use Sheikh's Charisma, *Times of India* December 28, p9, col 2-4

Anon, 1979, Threat of Regional Revivalism, *Link* 21 (28) February 18, p26-27

Anon, 1979, Unplanned Proliferation of Schools, *Commerce*

(Supplement) 139 (3557) August 18, p29-33, tables
Anon, 1979-80, Explorations and Excavations, *Indian Archaeology*, p32-33
Anon, 1979-80, Preservation of Monuments: Monuments of National Importance, *Indian Archaeology*, p139-140
Anon, 1980, Abdullah's Outborst Baffles Many in J&K, *Times of India* July 17, p5, col 4-5
Anon, 1980, Administrative Failures, *Link* 23 (16) November 30, p27
Anon, 1980, Arousing Parochial Sentiments, *Link* 22 (52) August 3, p18-20
Anon, 1980, Assembly Prorogued, Called again in J&K, *Times of India* October 6, p1, col 7-8 +
Anon, 1980, Censure Move against J&K Speaker Admitted, *Times of India* October 3, p1, col 4-5 +
Anon, 1980, Changes in Offing, *Link* 23 (38) April 27, p21
Anon, 1980, The Changing Landscape of Ladakh, *Times of India* October 13, p1, col 2-5 +
Anon, 1980, Compulsions of Change, *Link* 22 (24) January 20, p16-17
Anon, 1980, Dilemma before Sheikh, *Link* 22 (29) February 24, p23-24
Anon, 1980, Ex-Speaker, Opposition to Move SC Today, *Times of India* October 7, p1, col 1-2 +
Anon, 1980, Gujjar Leaders Want Cabinet Representation, *Economic Times* May 31, p3, col 1-4
Anon, 1980, J&K: Revival of Communalism, *Link* 23 (3) August 31, p16
Anon, 1980, J&K Assembly Crisis Deepens: New Speaker Chosen by NC Menbers, *Times of India* Octobers, p1, col 2-4
Anon, 1980, J&K to Nationalise Forests in 4 Years, *Economic Times* June 2, p4, col 5-7
Anon, 1980, JKIL to Transfer Brick Factory, *Economic Times* April 6, p7, col 4-7
Anon, 1980, Jammu and Kashmir: No Serious Tensions, *Link* 23 (17) December 7, p53-55
Anon, 1980, Kashmir Assembly Adjourned: Debate on Speaker Inconclusive, *Times of India* October 11, p1, col 6-8 +
Anon, 1980, Kashmir Assembly Removes Speaker, *Times of India* October 12, p1, col 1-2 +
Anon, 1980, Kashmir Drive against Secessionists: 178 Held, *Times of India* August 19, p1, col 5-6

Anon, 1980, Kashmiri, *Indian Literature* 23 (1-2) January-April, p248-260

Anon, 1980, Legislature Complex in Srinagar Gutted, *Times of India* October 10, p1, col 2-4 +

Anon, 1980, National Conference-Cong (I) Tussle, *Commerce* 140 (3586) March 15, p444-445

Anon, 1980, National Conference Steals the Show, *Commerce* 140 (3578) January 19, p21

Anon, 1980, New Taxes in J&K to Cover Deficit, *Economic Times* March 11, p1, col 5-8

Anon, 1980, Party Differences Take Serious Turn, *Link* 22 (50) July 20, p28-29

Anon, 1980, Rs 320 Crore New Taxes in J&K Budget, *Times of India* March 11, p5, col 1-2

Anon, 1980, Rs 41 Crore to be Earned from Excise, *Commerce* 140 (3587) March 22, p488

Anon, 1980, Regional Imbalanes: Tensions in the Wake of J&K Panels, *Economic Times* March 22, p3, col 2-3

Anon, 1980, SC Mediates in Kashmir Dispute, *Times of India* October 9, p1, col 7-8 +

Anon, 1980, SC to Hear J&K Speaker's Petition, *Times of India* October 8, p1, col 4-5 +

Anon, 1980, Sanjay Factor Absent in Kashmir, *Link* 23 (2) August 24, p12

Anon, 1980, Sheikh's Son-in-Law and His Antics, *Link* 22 (33) March 23, p23

Anon, 1980, Snowfall Cuts Short Campaign, *Link* 22 (22) January 6, p20

Anon, 1980, Three Claimants to the Gaddi of Sheikh Abdullah, *Organiser* 31 (39) February 17, p16

Anon, 1980, Two New Routes to Kashmir, *Times of India* June 15, p1, col 1-3 +

Anon, 1980, Unhealthy Developments, *Link* 22 (39) May 4, p17-18

Anon, 1980, Woes of Zanskaris, *Economic Times* November 11, p3, col 2-4

Anon, 1980-81, (Book Review), *Indian Historical Review* 7 (1-2), July 1980-January 1981, p328-330
Review of the Book:Khan, Ghulam Hassan, 1980, *Freedom Movement in Kashmir, 1931-1940,* Light and Life Pub, xivi 523p

Anon, 1980-81, (Book Review), *Indian Historical Review* 7 (1-2) July

1980-Januray 1981, p328-330
Review of the Book: Yasin, Mohammad and Rafiqi, A. Qaiyum, eds, 1980, *History of Freedom Struggle in Jammu and Kashmir,* Light and Life Pub, New Delhi, x, 256p

Anon, 1980-81, (Book Review), *Quarlerly Review of Historical Studies* 20 (1), p47-48
Review of the Book: Francke, A.H., 1977, *A History of Ladakh,* Sterling, New Delhi, 1, 182p

Anon, 1980-81, Explorations and Excavations, *Indian Archaeology,* p21-25

Anon, 1980-81, Preservation of Monuments: Monuments of National Importance, *Indian Archocology*, p139-140

Anon, 1981, Behind the Income Tax Raids, *Commerce* 142 (3647) May 9, p929

Anon, 1981, (Book Review), *National Herald* (Sunday Herald), November 22, p111, col 3-5
Review of the Book: Kak, B., 1981, *Kashmir: Past and Present,* Seema Pub, Delhi 173p

Anon, 1981, Cartel Operations Flourish in J&K, *Economic Times* October 31, p5, col 7-8

Anon, 1981, Changed Perception, *Economic and Political Weekly* 16(15) April 11, p639

Anon, 1981, Economic Development in Jammu and Kashmir: Centre's Contributions, *Southern Economist* 20 (5) July 1, p19-20, tables

Anon, 1981, Farooq is New NC Chief, *Times of India* August 22, p1, col 6 +

Anon, 1981, Gaps in Farm Credit Policy, *Capital* 187 (4666) July 20, p13 +

Anon, 1981, J&K: New Pulls and Pressure, *Link* 24 (10) October 18, p25

Anon, 1981, J&K Census Figures: Impact of Family Planning Meagre, *Economic Times* May 29, p7, col 3-6

Anon, 1981, J&K State Conference of CPI (M), *Peoples Democracy,* 5(47) November 22, p8 +

Anon, 1981, J&K's Dismal Performance, *Commerce* 143 (3670) October 17, p698-700

Anon, 1981, Jammu and Kashmir Budget: Tax on Professions, *Commerce* 142 (3639) March 14, p607-608

Anon, 1981, Kashmir in for Political Crisis, *Times of India* February 1, p1, col 1-4 +

Anon, 1981, Leh Power Project to Operate by '83, *Times of India* June 5, p5, col 5-6

Anon, 1981, Move Afoot for Merger of NC in Congress(I), *Times of India* October 7, p1, col 1-2 +

Anon, 1981, Muslim Karkhanas of Medieval Kashmir, *Islam and Modern Age* 14(3) August, p214-228

Anon, 1981, None Can Play with Kashmiris' Fate: CM, *Times of India* May 1, p1, col5-6 +

Anon, 1981, Profitabitity May be Hit, *Economic Times* April 16, p7, col 7-8

Anon, 1981, Projection of Conflicting Rate of Growth, *Economic Times* October 15, p6, col 5-8, tables

Anon, 1981-82, (Book Review), *Indian Historical Review* 8(1-2) July 1981-January 1982, p141-142
Review of the Book: Navdou, Jean, 1980, *Buddhist of Kashmir*, Agam Kala Prakashan, xvi, 308p

Anon, 1982, 10 J&K Minister Sworn in, *Times of India* September 15, p1, col 5-6 +

Anon, 1982, Abdullah on Warpath, *Organiser* 34 (6) June 27, p3

Anon, 1982, (Book Review), *Eastern Economist* 78 (1) January 1, p36; *Indian Express* September 26, p6, col 4-8; *Tribune* May 1, p4, col 3-6
Review of the Book: Khan, Ghulam Hassan, 1980 *Freedom Movement in Kashmir, 1931-1940*, Light & Life Pub, xvi 253p

Anon, 1982, (Book Review), *Economic Times* January 3, p6, col 1-4
Review of the Book: Ahluwalia, H.P.S., 1980, *Hermit Kingdom: Ladakh,* Vikas Pub, New Delhi, 186p

Anon, 1982, (Book Review), *Indian Journal of Political Science* 42 (3) July-September, p94-98; *Times of India* January 31, p8, col 5-8
Review of the Book: Puri, Balraj, 1981, *Jammu and Kashmir: Triumph and Tragedy of Indian Federalization,* Sterling, New Delhi, xx, 280p

Anon, 1982, (Book Review), *Journal of the Indian Anthropological Society* 17 (1), March, p89-90
Review of the Book: Basu, Arabinda and Anadi Pal, 1980, *Human Remains from Burzahom*, Anthropological Survey of India, 90p

Anon, 1982, (Book Review), *Link* 24 (30) March 7, p40

Review of the Book: Rashidov Sharaf, 1981, *Kashmir Song*, Navyug Pub, Delhi, 72p

Anon, 1982, (Book Review), *Tribune* May 8, p4, col 3-8
Review of the Book: Bedi, Rajesh and Bedi, Ramesh, 1982, *Ladakh: The Trans-Himalayan Kingdom,* Roli Books International, 192p

Anon, 1982, Communalism on Rise, *Link* 24 (27) February 14, p27-28

Anon, 1982, Farooq Admits Rift in Party, *Times of India* July 14, p1, col 3-4

Anon, 1982, Farooq Swearing in Raises Many Eye Brows, *Times of India* September 10, p7, col 7-8

Anon, 1982, Farooq Sworn in, Gets Health Portfolio, *Times of India* August 24, p1, col 1-2

Anon, 1982, Farooq for Better Centre-State Ties, *Times of India* September 29, p7, col 2-3

Anon, 1982, Food: From One Muddle to Another, *Economic Times* August 17, p3, col 3-6

Anon, 1982, GM Shah Quits, Farooq to Join Cabinet, *Times of India* August 19, p1, col 6-8 +

Anon, 1982, Harmless Sniping, *Economic and Political Weekly* 17 (31) July 31, p1215

Anon, 1982, Important Role of Public Sector Industries in Economy, *Times of India* (Supplement) September 27, pIII, col 1-8

Anon, 1982, Islamic Fundamentalists Call for Jehad against CPI(M), *People's Democracy* 6(31) August1, p4

Anon, 1982, The Isolationist Trait, *Link* 25(9) October 10, p12-13

Anon, 1982, J&K Citizenship Bill: Human Problem Becomes an Issue of Constitution, *Economic Times* May 15, p5, col 7-8

Anon, 1982, J&K Maintains Steady Urbanisation Trend, *Economic Times* September 9, p6, col 5-8

Anon, 1982, J&K Stabbing Secularism, *Link* 24 (37) April 25, p25

Anon, 1982, J&K's Annual Plan in Jeopardy, *Economic Times*, November 13, p5, col 7-8

Anon, 1982, Jammu and Kashmir, *Mysore Economic Review* 67 (3) March, p67

Anon, 1982, Kashmir Bill, *Times of India* May 18, p6, col 6, letter to the editor

Anon, 1982, Kashmir Bill to be Referred to SC, *Times of India* October 5, p1, col 5-7

Anon, 1982, Kashmir Exports May Hit New High, *Economic Times*

October 26, p5, col 7-8

Anon, 1982, Lack of Initiative in Promoting Industrial Units, *Times of India* (Supplement) September 27, pV, col 4-8

Anon, 1982, Legal Opinion Against Kashmir Bill: PM, *Times of India* October 4, p1, col 7-8

Anon, 1982, The New Team Gamble, *Link* 25(7) September 26, p30-31

Anon, 1982, No Stay of Operation of Resettlement Act, *Times of India* October 13, p1, col 7-8

Anon, 1982, Pay Commision: J&K Staff Dismayed, *Economic Times* April 12, p4, col 6-8

Anon, 1982, Putting the Clock Back, *Link* 24(45) June 20, p10-12

Anon, 1982, Resettlement Bill Infirm Says Governor, *Times of India* September 24, p1, col 2-3 +

Anon, 1982, Secessionist Forces at Work in J&K, *People's Democracy* 6(14) April 4, p3 +

Anon, 1982, Sheikh Creates Four More Muslim Majority Districts, *Onganiser* 34 (6) June 27, p10

Anon, 1982, Sheikh Questions Pak Annexation of 3 Areas, *Times of India* May 9, p1, col 4-5

Anon, 1982, Sheikh Stirring up Criris *Link* 24(45) June 20, p9

Anon, 1982, Signals from Kashmir, *Mainstneam* 22(37) May 15, p3-4

Anon, 1982, Situation Disquieting, *Commerce* 145(3714) August 14, p245-247, tables

Anon, 1982, Six J&K MLAs Suspended, *Times of India* March 30, p1, col 2-4

Anon, 1982, Study Shows Good Prospects for J&K Industrialisation, *Economic Times* March 27, p5, col 7-8

Anon, 1982, Television Still an Urban Phenomenon, *Times of India* (Supplement) September 27, pVI, col 1-5

Anon, 1982, Welcoming the Prodigals, *Economic and Political Weekly* 17(24) June 12, p966

Anon, 1983, 60 p.c. Turnout in J&K Poll, *Times of India*, June 6, p1, col 2-4

Anon, 1983, Ascending the Mountains, *Indian Railways* 28(11), April, p93-94

Anon, 1983, Big Shortfall in J&K Job Creation Plan, *Economic Times* November 1, p3, col 1-3

Anon, 1983, (Book Review), *Economic and Political Weekly*, 18(29) July 16, p1277-1279; *Indian Express*, Februray 2, p6, col 5-7,

Review of the Book: Puri, Balraj, 1982, *Jammu and Kashmir: Triumph and Tragedy of India Federalisation*, Sterling, New Delhi, x, 280p

Anon, 1983, (Book Review), *Economic Times*, August 7, p6, col 7-8
Review of the Book: Khan, Ghulam Hassan, 1980, *Freedom Movement in Kashmir, 1931-1940*, Light and Life Pub, New Delhi, xiv, 523p

Anon, 1983, (Book Review) *Hindustan Times* (Magazine), December 4, pIV, col 6-8
Review of the Book:Raghubir Singh, *Kashmir : A Garden of the Himalayas*, Perennial Press, Hong Kong, 99p

Anon, 1983, (Book Review) *Indian and Foreign Review* 20 (22), September 1, p28; *Link* 25 (52) August 7, p39: *Tribune,* September 3, p4, col 3-5
Review of the Book: Dhar, Somnath, 1982, *Jammu and Kashmir*, National Book Trust, New Delhi 200p

Anon, 1983, (Book Review), *Mysore Economic Review,* 68(2) Februray, p21-22
Review of the Book: Awasty, Indira, 1983, *Women in India: A Socio-Economic Profile of Jammu Women*, B.R. Pub, New Delhi

Anon, 1983, Confrontation in Kashmir, *Janata* 38(26), September 25, p3-5

Anon, 1983, Cong-I Group in J&K House Suspended, *Times of India*, July 24, p1, col 2-4

Anon, 1983, Cong (I) Sweep in Jammu Region: NC on Winning Spree in Kashmir Valley, *Times of India*, June 7, p1, col 6-8 +

Anon, 1983, Destabilising Game, *Economic and Political Weekly* 18(31), July 30, p1338

Anon, 1983, Development Priorities in Jammu and Kashmir, *Economic Times*, Februray 21, p4, col 1-3 +

Anon, 1983, Development Priorities not yet Clear, *Economic Times*, March 17, p7, col 7-8

Anon, 1983, Doda Poll Result Invalidated, *Times of India*, June 23, p1, col 8 +

Anon, 1983, An Effective Political Force, *Link* 26(11), October 23, p13

Anon, 1983, Election with High Stakes, *Link* 25(42), May 29, p10-11

Anon, 1983, Electioneering yet to Gain Monentum, *Times of India*, May 21, p9, col 1-2

Anon, 1983, Farooq-Mir Qasim Plan for NC-Cong(I) Alliance in

J&K, *Organiser* 34(44), March 20, p6

Anon, 1983, J&K: Farooq to Face Strong Opposition, *Link* 25(45), June 19, p13-14

Anon, 1983, J&K: Vision of an Ugly Culture, *Link* 25(46), June 26, p3

Anon, 1983, J&K Govt Rapped for Suppressing Congress-I, *Times of India* December 29, p1, col 1-2 +

Anon, 1983, Kashmir Hops Growers Face Severe Crisis, *Economic Times* Februray 12, p7, col 7-8

Anon, 1983, Kashmir Poll: Warning Signals, *Secular Democracy*, June, p1-2 +

Anon, 1983, Mineral Deposits of J&K, *Economic Times*, Februray 21, p5, col 4-8 +

Anon, 1983, Mirza Sahiban Tragedy being Re-enacted in J&K, *Organiser* 35(28) November 27, p6

Anon, 1983, Mrs Gandhi and Farooq Are Both Playing with Fire, *Organiser* 35(2), May 29, p4

Anon, 1983, A New Thrust in Kashmir Politics, *Radical Humanist* 48(4), July, p3-6

Anon, 1983, Phenomenon Named 'Double Farooq', *Link* 25(42), May 29, p13-14

Anon, 1983, Plea for Probe into J&K Election Reporting, *Times of India*, July 24, p5, col 2-5

Anon, 1983, Poll Prospects in Kashmir: A Battle of the Giants, *Illustrated Weekly of India* 104(19) June 5, p32-33

Anon, 1983, Qureshi, Others Hurt in Stone-Throwing: Srinagar PCC(I) Office Set Ablaze by Mob. *Times of India* May 20, p1, col 2-4 +

Anon, 1983, Rs 270 cr Outlay for J&K Plan Proposed, *Economic Times*, November 22, p3, col 4-6

Anon, 1983, Some Parties Vitiating J&K Poll Drive: PM, *Times of India*, May 22, p1, col 1-3 +

Anon, 1983, Teargas, Lathi Charge on Jammu Protester, *Times of India*, November 8, p1, col 1-3

Anon, 1983, Tourism in Kashmir, *Times of India*, Februray 21, p9, col 1-4

Anon, 1984, 13 J&K MLAs Disqualified, *Times of India* July 31, p1, col 1-3 +

Anon, 1984, 19 Parties Condemn J&K Govt Dismissal, *People's Democracy* 8(29) July 15, p1-2

Anon, 1984, Another Nerve Centre of Destabilisation Falls, *Link* 26(49) July 15, p12-14

Anon, 1984, Another Stroke for Hindu Vote, *Janata* 39(14) July 15, p1-3

Anon, 1984, A Battle of the Alliances, *Economic Times*, December 22, p3, col 1-4

Anon, 1984, (Book Review), *Economic and Political Weekly* 19(10), March 10, p420-421
Review of the Book: Khan, Mohammad Ishaq, 1983, *Perspectives on Kashmir: Historical Dimensions,* Gulshan Pub, Srinagar, 173p

Anon, 1984, (Book Review), *Financial Express* March 25, p5, col 5-6; *Indian Expess* February5, p6, col 1-2
Review of the Book: Raghubir Singh, n.d., *Kashmir: A Garden of the Himalayas*, Perennial Press, Hongkong, 99p

Anon, 1984, (Book Review), *Hindustan Times* (Magazine), Februray 19, p4, col 6-8,
Review of the Book: Bhupinder Singh, *Indo-Pak Conflicts over Kashmir*, B.C. Pub, Patiala, 22p

Anon, 1984, (Book Review), *India Quartely* 40(2), April-June, p244-247
Review of the Book: Puri, Balraj, 1981, *Jammu and Kashmir: Triumph and Tragedy of India Federalisation*, Sterling, New Delhi, x, 280p

Anon, 1984, (Book Review), *Indian Journal of Political Science* July 6-7, p108-110
Review of the Book: Puri, Balraj, 1983, *Simmering Volcano: Study of Jammu's Relations with Kashmir*, Sterling, New Delhi, x, 144p

Anon, 1984, (Book Review), *Times of India*, May 6, p8, col 1-4,
Review of the Book: Raghubir Singh, n.d, *Kashmir: Garden of the Himalayas*, Perennial Press, Hong Kong, 99p

Anon, 1984, (Book Review), *Tribune* Janurary 21, p4, col 4-8,
Review of the Book: Kapur, M.L., 1986, *Kingdom of Kashmir : A Complete History of Kashmir from Earliest Times to 1586 AD*, Kashmir History Publications, Jammu, 402p

Anon, 1984, A Chargesheet against Farooq Abdullah, *Link* 26(49) July 8, p17-20

Anon, 1984, Congress Blames It on Farooq's Policy, *Times of India* Februray 8, p9, col 7-8

Anon, 1984, Congress on Good Wicket at Udhampur, *Times of*

India, December 15, p11, col 1-2

Anon, 1984, Curb Secessionists, Farooq told, *Times of India* Januray 10, p1, col 1-2 +

Anon, 1984, Farooq Alleges Abduction, Intimidation, *Times of India* July 30, p1, col 7-8

Anon, 1984, Farooq Goes Underground, *Times of India* July 14, p1, col 7-8

Anon, 1984, Farooq Sacked for "Pro-Pak Attitude", *Times of India* July 29, p1, col 4-6 +

Anon, 1984, Farooq Wins Trust Vote, *Times of India* Januray 28, p1, col 7-8 +

Anon, 1984, Farooq's Politics of Convenience, *Link* 26(50) July 15, p24

Anon, 1984, GM Shah Wins Vote of Confidence, Ittoo Removed, *Times of India* August 1, p1, col 1-3 +

Anon, 1984, Governor, Farooq Summoned by PM, *Times of India* January 25, p1, col 2-4

Anon, 1984, The High-Drama: Some Tense Moments, *Link* 26(50) July 15, p26-27

Anon, 1984, High Intrigues, Menacing Dimensions, *Link* 26(26) Februray 5, p10-11

Anon, 1984, Hounded Out, *Economic and Political Weekly* 19(27) July 7, p1009

Anon, 1984, Jagmohan's Plan to Replace Farooq with Sister Khalida *Organiser* 36(2) May 27, p3

Anon, 1984, The Jammu and Kashmir Crisis,*Monthly Commentary on Indian Economic Conditions* 25(11) June, p3-4

Anon, 1984, Kashmir: On the Brink, *Janata* 38(40) Januray 29, p2-3

Anon, 1984, NC (F) Candidates Won by Big Margins, *Times of India* December 31, p9, col 6-7

Anon, 1984, NC(F) Has Edge in Srinagar, *Times of India* December 16, p11, col 2-4

Anon, 1984, NC(F) Stronger in Baramulla, *Times of India* December 17, p5, col 2-3

Anon, 1984, NC's White Paper: Truth Will Prevail, *New Age* 32(35) August 26, p11

Anon, 1981, Muslim Karkhanas of Medieval Kashmir, *Islam and Modern Age* 14(3) August, 214-228p

Anon, 1984, New Levies in J&K to Net Rs 1.25Crs, *Economic Times* March 6, p1, col 7-8 +

Anon, 1984, A New Phase in J&K Politics? *Link* 26(24) Januray 22, p9

Anon, 1984, President Urged to Intervene in J&K, *Times of India* Januray 24, p9, col 7-8

Anon, 1984, Rs 2,206 Cr J&K Plan Outlay, *Economic Times* December 19, p1, col 5-8

Anon, 1984, Respite for Farooq, *Times of India* January 26, p1, col 1-3+

Anon, 1984, Ruined beyond Redemption, *Link* 26(43) June 3, 15-16p

Anon, 1984, Set-back to J&K Tourist Inflow: State Loses Rs 81 Crores, *Economic Times* September 4, p1, col 2-5

Anon, 1984, The Shah of Kashmir, *Times of India*(Sunday Review) August 19, p1, col 3-6+

Anon, 1984, Shah Sworn in as Farooq is Dismissed: 15 Member Ministry Takes over as 12 NC MLAs Change Sides, *Times of India* July 3, p1, col 1-3+

Anon, 1984, Shah Yet to Find His Feet, *Times of India* October 6, p5, col 1-4

Anon, 1984, Situation in J&K: Mrs Gandhi Hints at Strong Action, *Times of India*, Januray 5 p1, col 2-4+

Anon, 1984, Three Parties Vie for 5 Seats, *Times of India*, December 23, p12, col 3-5

Anon, 1984, Tiger at Bay, *Times of India* (Sunday Review) July 8, p1, col 4-5+

Anon, 1984, Tug of War between NC (Farooq), Congress, *Times of India*, December 18, p13, col 1-4

Anon, 1984, Waiting for Action in J&K, *Organiser* 36(8) July 8, p1+

Anon, 1984, Wazir Commission Recommends More Dists for J&K, *Economic Times*, April 21, p9, col 1-8

Anon, 1984, Why Coup? *Janata* 39(14) July 15, p3

Anon, 1984, A Willing Governor, *Economic and Political Weekly* 19(13) March 31, p534

Anon, 1985, (Book Review), *Hindustan Times* (Magazine) July 21, p8, col 1-5,
Review of the Book: Abdullah, Farooq, 1985, *My Dismissal* Vikas Pub, New Delhi, 90p

Anon, 1985, (Book Review) *Indian Express* (Magazine), March 3, p4, col 1-4,
Review of the Book: Akbar, M.J., 1985 *The Seige Within, Challenges to a Nation's Unity*? Penguin Books, Middlesex

Anon, 1985, (Book Review), *National Herald*, March 31, p7, col 2-5, Review of the Book: Ahmad, S.Maqbul and Bano, Raja, 1984, *Historical Geography of Kashmir*, Ariana Pub House, 231p

Anon, 1985, Cabinet Report Indicts Farooq, *Times of India*, January 11, p1, col 7-8 +

Anon, 1985, Industrial Estates: Jammu is Second Largest, *Economic Times* July 7, p1, col 2-5

Anon, 1985, Is Farooq Guilty? *Illustrated Weekly of India* 105(44) March 10, p8-9

Anon, 1985, Jammu and Kashmir: Accent on Development, *National Herald*, November 3, p5, col 1-4

Anon, 1985, NC (K) Legislators' Meeting Backs Shah, *Times of India* October 4, p9, col 1-2

Anon, 1985, Pakistani Plot to Set up 'People's Republic of Kashmir, *Organiser* 37(20), September 29, p1-2

Anon, 1985, Power Crisis Haunts J&K, *Economic Times*, May 3, p1, col 6-7 +

Anon, 1985, Religious Issues Will Determine Ladakh Poll, *Times of India*, April 21, p16, col 3-5

Anon, 1985, Second J&K State Conference, *People's Democracy* 9(48), December 1, p12

Anon, 1986, Article 370 Must Go! *Organiser* 37(45), March 23, p1 +

Anon, 1986, (Book Review), *Indian Express* (Magazine) January 5, p5, col 6-8,
Review of the Book: Younghusband, Francis, 1986, *The Heart of a Continent*, Oxford University Press

Anon, 1986, (Book Review), *India Quarterly,* 42(4) October-December, p463-466
Review of the Book: Ray, Hemen, 1985, *How Moscow Sees Kashmir*, Jaico, Bombay, 100p

Anon, 1986, (Book Review), *India Quarterly* 42(2), April-June, p213-214
Review of the Book: Teng, M.K., 1985, *State Government and Politics: Jammu and Kashmir*, Sterling, New Delhi, 167p

Anon, 1988, (Book Review) *Times of India*, July 31, p 4, col 1-8
Review of the Book: Sender, Hennetta M., *The Kashmiri Pandits: A Study of Cultural Choice in North Inida*, Oxford University Press, Oxford, 358p, illustrations

Anon, 1986, Jamaat-e-Islami Poisoning Atmosphere, *New Age* 34(22), June 1, p 1 +

Anon, 1986, Kashmir Problem in Retrospect: When Dr Shyama Prasad Mookerjee Cornered Nehru on Article 370, *Organiser* 37(52), May 11, p6

Anon, 1986, NC (K) Facing Political Void, *Times of India* March 22, p4, col 1-2

Anon, 1986, Pak Aid to Terrorists, *Deccan Chronicle*, February 8, p 6

Anon, 1986, A Preacher in Bhindranwale Mould, *Times of India*, July 12, p1, col 2-5 +

Anon, 1986, Reincarnation of the Kashmir Accord, *Link* 29 (15), November 16, p 10-12

Anon, 1986, Scrap Article 370 and Bill for Resettlement of Pakistanis, *Organiser* 37 (45), March 23, p5

Anon, 1986, When Jagmohan Threatened to Resign, *Organiser* 37(46), March 30, p1 +

Anon, 1986, When Nehru Regretted Communal Rumour Mongering against Maharaja Bhagwan Singh, *Organiser* 37 (46) March 30, p 11

Anon, 1987, Blessed with Beauty in Bounty, *Hindu*, April 26, p 17, col 13 +

Anon, 1987, (Book Review), *Hindustan Times* (Magazine), November 1, p5, col 1-6
Review of the Book: Bamzai, P.N.K., n.d., *Socio-Economic History of Kashmir*, Metropolitan, New Delhi, 392 p

Anon, 1987, (Book Review), *Hindustan Times* (Magazine) May 24, p8, col 5-6; *Indian Express* (Magazine) October 4, p5, col 5-8
Review of the Book: Saraf, D.N., n.d., Arts and *Crafts of Jammu and Kashmir*, Abhinav Pub, New Delhi, 290p

Anon, 1987, (Book Review), *Indian Horizons* 36 (3-4), p55-55
Review of the Book: Dhar, Somnath, n.d., *Jammu and Kashmir Folklore*, Marwah Pub, 196 p

Anon, 1987, (Book Review), *Tribune* Feburary 22, p11, col 6-8
Review of the Book: Dogra, Ramesh Chander, n.d., *Jammu and Kashmir: A Select and Annotated Bibliography,* Ajanta Pub, New Delhi, viii, 417p

Anon, 1987, CPI (M) Appeal to the Jammu and Kashmir Electroate, *People's Democracy* 11(10) March 87, p 12

Anon, 1987, A Challenge to the Fundamentalists, *Link* 29 (33), March 22, p 15-16

Anon, 1987, Cooperative Credit Structure in J & K, *Co-operators Bulletin*, 30 (10), October, p 26-32

Anon, 1987, Erosion behind Apparent Alliance Vicotry, *Link* 29 (35) April 5, p 12-13

Anon, 1987, Farooq Scores over Congress, *Link* 29 (31), March 8, p6-7

Anon, 1987, Gujjar Vote a dominant factor, *Times of India* March 13, p 4, col 1-4

Anon, 1987, The Jammu and Kashmir Assembly Election, *Monthly Commentary on Indian Economic Conditions* 28(8) March, p 4-8

Anon, 1987, Wall Paintings from Alchl Monastery : Ladakh, *Rooka-Lekha* 59 (1-2) August, p 80-81

Anon, 1987, Winter of Discontent, *Hindu*, November 26, p 18, col 1-5

Anon, 1988, Achievement of Cooperative Department of Rajouri, *Co-operators Bulletin*, 31(8) August, p 21-22

Anon, 1988, (Book Review), *Economic and Political Weekly*, 23 (19), May 7, p 953-954,
Review of the Book: Zutshi, U.K., 1986, *Emergence of Political Awaking in Kashmir*, Manohar Pub, New Delhi, 252p

Anon, 1988, (Book Review), *Economic Times* November 27, p 5, col 19-22
Review of the Book: Khullar, Rupinder, 1988, *Kashmir: The Pageant of the Seasons*, Media Transasia Ltd, 114p

Anon, 1988, (Book Review), *Financial Express*, October 2, p5, col 6-8
Review of the Book: Raina, N.N., 1988, *Kashmir Politics and Imperialist Manoeuvres, 1842-1980,* Patriot Pub, New Delhi, vii, 276p

Anon, 1988, (Book Review), *Indian Express* (Magazine) May 29, p 5, col 1-4,
Review of the Book: Prasad, S.N and Dharam Pal, n.d. *History of Operation in Jammu and Kashmir (1947-1948)*, Controller of Publications, Government of Iinda, Delhi, 3 vols

Anon, 1988, (Book Review), *Sunday Statesman* (Misc), June 5, p 12, col 3-5
Review of the Book: Madhok, Balraj, 1988, *Jammu and Kashmir and Ladakh: Problem and Solution*, Reliance, New Delhi, xviii, 83p

Anon, 1988, (Book Review), *Hindustan Times,* (Magazine) January 31, p8, col 1-8; *Times of India* (Sunday Review), July 31, p 4, col 1-8
Review of the Book: Pant, Kusum, 1987, *The Kashmiri Pandits: Story of Community in Exile in the 19th and 20th Centuries*,

Allied, Bombay, 200p

Anon, 1988, (Book Review), *Tribune* (Sunday Magazine) November 13, p2, col 4-8

Review of the Book: Vas, E.A., 1988, *Without Baggage*, Natraj Pub, Dehradun, 173p

Anon, 1988, Farooq Lashes out at Centre, *Times of India* November 4, p1, col 4-5 +

Anon, 1988, Jammu and Kashmir Marches ahead, *Co-operators Bulletin* 31(4), April, p 17-21

Anon, 1988, The Jammu Central Cooperative Bank Marches ahead, *Co-operators Bulletin* 31(1), January, p 62-74

Anon, 1988, Kashmir Riots, *Commerce* 157 (4035) October 3, p 21-22

Anon, 1988, Role of Cooperative in Horticulture Planning and Marketing in J&K, *Co-operators Bulletin* 31(1) January, p75-76

Anon, 1989, 8 Congress Men Join Farooq Cabinet: Qureshi to Head New PCC, *Times of India*, May 1, p 1, col 1-3 +

Anon, 1989, (Book Review), *Indian Express* (Magazine) January 15, p5, col 1-4

Review of the Bool: Sender, Hennetta M., 1988, *The Kashmiri Pandits: A Study of Cultural Choice*, Oxford University Press

Anon, 1989, (Book Review), *Patriot*, January 15, p 4, col 1-2; January 22, p 4, col 1-2; *Tribune* January 8, p 2, col 1-3

Review of the Book: Raina, N.N., 1988, *Kashmir Politics and Imperialist Manoeuvers 1846-1980*, Patriot Pub, New Delhi, xii, 276 p

Anon, 1989, (Book Review), *Times of India* (Sunday Review) February 12, p 2, col 1-5

Review of the Book: Keenam, Brigid, 1989, *Travels in Kashmir: A Popular History of Its People*, Oxford University Press, xi, 226 p, Illustrations

Anon, 1989, Coalition: A Colossal Failure, *Line* 31(41) May 31, p30-31

Anon, 1989, Professionalizing Public Relations, *Link* 31 (39), May 7, p 22-23

Anon, 1989, The Valley Defies the Republic, *Economic Times*, September 3, p-3, col 1-6

Anon, 1989, Why Kashmir is Burning, *Link* 31 (37), April 23, p 4-6

Anon, 1989-91, (Book Review), *Journal of the Indian Society of Oriental Art* (New Series), 18-19, p 109-110

Review of the Book: Pal, Pratapaditya, ed, 1989, *Art and*

Architecture of Ancient Kashmir, Marg Pub, Bombay

Anon, 1990, One Step Closer to War (Killing of M. Farooq Triggers Kashmir Fervor), *Newsweek*, 115, June 4, p30, illustrations

Anon, 1991, *Genocide of Hindus in Kashmir*, J.K. Sahayata Samiti; Suruchi Prakashan, New Delhi

Anon, 1992, (Book Review), *USI Journal* 122 (508) April-June, p276-277
Review of the Book: Akbar, M.J., 1991, *Kashmir: Behind the Vale,* Penguin Books/Viking, New Delhi, 232 p

Anon, 1992, Brief Note on the Working of the Jammu and Kashmir Cooperative Central Land Development Bank Limited, Srinagar, *Co-operator's Bulletin* 35(5) May, p 13-18, tables

Anon, 1992, Human Rights Situation in the Kashmir Valley, *Other Side*, 101, October, p 31-39

Anon, 1992, Pro-Pak Terrorists Tightening Hold over Doda, Rajaori and Poonch Districts of Jammu Region, *Organiser* 44(5) September 6, p5

Anon, 1992, Sericulture in Kashmir, *Social Welfare* 39(2) May, p 15

Anon, 1993, (Book Review), *Book Review* 17(1) January, p8
Review of the Book: Lamb, Alastair, 1991, *Kashmir: A Disputed Legacy, 1846-1990*, Oxford Books, London, 368p

Anon, 1993, (Book Review), *Book Review* 17(1) January, p11
Review of the Book: Kadian, Rajesh, 1992, *The Kashmir Tangle: Issues and Options*, Vision Books, New Delhi, 200p

Anon, 1993, (Book Review), *Economic Times* September 5, p13, col 2-6
Review of the Book: Shali, S.K., 1993, *Kashmir: History and Anchaeology through the Ages*, Indus Pub, New Delhi, 289p

Anon, 1993, (Book Review), *Economic Times*, October, pII, col 2-6
Review od the Book: Abdullah, Sheikh Mohammad, 1993, *Flames of the Chinar: An Autobiography*, abridged and tr from Urdu by Khuswant singh, Viking, New Delhi, 186 p

Anon, 1993, I Am Nothing: Torture of Kashmiri Student M. Sultan by India's Border Security Forces, *Scholastic Update* (Teachers' Edition) 126, December 3, p17-19, illustrations

Anon, 1993, Kashmir Integral Part of India, *National Herald* May 10

Anon, 1993, Piloting a Course for Kashmir, *Economic Times* June 6, p6, col 3-7

Anon, 1993, Setback to Pak Stand on Kashmir, *National Herald* May1

Anon, 1993, Solve Kashmir Tangle through Talks, *Patriot* May 5

Ansari, Abdul Aziz, 1988, The Silk Weaving Industry in Kashmir, *Co-operators Bulletin* 31(4), April, p 12-13+

Appadorai, 1967, Chinese Aggression and India: An Introductory Eassay, *International Studies* 5(1-2), July, p 3-18

Ara, Tabasum and Tantray, A.M., 1988, Agriculture and Women, *Co-operators Bulletin*, 31(7), July, p 22-25, tables

Armstrong, Rath Gallup, 1964, *Sisters under the Sari,* Iowa State University Press, p216-340

Arora, R.C., 1933, *New Guide to Kashmir: With Its History, Lakes, Places of Interest*, R.C.Arora, Calcutta, 97p, appendix, maps, plates

Arora, R.C., 1938, *Kashmir: The Land of Celestial Charm*, 2nd edn, Unique Literature Publishing House, Aligarh

Arora R.C., 1940, *In the Land of Kashmir with Their History, Places of Interest, Routes, Lakes and Exhaustive Information for the Guidance of Visitors to Kashmir, Ladakh, Gilgit, Astor, Skardu, etc.*, C.M.S. Press, Calcutta, 303p, map, plates

Asghar Khan, M.
see Khan, M. Asghar

Ashok Dilwali
see Dilwali, Ashok

Aslam, Mohammed
see, Mohammed Aslam

Atal, Hiralal, 1972, *Nehru's Emissary to Kashmir (October 1947)*, Army Educational Stores, New Delhi, v, 183p

Atri, S.K., 1931, *Kashmir Guide*, 2nd edn, Kashmir Book Depot, 94p

Attar Chand, 1994, *Islamic Nation and Kashmir Problem*, Raj Publication, Delhi, 301p

Aubertin, J.J., 1892, *Wanderings and Wondering: India, Burma, Kashmir, Ceylon, Singapore, etc,* Kegan Paul, London, p136-186

Ashok Rudra
see Rudra, Ashok

Aslam, Mohammed
see Mohammed Aslam

Awasty, Indira, 1983, *Rural Women in India: A Socio-Economic Profile of Jammu Women*, B.R. Pub, New Delhi

Ayesha Jalal
see Jalal, Ayesha

Ayoob, Mohammed

see Mohammed Ayoob

Ayub Khan, M.
see Khan, Muhammad Ayub

Ayyar, S.R. Narayana
see Narayana Ayyar, S.R.

Azad, Abdul Kalam, 1959, *India Wins Freedom,* New Delhi

Aziz, M.A., 1966, *Struggle for the Liberation of Kashmir,* Revolutionary Council of the People of J&K, Lahore, 8p

Aziz, Mir Abdul, 1967, Abdullah's Birthday in Jail, *Morning News* December 5

Azizuddin S.M. Husain
see Husain, Azizuddin S.M.

Bacha, G.Q., 1988, Cooperative Movement in Jammu and Kashmir, *Co-operator Bulletin* 31 (11) January, p41-52

Bahl, M., n.d., *Whither Kashmir*, New Delhi

Bahl, Mohinder, n.d., *I Was on the Kashmir Front*, New Delhi

Bakaya, N.L., 1969, *Holidaying and Trekking in Kashmir*, Nawin Press, New Delhi, 150p

Bakaya, N.L., 1957, 'Wanderings in the Happy Valley, *KT* 2(6) July-August, p21-24, illustrations

Bakaya, N.L., 1961, From the Lidder Valley into the Sindh Valley, *KT* 5(3) Sepetember, p10-12

Bakhsi
see Bakshi

Bakshi, G.A., 1972, Tourism in Kashmir : New Look, *Link* 14 (46) June 25, p37

Bakshi G.A. and Kilam, K.K., 1979, *Jammu and Kashmir, 1975-79*, Directorate of Information, Government of Jammu and Kashmir, Srinagar, 138p

Bakshi, Ghulam Mohammed, 1964, I Am Not Going to Talk to Shastriji, or Nandaji or Any Ji : Bakshi, *Organiser* 18 (8) October 5, p1 +

Bakshi, S.P., 1956, Tour of the Lolab Valley, *Kashmir* 6(4) April, p95-97

Bakshi, Tasneem, 1984, The Political Ideas of Mehjoor, *Indian Literature* 27 (1) January-February, p96-108

Bamzai, P.N.K., n.d., *Socio-Economic History of Kashmir*, Metropolitan, New Delhi, 392p

Bamzai, P.N.K., 1966, *Kashmir and Power Politics : From Lake Success to Tashkent*, Metropolitan, Delhi, 314p

Bamzai, P.N.K., 1971, Kashmiri Muslims, *Illustrated Weekly of India* 92 (47) November 21, p40-45, illustrations

Bamzai, P.N.K., 1972, *History of Kashmir : Political, Social, Cultural from the Earliest Times to the Present Day*, 2nd edn, Metropolitan, Delhi, xxii, 866p

Bamzai, P.N.K., 1975, *Jammu and Kashmir*, Publications Division, Government of India, New Delhi, 62p,

Bamzai, P.N.K., 1980, *Kashmir and Central Asia*, Light and Life Pub, New Delhi, viii, 125p

Bamzai, P.N.K., 1994, Cultural and Political History of Kashmir, M.D. Pub, New Delhi, 882p, 3vols

Banerji, Adris, 1958, Kashmir in Jahangir's Memoirs, *Kashmir* 8(7) July, p187-188, illustrations

Banerji, Shibdas, 1951, Kashmir, U.N. and Power, *Organiser* 5 (20) December 31, 11p

Banka Behari Das
 see Das, Banka Behari

Bano, Hanifa, 1986, Economic Exploitation by Way of Agriculture in Dal Lake (Srinagar), *Annals of the National Association of Geographers, India* 6 (1) June, p38-42

Bano, Razia, 1991, *History of Kashmir*, Bhavana Prakashan, Delhi, xv, 107p

Bano, Razia, *jt author*
 see Ahmad, S. Maqbul and Bano, Razia

Bargotra
 see also Anon, 1969, Bargotra Joins Issue with C.R.

Barry, N., 1966, Going Places, Finding Thing in Kashmir, *House & Gardens* October, p54-56

Bashir Akhtar
 see Akhtar, Bashir

Basu, Arabinda and Anadi Pal, 1980, *Human Remains from Burzahom*, Anthropological Survey of India, 90p

Bates, Charles Ellison, comp, 1980, *Gazetteer of Kashmir and the Badrewar, Jammu, Naoshgn, Punch and the Valley of the Kishen Ganga*, Light and Life Pub, New Delhi, ii, 560p, reprint

Bauer Paul, ed, 1938, *Himalayan Guest : The German Expeditions to Siniolchum and Nanga Parbat*, Tr From German by E.C. Hall, 150p, map

Bawa Satinder Singh, 1975, *The Jammu Fox : A Biography of Maharaja Gulab Singh of Kashmir (1792-1857)*, Southern

University Press

Bayley, Viloa, 1956, *Kashmir Adventure*, J.M.Dent, London, 151p

Bazaz, Prem Nath, 1941, *Inside Kashmir*, Kashmir Pub Co, Srinagar, 412p

Bazaz, Prem Nath, 1959, Can India Save Tibet? *RH* August 16

Bazaz, Prem Nath, 1964, *Natural Environments, Political Vicissitudes and People in Kashmir*, Pamposh Pub, New Delhi, 88p

Bazaz, Prem Nath, 1965, Kashmir, *Swarajya* 10 (10) September 4, p29-31

Bazaz, Prem Nath 1967, *Kashmir in Crucible*, Pamposh Pub, New Delhi, 318p

Bazaz, Prem Nath 1971, The Unsolved Problem of Kashmir, *Swarajya* 15 (32) February 6, p2-3

Bazaz, Prem Nath 1973, Influence of Shaivism on Nund Rishi, *Indian Literature* 16 (1-2) January-June, p256-257

Bazaz, Prem Nath 1978, He Wrote History in Verse, *Times of India* July 16, p8, col 2-6

Bazaz Malik, Gauri, 1986, February Riots in Jammu and Kashmir and Their Aftermath, *Radical Humanist* 50 (15) August, p19-26

Bazaz Malik, Gauri, 1988, The Kashmir Imbroglio : A Shiya-Suni Conflict, *Radical Humanist* 52 (7) October, p19-22

Bedi, Rahul, 1993, Kashmir : Ground Realities, *Economic Times* March 6, p8, col 3-8

Bedi, Rajesh, *jt author*
see Bedi, Ramesh and Bedi, Rajesh

Bedi, Ramesh and Bedi, Rajesh, 1982, *Ladakh : The Trans-Himalayan Kingdom*, Roli Bks International, New Delhi, 192p

Beg, 1975, Article 370 to Be Made Permanent : Beg, *Times of India* February 13, p1, col 1-3

Beg, 1974, Concrete Stage in Kashmir Talks : Beg, *Times of India* July 4, p1, col 6-7

Beg, Afzal
see Beg, Mirza Afzal

Beg, Arif, n.d, *Muslim Dilemma in India*

Beg, Aziz, 1957, *Captive Kashmir*, Allied Business Corporation, Lahore, 202p

Beg Aziz, 1966, *Pakistan Faces India*, Babur and Amer Publications, Lahore, 280p, map

Beg Aziz, 1966, *Seventeen September Days*, Lahore

Beg Aziz, 1969, The *Wailing Vale : The Blood Stained Story of*

Kashmir, Babur and Amer Publications, Lahore, 376p, bibliography, illustrations

Beg, Mohammad Mirza Afzal, 1976, Land Reforms in Jammu and Kashmir, *Mainstream* (Annual Number) 15 (1-6), p27-29

Beg, Mirza Mohammad Afzal, 1978, Beg Says He Can Topple Sheikh Govt, *Times of India* October 17, p1, col 7-8

Begum Zafar Ali
see Ali, Begum Zafar

Bellew, H.W., 1875, *Kashmir and Kashgar : A Narrative of the Journey of the Embassy to Kashgar in 1873-74*, Trubner, London, reprint, 1989, Asian Educ Services

Berindranath, 1968, Azad Kashmir : Problems and Perspectives, *Mainstream* (Annual Number) 7 (1-3), p55-58

Berindranath, 1968, Pakistan-Occupied Kashmir, *Indian and Foreign Review* 5(22) September 1, p18-19

Berindranath Dewan, 1966, *The War with Pakistan*, Asia Press, New Delhi

Berindranath Dewan, 1969, Restraiant on Kashmir : Anti Soviet Sentiment, *Tribune* (Ambala), February 15

Bernier, Francois, 1914, *Travels in India AD 1656-1668: Containing Series of Letters Concerning His Jounmey*, tr by Archibald Constable, 2nd edn, Oxford University Press, p391-431, originally published 1891

Beveridge, Henry, 1888, Father Jerome Xavier, *JASB* 7(1), p37-39

Bhagat, P.S., 1974, *The Sheild and the Sword,* Vikas Pub, Delhi

Bhagwan Singh, 1969, What is Wrong with the People of Jammu? *Organiser* 22 (36) April 19, p6 +

Bhagwan Singh, 1974, P.M.'s Partisan Compulsions for Dialogue with the Anti-National Sheikh, *Organiser* 28 (15) October 23, p7 +

Bhagwan Singh, 1975, *Political Conspiracies of Kashmir*, Light and Life Pub, 158p

Bhan, Jai Kishori, 1988, Twenty Seven Years ago Cooperative Organisation of Women Spinners, *Co-operators Bulletin* 31 (7) July, p11-13

Bhan, Kiran Sumbali and Puri, Kiran, 1985, A Study of Values of New Entrants to Police Force, *Police Research and Development Quarterly*, 11, p5-7

Bhan, Susheela, et al, comps, 1989, *Terrorism : An Annotated Bibliography*, Concept Publishing Company, New Delhi, 338p,

Concepts in Communication Informatics and Librarianship, 9

Bharat Singh, 1963-64, Ancient Kashmir upto 940 AD : Political and Cultural, *Quarterly Review of Historical Studies* 3 (1-2), p88-93

Bharati, Princy, 1986, Kashmir Is on Its Way to Becoming a Mini Iran, *Organiser* 38 (16) August 31, p5

Bharati, R.K., 1981, The Anti-Hindu Bias of J&K Agrarian Reforms, *Organiser* 33 (11) August 2, p6

Bhardwaj, A.N., 1979, Carpet Industry in Jammu and Kashmir, *Yojana* 23 (4) March 1, p32

Bhargava, G.S., 1964, Another Opportunity, *Seminar*, 58, June, p20-23

Bhasin, Prem, 1968, A New Begining in Kashmir, *Janata* 23 (8) March 17, p7-8

Bhasin, Prem, 1972, Stalemate on Kashmir, *Janata* 27 (32) August 27, p3-5 +

Bhasin, Prem, 1973, Bhutto, Jana Sangh and Kashmir, *Janata* 28 (10) April 1, p3-4

Bhasin, Prem, 1974, Let's Settle in with Sheikh Abdullah, *Janata* 29 (39) November 10, p 8-10

Bhasin, Prem, 1975, The Kashmir Accord, *Janata* 30 (5) March 2, p12-13

Bhat
see also Bhatt

Bhat, G.M. and Dhar, M.K., 1988, Resource: Use Efficiency of Apple Cultivation in Jammu and Kashmir State, *Indian Journal of Economics* 69 (1) July, p51-58, appendices, bibliography, tables

Bhat, M.L., 1964, Livestock in Jammu and Kashmir : Some Problems, *Khadi Gramodyog* 10 (12) September, p824-832, footnotes, tables

Bhat, M.L., 1965, Fruit Industry In Jammu and Kashmir, *Khadi Gramodyog* 11 (9) June, p709-720, bibliography, footnotes

Bhat, M.S., 1977, Kashmir Forests : Use and Prospects, *Mainstream* 15 (52) August 27, p23-26

Bhat, Mohammed Sultan, 1976, Planning in Jammu and Kashmir, *Mainstream* 14 (52) August 28, p18-22

Bhat, Mohammed Sultan, 1982, Kashmir's Finances : Thoughts for 8th Finance Commission, *Economic Times* December 24, p5, col 3-6, tables

Bhat, Prem Nath, 1986, Anti-National Elements Mustering under

Farooq Abdullah's Umbrella, *Organiser* 38 (19) September 21, p31

Bhat, Prem Nath, 1986, Wanted a Sardar Patel to Crush Anti-India Elements in Kashmir, *Organiser* 37 (43) March 9, p5

Bhat, Roopkrishan, 1987, *Descriptive Study of Kashmir*, Amar Prakashan, Delhi, vi, 172p

Bhatia, K.L, 1981, Legal Aid to Victims of Industrial Accidents : An Empirical Study of the Administration of Workmen's Compensation Law in the States of Jammu and Kashmir and Punjab, *Journal of Indian Law Institute* 23 (1) January-March, p120-127, footnotes

Bhatia, K.L, 1981, Settlement of Disputes : Informal Methods on Empirical Study of the Administration of Workmen's Compensation Law in the States of Jammu and Kashmir and Punjab, *Journal of Indian Law Institute* 23 (3) July-September, p431-445, tables

Bhatia, Prem, 1962, Focus on India, *Times of India* March 8

Bhatia, Prem, 1962, A Search for Amity, *Times of India*, December 19

Bhatia, Sudarshan, 1969, Danger Signals in Kashmir : Plebiscite Front Gaining Ground, *Times of India* October 7,p6, col 3-5 +

Bhatnagar, Y., 1965, Kashmir and Its Ecocnomic Growth, *AICC Economic Review* 17 (2) July 1, p25-27, bibliography

Bhatt
see also Bhat

Bhatt, K.K., 1972, Ladakh and Kashmir : Stray Musings on Ancient Links, *Inquiry* 1(3) July

Bhatt, V.R., 1964, British Sop to Pakistan, *Hindustan Times* February 15

Bhattacharjea, Ajit, 1963, Re-thinking on Kashmir, *Hindustan Times* August 21

Bhattacharjea, Ajit, 1972, Story of Kashmir's Accession : Patel's Letters Throw Some New Light : A Review Article on Sardar Patel's Correspondence 1945-50, Vol 1; New Light on Kashmir ed, by Durga Das, *Times of India* March 1, p6, col 3-6

Bhattacharjea, Ajit, 1994, *Kashmir : The Wounded Valley*, UBS Publishers and Distributors, New Delhi, 312p

Bhattacharjea, S.S., 1965, The McMohan Line, *Modern Review*, 117, February, p140-145

Bhattacharjea, Shubhabrata, 1989, The Kashmir of Kalashnikovs,

Hindustan Times (Magazine) May 14, p1, col 1-8

Bhattacharyya, Som Nath, 1968, Sheikh on War Path, *Link* 11 (11) October 27, p2

Bhaumik

see also Bhowmik

Bhaumik, Kiriti, 1989, Kashmir Presents a Political Challenge, *Times of India* April 18, p6, col 7-8

Bhowmik

see also Bhaumik

Bhowmik, D.C. and Huq, F., 1971, Occipital Hair Whorl in Brahmans and Muslim of Kashmir Valley, *Man is India* 51 (12) April-June, p151-156, tables

Bhupinder Singh, 1983, *Indo-Pak Conflict over Kashmir*, B.C. Pub, Patiala, 221p

Bhushan

see under full name/surname of the author, e.g., Vidya Bhushan

Bhutto, Z.A., 1962, The Kashmir Case, *Pakistan Quarterly* 11 (1) Summer, p4-7, 46-47, illustrations

Bhutto, Z.A., 1962, Statement in the National Assembly on the Joint Communique Signed 29 November, 1962 and 4 December, 1962, Rawalpindi, *Pakistani National Assembly Debates* 2 (9) November 30, p267-271

Bhutto, Z.A., 1969, *The Myth of Independence*, London

Bilainkin, George, 1965, Mankind's Cross Roads in Kashmir, *Contemporary Review* 207 (1197) October, p175-178

Bindra, 1981, Mediatory Efforts of the U.N. : A Case Study of the Kashmir Problem (1947-65), *International Review of History and Political Science* 18 (2) May, p58-70, footnotes

Birdwood, Christopher Bromhead, 1953, *A Continent Decides : Introducting Two New Members in the Great and Diverse Family of the Commonwealth, and Some of the Problems Which They Offer for Our Understanding and Solution*, Hale, London, 315p

Birdwood (Lord), 1956, *Two Nations and Kashmir*

Biscoe, Cesil Earle Tyndale

see Tyndale-Biscoe, Cesil Earle

Biswas, Sukumar, 1966, *The Three Weeks War,* Calcutta

Bose, Ajoy, 1989, Doctor in Trouble, *Indian Express* (Magazine) December, p4, col 1-4

Bose, Ajoy, 1989, The Pro-Delhi Line Has Cost Farooq Abdullah Dear, *Times of India* (Sec II) April 18, p3, col 3-8

Bose, S.C, 1972, Glaciated Valley of Lambodri, *GERE* 34(1) March, p36-45

Boulnois, Helen Mary, 1923, *Into Little Thibet*, Simpkin, Marshall, London, 256p, plates

Boulnois, Helen Mary, 1935, *Mystic India*, Methuen, London, 255p

Boyle, George
see Markham, Clements R.

Boys, H.S., 1886, *Seven Hundred Miles in Kashmir*, Lucknow

Bray, John, 1986, *Culture and Society in Ladakh,* ESS ESS, New Delhi, 207p

Brecher, Michael, 1953, *The Struggle for Kashmir*, Toronto

Bright, Jagat S., 1958, *Kashmir for Ever,* Bright Inst, Delhi, viii 240p

Brines, Russel, 1968, *The Indo-Pak Conflict*, London

British Survey (Periodical), 1968, Kashmir, *British Survey*, 228, March, p10-20, editorial

Brown, B.L, 1921, *Camera Shikar in Kashmir,* Times of India Press, Bombay

Bruce, Charles Granville, 1934, *Himalayan Wanderer*, Alexander Maclehose, London, p309, illustrations

Bruce, Finetta Madelina, 1911, *Kashmir: With 12 Full Page Illustrations in Colour, by Maj E. Molyneux*, A&C Black, London, 25p

Brunel, Francis, 1977, *Kashmir*, Rupa, Calcutta, 233p

Buddha Prakash, 1970, Kashmir and Haryana in the Eleventh Century, *Journal of Haryana Studies* 2 (1-2), p13-17, bibliography

Burford, Robert, 1849, *Description of View of the Valley and City of Cashmere Now Exhibiting at the Panorama, Leicester Square*, W.J. Colburn, London, 15p

Burke, S.M., 1973, *Pakistan's Foreign Policy : An Historical Analysis*, London

Burns, John F., 1994, U.S. Remarks over Kashmir Anger Indians (Human Rights Concerns), *New York Times* March 10, p A9

Burton, E., 1954, Kashmir, *Labour Monthly* 36 (2) February, p81-84

Burton, Reginald George, 1898, *Tropics and Snow : A Record of Travel and Adventure,* illustrations by Miss Clare Burton, Edward Arnold, London, 349p

Business Week (Periodical), 1965, War Ends in Kashmir, but Issue Still Simmers, *Business Week*, September 25, p31, editorial

Buth, G.M., ed, 1986, *Central Asia and Kashmir Himalaya : A Forgotten Link*, Scientific Publications (IA), St Mut

Cadogan, Edward, 1933, *The India We Saw*, John Murray, London, 310p

Cameron, N., 1958 Emperor's Private Garden, *National Geographic Magazine*, November, p 606-647

Campbell, Jeffery Y., 1982, A Life of Solitary Confinement? *India Magazine* 2 (8) July, p28-35

Campbell Johnson, A., 1951, *Mission with Mountbatten*, London

Candler, Edmund, 1919, *On the Edge of the World*, Cassell, London, 267p, plates

Capital (Periodical), 1966, The Kashmir Imbroglio, *Capital* 157 (3922) August 4, p235, editoral

Caroe, O., 1961, The Indian-Chinese Boundary Dispute, *Geographical Journal*, 127, p345-347

Caruswilson, Ashley, 1901, *Irene Petrie: Missionary to Kashmir*, Hodder and Stoughton, London, 343p, map

Chadha, Kum Kum, 1986, The Return of Farooq Abdullah, *Hindustan Times* (Magazine) November 16, p1, col 1-6 +

Chadha, S.K., ed, 1991, *Kashmir : Ecology and Environment*, Mittal Publications, New Delhi, 134p, bibliography, illustrations, maps

Chadurah, Haider Malik 1991, *History of Kashmir*, Bhavna Prakashan, Delhi, xv, 107p

Chagla, M.C., 1965, *Kashmir, 1947-1965*, Publications Division, Ministry of Information and Broadcasting, Government of India, New Delhi, 125p

Chakravartty, Nikhil, 1992, Kashmir Crisis, *Mainstream* 30 (46) September 5, p3-4

Chakuu, O.P., 1983, Behavioural Aspects of Member Patrons : Special Reference to J&K Marketing Cooperative, *Indian Cooperative Review* 21 (2) October, p146-158

Chakuu, O.P., 1983, Operational Problems of the Marketing Co-operative of J&K State, *Indian Cooperative Review* 20 (3) January, p237-247

Chalmers, M.H., 1929, *A Walking Tour through the Heart of the Himalayas and the Middle Tibet*, Pioneer Press, Allahabad

Chaman Lal Datta
see Datta, Chaman Lal

Chanakya Sen
see Sen, Chanakya

Chand
see also under full name/surname of the author, e.g., Sansar Chand

Chandra
see also under full name/surname of the author, e.g., Ramesh Chandra

Chandramohan, A.T., 1970, Dateline Srinagar : Press More Alert in Kashmir, *Vidura* 7 (1) Feburary, p17-18

Channing, Mark, 1936, *Indian Mosaic*, George G. Harrap, London, 282p

Charak, S.D.S., *jt author*
see Chhabra, G.S. and Charak, S.D.S.

Charak, Sukhdev, Singh, 1977, *Jammu and Kashmir*, Light and Life Pub, New Delhi, vii, 159p, plates

Charak, Sukhdev Singh, 1985, *Short History of Jammu Raj from Earliest Times to 1846 AD*, Ajaya Prakashan, Jammu, xiv, 358p

Charak, Sukh Dev Singh, *translator*
see Kirpa Ram (Diwan), 1977

Charan Singh, 1977, Charges against Abdullah under Study, *Times of India* June 20, p1, col 4-5 +

Chari, A.S.R., *Kashmir Problem*, M. Kalimullah, New Delhi, vi, 70p

Chari, A.S.R., 1965, Plebiscite in Kashmir : Whose Demand? *Afro-Asian and World Affairs* 2 (4) November, p311-321

Chatterjee, Basant, 1970, Kashmir: The Land and Its People, *Caravan* September 15, p 19-20

Chatterjee, P.C., 1956, Assam and Kashmir: As a Tourist Looks at Them, *AT* February 26, p8

Chatterji, J.C., 1986, *Kashmir Shaivism*, State University NY Pr, 175p, Cultural Perspectives Series

Chattopadhyay, Kamala Devi, 1949, Kashmir Today, *MI* 2(2) November-December, p 27-29

Chaudhri Mohammed Ali
see Mohammad Ali, Chaudhri

Chawla
see also Chowla

Chhabra G.S. and Charak S.D.S., 1986, *Jammu and Kashmir : Aspect of Socio Political History*, Archives Pub, New Delhi, 104p

Chib, S.N., 1966, Kashmir from a Tourist Point of View, *Illustrated Weekly of India* 87 (12) March 20, p13-15

Chisti
see Chishti
Chishti, B.A., 1969, Kashmir's Village of Shepherds, *Mainstream* 7 (40) June 7, p37-38
Chishti, B.A., 1969, Village of Shepherds: A Fascimile Paradise, *Contemporary* 13(6) June, p39-40, 42
Chitale, K.A., 1968, Kashmir, *India Quarterly* 24 (1) January-March, p1-5
Chohan, Amar Singh, 1984, *Gilgit Agency, 1877-1935*, Atlantic, New Delhi, 250p
Chopra, Maharaj K., 1967, A Fresh Look at Jammu and Kashmir, *Organiser* 21 (15) November 19, p5 +
Chopra, Pran, 1983, How Green Was My Valley, *Indian Express* (Magazine) September 4, p3, col 1-8; September 11, p8, col 1-8
Chopra, Surendra, 1964, Kashmir in the United Nations, *Indian Journal of Political Science* 25 (3-4) July-September, p124-135, bibliography, footnotes
Chopra, Surendra, 1968, Chinese Diplomacy and Kashmir, *Indian Journal of Political Science* 29 (3) July-September, p244-251, bibliography, footnotes
Chopra, Surendra, 1968, Sheikh Abdullah's Kaleidoscope, *Journal of African and Asian Studies* 2 (1) Autumn, p81-85
Chopra, Surendra, 1970, U.S. Intervention in the Indo-Pakistan Dialogue, 1953-1955, *Kurukshetra University Research Journal* 4 (1-2) April-September, p165-175, bibliography, footnotes
Chopra, Surendra, 1971, *U.N. Meditating in Kashmir : A Study in Power Politics*, Vishal Pub, Kurukshetra, viii, 285p
Chopra, Surendra, 1978, U.S. Foreign Policy in Kashmir, *Indian Journal of Political Studies* 2 (2) July, p130-145, bibliography
Chopra, Surendra, 1979, Kashmir as a Factor in Indo-Soviet Relations, *Punjab Journal of Political Science* October, 3, p176-210
Chopra, V.D., 1990, *Genesis of Indo-Pakistan Conflict on Kashmir*, Patriot, New Delhi
Choudhary, A.K., *September 65 : Before and after*
Choudhary, G.W., 1968, Pakistan's Relations with the West, *Eastern World* 12 (17) July, p20-21
Choudhary, J.N. n.d., *Arms, Aims and Aspects*
Chowla
see also Chawla

Chowla, N.L.. 1970, Changing Pattern of Tourism in Kashmir, *Indian and Foreign Review* 7 (20) August 1, p14

Chowla, N.L., 1978, The Media in Kashmir : The Social Context, *Times of India* July 7, p6, col 7-8; July 8, p6, col 7-8

Clanson, Gerald L.M., comp, 1912, Catalogue of the Stein Collection of Sanskrit MSS from Kashmir, with Indtroductory note by Prof. A.A. Marshall, *JRAS*, July, p 587-629

Cobbold, Ralph P., 1900, *Innermost Asia: Travel and Sport in the Pamirs*, William Heinemann, London, 354p, plates

Cohen, M., 1970, *Thunder over Kashmir*, Orient Longmans, New Delhi, 220p

Collet, John, 1898, *Guide for Visitors to Kashmir*, enl rev and corrected up-to-date by A Mitra, 2nd edn, Newmans, Calcutta, 205p

Commerce (Periodical), 1975, Great Opportunity for Abdullah, *Commerce* 130 (3328) March 1, p 263-265, editorial

Commerce (Periodical), 1983, Status Quo in Jammu and Kashmir, *Commerce* 146 (3759) June 18, p1001, editorial

Confield, C., 1957, The Problem of Kashmir, *Listener* 58 (1488) October 3, p497-499

Conway, Beatrice, 1962, *Kashmir Holiday*, Macmillan, Mardas, 71p

Conway, William Martin, 1920, *Mountain Memories: A Pilgrimage of Romance*, Cassell, London, 282p, plates

Critic, (pseud), 1970, A Fascinating Experience, *IARC* 12(10), October, p168

Crowly, Carolyn Hughes, 1988, On the Roof of the World, *Saturday Evening Past*, 260, March, p64-66

Csemendra

see also Ved Kumari, 1975, *Csemendra's Views about Education*

Cunningham, Alexander, 1854, *Ladak : Physical, Statislical and Historical Notices of the Surrounding Countries*, W.H. Allen, London, 485p, illustrations, reprinted in 1970

Daily Telegraph (News paper), 1962, Kashmir Barrier, *Daily Telegraph* November 28, editorial

Damle, P.R., 1957, Kashmir, *Times of India* February 25

Dang, Satyapal, 1989, Analysis of Communal Clashes in Jammu, *Mainstream* 27 (20) February 11, p4-5 +

Dang, Satyapal, 1989, Forces behind Jammu Communal Clashes, *New Age* 37 (8) February 19, p5

Dang, Satyapal, 1993, Lessons of Punjab for Kashmir, *Times of India*

May 31, p8, col 7-8

Dange, S.A., 1964, Withdraw Kashmir Issue from the U.N.: Dange Suggests Immediate Steps for Solving the Present Impasse, *New Age* 12(20) May 17, p1

Dange, S.A., 1965, Kutch, Kashmir, NEFA, Nagaland Imperialist Plot against India, *New Age* 13(20) May 16, p1+

Dar, A.N., 1982, In the Shadow of the Giant Chinar, *Indian Express* (Magazine) September 26, pVI, col 1-8

Dar, Prem Nath, 1968, Kashmiri : A Total of Ten Books, *Indian Literature* 11 (4) October-December, p42-45

Daroboo, M.A., Cooperative Credit in Jammu and Kashmir, *Co-operators Bulletin*, 31 (1) January, p19-23

Das, Banka Behary, 1968, A Few Days on the Border in Kashmir, *Janata* 23 (3) February 11, p5-7+

Das, Manoj, 1981, The Rajatarangini, *Indian and Foreign Review* 18(17) June 15, p21-22

Das, S.M., 1966, Kashmir's Contribution to Science, *Illustrated Weekly of India* 87 (13) March 27, p44-45

Das, Taraknath, 1955, No Plebiscite on Kashmir Issue, *Organiser* 9(75) November 28, p6, 14

Das, Taraknath, 1956, The Kashmir Issue To-day, *Modern Review* 99(2) February, p165-167

Das Gupta, J.B., 1958, *Indo-Pakistan Relations, 1947-1955,* Amsterdam

Das Gupta, S., 1992, Pakistan's Indian Baiting Continues, *National Herald* September 28

Dass, Thakar
see Thakar Dass

Dat, T., 1972, *Sino-Pak Collusion and U.S. Policy,* New Delhi

Datar, B.N., 1961, *Himalayan Pilgrimage*, Publications Division Government of India, Delhi, 55-60p

Datta
see also Dutt

Datta, Chaman Lal, 1966, *Kashmir in Stories*, Kitab Mahal, Allahabad, 112p

Datta, Chaman Lal, 1973, *Ladakh and Western Himalayan Politics, 1819-1848 : The Dogra Conquest of Ladakh, Baltistan and West Tibet and Reactions of Other Powers*, Munshiram Manoharlal, New Delhi, xix, 239p

Datta, Chaman Lal, 1982, *Jammu and Kashmir*, rev edn, National

Book Trust, New Delhi, 200p

Datta, Chaman Lal, 1984, *Historical Tales of Kashmir*, Sagar, New Delhi, 132p

Dattatreya, P., 1955, Why Kashmir, *Kashmir* 5(3) March, p45-49, illustrations

Daval, John, 1984, Change in Kashmir, *Link* 26 (49) July 8, p15-16

Davidge Brothers, 1872, *Traveller's Compainion and Guide to Kashmir*, Murree

Dawn (Newspaper), 1962, The Imperverse Truth, *Dawn* (Pakistan) June 6, editorial

Dawn (Newspaper), 1962, Moment for Decision, *Dawn* (Pakistan) June 2, editorial

Dawn (Newspaper), 1962, Talks or a Trap, *Dawn* (Pakistan) December 17, editorial

Dawn (Newspaper), 1962, The Unvarinshed Truth, *Dawn* (Pakistan) June 8, editorial

Dawn (Newspaper), 1963, The Three Approaches, *Dawn* (Pakistan) April 23, editorial

Deambi, B.K., 1969-70, Sharada Inscriptions in Kashmir : A Socio-Political Study, *Quarterly Review of Historical Studies* 9 (1) p26-32

Deambi, B.K., 1979, Khonamoh Inscription of Times of Jayanolabadenasaha, Kali 4530, *Vishveshvaranand Indological Journal*, 17, p220-224

De Filippi, F., 1912, *Karakoram and Western Himalaya: An Account of Expedition of HRH Prince Luigi Amedeo of Savoy, 1909*, Constable, London, 469p, illustrations

De Filippi, Filippo, 1932, *Italian Expedition to the Himalaya, Karakoram and Eastern Turkestan, 1913-1914*, Edward Arnold, London, 528p, illustrations, map

Delmar, Walter, 1906, *Romantic East: Burma, Assam and Kashmir*, A&C Black, London, 211p, illustrations

De Mello, Melville, 1969, Kashmir Trout Waters, *Illustrated Weekly of India* 90 (48) November 30, p36-40

De Mello, Melville, 1969, Kashmir: In Search of the Rainbows, *Hindustan Times* October 5, pIV

De Mhafe, A., 1948, *Road to Kashmir*, Ripon Press, Lahore, 206p

Denys, Fredrick Ward, 1915, *Our Summer in the Valley of Kashmir*, James William Bryan Press, Washington, 232p

Deora, Man Singh and Grover, Rajinder, eds, 1991-94, *Documents on Kashmir Problem*, Discovery Publishers, various pagination, 19 vols

Deotare, B.C. and Kshirsagar, Anupama, 1985, Chemistry of Archaeological Deposits and Animal Bones from Jammu and Kashmir, *Bulletin of Deccan College Research Institute*, 44, p45-49

Dermot, Norris, 1932, *Kashmir: The Switzerland of India*, Newmans, Calcutta, 271p, illustrations, maps

Des Raj, *jt author*
see Karam Singh and Des Raj

Desh Bandhu, 1989, *Jammu and Kashmir and Ladakh* (*Tourist Attractions and Tourisa*), Akashdeep, Delhi, v, 264p

Deshmukh, Yadavrao, 1968, Sheikh Abdullah Admits Receiving Pak Money : Special Interview, *Organiser* 22 (5) September 14, p4

Desmond, Edward W., 1990, Taking the Road to War? (Assassination of M. Farooq), *Time*, 135, June 4, p62-63 illustrations, map

Deshpande, G.T., 1992, *Abhinavagupta*, Sahitya Akademi, New Delhi

De Souza
see after Drieberg

Dethe, V.K., 1980, Kashmir's Rs. 25 Crore Plan to Promote Tourism, *Times of India* July 28, p6, col 7-8

Dethe, V.K., 1980, Seething Discontent in Ladakh, *Times of India* December 15, col 2-4 +

Dethe, V.K., 1981, Smooth Transition in Kashmir, *Times of India* September 9, p8, col 7-8

Dethe, V.K., 1982, The G.M. Shah Factor in Kashmir Politics, *Times of India* May 17, p6, col 7-8

Dethe, V.K., 1982, Thirty Five Years of Momentous History, *Times of India* (Supplement) September 27, p1, col 3-8 +

Dethe, V.K., 1985, Leh, Kargil Tussle for Dominance, *Times of India* April 24, p5, col 1-4

Dewan
see also Diwan

Dewan, Berindranath
see Berindranath Dewan

Dewan, Gurbaksh Singh, 1984, CPI and NC Volunteers Defended Kashmir, *New Age* 32 (9) February 16, p15

Dewan, P. Dutt
see Dutt, Dewan P.

Dhami, Ida, 1965, Kashmir : An International View, *Freedom First* (163) December, p2-3

Dhar, D.N., 1970, Plan for High Court Building Srinagar That Was, *Indian Architect* 12 (9) September, p154-156

Dhar, D.P., 1966, The Law and Order Situation, *Illustrated Weekly of India* 87 (13) March 27, p16-17

Dhar, K.N., 1976, *Glimpses of Kashmiri Culture*, Shri Parmananda Research Institute

Dhar, M.K., *jt author*
see Bhat, G.M. and Dhar, M.K.

Dhar, P.N., 1964, Historical Realities, *Seminar,* 58, June, p12-15

Dhar, S.N., 1945, *Kashmir: Eden of the East: With an Introductory Essay by J.L. Nehru*, Kitab Mahal, Allahabad, 139p, map, plates

Dhar, Somnath, n.d., *Jammu and Kashmir Folklore*, Marwah Pub, 196p

Dhar, Somnath, 1978, Art and Crafts of Kashmir, *Social Welfare* 25(4) July, p17-19

Dhar, Somnath, 1982, *Jammu and Kashmir*, National Book Trust, New Delhi, 200p

Dharm Paul
see Paul, Dharm

Digby, Simon, 1964, Pir Hasan Shah and the History of Kashmir, *Indian Economic and Social History Review* 1 (3) January-March, p95-100, bibliography, footnotes

Dikshit, 1974, No Need for Anxiety over Kashmir Talks,*Times of India* August 31, p1, col 7-8 +

Dilwali, Ashok, 1986, Winter of Kashmir's Discontent, *Sunday Statesman* March 16, p1, col 1-5 +

Discoe, n.d., *Kashmir in Sunlight and Shade*, Sagar, New Delhi

Diwan
see also Dewan

Diwan Kirpa Ram
see Kirpa Ram Diwan

Dixtt
see also Dikshit

Dogra, G.L., 1969, Kashmir Turns Corner, *Times of India* (Magazine) January 26, pIX, col 5-8

Dogra, Hari Saran, 1967, Behind Kashmir's Communal Flare-up, *New Age* 15 (39) September 24, p11

Dogra, Ramesh Chander, 1986, *Jammu and Kashmir : A Select and Annotated bibliography*, Ajanta Pub, New Delhi, viii, 417p

Doughty, Marton, 1902, *Afoot through the Valley, of Kashmir,* Sands, London, 276p, illustrations, reprint, 1971, Sagar, New Delhi, 276p

Drabu, V.N., 1984, *Kashmir Polity C 600 to 1200 A.D.*, Bahri, New Delhi

Drabu, Vishva N., 1990, *Saivagamas : A Study in the Socio-Economic Ideas and Insitutions of Kashmir*, Indus Pub

Drew, Frederic, 1971, *Northern Barrier of India : A Popular Account of the Jammu and Kashmir Territories with Illustrations*, Light and Life Pub, New Delhi, v, 336p

Drew, Frederic, 1986, *Jammu and Kashmir Territorites : A Geographical Account*, Scientific Publishers, Jodhpur, 602p

Drieberg, Trevor, 1968, Illusion and Reality in Kashmir, *Now* 4 (41) June 28, p17-18

Drieberg, Trevor, 1968, Kashmir in Search of Its Identity, *Now* 4 (48) August 16, p8-9

Drieberg, Trevor and Sahni, Sat Pal, 1978, *Jammu and Kashmir : A Tourist Guide*, Vikas Pub, New Delhi, 140p

D'Souza, Marie and Saith, Sanjeev, 1990, *Kashmir : The Himalayan Paradise*, Lustre Press, New Delhi, 40p

Dube, D.N., 1989, *Kashmir, Jammu and Ladakh : The Trefoil Land*, Spantech, New Delhi, 132p

Dubey, K.P., 1987, Lingering Shadow of Terrorism in India, *Indian Nation*, January 11

Dugsal, 1874, *Letters from India and Kashmir,* George Bell, London, xvi, 252p, illustrations

Duke, Joshua, 1910, *Kashmir and Jammu: A Guide for Visitors*, 2nd edn, Thacker Spink, Calcutta, 387p, maps, plans, plates

Duncan, Jane E., 1906, *A Summer Ride through the Western Tibet,* Smith, Elder, London, 341p, illustrations

Dundas, Lawrence John Lumbley, 1902, *Sport and Politics under an Eastern Sky, by the Earl of Ronaldshay*, William Blackwood, Edinburgh, 423p, maps

Dupree, Louis, 1966, Further Reflection on the Second Kashmir War, *American Universities Field Staff Reports Service* (South Asia Series) 10 (3) May, p1-23

Durga Das, *editor*
see Patel, Ballabhbhai, 1971

Dutt

see also under fuli name/surname of the author, e.g., Iswara Dutt, K.

Dutt, Anuradha, 1988, Farooq vs Farooq, *Illustrated Weekly of India* 109 (31) July, p20-23

Dutt, Dewan P., 1989, The Maelstrom in Kashmir Is a Cry for Democracy, *Times of India* (Sec II) July 17, p3, col 3-8

Dutt, Jogesh Chunder, *translator*

see Kalhana

Dutt, R. Palme, 1965, A British Communist Solution for Kashmir, *Thought* 17 (39) September 25, p11-12

Dutt, R. Palme, 1965, Kashmir: The Only Solution, *New Age* 13 (44) October 31, p8-9

Dutta

see also Datt

Eastern Economist (Periodical), 1962, The Kashmir Debate, *Eastern Economist* 38 (19) May 11, p1147-1148, editorial

Eastern Economist (Periodical), 1965, A for Abdullah, *Eastern Economist* 44 (15) April 9, p879-880, editorial

Eastwick, Edward B., 1893, *Handbook of the Punjab, Western Rajaputana, Kashmir and Upper Sindh*, John Murray, London

Eckenstein, Oscar, 1896, *Karakorams and Kashmir: An Account of Journey*, T. Fisher Unwin, London, 253p

Economic and Political Weekly (Periodical), 1968, Dealing with Abdullah, *Economic and Political Weekly* 3 (3) January 20, p181, editorial

Economic and Political Weekly (Periodical), 1968, Fresh Chance, *Economic and Political Weekly* 3 (42) October 19, p1603, editorial

Economic and Political Weekly (Periodical), 1972, Kashmir Elections, *Economic and Political Weekly* 7 (38) September 16, p1897, editorial

Economic and Political Weekly (Periodical), 1976, A Deviation, *Economic and Political Weekly* 11 (36) September 4, p1442-1443, editorial

Economic Times (Newspaper), 1978, Kashmir Crisis, *Economic Times* September 28, p5, col 1-2, editorial

Economic Times (Newspaper), 1986, Transition in Kashmir, *Economic Times*, March 8, p5, col 1-2, editorial

Economic Times (Newspaper), 1993, Despite Clinton, *Economic*

Times November 1, p6, col 1-2, editorial

Economic Weekly (Periodical), 1964, Eliminating Bakshi, *Economic Weekly* 16 (39) September 26, p1547, editorial

Economic Weekly (Periodical), 1965, Aggression Will Not Pay, *Economic Weekly* 17 (36) September 4, p1359-1360, editorial

Economic Weekly (Periodical), 1965, New Turn in Kashmir, *Economic Weekly* 17 (20) May 15, p800-801, editorial

Economic Weekly (Periodical), 1965, What Next on Kashmir, *Economic Weekly* 17 (47) November 20, p1716-1717, editorial

Economic Weekly (Periodical), 1965, What Are We Defending, *Economic Weekly* 17 (43) October 23, p1611-1612; 17(44-45) November 6, p1652, editorial

Economic Weekly (Periodical), 1965, Winning the Peace, *Economic Weekly* 17 (39) September 25, p1463, editorial

Economist (Periodical), 1965, Pakistan Can't Win, *Economist* 216 (6367) September 4, p853-854, editorial

Edmead, Frank, 1967, Conflicts in Asia : Kashmir Problem, *Manchester Guardian Weekly* (Air Edition) 96 (26) June 29, p6

Eisenberg, Joyce, 1986, Houseboating in Kashmir : Life on and off the Water, *Travel Holiday*, 166, November, p56-61, illustrations, map

Ejaj Husain, 1959, Prospect of Kashmir Case in the U.N. Council, *Dawn* (Pakistan), January 7

Engineer, Asghar Ali, ed, 1991, *Secular Crown on Fire : The Kashmir Problems*, Ajanta, Delhi, xi, 344p

Enriquaz, C.M, 1915, *The Realm of Gods: A tale of Travel in Kangra, Mandi, Kulu, Chamba, Kishtwar, Kashmir, Ladakh and Baltistan*, Thacker Spink, Calcutta, 223p, map

Ernest (Dr), *Beyond the Pir Panjal*

Etherton, P.T., 1911, *Across the Roof of the World*, London

Faizee, Shameem, 1977, Issue of Land Reforms in Jammu and Kashmir, *New Age* 25 (43) October 23, p6

Far Eastern Economic Review (Periodical), 1965, Understimated Perils, *Far Eastern Economic Review* 50 (3) October 21, p112, 127-129, editorial

Farmer and Parliament (Periodical), 1968, Kashmir Problem, *Farmer and Parliament* 3 (11) November, p4, editorial

Farooq Abdullah
see Abdullah, Farooq

Farooqi, M., 1975, Kashmir : A New Chapter Opens, *New Age* 23 (9)

March 2, p3+

Farooqi, M., 1980, Kashmir : Ominous Developments, *New Age* 28(32) August 10, p3

Farooqi, M., 1983, Indira Gandhi's Dangerous Course in Jammu-Kashmir, *New Age* 31 (47) November 20, p3

Farooqi, M., 1983, J&K : Need to Repair Damage to Secular Traditions, *New Age* (26) June 26, p8

Farooqi, M., 1983, Kashmir : Confrontationist Policy a Perilous Pasttime, *New Age* 21 (22) May 29, p1+

Farooqi, M., 1984, Express Solidarity with J&K People, *New Age* 32(33) August 12, p3

Fazili, Manzoor, 1988, *Kashmir Predilection*, Gulshan Pub, Srinagar, 158p

Featherstone, B.K, 1926, *An Unexplored Pass: A Narrative of a Thousand Mile Journey to the Karakoram Himalayas*, Hutchinson, London, 295p, illustrations, map

Fevre, George, 1935, *Eastern Odyssey: The Third Expedition of Haardt and Audouin-Dubreuit, Tr and adapted by Sir E.D. Swinton*, Victor Gollancz, London, 368p, plates

Fida Mohammed Hassnain
see Hassnain, Fida Mohammad

Fielden, L., 1950, Kashmir : Bone of Contention, *Listener*, 43, April 20, p683-684

Fillippi, F. De
see De Fillippi, F.

Fisher, Robert E., n.d., Buddhist Architecture, *Marg* 40 (2), p17-28

Fisher, Robert E., n.d., Stone temples, *Marg* 40 (2), p29-40

Fisher, Robert E., 1989, The Enigma of Harwan, *Marg* 40 (2), p1-16

Fitze, Kenneth, 1956, *Twilight of the Maharajas*, John Murray, London, p42-66

Fitzgerald-Lee, G., 1951, Kashmir, *Contemporary Review*, 179, February, p93-97

Fleming, Peter, 1937, *News from Tartary: A Journey from Peking to Kashmir*, Jonathan Cape, London, 384p

Forster, George, 1898, *Journey from Bengal to England: Through the Northen Part of India, Kashmir, Afghanistan, Persia and into Russia by the Caspian Sea,* R. Foulder, 314+297p, 2 vols, reprint, 1970, Department of Languages, Patiala

Forsyth, T.D., 1873, *Lahore to Yarkand: Incidents of the Route and Natural History of the Countries Traversed by the Expedition of*

1870, under T.D. Forsyth, by George Henderson and Allah H. Hume, Reeve, London, 370p, illustrations, map

Foster, William, ed, 1968, *Early Travels in India, 1583-1619*, S. Chand, Delhi, 351p, illustrations, map, originally published 1922, London

Francke, A.H., 1977, *A History of Ladakh*, Sterling, New Delhi, 1,182p

Francke, August Hermann, 1978, *Ladakh : The Mysterious Land : History of Western Himalayas*, Cosmo, New Delhi, iv, 191p

Fulton, Robert Edison, 1939, *One-man Caravan,* Travel Book Club, London, 271p, illustrations, map, photographs, sketchs

Fyzee, A.A.A., 1964, Communication, *Seminar,* 58, June, p41-43, appendices

Gadgil, D.R., 1969, Planning in Jammu and Kashmir, *Yojana* 13 (24) December 14, p3-4

Gajendragadakar, P.B., 1967, *Kashmir : Retrospect and Prospect*, Manaktalas, Bombay, 147p, Patel Memorial Lecture

Gajendragadkar Commission
see Anon, 1969, Early Implementation of Gajendragadkar Body Report Urged; Anon, 1969, Gajendragadkar Body's Suggestion Opposed; Anon, 1969, The Gajendragadkar Commission Report; Anon, 1969, Gajendragadkar's Views on Article 370; Anon, 1969, Kashmir May Not Accept Suggestions on Cabinet Set-up; Anon, 1969, Regional Staff Quota Unconstitutional; Anon, 1969, Report on Kashmir Next Week; Anon, 1969, Uproarious Document; Bhagwan Singh, 1969, What Is Wrong with the People of Jammu; Suresh Chander, 1969, Gajendragadkar Commission Report; Times of India (Periodical), 1969, Mr Sadiq's Task

Ganai, Abdul Jabbar, 1984, *Kashmir National Conference and Politics*, Gulshan Pub, Srinagar, 168p

Ganai, Nisar Ahmad, 1985, Privileged Position of Dukhtar Khana Nashin among Muslim Female Heirs in Kashmir : An Empirical Study, *Journal of Indian Law Institute* 27 (3) July September, p387-422, footnotes

Ganai, Nisar Ahmad, 1988, Familial Rights of Muslim Women under Customary Law in Kashmir : Myth and Reality, *Cochin University Law Review* 12 (4) December, p359-390

Ganeshi Lal, 1955, *Siaht-I-Kashmir: Being an Account of a Journey to Kashmir, March-June 1846,* tr into English by Vidya Sagar Suri,

Controller Printing Punjab, Shimla, 58p reprint 1967, *Siyahat-Kashmir : Kashmir Nama, or Taikh-i-Kashmir*, etc., 2nd edn, Punjab Ithas Prakashan, Chandigarh, viii, 66p

Ganguli

see also Razdan, Prithvi Nath, 1967, Educational Standards Ganguli Report

Ganguly, Sumit, 1990-91, Avoiding War in Kashmir, *Foreign Affairs*, 69, Winter, p57-73, bibliography, footnotes

Ganhar, J.N., 1974, *Jammu : Shrines and Pilgrimages*, Ganhar Pub, 180p

Ganhar, J.N., 1986, Hasan : Doyen among Kashmiri Historians, *Patriot*, February 23, p4, col 3-7

Ganjo, Satish, 1990, *Kashmir Politics*, Anmol, New Delhi, xi, 84p

Ganju, Shanta, 1957, Charm of Kashmir, *KT* 2(7) September-October, p24-26, illustrations

Gargan, Edward A., 1992, Where Violence Has Silenced Verse (Kashmir), *New York Times* November 22, p46-50+, illustrations, map

Gargan, Edward A., 1993, Indian Troops Surround Mosque in Kashmir (Srinagar), *New York Times* (Sec 1) October 17, p11, maps

Gargan, Edward A., 1993, Kashmir Clashes Kill atleast 25, *New York Times* October 23, p6, illustrations, maps

Garstin, W.A., 1952, The Kashmir Tension, *Eastern World*, 6, March, p 14-16

Gee, E.P, 1947, Kashmir Holiday, *JKI* 4(5) May, p14-18

Gervis, Pearce, 1954, *This is Kashmir*, Cassell, London, 330p, reprint, 1974, Universal Book and Stationery Co, Delhi, 356p

Gervis, Pearce, 1977, The Hindu and Muslim Festivals in Kashmir, *Vivekananda Kendra Patrika* 6(1) February, p297-301

Ghaznavi, Khalid, 1966, *Story of Indian Aggressim against Pakistan*, Lahore

Ghose, D.K., 1969-70, Source-Material for the History of Kashmir, *Quarterly Review of Historical Studies* 9(1), p7-12

Ghose, Dilip Kumar, 1967-68, The Kashmir Residency Question, *Quarterly Review of Historical Studies* 7(4) p269-275, bibliography

Ghose, Dilip Kumar, 1968-69, The Kashmir Residency Question, *Quarterly Review of Historical Studies* 8(1), p25-31, bibliography

Ghose, Dilip Kumar, 1975, *Kashmir in Transition, 1885-1893*, World

Press, Calcutta, xiv, 26p
Ghose, Indra, *jt editor*
see Ghose, Partha and Ghosh, Indra
Ghose, Nripendranath, 1979, Kashmir Today, *Janata* 33(44) January 21, p12-13 +
Ghose, Partha S. and Ghosh, Indra, 1983, Some Reflections on Kashmir Politics, *Mainstream* 21 (45) July 9, p31-33
Ghose, Sailen, 1965, The Essence of It, *Seminar*, 75, November, p10-18
Ghulam
see also Gulam
Ghulam Hassan Khan
see Khan, Ghulam Hassan
Ghulam Mohammed
see Mohammed, Ghulam
Ghulam Mohammed Bakshi
see Bakshi, Ghulam Mohammed
Ghulam Mohammad Sadiq
see Sadiq, Ghulam Mohammad
Ghulam Mohuddin Kara
see Kara, Ghulam Mohiuddin
Ghulam Nabi, 1970, Mahjoor: His Age and Poetry, *Cultural Forum* 12(3-4) April-July, p52-55
Ghulam Nabi Khayal
see Khayal, Ghulam Nabi
Giasuddin
see also Giyas-ud-din
Gias-ud-Din, 1968, Industrial Profile of States-6: Kashmir: A Package of Incentives, *Commerce* (Annual Number) 117(3009), p250
Gilbert, C.F, 1887, *Hints to Travellers in Kashmir*, Newmans, Calcutta
Gillibran, Patrick, 1959, Beyond the Gateway of Banihal, *KT* 3(6) July-August, p34-35
Giyasuddin
see also Gias-ud-din
Giyas-ud-din, Peer, n.d., *Understanding the Kashmir Insurgency*
Giyas-ud-din, Peer, 1974, Reassertion of Democratic Movement, *Mainstream* 13(5) October 5, p21-22
Goldberg, Arthur J., 1966, Remark on Kashmir Dispute in an Address before Economic Club, Detroit, Michigan, *Department*

of State Bulletin 54 (1404) May 23, p799-800

Gokhale, M.S., 1981, Federalisation and J&K State, *Janata* 36(39) November 29, p5-6

Gonway, Beatric, 1962, *Kashmir Holiday*, Macmillan, Madras, 71p

Goray, N.G., 1975, Kashmir: An Accord Full of Hope, *Janata* 30(8) March 23, p3-4

Goyal, D.R., 1964, *Kashmir*, R and K Publishing House, New Delhi, viii 141p, illustrations

Goyal, D.R., 1983, Silver Lining in Kashmir? *Mainstream* 21 (45) July9, p9-10

Goyal, Narendra, 1960, Himalayan Border, *Australian Quarterly* 31(1), March, p54-65

Grant, R.L.C, 1953, Kashmir: A Land of Peace and Beauty, *ODT* April 9

Grierson, G.A, 1912, Kashmiri Almanacs, *JRAS* July, p719-712

Grover, Rajinder, *jt author*
see Deora, Man Singh and Grover, Rajinder

Guardian (Newspaper), 1962, An End to Two Conflicts, *Guardian* (Manchester) November 8, editorial

Guardian (Periodical), 1962, Hopes for Kashmir, *Guardian* (Manchester) November 30, editorial

Guha
see also Kaul, Pyare lal, 1971, The Mistake Kashmir Did Not Make

Gulam
see also Ghulam

Gulam Rasook Kochak
see Kochak, Gulam Rasook

Gulam Rasool Matto
see Matto, Gulam Rasool

Gulzar Ahmed
see Ahmed, Gulzar

Gundeviya, Y.D., 1974, *The Testament of Sheikh Abdullah*, Palit and Palit, New Delhi, 156p

Gupta, Arun Kumar, 1975, Status Values of Professions on Vocational Preferences of School Pupils, *Indian Journal of Applied Psychology* 12(2) July, p55-64, tables, bibliography

Gupta, H.R., 1967, *The India-Pakistan War, 1965*, Delhi, 2 vols

Gupta, K.L., 1993, The Citizens Cooperative Bank Limited, Jammu, Marches ahead, *Co-operator's Bulletin* 35(7) July, p5-7

Gupta, N.S., 1967, People of Chhamb and Jaurian: A Demographic Study, *Quarterly Journal of Indian Studies in Social Sciences* 1(1) January, p68-76, tables.

Gupta, N.S., 1968, Agricultural Growth in Kashmir, *Productivity*, 8(4)-9(1) Spring, p573-579, tables

Gupta, N.S., 1968, Economic Growth of Jammu and Kashmir State : A Study of Investment, Saving and Capital Formation, *Quarterly Journal of Indian Studies in Social Sciences* 2(3-4) July-October, p18-28, bibliography, footnotes, tables

Gupta, N.S., 1968, People of Chhamb and Jaurian: An Income Study, *AICC Economic Review* 19(19) April 15, p 12-14, tables; 19(20) May 1, p24-28, footnotes, tables

Gupta, Nand Lal, 1964, Kashmir and Jan Sangh, *Mainstream* 2(19) January 11, p 8-9

Gupta, Pitamber, 1982, Don't Count on Farooq yet, *Janata* 37(36) October 31, p 9-10

Gupta, Pitamber, 1982, Kashmir Livelier but Uncertain, *Janata* 37 (29) September 12, p 13-14

Gupta, R.D., et al, 1986, Clay Mineralogy of Some Soil Profiles of Jammu and Kashmir State, *Journal of the Indian Society of Soil Science* 34(3) September, p 577-584, bibliography, tables

Gupta, Sisir, 1964, Forgotten Facts, *Seminar*, 58, June, p24-28

Gupta, Sisir, 1965, Issues and Prospects in Kashmir, *India Quarterly* 21 (3) July-September, p 253-284, footnotes

Gupta, Sisir, 1965, The Kashmir Question Today, *International Studies* 6(3) January, p217-253, bibliography, footnotes

Gupta, Sisir, 1966, *Kashmir: A Study in India-Pakistan Relations*, Asia, Bombay, 511p

Gurbaksh Singh Dewan
see Dewan, Gurbaksh Singh

Gurmani, Mushtaq Ahmad, 1951, *Kashmir : A Survey*, Minister for Kashmir Affairs, Government of Pakistan, Karachi, 47p, illustrations

Gurmani, Mushtaq Ahmad, 1951, The Kashmir Dispute, *Vital Speeches of the Day*, 17, May 15, p 466-468

Gurmani, Mushtaq Ahmad, 1951, *The Kashmir Dispute and Its Solution*, Minister for Kashmir Affairs, Government of Pakistan, Karachi, 23p, illustrations

Gururaj Rao, H.S., 1967, *Legal Aspects of the Kashmir Problem*, Asia, Bomaby, 379p

Habibullah, E., 1985, Why Kashmir Came to India, *National Herald,* October 20, p5, col 5-8

Hafizullah, Muhammad, 1948, *Towards Azad Kashmir,* Bazam-U-Firogh, Lahore, xii, 170 p

Haider Malik Chadurah
see Chadurah, Haider Malik

Hajini, Mohy-ud-din, 1970, Historical Background of Kashmiri Language, *Cultural Forum* 12(3-4) April-July, p20-23, bibliography

Hall, E.C., *translator*
see Bauer, Paul, ed, 1938, *Himalayan Guest*

Hamidullah, Zeb-un-Nissa, 1957, Turn a Woman's Eyes, *Dawn* (Pakistan) Februry 4

Handoo, Jawaharlal, 1979, Contemporary Kashmiri Poetry, *Indian Literature* 22(5) September-October, p 145-154

Hanifa Bano
see Bano, Hanifa

Harbaksh Singh (Lt Gen), 1965, *War Despatches: Indo-Pak Conflict*

Har Dev Singh, 1978, Jammu and Kashmir: An Era of Stability, *Eastern Economist* (Annual Number), p1329-1333

Hari Om, 1992, Article 370: Myth and Reality, *Organiser* 44(6) September 13, p8 +

Hari Om, 1993, A Return to 1952 Will Hurt J and K, *Times of India* July 28, p10, col 7-8

Hari Ram, 1983, *Special Status in Indian Federalism: Jammu and Kashmir,* Seema Pub, Delhi, viii, 230 p

Harrer, Heinrich, 1988, *Ladakh,* Himalayan, New Delhi, 170p

Harris, Barbara, 1969, Amid the Glaciers in Kashmir, *Hindustan Times Weekly,* November2

Harvey (Mrs), 1854, *Adventures of a Lady in Tartary, Thibet, China and Kashmir, through Portions of Territory never before Visited by Europeans, etc.,* Hope, London, appendix, maps, plates, 3vols

Hasan
see also Hassan

Hasan Khan, Noorul
see Khan, Noorul Hasan

Hasan, K. Sarwar
see Sarwar Hasan, K

Hasan, Muhibbul
see Muhibbul Husan

Hasan, Zubeida
see Zubeida Hasan

Hassan
see also Hasan

Hassan Khan, G.
see Khan, G. Hassan

Hassnain, F.M., 1970, Lakes and Gardens of Kashmir, *Cultural Forum* 12 (3-4) April-July, p77-79

Hassnain, F.M., 1972, A Note on the State Archives Department, Jammu and Kashmir, *Indian Architect* 21(2) July-December, p1-5

Hassnain, F.M., 1975, *British Policy towards Kashmir*, Sterting, New Delhi, 148p

Hassnain, F.M., 1977, *Hindu Kashmir*, Light and Life Pubs, New Delhi, xvi 149p

Hassnain, F.M., 1978, *Gilgit: The Northern Gate of India*, Sterling, New Delhi, vi, 195, (12)p

Hassnain, F.M., 1980, *Heritage of Kashmir,* Gulshan Pub, Srinagar, 239 p

Hassnain, F.M., 1992, *Cultural History of Kashmir and Kishtawar*, Rima

Hassnain, F.M., *editor*
see Thorp, Robert, 1980

Hassnain, Fida Mohammad, 1969-70, Kashmir Archives, *Quarterly Review of Historical Studies* 9(1), p13-16

Hazarika, Sanjoy, 1993, Afghans Joining Rebels in Kashmir, *New York Times* August 24, p 45

Heddurshetti, B.V., 1978, The Status of Jammu and Kashmir under the Constitution of India, *Janata* 33(17) June 11, p13-16; 33(18) June 18, p13-15, bibliography, footnotes

Henderson, *translator*
see Izzatullah, Mir, 1872, Safar Nama-I-Izzatullah

Hilaly, Agha, 1964, Pakistan and Kashmir, *Commonwealth Journal* 7(3) June, p119-120

Hindu (Newspaper), 1957, Kashmir, *Hindu* February 16, editorial

Hindu (Newspaper), 1961, Kashmir and Goa, *Hindu* February 24, editorial

Hindu (Newspaper), 1962, Fresh Approach Wanted, *Hindu* December 5, editorial

Hindu (Newspaper), 1962, Indo-Pakistan Relations, *Hindu*

December 23, editorial

Hindu (Newspaper), 1962, Kashmir Pointers, *Hindu* June 24, editorial

Hindustan Standard (Newspaper), 1957, Kashmir Perspective, *Hindustan Standard* February 15, editorial

Hindustan Standard (Newspaper), 1957, Trial at Kagmari, *Hindustan Standard* February 9, editorial

Hindustan Times (Newspaper), 1955, Kashmir, *Hindustan Times* December 13, editorial

Hindustan Times (Newspaper), 1956, Question of Kashmir, *Hindustan Times* December 24, editorial

Hindustan Times (Newspaper), 1962, A Pause for Reflection, *Hindustan Times* June 30, editorial

Hindustan Times (Newspaper), 1963, Line Clear, *Hindustan Times* May 6, editorial

Hitschmann, Marcelle, 1956, Kashmir Issue at the U.N., *Pakistan Times*, June 3.

Hochberg, F, 1910, *An Eastern Voyage*, London, 2 vols

Hodson, H.V., 1948, Roots of the Kashmir Crisis, *Listener*, 39, January 22, p 125-126

Hodson, H.V., 1969, *The Great Divide: Britain, India-Pakistan*, London

Holloway, James, 1965, Vale of Kashmir Is an Emerald Set in Pearls, *Auckland Star* (New Zealand) May 15

Holkar, Shalini Devi, 1987, Wazwan: A Kashmiri Feast, *India Magazine* 7(5) April, p 33-39

Holt, E., 1973, My Asian Friends, *Holiday* Februray, p34

Honiberger, John Martin, 1905, *Thirty-Five Years in the East: Adventures, Discoveries, Experiments and Historical Sketches Relating to the Punjab and Cashmere in Connection with Medicine, Botany, Pharmacy, etc.*, Bangabasi Office, Calcutta, 214p

Hook, Peter Edwin, 1976, Is Kashmiri an SVO Language? *Indian Linguistics* 37(2) June, p133-142, bibliography, footnotes

Hook, Peter Edwin and Koul, Omkar Nath, 1986-87, Subject versus Agent: A Study of the Kashmiri Phasal Verb HYE 'Begin to', *Journal of Oriental Institute* September-June, p115-132, bibliography

Hugel, B.C., 1972, *Kashmir and the Punjab*, Light and Life Pub, Jammu, 423p

Hugel, Baron Charles, 1845, *Travels in Cashmere and the Punjab, Containing a Particular Account of the Govt and Character of the Sikhs,* tr from German by T.B. Jevis, John Methuen, London, 423p, map, reprint, 1970, Department of Languages, Patiala

Hugel, Charles von
see von Hugel, Charles

Hugh-Jones, Stephen, 1965 British Attitude to the Indo-Pak War, *Economic Weekly* 17(42) October 16, p1589-1590

Huq, F., *jt author*
see Bhowmik, D.C and Huq, F.

Husain
see also Hussain

Husain, Azizuddin S.M., 1981, Inayatullah Khan Kashmiri: A Biographical Study, *Studies in Islam*, 18(1-2) Junaury-April, p9-17, F + -n

Husain, Ejaj
see Ejaj Husain

Husain, Majid, *jt author*
see Mir, Ali Mohammed and Husain, Majid

Husain, Majid, *jt editor*
see Kehra, M.K., et al, eds

Husband, Francis Edward Young
see Young-Husband, Frances Edward

Hussain
see also Husain

Hussain, S.A., 1976, In Quest of a Himalayan Crane, *Times of India* September 26, p8, col 2-6

Hussain, Syed T., 1987, *Reflections on Kashmir Politics*, Usha; Sundeep

Hutchinson, J., 1923, *Guide to Dalhousie, Chamba and the Inner Mountains between Simla and Kashmir*, Lahore

Ibrahim, M. Mohammad, 1969-70, Manuscript Source Material of Kashmir History of the Mughal Period in the Research and Publication Department, Jammu and Kashmir Government, *Quarterly Review of Historical Studies* 9(1), p23-25

Ibrahim Khan, M.
see Khan, M. Ibrahim

Ikle, Fred Charles, 1971, *Every War Must End*, New York

Inder Jit, 1980, Brinkmanship in Kashmir, *Economic Times* July 29, p5, col 7-8

Inder Jit, 1984, Playing with Fire in Kashmir, *Economic Times* Januray 10, p5, col 7-8

Indian and Foreign Review (Periodical), 1975, Kashmir Settlement within Framework of Indian Constitution: Prime Minister's Statement in Parliament, *Indian and Foreign Review* 12(11) March 15, p7-9, editorial

Indian Express (Newspaper), 1962, Perverse Tactics, *Indian Express* May7, editorial

Indian Express (Newspaper), 1962, Pouring Oil, *Indian Express* June 30, editorial

Indian Express (Newspaper), 1962, Pressure Tactics, *Indian Express* December 22, editorial

Indian Express (Newspaper), 1962, The Rawalpindi Talks, *Indian Express* December 31, editiorial

Indian Express (Newspaper), 1962, Thieves' Kitchen, *Indian Express* June 25, editiorial

Indian Express (Newspaper), 1962, Working in the Park, *Indian Express* December 19, editiorial

Indian Express (Newspaper), 1963, The Perennial Problem, *Indian Express* May 3, editorial

Indian Express (Newspaper), 1963, The U.S. Plan, *Indian Express* April 19, editorial

Indo-Asian Culture (Periodical), 1965, India, Pakistan and Kashmir, *Indo-Asian Culture* 14(4) October, p280-286, editorial

Inge, J., 1888, *Kashmir Handbook,* rewritten by J. Duke, 4th edn, Calcutta, 337p

Iqbal, S.M., *jt author*
see Nirash K.L and Iqbal, S.M.

Iqbal Khan, Mohammed
see Khan, Mohammed Iqbal

Iqbal Singh, 1963, Kashmir, *National Herald* May 19

Ireland, John B., 1859, *From Wall Street to Kashmere: Five Years in Asia, Africa and Europe during 1851-1856,* S.A. Roll, New York, 531p

Ishaq Khan, Mohammad
see Khan, Mohammad Ishaq

Ismay (Lord), 1960, *The Memoirs of Lord Ismay*, London

Iswara Dutt, K. 1965, Sheikh Abdullah's Right Place, *Onganiser* 18(37) April 26, p7

Izzatullah, Mir, 1872, *Safar Nama-I-Izzatullah,* tr into English from

Persian by Capt Henderson, entitled *Trevels in Central Asia in the Years 1812*, Foreign Department Press, Calcutta

Jackson, A. John; 1955, *More than Mountains*, George G. Harrap, London, 213p, illustrations

Jackson, R., 1975, *South Asian Crisis: India-Pakistan-Bangladesh,* London

Jacquemnt, Victor, 1835, *Letters from India, Describing a Journey in the British Dominions of India, Tibet, Lohore and Kashmir during the Years 1828-31,* Edward Churton, London, 2vols

Jacquemont, Victor, 1936, *Letters from India, 1829-32: Being a Selection from His Correspondence, tr by Catherine Alison Philips,* MacMillan, London, 372p

Jahangir (Emperor), n.d., *Memoirs of the Emperor Jahangir*, tr. from Persian Manuscript by Maj David Price, Delhi, p220-246

Jefery, S.M., 1988, Consumer Cooperative in Jammu Region, *Co-operators Bulletin* 31(1) January, p17-18

Jaffer, S.M., n.d., *Kashmir Sold and Resold*, Book Traders, Lahore

Jafri, Fareed S., 1964, Kashmir Case and the Arabs, *Pakistan Times* Februray 20

Jagmohan, 1992, *My Frozen Turbulence in Kashmir*, 2nd edn, Allied Publishers, New Delhi, xx, 749p, appendices

Jai Krishen, Raja
See Raja Jai Krishen

Jain, A.K., 1970, The Rural Houses of Kashmir, *Design* 14(11) November, p15-18

Jain, A.P., 1972, *Kashmir : What Really Happened,* Jaico, Bombay, 242p

Jain, Ajit Prasad, 1971, Kashmir: Fact and Fiction, *Times of India* August 1, p6, col 2-5; August 8, p6, col 2-5

Jain, Balbir K., 1971, Forests: A Source of Revenue in Jammu and Kashmir, *Political and Economic Review* 2(7) April 21, p15, table

Jain, Balbir Kumar, 1975, Withdrawal of Food Subsidy in J&K at the Cost of the Poor, *Janata* 30(13) April 27, p8-9

Jain, Girilal, 1962, B.B.C. Debate on Kashmir, *Times of India* May 21

Jain, Girilal, 1962, Indifference to Kashmir, *Times of India* April 28

Jain, Girilal, 1962, Policy of Playing It Cool, *Times of India*, December1

Jain, Girilal, 1974, Pandora's Box in Kashmir: Putting Back the Lid Won't be Easy, *Times of India* July 17, p4, col 3-5

Jain, Girilal, 1977, Violence in Kashmir Valley: Centre Must Ensure

Free Elections, *Times of India* June 15, p6, col 3-5

Jain, Girilal, 1983, Momentous Poll in Kashmir: Major Implications for the Country, *Times of India* June 9, p6, col 3-5

Jain, Girilal, 1983, Two Faces of Farooq : Compulsions of Kashmir's Politics, *Times of India* May 4, p8, col 3-5

Jain, Girilal, 1984, Anatomy of Fight in Kashmir : Limits That Must Not be Crossed, *Times of India* January 18, p8, col 3-5

Jalal, Ayesha, 1990, Kashmir Scars, *New Republic,* 203, July 23, p17-20

Jalali, Bansi Lal, 1956, Sight Seeing in Kashmir, *Kashmir* 6(3) March, p59-60, illustrations

Jalali, J.L.K, 1940, *Handbook for Visitors to Kashmir,* Srinagar, 180p

Jalali J.L.K, 1958, Two Notable Sons of Kashmir, *Kashmir* 8(10), October, p248

Jalali, P. N., 1971, Kashmir's Glorious October, 1947, *Mainstream* (Annual Number) 10(1-4), p23-25

Jalali, P.N., 1979, Quit Kashmir Movement in Retrospect, *Mainstream* (Republic Day Number) 17(2-23), p65-70

Janak Singh, 1975, Cleaning the Air in Kashmir : Gains of P.M.'s Visit, *Times of India* October 18, p4, col 7-8

Janak Singh, 1975, Development Has Bypassed Gurez Valley in Kashmir, *Times of India* January 29, p4, col 7-8

Janak Singh, 1975, Drive to Increase Production of Kashmir Shawls, *Times of India* January 11, p4, col 7-8

Janak Singh, 1975, Kashmir Needs New Development Priorities, *Times of India* May 16, p4, col 7-8

Janak Singh, 1975, Kashmir Tourist Meet: Plans to Attract More Visitors, *Times of India* September 17, p4, col 7-8

Janak Singh, 1975, New Political Alignments in Kashmir Likely, *Times of India* May 30, p4, col 7-8

Janak Singh, 1975, Public Health Facilities in Kashmir Bypass the Common Man, *Times of India* December 26, p6, col 7-8

Janak Singh, 1975, Sheikh Abdullah Stands Firm against Communalism, *Times of India* August 7, p4, col 7-8

Janak Singh, 1975, Steps to Clean up Administration in Kashmir : Reform Measures, *Times of India* March 29, p6, col 7-8

Janak Singh, 1975, Woes of Kashmir Craftsmen : Menace of Middlemen, *Times of India* Novemebt 29, p6, col 7-8

Janak Singh, 1976, Acute Shontage of Drinking Water in Jammu and Kashmir, *Times of India* July 17, p6, col 7-8

Janak Singh, 1976, Checking Rampant Corruption in Kashmir : More Stringent Law, *Times of India* May 7, p4, col 7-8

Janak Singh, 1976, Kashmir Co-ops: Poor Record : New Rules in Force, *Times of India* June 16, p4, col 7-8

Janak Singh, 1976, Kashmir Reduces Subsidy Burden, *Times of India* April 16, p6, col 7-8

Janak Singh, 1976, Kashmir's Backward Areas Suffer from Lack of Power, *Times of India* December 3, p6, col 7-8

Janak Singh, 1976, Power Paucity Slows Down Pace of Industrialisation in Kashmir, *Times of India* March 20, p6, col3-5

Janak Singh, 1976, Severe Setback to Sericulture: Kashmir Lags behind, *Times of India* January 9, p6, col 7-8

Janak Singh, 1977, Borderline Life-1 : Tangdhar Steeped in Abject Poverty, *Times of India* December 2, p1, col 2-4; December 3, p1 col, 2-4, December 4, p1, col 2-4 +

Janak Singh, 1977, Kashmir on Eve of Elections : Janata to the Fore, *Times of India* May, p6, col 7-8

Janak Singh, 1977, The Sheikh and the Janata : Why Secession Bogey? *Times of India* June 3, p4, col 7-8

Janak Singh, 1977, Small Sector in Kashmir Faces Serious Finance Problems, *Times of India* November 21, p6, col 7-8

Janak Singh, 1977, Why the Congress Supports Sheikh Abdullah, *Times of India* September 7, p6, col 7-8

Janak Singh, 1978, Abdullah Unshaken by Beg's Exit : Kashmir Stays Stable, *Times of India* October 10, p8, col 7-8

Janak Singh, 1978, Gulmarg: A Booming Winter Sports Centre, *Times of India* December 27, p6, col 1-6

Janak Singh, 1979, Jammu's Deep-Seated Resentments: Big Dangers ahead, *Times of India* February 10, p8, col 7-8

Janak Singh, 1979, People's Feelings Not Heeded in Kashmir, *Times of India* May 21, p6, col 7-8

Janata (Periodical), 1956, Kashmir and the SEATO, *Janata* 11(7) March 11, p1, editorial

Janata, (Periodical), 1968, Abdullah Drunk and Abdullah Sober, *Janata* 23(9) March 24, p1 +, editirial

Janata (Periodical) 1968, Astoundingly Ignorant, *Janata* 23(44) December 1, p2, editorial

Janata (Periodical), 1968, Realities in Kashmir, *Janata* 23(39) October 27, p1-2, editorial

Janata (Periodical), 1975, In Kashmir : A New Chapter, *Janata* 30(5)

March 2, p1 +, editiorial

Janata (Periodical), 1977, The Kashmir Ordinance, *Janata* 32(40) November 20, p1, editorial

Janata (Periodical), 1977, Sheikh Saheb : The Secessionist, *Janata* 32(9) June 5, p1-3, editorial

Janata (Periodical), 1978, Sons and Son-in-Law in Kashmir, *Janata* 33(31) October 15, p1-2, editorial

Janata (Periodical), 1979, The Jammu Accord, *Janata* 34(7) March 18, p1-2, editiorial

Janata (Periodical), 1979, A Plea for Restraint, *Janata* 34(2) February 11, p1-2, editorial

Janata (Periodical), 1982, Ominous Precedent, *Janata* 37(31) September 26, p3-4, editorial

Janata (Periodical), 1982, A Planned Exercise, *Janata* 37(33) October 10, p1, editorial

Janata (Periodical), 1982, Trust Begets Trust, *Janata* 37(19) June 20, p1-2 +, editorial

Janata (Periodical), 1983, J&K Elections, *Janata* 38(16) June 12, p3-4, editorial

Janata (Periodical), 1984, Playing with Fire, *Janata* 39(15) July 22, p1-2, editorial

Jasbir Singh, 1992, Attempt for Rural Development in J&K: A Survey-II, *Co-operators Bulletine* 35(11) November, p13-19, bibliography, table

Jayaprakash Narayan
 see also Anon, 1965, Jayaprakash Narayan's Views

Jayaprakash Narayan, 1964, Our Great Opportunity in Kashmir, *Swarajya* 8(44) May 2, p20

Jayaprakash Narayan 1968, Need for Settlement in Kashmir, *Janata* 23(45) December 8, p9-11

Jensen, Holger, 1990, A Threat of Nuelear War (Tensions over (Kashmir), *Maclean's*, 103, June 11, p52-53, illustrations, p52-53,

Jha, Prem Shanker, 1984, Punjab and Kashmir : Relevance of Opposition Stand, *Times of India* August 6, p8, col 3-5

Jha, Srinand, 1984, Cong I MP G.R. Kar is a Nucleus of Pro-Pakistani Elements in J&K, *Organiser* 36(10) July 22, p5

Jha, Srinand, 1984, Farooq's Dream of an Islamic Kashmir, *Organiser* 36(11) July 29, p8 +

Jinnah, Muhammad Ali, 1947, Extract from Jinnah's Statement on the Muslim League Position vis-a-vis Indian States (June 17,

1947), *Indian Annual Register* (Calcutta), p112

Jinnah, Muhammad Ali, 1966, *Selected Speeches and Statement of the Quaid-i-Azam Muhammad Ali Jinnah (1911-1934 and 1947-1948),* ed by M. Rafique Afzal, Research Society of Pakistan, Lahore, xvii, 475p

Jit, Inder
see Inder Jit

Johnson, A. Campbell
see Campbell Johnson, A.

Johri, Sita Ram, 1967, *The Indo-Pak Conflict of 1965,* Lucknow

Jonaraja
see also Kalhana

Jones, Constance, 1930, *Thin Air: A Himalayan Interlude*, Brewer and Warren, New York, 384p

Jones, Stephen Hugh
see Hugh-Jones, Stphen

Joseph, George, 1989, Kashmir: Turmoil in the Valley, *Indian Express* (Magazine) April 30, p1, col 1-8

Joseph, Pothan, 1965, Abdullah: No Lawyers? *Swarajya* 10(3) July 17, p4

Joseph, Pothan, 1965, Diplomatic Ditherings, *Swarajya* 10(19) November 6, p2

Joseph, Pothan, 1965, Haji Sheikh Abdullah at Ooty, *Swarajya* 9(47) May 22, p2-3

Joseph, Pathan, 1965, Intimidating Citizens, *Swarajya* 9(51) June 19, p2-3

Joseph, Pothan, 1965, Kashmir : Secularism vs Jehad, *Swarajya* 10(12) September 18, p2

Joshee, O.K, 1967, Lure of Kashmir, *Times of India* October 29, p2

Joshi, D. K., 1978, *A New Deal for Kashmir,* New Delhi

Kabotra, Devi Chand, 1957, Kashmir, *Hindustan Standard* March 7

Kachru, D.N., 1973, The Kashmir Valley : One That Is Paradise on Earth, *Times of India* (Supplement) March 27, p vi, col 2-3

Kadian, Rajesh, 1992, *The Kashmir Tangle : Issues and Options,* Vision Books, New Delhi, 200p

Kagal, Ayesha, 1980, Rumbling in the Valley, *Times of India* (Sunday Review) November 16, p v, col 1-8

Kagal, Nandan B., 1963, Diplomany in a Low Key, *Times of India* May 15

Kak. B.L., n.d., *Kashmir : Past and Present*, Seema Pub, Delhi, 173p

Kak, B.L., 1978, *Chasing Shadows in Ladakh*, Light and Life Pub, New Delhi, 151p

Kak, B.L., 1981, *Kashmir : Problems and Politics,* Delhi

Kak, B.L., 1987, *Kashmir : The Untold Story of Men and Matters,* Jay Jay B. K. House, Jammu Tawi, 144p

Kak, R.C., 1923, *Handbook of the Archaeological and Numismatic Section of Sri Pratap Singh Museum, Srinagar*, London

Kak, R.C., 1924, A Bird's Eyeview of Kashmir, *CR* November, p205-227

Kak, R.C., 1933, *Ancient Monuments of Kashmir*, London

Kak, R.K., 1979, Education for Employment, *Indian Express* July 16, p9, col 6-8

Kak, Ram Chandra, 1971, *Memoirs of the Archaeological Survey of Kashmir,* Vol 1 *: Antiquities of Marew-Wadwan,* Sagar, New Delhi, 32p

Kak, Ram Chandra and Shatri, Harabhatta, 1927, *Descriptive Catalogue of Sanskrit MSS in the Private Library of Maharaja Shri Hari Singh Ji*, Aryabhushan Press, Puna, 106p

Kakar, V.N., 1970, To Die in Kashmir, *Indian Express* September p6

Kalhana, 1990, *Rajatarangini: Kings of Kashmira,* tr by Jogesh Chunder Dutt, Mittal Publication, New Delhi, (1083p), 3 vols, originally published 1879-1898, Calcutta; tr by Jogesh Chander Dutt, Gian Publishing House, 1986, xv, 452p; tr by Ranjit Sitaram Pandit, Sahitya Academy, New Delhi, 1977, xiii, 784p; tr by M.A. Stein, Motilal Banarsidas, Delhi, 1961-87, 1083p, 3 vols

Kalim, Jialal, n.d., *A History of Kashmiri Pandit*

Kalkat, O.S., 1983, *The Far Flung Frontiers*, New Delhi

Kalla, Aloke K., 1985, *Kashmir Pandits and Their Diversity,* BR Pub, New Delhi, 244p

Kamath, H.V., 1951, Kashmir Truth Must be Told, *Organiser* 4(33) April 2, p5, 12

Kamli, S.A., 1982, Industrial Cooperatives in Jammu and Kashmir, *Co-operators Bulletin* 25(5) May, p5-8

Kanramal, Manohar Das, 1933, *My Trip to the Valley of Kashmir,* Imperial Press, Kasur

Kapoor

see also Kapur

Kapoor, D.R., 1987, Out of the Cult of Defunctism Proposal Discussed in District Board Meeting and Recommended to Govt for Approval, *Co-operations Bulletin* 30(8) August, p9-14, appendix

Kapoor, D. R. and Rajouri, D.R., 1987, Cooperative Movement Marches ahead in Rajouri District, *Co-operators Bullelin* 30 (6) June, p15-16

Kapur

see also Kapoor

Kapur, G.C., 1942, Visit to Kashmir, *Indian Geographic Journal* 17(2), p137-146

Kapur, M.L., 1969, *Kashmir Sold and Snatched*, M.L. Kapur, Jammu Tawi, 180p

Kapur, M.L., 1971, A *History of Medieval Kashmir,1320-1586 A.D., A.R.B. Pub, Jammu, 272p*

Kapur, M.L., 1977, *Studies in History and Culture of Kashmir*, Trikuta Pub, Jammu, 229p

Kapur, M..L, 1986, *Kingdom of Kashmir: A Complete History of Kashmir from Earliest Times to 1586 AD,* Kashmir History Publications, Jammu, 402p

Kapur, M.L., 1992, *Social and Economic History of Jammu and Kashmir State 1885-1925 AD,* Anmol, New Delhi, xi, 451p

Kapur, Teg Bahadur, 1987, *Ladakh: The Wonderland: A Geographical, Historical and Sociological Study*, Mittal, Delhi, vi, 175p

Kara, Ghulam Mohiuddin, 1964, The Jammu Hindus Have Won the Hearts of Kashmir Muslims : Statement, *Organiser* 17(35) March 30, p16

Karam Singh and Des Raj, 1978, Integrated Area Development Planning : Suggested Approach and Its Application, *Indian Journal of Industrial Relations* 13(4) April, p525-539, appendix, biliography, figure

Karan Singh, 1964, *Selected Writings and Speeches, 1960-1964*, Information Department, Government of Jammu and Kashmir, 109p

Karan Singh, 1977, Karan Singh Warns Janata to Prove Its Worth, *Times of India* February 23, p2, col 5-6

Karan Singh, 1982, *Heir Apperent : An Autobiography*, Delhi

Karim, Afsir, 1994, *Kashmir : The Troubled Frontiers*, Lancer International, New Delhi, 396p

Karim, Baz Le, 1971, Industrial Relations in Public Untertakings in Jammu and Kashmir, *Indian Journal of Industrial Relations* 7(2) October, p269-272, bibliography, footnotes

Karnail Singh, 1988, Handicraft in Jammu Province: Tradition and Development, *Co-operators Bullelin* 31(1) January, p77-79

Karnik, Anant Sridhar, 1959, *Kashmir Princess*, Jaico, Bombay, 171p

Kartar Singh, 1953, *Kashmir and Imperialist Intervention*, People's Publishing House, Bombay, 38p

Kaul
 see also Koul

Kaul, A.K., 1979, Seasons of Kashmir Valley, *Geographical Review of India* 41(2) June, p123-130, bibliography, tables

Kaul, Anand, n.d., *The Kashmiri Pandit*

Kaul, B.M., 1971, *Confrontation with Pakistan*, Delhi

Kaul, C.B, 1983, Battle for a Mountain State, *Indian Express* (Magazine) May 29, p1, col 1-8 +

Kaul, D.N, 1992, Kashmir: The Sub-Continent's Dark Spot, *Pioneer* September 22

Kaul, G.L., 1978, Schemes of Minimum Needs in J&K, *Yojana* 22(14-15) August 15, p59

Kaul, Gwasha Lal, 1967, *Kashmir through the Ages (500 BC-AD1967)*, Chronicle Pub House, Srinagar, ix, 304p

Kaul, Gwasha Lal, 1969, *Six Millemium Review of Kashmir Describing Physical, Political, Social, Cultural, Economic and Religious Up-Heavals*, Chronicle Pub, ix, 304p

Kaul, Gwasha Lal, 1970, Shrines, Temples and Mosques in Kashmir, *Cultural Forum* 12(3-4) April-July, p28-32

Kaul, Gwasha Lal, 1972, *Kashmir: Then and Now (500 BC to AD 1972) : A Historical Survey,* Chronicle Pub, Srinagar, xiv, 312p

Kaul, Hari Krishna, 1973, The Kashmir Short Story, *Indian Literature* 16(1-2) January-June, p285-291

Kaul, Hari Kishan, 1980, Sunshine, *Indian Literature* 23(3-4) May-August, p384-393

Kaul, Ikbal
 see Kaul, Iqbal

Kaul, Iqbal, 1971, In the Valley of the Lidder, *Times of India* June 27, p9, col 1-5

Kaul, Iqbal, 1971, Women Poets of Kashmir, *Times of India* March 21, p7, col 1-5 +

Kaul, J.L., 1965, Annual Review of Indian Writing in 1964: Kashmiri, *Indian Literature* 8(2), p76,78

Kaul, J.L., 1967, *Kashmir Guide and Album,* Chronicle Pub, Srinagar

Kaul, Jayalal, 1969, *Studies in Kashmiri*, Kashmir Book Shop

Srinagar, 312p

Kaul, Jayalal, 1970, Sahitya Akademi Award Winners: Taak Zainageri, *Illustrated Weekly of India* 91(31) August 2, p35

Kaul, Jayalal, 1973, Kashmiri: The Facts, *Indian Literature* 16(1-2) January-June, p247-255

Kaul, M.K., 1886, *Weed Flora of Kashmir Valley*, Scientific, St. Mut, 422p

Kaul, Manohar, 1971, *Kashmir : Hindu, Buddhist and Muslim Architecture*, Sagar Pub, New Delhi, 139p, plates

Kaul, P.N, 1981, The Ladakh Karakorams and Their Explorers, *Link* 24(5) September 13, p25-26

Kaul, Pyare Lal, 1968, Kashmir PSP Conference: A Report, *Janata* 23(13) April 21, p9-10

Kaul, Pyare Lal, 1971, The Mistake Kashmir Did Not Make : Guha Draws a Parallel, *Janata* 26(4) December 5, p7

Kaul, Pyare Lal, 1991, *Crisis in Kashmir*, Suman Pub, Delhi, v, 330p

Kaul, S.C., 1932, *A Holiday Trip in Kasmir*, K.P. Press, Srinagar

Kaul, Samvit S., 1967, Blessings in the Kashmiri Proverbs, *Folklore* 8(2) February, p51-54

Kaul, Sansar Chand, 1982, *Beautiful Valleys of Kashmir and Ladakh*, Utpal Pub, Srinagar, 239p

Kaul, Santosh, 1979, Constitution of Kashmir : General Features, *Journal of Political Studies* 12(1) February

Kaul, T.N, 1984, Mehjoor: The Solitary Reaper, *Indian Literature* 27(2) March-April, p83-101

Kaul, Vijay K., 1973, *Kashmir Greets You,* Chronicle Pub, Srinagar, 84p

Kaul, Vijay K., 1982-83, Semantic Study of the Verb *Tshunun* 'To Wear' in Kashmiri, *Kurukshetra University Research Journal,* 16-17, 134-141p

Kaula, M.S., 1923, *Short Review of Research Publications, Kashmir State,* Srinagar

Kaula, P.N., 1966, The First Kashmir Library Conference, *Herald of Library Sciences* 5(3) July, p226-231

Keenan, Brigid, 1989, *Travels in Kashmir: A Popular History of Its People, Places and Crafts*, Oxford University Press, Delhi, ix, 226p, illustrations

Kemp, Emily Georgiana, 1913, *An Artist's Impressions of Western Tibet and Turkestan,* Central Asian Society, London

Khajuria, R.R., 1988, A Bird's Eye View of the Jammu Cooperative

Milk Federation Ltd, *Co-operators Bulletin* 31(1) January, 55-56p

Khan, Abdul Majid, 1957, Kashmir: Confluence of Culture, *Tribune* October 27

Khan, Akbar, 1970, *Raiders in Kashmir: Story of the Kashmir War (1947-48)*, Karachi

Khan, Ali Mohammad, 1959, The Lolab Valley, *KT* 3(6) July-August, p28

Khan, Ali Mohammad, 1961, The Sindh Valley, *KT* 5(8) September, p6-7

Khan, G. Hassan, 1973, *The Kashmiri Mussalman*, Srinagar

Khan, G.M., *jt author*
see Shah, M.H. and Khan, G.M.

Khan, Ghulam Hassan, 1980, *Freedom Movement in Kashmir, 1931-1940*, Light and Life Pub, New Delhi, xiv, 253 p

Khan, J.A., 1983, J and K's Changing Industrial Scené, *Economic Times*, February 21, p4, col 6-8 +

Khan, Liaquat Ali, 1950, *Kashmir and the Inter-Dominion Relations : Statement of the Prime Minister in the Dominion Parliament on January 19, 1950*, Department of Films and Publications, Government of Pakistan, Karachi

Khan, M.A., 1973, Development and Entrepreneurship in Jammu and Kashmir, *SIET Studies* Spring, p51-56

Khan, M. Asghar, 1979, *The First Round: Indo-Pakistan War, 1965*, London

Khan, M. Ibrahim, 1965, *The Kashmir Saga*, Ripon, 228p

Khan, Mahmood Ahmed, 1987, Elementary Education in Jammu and Kashmir : A Review, *Educational Reivew* 93 (10) October, p167-170, bibliography, tables

Khan, Mohammad Ishaq, 1983, *Perspectives on Kashmir: Historical Dimensions*, Gulshan Pub, Srinagar, 173p

Khan, Mohammad Ishaq, 1994, Kashmir's Transition to Islam, : The Role of Muslim Rishis (Fifteenth to Eighteenth century), Manohar Publishers and Distributors, Delhi, viii, 302p

Khan, Mohammed Iqbal, 1977, Persian Influences in Kashmir in the Sultunate Period (1320-1586), *Islamic Culture* 51(1) January, p1-10, bibliography, footnotes

Khan, Mohammed Shahidullah
see Shahidulla Khan, Mohammed

Khan, Muhammad Ayub, 1964, The Pakistan American Alliance: Stresses and Strains, *Foreign Affairs* 42(2) January, p119-206

Khan, Muhammad Ayub, 1965, Address on the Kashmir Dispute; Peace with India, Karachi, October 2, 1965, *Vital Speeches of the Day* 32(1) October 15, p8-9

Khan, Muhammad Ayub, 1967, *Friends Not Masters: A Political Antobiography,* London

Khan, Noorul Hasan, 1977, Library Legislation on the Anvil : Public Libraries in Jammu and Kashmir State, *Indian Library Association Bullentin* 13(1-4) January-December, p5-10

Khan, Rahmatullah, 1969, *Kashmir and the United Nations*, Vikas Pub, New Delhi, vii, 199p,

Khan, Rahmatullah, 1969, The Kashmir Problem: Its Handling in the United Nations, *Journal of Indian Law Institute* 2(3) July-September, p 293-292, bibliography, footnotes

Khan, Rasheeduddin, 1965, A Battle of Principles, *Seminar,* November, p19-25, bibliography

Khanna, K.C., 1973, New Hope in Kashmir : Back from the Wilderness, *Times of India* May 29, p6, col 3-5; May 30, p6, col 3-5

Khare, Harish, 1989, Stalemate in Kashmir : Battle for Minds and Hearts, *Times of India* September, 4, p6, col 3-5

Khare, N.B.
see also Rajagopalachari, C., 1965, Dr N.B. Khare's Prophecy

Khayal, Ghulam Nabi, 1985, A Family Goes to War, *Indian Express* August 5, p1, col 1-8 +

Khayal, Ghulam Nabi, 1985, Pakistan-Occupied Kashmir: What's up? *Illustrated Weekly of India* 105(51) April 28, p20-30

Khayal, Ghulam Nabi, 1986, Winds of Change, *Illustrated Weekly of India* 107 (13) March 30, p20-23

Khayal, Ghulam Nabi, 1989, The Troubled Valley, *Illustrated Weekly of India* 110 (38) September 17, p 30-33

Khazanchi, Ramesh, 1993, Plight of Hindus in Kashmir, *Times of India* July 15, p8, col 7-8

Khera, M.K., et al, eds, 1991, *Energy Problems and Prospects : Studies on Jammu and Kashmir*, Concept Publishing Company, 405p, bibliography, illustrations, maps

Khokhar, B.M., 1972, Fabulous Kashmir, *TW* May 14, p7

Khosla, K.S., 1968, Traveller's Delight : Beautiful Valley of Kashmir, *Times of India* May 12

Khosla, K.S., 1969, Family Planning : Kashmir, *Times of India* (Magazine) October 19, p1, col 2-5

Khosla, K.S., 1969, Kashmir's Power Needs: No Proper Planning, *Times of India* July 26, p8, col 7-8

Khosla, K.S., 1969, Plebiscite Front's Threat: Testing Time for Kashmir Congress, *Times of India* June 11, p6, col 7-8

Khosla, K.S., 1969, The Unchanging Village: Kashmir, *Times of India* (Magazine) July 13, p 1, col 5-8

Khosla, K.S., 1969, A Whiff of Change: Kashmir, *Times of India* (Magazine) August 10, p1, col 6-8

Khosla, K.S., 1971, Eve-of-Poll Survey-XI : It Will be Tough Going for New Congress in Kashmir, *Times of India* February 26, p6, col 4-6

Khosla, K.S., 1971, Reconciliations between Qasim and Sadiq: Tasks Ahead, *Times of India* October 14, p8, col 7-8

Khosla, K.S., 1972, Election Preview-X: Cong Confidence in Victory in Kashmir Well Founded, *Times of India* February 25, p1, col 2-4 +

Khosla, K.S., 1972, Kashmir: Pioneer in Radical Reforms, *Times of India* November 4, p1, col 1-4 +

Khosla, K.S. 1974, Cautions Optimism on Kashmir : Some Advances Made, *Times of India* July 16, p4, col 7-8

Khosla, K.S., 1974, Kashmir Encourages Vegetables Production, *Times of India* September 30, p4, col 7-8

Khosla, K.S., 1974, Kashmir Left Out in the Cold, *Times of India* February 23, p4, col 7-8

Khosla, K.S., 1974, Mr. Swaran Singh's Srinagar Visit Changes Forecast, *Times of India* June 8, p4, col 7-8

Khosla, K.S., 1974, New Measures Taken to Check Corruption in Kashmir, *Times of India* July 2, p4, col 7-8

Khosla, K.S., 1974, Relaxed Atmosphere in Kashmir Valley: Sheikh's Role, *Times of India* May 3, p4, col 7-8

Khrushchev, Nikita Sergeyevich
see also Anon, 1955, Khrushchev Explains Soviet View on Kashmir Question

Khrushchev, Nikita Sergeyevich, 1955, *Extract from N.S. Khrushchev on Kashmir, December 10: Kashmir: An Open Book*, Srinagar

Khullar, L.C., 1978, Channels of Dirstribution in J and K Enterprises, *Indian Journal of Commerce* 31(1) March, p93-100

Khullar, Rupinder, 1988, *Kashmir: The Pageant of the Seasons*, Media Transasia, 114p

Khurshid Ali, 1981, Is State Sector in J&K Efficient, *Capital* 186

(4659) June 1, p15

Khushwant Singh, 1974, Valley of the Jhelum, *Illustrated Weekly of India* 95(8) April 21, p6, col 13 +

Kilam, K.K., *jt author*
see Bakshi, G.A. and Kilam, K.K.

Kilne, James, 1929, *Road to Kashmir,* Hodder and Stoughton, London

Kind, Christian, 1964, More on Kashmir, *Swiss Review of World Affairs* 14(7) October 1964, p10-12

King, Robert Moss, 1884, *The Diary of a Civilian's Wife in India, 1877-82,* Richard Bentley, London, 2 vols

Kirpa Ram (Diwan) 1977, *The Gulabnama of Diwan Kirpa Ram: A History of Maharaja Gulab Singh of Jammu and Kashmir*, tr from Persian by Sukhdev Singh Charak, Light and Life Pub, New Delhi

Kishinchandani, K.M., 1976, J&K State Financial Corporation Makes Progress, *Eastern Economist* 67(21) Novermber 19, p1008-1009

Kishwar, Mahdu and Kothari, Smita, 1989, Violence on Gurparab in Jammu and Its Aftermath, *Economic and Political Weekly,* 24(15), April 15, p 769-777

Knight, E.F, 1893, *Where Three Empires Meet: A Narrative of Recent Travel in Kashmir, Western, Tibet, Gilgit and Adjoining Countries,* Longmans Green, London, 495p, illustrations, map

Knight, William Henry, 1863, *Diary of a Pedestrian in Cashmere and Thibet,* R. Bentley, London, 385p, illustrations

Knowles, J. Hinton, 1985, *Folk-tales of Kashmir*, Jay Jay Book House, Jammu Tawi, x, 510p

Kochak, Gulam Rasook, *The Kashmir Consipiracy Case*

Korbel, J. 1954, *Danger in Kashmir*, Princeton

Korbel, Josef, 1954, The National Conference Administration of Kashmir 1949-54, *Middle East Journal*, Summer

Kotak, H.M., n.d., *AISA Kashmir Guide,* All India Srinagar Spinner's Association, 122p

Kothari, Smita, *jt author*
see Kishwar, Madhu and Kothari, Smita

Koul
see also Kaul

Koul, M.L. , 1976, Sprinkler Irrigation in Jammu and Kashmir, *Social Welfare* 23(4) July, p23

Koul, O.N., 1974, Transport Cartels Batten at Industry's Cost, *Commerce* 129 (3296), July 13, p69

Koul, O.N., 1978, Citric Acid from Sugar, *Commerce* (Annual Number) 137 (3526), p218-220

Koul, O.N., 1978, Moon's Surface and Meadow of Flowers, *Economic Times* April 2, p4, col 1-3 +

Koul, O.N., 1978, Who Will be Successor to Sheikh? *Commerce* 137 (3513) October 7, p648-649

Koul, O.N., 1979, Karakul Sheep Farm at Kharbathang, *Economic Times* December 2, p4, col 6-8 +

Koul, O.N., 1979, Regional Imbalances Issue Hots up, *Commerce* 138(3527) January 20, p19-20

Koul, O.N., 1979, Why do Ladakhi Feel Insecure? *Economic Times* December 9, p4, col 4-8

Koul, O.N., 1980, J&K Land Reforms: Progress Less than Satisfactory, *Economic Times* April 7, p5, col 8

Koul, O.N., 1980, Jammu and Kashmir : Inadequate Power and Communication Facilities, *Commerce* (Annual Number) 141(3628), p251-253

Koul, O.N., 1980, Jammu and Kashmir : Low Literacy Minimises Progress, *Commerce* (Supplement) 141 (3608) August 16, p41-42

Koul, O.N., 1980, Jawans Take Law into Their Hands, *Commerce* 141(3608) August 16, p 314-315

Koul, O.N., 1980, Rs 976 Crore Plan Outlay for J&K Proposed, *Economic Times* December 11, p5, col 7-8

Koul, O.N., 1980, The Speaker Episode and Implications, *Commerce* 141 (3619) November 1, p 854-856

Koul, O.N., 1980, What's Happening in Kashmir : Chauvinism or Blackmail? *Commerce* 141 (3606) August 2, p217-220

Koul, O.N., 1981, Centre-Kashmir Relations, *Economic Times* November 30, p4, col 5-8

Koul, O.N., 1981, Dynastic Rule in Kashmir? *Commerce* 142 (3642) April 4, p750-751

Koul, O.N., 1981, Higher Levels of Consumption, *Commerce* (Supplement) 143 (3661) August 15, p33-34, tables

Koul, O.N., 1981, Power Transmission Loss, *Economic Times* October 5, p4, col 5-8

Koul, O.N., 1981, Study Calls for Organisation to Develop J&K Carpet Industry, *Economic Times* January 21, p7, col 5-8

Koul, O.N., 1982, In Search of Resources, *Commerce* 144 (3689)

February 20, p334-335

Koul, O.N., 1982, Kashmir after Sheikh, *Commerce* 145 (3719) September 18, p450-451

Koul, O.N., 1982, Sericulture in J&K, *Economic Times* (Supplement) May 26, p III, col 8 +

Koul, O.N., 1982, Why G.M. Shah had to Go, *Economic Times* August 23, p4, col 5-8

Koul, O.N., 1983, Beer Makers Lose Battle with Hops Growers of Kashmir, *Economic Times* Septemner 30, p5, col 7-8

Koul, O.N., 1983, Dr. Farooq Abdullah Gets a Big Boost, *Commerce* 147 (3777) October 22, p 626 +

Koul, O.N., 1983, J&K Lures Industrialists, *Economic Times* May 16, p4, col 4-5

Koul, O.N., 1983, Jammu and Kashmir Poll: A Fight to Finish between NC and Congress (I)? *Commerce* 146 (3754), May 14, p829-830

Koul, O.N., 1983, Private Sector to Build Captive Hydel Units, *Economic Times*, November 14, p4, col 6-8

Koul, O.N., 1983, Stagnation in J&K Sericulture Industry, *Economic Times* January 31, p5, col 7-8

Koul, O.N., 1984, Beneficial to Small Scale Entrepreneurs, *Commerce* 148 (3800) March 31, p 497

Koul, O.N., 1984, Dismissal of Farooq Government, *Commerce* 149(3814) July 7, p15-16

Koul, O.N., 1984, Lack of Entrepreneurial Will, *Commerce* 149(3820) August 18, p 245-246 +

Koul, O.N., 1984, Manipulation Feared, *Commerce* 149 (3837), December 15, 919, 922p

Koul, O.N., 1985, Cong (I) in an Unenviable Position in J&K *Economic Times* July 18, p5, col 7-8

Koul, O.N., 1985, Highest Priority to Energy, *Commerce* 151 (3873) August 17, 317-318p

Koul, O.N., 1985, Low River Discharge Affects Power Generation, *Commerce* 150 (3842) January 12, p 82-83

Koul, O.N., 1985, Mass Verdict in Dr. Farooq's Favour, *Commerce* 150 (3842) January 12, p66-67

Koul, O.N., 1985, Priority to Power Generation, *Commerce*, 151(3876) September 7, p476

Koul, O.N., 1986, J&K: Unimaginaive Policies Strifle Modernisation, *Commerce* 153 (3926) August 16, p315-317

Koul, O.N., 1986, Jagmohan Cuts Loops Clearning up, *Economic Times* April 2, p3, col 4-6

Koul, O.N., 1986, Will Gul Shah Bloom again? *Economic Times* March 26, p3, col 4-6

Koul, O.N., 1987, J&K: Are Foodgrains Production Data Reliable? *Commerce* 154 (3961) April 18, p22-23

Koul, O.N., 1987, Muslim United Front Shows Mass Support, *Commerce* 154 (3960) April 11, p 21

Koul, O.N., 1987, Rs 375 Crore Annual Plan Outlay Approved, *Commerce* 154 (3950) January 31, p 23

Koul, O.N., 1987, Salal Project: Elusive Targets, *Commerce* 154(3969) June 13, p 26-27

Koul, Omkar Nath, 1959, Kashmir Welcomes You, *KT* 3(5) May June, p16-19, illustrations

Koul, Omkar Nath, 1976, Noun Phrase in Kashmiri, *Indian Lingusitics* 37(3-4) September-December, p187-195

Koul, Omkar Nath, *jt author*
see Hook, Peter Edwin and Koul, Omkar Nath

Krishan Prasad, 1956, *The United States and the Power Politics,* Seal Publication Centre, Agra

Krishna, Akbar
see Akbar Krishna

Krishna, B., 1975, Jammu and Kashmir, *Illustrated Weekly of Inida* 96(50) December 14-20, p16-23

Krishna, Mohan
see Mohan Krishna

Krishna Menon, V.K., 1964, What is at Stake? *Seminar*, 58, June, p32-40

Krishna Rao, D.V.L.N. and Sharma, R.C., eds, 1991, *Indian Borders: Ecology and Security Perspectives,* Promilla and Co, New Delhi, ix, 230p

Krishna Rao, K., 1962, Sino-Indian Boundary Question and International Law, *International and Comparative Law Quarterly* 2(2) April, p375-415

Krishnan, M.K., 1965, Self-Determination for Kashmir, *New Age* 13(39) September 26, p3

Ksemendra
see Csemendra

Kshirsagar, Anupama, *jt author*
see Deotare, B.C. and Kshirsagar, Anupma

Kulkarni, S.R., 1957, *Truth and Kashmir*, Krishna Pub, New Delhi, xiv, 131p

Kulkarni, V.B., 1965, Kashmir : What about It? *United Asia* 17(3) May-June, p208-213

Kulkarni, V.B., 1988, *Pakistan : Its Origin and Relations with India*, London

Kulshreshtha, Akhilesh and Sharma, B.L., 1988, Fertiliser in Coop Sector: Why? *Co-operators Bulletin* 31(7), July, p14-16

Kulwant Singh, 1988, Railway Crimes: Theft and Pilferage of Railway Property at Jammu Tawi Railway Station, *Indian Journal of Criminology* 16(1) January, p 31-40, tables

Kumar
see also under full name/surname of the author, e.g., Pradeep Kumar

Kumar, D.P., n.d., *Pakistani Proxy War*, Har-Anand Pub, New Delhi

Kumar, V., 1954, *Anglo American Plot against Kashmir*, Bombay

Kumaramangalam, Mohan, 1965, American Approach to Kashmir, *Mainstream* 4(11) November 13, p 25-26

Kumari
see also under full name of the author, e.g. Ved Kumari

Kuppusami, Kurumbai 1991, *Kashmir, Jaipur and Kashi, Rameshwaram*, Vanathi Pathippakam

Lakhanpal, P.L., 1958, *Essential Documents and Notes of Kashmir Dispute*, International Pubs, Delhi, 272p

Lakshmi Narayan and Sansar Chand, 1985, *Introduction to Dogri Folk Literature and Pahari Art*, Academy of Art and Culture and Languages, Jammu, xxii, 17p

Lal
see also under full name/surname of the author, e.g. Mukut Behari Lal

Lal, H.H., 1954, An Emperor Visits Kashmir, *Kashmir* 4(5) May, p107-111, route map

Lamb, Alastair, 1966, *Crisis in Kashmir (1949-1966)*, Routledge and Kegan Paul, London, 163p

Lamb, Alastair, 1991, *Kashmir: A Disputed Legacy, 1846-1990*, Oxford Books, London, 368p

Lambert, Cowley, 1877, *Trip to Cashmere and Ladakh*, Henry and King, London, 199p

Langar, M.L., 1921, *Handy Guide to Kashmir*, Star Press,

Latif Abdul Wani
see Wani, Latif Abdul

Lattimore, Owen, 1954, Pakistan Pact: Two Views: Battle of Corridors, *Nation*, January 23

Lawrence, Walter Roper, 1895, *The Valley of Kashmir*, H. Frowde, London, 478p, map, tables, reprint, 1967, Kesar Pub, Srinagar, 278p

Lee, G. Fitzgerald
see Fitzgerald-Lee, G.

Leitner, G.W, n.d., *Results of Tour in Dardistan, Kashmir, Little Tibet, Ladakh, Zanskar & C.*, Robsthain, London, 4vols

Levi, Werner, 1958, Kashmir and India's Foreign Policy, *Current History* June

Liaquat Ali Khan
see Khan, Liaquat Ali

Lifbor, Reginali, 1956, The Kashmir Issue in Swedish Press, *Scandinavian Newsletter* January 14

Lilienthal, D., 1951, Another Korea in the Making, *Colliers Journal* (New York) August 4

Limaye, Madhu, 1962, India's Defence: National Apathy, *Seminar*

Link (Periodical), 1964, The Week, *Link* 6(40) May 17, p5, editorial

Link (Periodical) 1985, G.M. Shah's Overtures to Farooq Abdullah, *Link* 28(14), November 10, p17, editorial

Little, Gertrude, 1955, A River Trip, *Kashmi*r 5(3) March, p70-73, illustrations

Lohia, Ram Monohar, 1951, Indian Socialist View on Kashmir, *Socialist International Information* August 18

Loman, J.R.A., 1967-68, Types of Kashmiri Society in Ksemendra's Despoadesa, *Adyar Library Bulletin*, 31-32, p171-184, footnotes

Longone, R., 1957, A Week in Kashmir, *KT* 2(5) May, p14-15

Longone, Riccordo, 1957, Kashmir: An Italian View, *KT* 2(3-4) March-April, p1-3

Luthra, G.L., 1968, Amazing Possibilities in High Altitude Farming, *Lok Rajya* 24(15) December 16, p2-4

Mac
See also Mc

MacFarquhar, Emily, 1990, Bleeding Kashmir, *U.S. News and World Report,* 109, November 19, p 53, illustrations

MacFarquhar, Emily, 1990, The Kashmir Question, *U.S. News and World Report*, 108, June 11, p42-44, illustrations, map

MacFarquhar, Roderick, 1965, China and the Ceasefire, *New Statesman*, 70, September 24, p 423-424

Macmunn, George, 1931, *Romance of Indian Frontiers,* Jonathan Cape, London, p25-31

Macmunn, G.F., 1915, *A Freelance in Kashmir: A Tale of the Great Anarchy*, Smith Elder, London, 344p

Madan, T.N., 1972, Religious Ideology in a Plural Society: The Muslims and Hindus of Kashmir, *Contributions to Indian Sociology* (New Series), 6, p106-141, bibliography, diagrams, footnotes, tables,

Madan, T.N., 1975, Structural Implications of Marriage in North India: Wife Givers and Wife Takers among the Pandits of Kashmir, *Contributions to Indian Sociology* (New Series) 9(2) July-December, p217-243, bibliography, foontotes

Madan, T.N., 1985, *Family and Kinship: A Study of the Pandits of Rural Kashmir*, Asia, Bombay, xx, 259 p

Madhava Wariar, A. , 1965, Let the U.N. Take Charge, *Swarajya* 10(17) October 23, p23-24

Madhok, Balraj, 1950, *Kashmir Divided*, Rashtra Dharma, Lucknow, 208p

Madhok, Balraj, 1963, *Kashmir: Centre of New Alignments*, Deepak Prakashan, New Delhi, 196p

Madhok, Balraj, 1964, Kashmir and Indo-Pak Tension, *Organiser* 18(6) September 21, p7

Madhok, Balraj, 1965, What We Saw and Heard in Jammu and Kashmir : A First Hand Account, *Organiser* 19(5) September 12, p9 +

Madhok, Balraj, 1972, *A Story of Bungling in Kashmir*, Young Asia Publications, New Delhi, iii, 197p

Madhok, Balraj, 1988, *Jammu and Kashmir and Ladakh: Problem and Solution*, Reliance, New Delhi, xviii, 83p

Madhok, Balraj, 1992, *Kashmir: The Storm Centre of the World*, A Ghosh, 280 p

Madhok, Balraj and Abhayavardhan, Hector, 1959, Tibet and Kashmir: A Forum, *KA* 1(11) August-September

Madhu Limaye
see Limaye, Madhu

Mahadevan, P., 1964, A Great Victory, *Swarajya* 8(34) February 29, p6-7

Mahadevan, P., 1965, A Diplomatic Triumph, *Swarajya* 10(8) 30

October, p9-10
Mahadevan, P., 1965, The Story of Kashmir, *Organiser* 19(11) October 24, p23-26
Mahadevan, T.M.P., 1966, Adi Samkara in the Land of Sarada, *Illustrated Weekly of India* 87(13) March 27, p41-43
Mahajan, M.C., n.d. *Accession of Kashmir to India*
Mahajan, M.C., 1963, *Looking Back*, London
Mahajan, R.K., *jt author*
see Sadhu, A.N. and Mahajan, R.K.
Maheshwari, Anil, 1993, *Crescent over Kashmir: Politics of Mullaism*, Rupa & Co, New Delhi, 303 p
Mahfoozur Rahman
see Rahman, Mahfoozur
Mahmood Ahmed Khan
see Khan, Mahmood Ahmed
Maillar, Ella K., 1937, *Forbidden Journey from Peking to Kashmir*, William Heinmann, London, 312p
Mainstream (Periodical), 1964, Mountbatten and Kashmir, *Mainstream* 2(25) February 22, p 9-10, editorial
Mainstream (Periodical), 1968, Sheikh Abdullah: The Moment of Decision, *Mainstream* 6(19) January 6, p5-6, editorial
Mainstream (Periodical), 1970, Kashmir Wrangling, *Mainstream* 8(30) March 28, p5-6, editorial
Mainstream (Periodical), 1975, Kashmir and US Arms, *Mainstream* 13(26) March 1, p4-5, editorial
Mainstream (Periodical), 1982, The Lead from Kashmir, *Mainstream* 21 (13), November 27, 1-2p, editorial
Mainstream (Periodical), 1982, Stakes in Kashmir,*Mainstream* 20(44) July 3, p1-3, editorial
Mainstream (Periodical), 1983, Danger in Kashmir, *Mainstream* 21(34) April 23, p1-2, editorial
Mainstream (Perodical), 1983, Kashmir : What Next, *Mainstream* 21(41), June 11, 1-2p, editorial
Mainstream (Perodical), 1984, Musings on Kashmir, *Mainstream* 22(49), August 4, p1-4
Majid Husain
see Husain, Majid
Majid Khan
see Khan, Majid

Majid Khan, Abdul
see Khan, Abdul Majid
Mala Singh, 1979, *Kashmir*, National Book Trust, New Delhi, 48p, illustrations
Malhotra, Inder, 1964, The Separatists, *Seminar,* 58, June, p 29-31
Malhotra, Inder, 1975, The Lion Roars again in Kashmir, *Illustrated Weekly of India* 96(11) March 16, p4-11 +
Malhotra, Inder, 1978, Sordid Drama in Kashmir : Uncertainty in a Sensitive State, *Times of India* September 28, p6, col 3-5
Malhotra, Inder, 1979, Kashmir's Multiple Problems : Need for Careful Handlings, *Times of India* April 12, p8, col 3-5
Malhotra, Inder, 1980, Gen Zia and Kashmir Issue: Highly Negative Stance, *Times of India* May 29, p6, col 3-5
Malhotra, Inder, 1981, The Current Kashmir Scene: Delhi's Worries and Responsibilities, *Times of India* February 5, p8, col 3-5
Malhotra, Inder, 1981, Succession in Kashmir : Local and Wider Implications, *Times of India* February 12, p8, col 3-5
Malhotra, Inder, 1982, Beyond Farooq's Good Start : Real Task in Kashmir, *Times of India* September 23, p8 col 3-5
Malhotra, Inder, 1982, Sheikh Abdullah's Tantrums : Enough is Enough, *Times of India* June 3, p8, col 3-5
Malhotra, Inder, 1983, New Delhi and Srinagar: What Not to do in Kashmir, *Times of India*, November 10, p8, col 3-5
Malhotra, Inder, 1983, Wild Rhetoric in Kashmir : Farooq Ought to Know Better, *Times of India* April 21, p6, col 3-5
Malhotra, Inder, 1984, Farooq Abdhullah's Ouster: Problems and Prospects, *Times of India* July 5, p6, col 3-5
Malhotra, Inder, 1984, Kashmir Drama: Act Two after the Trust Vote, What? *Times of India* August 2, p8, col 3-5
Malhotra, Inder, 1985, Marking Time in Kashmir : G.M. Shah's Second Reprieve, *Times of India* July 25, p8, col 3-5
Malhotra, Inder, 1986, High Stakes in Kashmir : Political Commentary, *Times of India* September 11, p8, col 3-5
Malhotra Inder, 1986, Kashmir's Shame and Agony: Bitter Truth Must be Faced, *Times of India* March 6, p8, col 3-5
Malhotra, Inder, 1988 Facing Facts in Kashmir : Political Commentary, *Times of India* September 1, p6, col 3-5
Malhotra, Inder, 1988, Mischief of Valley : Political Commentary, *Times of India* April 21, p6, col 3-5
Malhotra, Inder, 1989, Mess and Mischief in Kashmir : Political

Commentary, *Times of India* August 24, p4, col 3-5

Malhotra, Inder, 1993, Of Human Rights and Wrongs: U.S. Mood and Vienna Meet, *Times of India* June 11, p8, col 3-5

Malhotra, Prakash Chandra, 1951, *Kashmir and Imperialist Powers*, New Asia Book Club, New Delhi

Malik
see also Mallik

Malik, Gauri Bazaz
see Bazaz Malik, Gauri

Malik, Keshav, 1970, Valley of the Imagination, *Thought* September 12, p14-16

Malik Chadurah, Haider
see Chadurah, Haider Malik

Malla, Bansi Lal, 1985, A Note on Vaishnavite Ayudhapursas in Medieval Kashmiri Sculptures, *Indian Museum Bulletin*, 20, p28-31, bibliography, figures

Malla, Bansi Lal, 1989-91,Some Lakshmi-Narayana Images from Kashmir, *Journal of Indian Society of Oriental Art* (New Series) 18-19, p33-36

Mallet, Pascaline, 1938, *Turn Eastwards: Glimpses into Indian Life*, Pt 4: *Kashmir*, Rider, London, 191p, map, plates

Mandal, Bankim C., 1992, *Srikanthacarita : A Mahakavya of Mankhaka*

Manegole, Catherine S., 1990, A New Clash over Kashmir, *Newsweek*, 115, April 30, p33-34, illustrations

Mangat Rai, 1972, Kashmir Revisited, *Statesman* December 10, p13

Mankekar, D.R., 1966, *Twenty Two Fateful Days*, Bombay

Mann, R.S., 1979, Anthropo-geography : An Important Methodological Issue, *Man in India* 59(3) July-September, p261-273, bibliography

Mann, Ram Singh, 1986, *Ladakhi: A Study in Ethnography and Change*, Anthropological Survey of India, Calcutta, vii, 181p

Manning Thomas
see under Markham, Clements R.

Manoj Das
see Das, Manoj

Maqbul Ahmad, S.
see Ahmad, S. Maqbul

Markham, Clements R., 1876, *Narrative of Mission of George Boyle to Tibet and of the Journey of Thomas Manning to Lhasa*, Trubner,

London, 354p

Marsden, Philip, 1946, *Kashmir Calls*, Today and Tomorrow, Leeds, 48p

Marshall, A.A., *introduction writer*
see Clanson, Gerald L.M., comp, 1912, *Catalogue of Stein Collection. . .*

Martin, Kingsley, 1963, China and the Kashmir Deadlock, *New Statesman* 65 (1680) May 24, p788

Martin, Kingsley, 1965, Kashmir : The Lion at Large, *New Statesman* 69(1775) March 19, p427-428

Martin, Kingsley, 1965, Reflections on Kashmir, *New Statesman* 70(1801) September 17, p 385

Mascarenhas, Lambert, 1978, Kashmir : A New World : An Experience, *Goa Today* 12(12) July, p17-18 +

Mather, Berkeley, 1969, *Pass Beyond Kashmir,* Collins, London, 252p

Mathew, George, ed, 1990 *Panchayati Ray in Jammu and Kashmir*, foreword by Farooq Abdullah, Institute of Social Sciences; Concept Publishing Company, New Delhi, xxii, 165 p, bibliography

Mathur, R.B., 1961, Kashmir and Switzerland, *Leader* October10

Matto, Gulam Rasool, 1968, Regional Disparities in Kashmir, *Mainstream* 6(47) July 20, p32-35

Maya Rallia Ram
see Rallia Ram, Maya

Mayfield, R.C., 1955. A Geographic Study of the Kashmir Issue, *Geographical Review*, April

Mazumdar, Sudip, 1990, The Ring around Singh (Kashmir), *Newsweek*, 114, February 5, p 36, illustrations, map

Mc
see also Mac

Mc Callum, Duncan, 1930, *China to Chelasa : A Modern Pilgrimage long Ancient Highways,* Ernest Benn, London, 283p, maps, plates

Mc Cormic, Arthur David, 1895, *An Artist in the Himalayas*, Macmillan, New York, 306p, illustrations, map

McLeish, Alexander, 1931, *Frontier Peoples of India: A Missionary Survey*, World Dominion Press, London

Megub, George, 1971, Trout Fishing in Kashmir, *Times of India* January 31, p9, col 1-4

Mehjoor
see also Bakshi, Tanseem, 1984, The Political Ideas of Mehjoor;

Kaul, T.N., 1984, Mehjoor

Mehrajuddin, 1977, A Study of the Central Jail, Kashmir, *Social Defence* 12(48) April, p49-60

Mehta, Chandralekha, 1954, Glimpses of Kashmir, *Kashmir* 4(3), p43-44

Mehta, Krishna, 1966, *This Happened in Kashmir*, Publications Division, Government of India, New Delhi, 171p

Mehta, R.L., 1956, Discovery of Kashmir, *MI* 8(12) December, p9-13

Mehta, R.L., 1957, Homage to a Hero: Baba Jito : An Agrarian Revolutionary about Six Centuries ago, *KT* 2(7) September-October, p7

Mehta, R.L., 1964, Mineral Resources of Jammu and Kashmir State, *Modern Review* 115(5) May, p354-359, illustrations

Mello, Melville de
see, De Mello, Melville

Menon
see also under full name/surname of the author, e.g., Krishna Menon, V.K.

Menon, V.P., 1956, *The Story of Integration of the Indian States*, London

Menon, V.P., 1957, *The Transfer of Power in India*, London

Menteth, S., 1949, Kashmir, *New Commonwealth*, 9, December, p244-249

Merrick, Henrietta Sands, 1931, *In the World's Attics*, G.P. Putnams, New York, 259p, illustrations

Messervy, F., 1949, Kashmir, *Great Britain and the East*, 65, January, p 37-38

Messervy, Frank, 1949, Kashmir Problem, *Asiatic Review*, 45, January, p 469-483

Mhafe, A. De
see De Mhafe, A.

Mikoyan, S., 1956, Kashmir People Should Decide Their Future, *Dawn* (Pakistan), March 26

Mikoyan, S., 1965, Kashmir : The Apple of Discord, *Now* 2(5) November 19, p7-8, 10

Milks, Harold K., 1955, Kashmir : Bone of Indo-Pakistan Contention, *New Times of Burma*, June 1

Miller, T.B., 1963, Kashmir : The Commonwealth and the United Nations, *Australian Outlook* 17(1) April, p54-73

Milne, James, 1929, *Road to Kashmir: With a Gallery of Special*

Pictures, Hodder & Stoughton, London, 159p

Mir, Ali Mohammad and Husain, Majid, 1984, The Assembly Election in Jammu and Kashmir : A Study in Spatial Structure of Voting Behaviour in 1983, *National Geographical Journal of India* 30(1) March, p53-62, figures

Mir Abdual Aziz
see Aziz, Mir Abdul

Mir Qasim, Syed
see Qasim, Syed Mir

Mirchandani, B.D., 1965, Chack-Nama: Reference to Persia, Kabul, Kashmir and Kanauj, *JIH* 43(2) August, p369-385

Mishra
see also Misra

Mishra, Mandan, 1968, *Kasmiretihas*, Shri Lal Bahadur Shashtri Rashtriya Sanskrit Vidyapeetha, New Delhi, 14, 310p

Mishra, R.K., 1984, 'I' am being Maligned, Says Farooq Abdullah, *Link* 26(50) July 15, p 19-20

Mishra, R.K., 1984, Will Kashmir Remain Peaceful? *Link* 26(50) July 15, p 16-18

Misra
see also Mishra

Misra, K.K., n.d., *Kashmir and India's Foreign Policy* Chugh, Allahabad, 615p

Misra, M.M., 1980, Emergence and Growth of Municipal Government and Finance in Jammu and Kashmir, *Quarterly Journal of Local Self-Government Institute* 50(3) January-March, p557-573, bibliography

Mistri, Motilal, 1974, Kashmir: A New Down, *Mainstream* 12(50) August 10, p14 +

Mitchell, Jared, 1984, Gandhi Ousts an Opponent (Troops to Kashmir), *Maclean's*, 19, July 16, p 21-22

Mitra, A.
see also Collet, John, 1898, *Guide for Visitors to Kashmir*

Mohammad
see also Mohammed; Muhammad

Mohammad Ali, Chaudhri, 1967, *The Emergence of Pakistan*, London

Muhammad Hafizullah
see Hafizullah, Muhammad

Mohammad Ibrahim, M.
see Ibrahim, M. Mohammad

Mohammad Ishaq Khan
see Khan, Mohammad Ishaq

Mohammad Khan, Ali
see Khan, Ali Mohammad

Mohammad Mir, Ali
see Mir, Ali Mohammad

Mohammad Musa, *My Version: India-Pakistan War*, 1965

Mohammad Shafi
see Shafi, Mohammad

Mohammad Syeed, Syed, 1978, The Himalayan Way of Breathing the Last: On the Neutralising Status of the Wone: Final Aspiration in Kashmiri, *Eastern Anthropologist* 31(4) October-December, p531-541, bibliography

Mohammad Yasin
see Yasin, Mohammad

Mohammed
see also Mohammad

Mohammed Abdullah, Sheikh
see Abdullah, Sheikh Mohammed

Mohammed Aslam, 1977, Community Development in Jammu and Kashmir, *Kurukshetra* 25(14) April 16, p14-15

Mohammed Aslam, 1977, Land Reforms in Jammu and Kashmir, *Social Scientist* 6(4) November, p59-64, footnotes

Mohammed Ayoob, 1968, Pakistan: New Move on Kashmir, *Mainstream* (Annual Number) 7(1-3), p59-60

Mohammed Ayoob and Subrahmanyan, 1972, *The Liberation War*, New Delhi

Mohammed, Ghulam, 1971, Action against Secessionists, *Mainstream* 9(23) February 6, p28-30 +

Mohammed Hassnain, Fida
see Hassnain, Fida Mohammed

Mohammed Iqbal Khan
see Khan, Mohammed Iqbal

Mohammed Sadiq, Ghulam
see Sadiq, Ghulam Mohammad

Mohammed Sayeed
see also Sayeed, Mohammed

Mohammed Sayeed, Mufti, 1983, Exit of Mir Qasim a Technicality,

Link 26(7) September 25, p 8+

Mohammed Sayeed, Mufti, 1985, Why the High Command Distrusts, *Organiser* 37 (28) November 24, p7+

Mohammed Sayeed, Mufti, 1989, Kashmir Situation Is Explosive, *Link* 31(29) February 26, p13-14

Mohammed Shahidullah, Khan
see Shahidullah, Khan Mohammed

Mohammed Shahwar Alam
see Alam, Mohammed Shahwar

Mohammed Sultan, 1983, Farming in J&K: Land Reforms and Agrarian Set-up, *Economic Times* July 7, p5, col 3-6+; July 8, p5, col 7-8

Mohan,
see also under full name/surname of the author, e.g., Surendra Mohan

Mohan Krishna, n.d., *Early Medieval History of Kashmir with Speical Reference to the Loharas, AD 1003-1171*, New Delhi

Mohi-ud-din, Akhtar, 1977, Social Ideals and Patriotism in Kashmiri Literature (1900-1930), *Indian Literature* 20(3) May-June, p80-89

Mohi-ud-din, Akhtar, 1980, Light and Shade, *Indian Literature* 23(3-4) May-August, p350-353

Mohi-ud-Din, Akhtar, 1987, The Houri of Paradise; A Kashmiri Story, *Indian Literature* 30(1) January-February, p38-46

Mohi-ud-din, Gh., 1986, Kargil and Its Inhabitants : A Historical Background, *Quarterly Review of Historical Studies* 25(4) January-March, p49-58

Mohi-ud-din-Dar, Ghulam, 1992, *Social and Religious Conditions on the Eve of Spread of Islam in Kashmir*, Gulshan Pub, Srinagar 92p

Mohi-ud-din-Kara, Ghulam
see Kara, Ghulam Mohiuddin

Mohy-ud-din Hajini
see Hajini, Mohy-ud-din

Moonis Raza
see Raza, Moonis

Moraes, Frank, 1965, Self-Reliance, *Seminar*, 75, Novermber, p34-36

Moraes, Frank, 1970, An Ambassador's Dairy-I, *Indian Express*, January 6

Morrisby, Edwin S., 1957, An Australian View of Kashmir, *Eastern World* (London) 11(4) April, p23-24

Mufti Mohammed Sayeed
see Mohammed Sayeed, Mufti

Muhammed Ayub Khan
see Khan, Muhammed Ayub

Muhibbul Hasan, 1959, *Kashmir under the Sultans*, Iran Society, Calcutta, xiv, 338p

Mujahid, Sharif-al, n.d., *The Issue behind India-Pakistan Conflict*, Pakistan High Commission, London, 5p

Mujahid, Sharyal, 1965, *Is Kashmir an Internal Matter of India*, Sharyal Mujahid, London, 5p

Mukerjee, Dilip, 1965, India and Pakistan: The Other Half of Our Task, *Economic Weekly* 17(42) October 16, p1597-1588

Mukherjee, Dilip, 1973, Mr. Bhutto on Kashmir : A Matter of Dramatics, *Times of India* December 1, p4, col 3-4

Mukerjee, Dilip, 1974, Dialogue in Kashmir-II : Problems of the Future, *Times of India* November 9, p4, col 3-5

Mukherjee, S.K., 1955, Problems of International Law Involved in the Kashmir Dispute, *Calcutta Review* August, p 157-170, September, p302-316

Mukherji, Saradindu, 1992, Subservience to Pan-Islam Must End, *Pioneer*, September 18

Mukut Behari Lal, 1965, The Kashmir Issue, *Indian Quarterly* 21(4) October-December, p345-374

Mullik
see also Malik

Mullik, B.N., 1971, *My Years with Nehru-Kashmir*, Allied, New Delhi, 320p

Munshi, D.N., 1992, *Agony of Kashmir*, Suruchi Prakashan, New Delhi

Murty, B.S.N., 1968, India's Complaint to the World Court on Judge Zafarulla Khan's Political Speeches on Kashmir, *Indian Journal of International Law* 8(4) October, p547-548

Musa, Mohammad
see Mohammad Musa

Mushtaq Ahmad Gurmani
see Gurmani, Mushtaq Ahmad

Muthoo, M.K., 1970, Impact Analysis of a Renewable National Resources Plan with Reference to Kashmir, *Artha Vijnana* 12(1-2) May-June, p270-299, appendix, bibliography, figures, footnotes, tables,

Muthoo, M.K., 1970, Optional Systems Designing for Efficiency in Kashmir's Renewable Resource Use, *Artha-Vikas* 6(2) July p1-31, appendix, bibliography, footnotes

Muzaffar Aazim
see Aazim, Muzaffar

N.J.N. (psued), 1962, Pipe-Dreams from Marvard, *Times of India* December 24

Nabi, Ghulam
see Ghulam Nabi

Nabi Khayal, Ghulam
see Khayal, Ghulam Nabi

Naik, J.A., 1968, Indo-Soviet Relations and Kashmir, *Janata* 23(10) March 31, p4

Naik, J.A., 1968, Soviet Policy on Kashmir, *Foreign Affairs Reports* 17(1) January, p5-7; *India Quarterly* 24(1) January-March, p50-61

Nambiar, A.C.N., 1963, Kashmir Negotiations: Echoes in Europe, *National Herald* June 10

Nanda, K.K., 1994, *Conquering Kashmir: A Pakistani Obsession*, Lancers Books, xvi, 400p, bibliography

Nandakumar, Prema, 1965, Blurred Vision, *Swarajya* 10(19) November 6, p9-10

Nandi, Satyananda, 1965, Towards Peaceful Change, *Swarajya* 10(20) November 13, p27

Narain
see also *under* full name/surname of the author, e.g., Virendra

Narain
see also Narayan

Narayan
see also under full name/surname of the author, e.g., Lakshmi Narayan; *see also* Narain

Narayana Ayyar, S.R., 1968, The Only Way of Dealing with Sheikh Abdullah, *Organiser* 21(27) February 11, p6

Narayanan, K.R., 1986, Kashmir and Secularism, *Mainstream* 24(38) May 24, p9-10 +

Narinder Singh, 1992, *Political Awakening in Kashmir*, H.K. Pubs, Delhi, 202p

Nasim Ahmed
see Ahmed, Nasim

Nath, S.K., 1965, The Aftermath, *Economic Weekly* 17(40) October

2, p1509-1510

National Herald (Newspaper), 1962, Timely Warning, *National Herald* May 19, editorial

National Herald (Newspaper), 1963, Failure and Third Party, *National Herald* May 17, editorial

National Herald (Newspaper), 1963, Kashmir, *National Herald* May 27, editorial

National Herald (Newspaper), 1963, Kashmir and the Sub-Continent, *National Herald* May 18, editorial

Navdou, Jean, 1980, *Buddhist of Kashmir*, Agam Kala Prakashan, xvi, 308p

Nawang, Tsering Shakspo, 1993, *Insinght into Ladakh*, Tsering Shakspo Nawang, Sabu-Leh, iii, 159p

Nayar, Kuldip, 1971, *India: The Critical Years*, Delhi

Nayar, Kuldip, 1972, *Distant Neighbours*

Nedou, Harry, 1966, Big and Small Himalayan Game, *Illustrated Weekly of India* 87(13) March 27, p29

Nedou, Freddie, 1978, Meadow of Flowers, *Times of India* December 27, p6, col 3-4

Nehru, Jawaharlal, 1946, *The Discovery of India*, Oxford University Press

Nehru, Jawaharlal, *introduction writer*
see Dhar, S.N., 1945, *Kashmir*

Neve, Arthur, 1984, *Thirty Years in Kashmir*, Asian Pub, Lucknow, 316p

New Age (Periodical), 1964, The Nation's Wrath, *New Age* 12(8) February 23, p4, editorial

New Age (Periodical), 1974, Clinch the Issue Now, *New Age* 22(47) November 24, p2, editorial

New Age (Periodical), 1977, Janata's Shadow over Kashmir, *New Age* 25(27) July 3, p2, editorial

New Age (Periodical), 1984, Farce in Srinagar, *New Age* 32(32) August 5, p2, editorial

New Age (Periodical), 1984, Thirteen Musketeers, *New Age* 32(28) July 8, p2, editorial

New Age (Periodical), 1986, Good Riddance but Not Enough, *New Age* 34(11), March 16, p2, editorial

New Republic (Periodical), 1965, Fighting in Kashmir, *New Republic* 153(11) September 11, p7-8, editorial

New York Times (Periodical), 1955, The Russians in Kashmir, *New*

York Times December 11, editorial

New York Times (Perodical), 1957, A Veto on Kashmir, *New York Times* February 22, editorial

New York Times (Periodical), 1962, Hope for a Kashmir Solution, *New York Times* November 30, editorial

New York Times (Perodical), 1962, India, Pakistan and Kashmir *New York Times* November 27, editorial

New York Times (Periodical), 1962, Mr. Nehru's Double Standard, *New York Times* June 26, editorial

New York Times (Periodical), 1961, New Try on Kashmir, *New York Times* July 15, editorial

New York Times (Periodical), 1962, A U.N. Resolution on Kashmir, *New York Times* June 18, editorial

Nirash, K.L. and Iqbal, S.M., 1978, *The Culture of Kashmir*, Asia Book Corp

Nisar Ali, 1978, Deteriorating Agrarian Situation in Jammu and Kashmir, *Eastern Economist* 71(24) December 15, p1227-1273, bibliography, tables

Nisar Ali, 1982, A Study of Economic Optima and Resource Use, *Kurukshetra* 30(20) July 16, p17-20

Nizam-ud-din-Wani, 1993, *Muslim Rule in Kashmir (AD 1554-1568)* Anmol, New Delhi, 308 p

Noorani, A.G., 1964, *Kashmir Question*, Manaktalas, Bombay, 125p

Noorani, A.G., 1986, Kashmir: The Lost Opportunity, *Illustrated Weekly of India* 107(35) September 7, p50-53

Noorul Hasan Khan
see Khan, Noorul Hasan

Obradovic, Vlada, 1965, The Dispute over Kashmir, *Review of International Affairs* 16(370) September 5, p8-10

Ogra, Ashok, 1976, Need to Develop Low Budget Tourism, *Mainstream* 14(38) May 22, p 31

Olver, A.S.B., 1964, Kashmir, *World Today* 20(11), p461-464

Om, Hari
see Hari Om

Organiser (Periodical), 1949, Our Kashmir, *Organiser* 3(3) September 6, p3 +, editorial

Organiser (Periodical), 1950, Kashmir, *Organiser* 3(45) July 3, p3, 18, editorial

Organiser (Periodical), 1951, Kashmir, *Organiser* 4(96) July 2, p3, editorial

Organiser (Periodical) 1951, Over Unforgettable Lesson, *Organiser* 4(34) April 9, p3, editorial

Organiser (Periodical), 1953, India is No Turkey *Organiser* 7(2) August 24, p3, editorial

Organiser (Periodical), 1964, All Looking and No Leaping, *Organiser* 17(27) February 10, p3, editorial

Organiser (Periodical), 1964, The Big Lie, *Organiser* 17(43) May 25, p3, editorial

Organiser (Periodical), 1964, The Caravan Must Go on, *Organiser* 17(23) January 13, p3, editorial

Organiser (Periodical), 1964, The Economic Consequences of Abdullah, *Organiser* 17(54) August 10, p3, editorial

Organiser (Periodical), 1964, Enter Sadiq, *Organiser* 17(31) March 9, p3, editorial

Organiser (Periodical), 1964, Haji or Ghazi? *Organiser* 18(20) December 28, p3, editorial

Organiser, 1964, Hitch over 'Sadar-i-Riyasat' *Organiser* 18(11) October 26, p3, editorial

Organiser (Periodical), 1964, Mr. Nanda and His Three Rats, *Organiser* 17(29) February 24, p3, editorial

Organiser (Periodical), 1964, Panditji, Hands off Kashmir, *Organiser* 17(42) May 18, p3, editorial

Organiser (Periodical), 1964, The Time to Act is Now, *Organiser* 17(24) January 20, p3+, editorial

Organiser (Periodical), 1964, Too Much, too Soon, too Fast, *Organiser* 17(38) April 20, p3, editorial

Organiser (Periodical), 1964, We Can Do It? *Organiser* 17(29) February 24, p3, editorial

Organiser (Periodical), 1964, When Bhutto Was Still at School, *Organiser* 17 (48) June 29, p3, editorial

Organiser (Periodical), 1965, Agni Pariksha, *Organiser* 19(7) September 26, p3, editorial

Organiser (Periodical), 1965, Cooling His Heels, *Organiser* 18(40) may 17, p3, editorial

Organiser (Periodical), 1965, Have Mercy on the Sheikh, *Organiser* 18(35) April 13, p7, editorial

Organiser, 1965, JP's Contradictions, *Organiser* 19(16) December 5, p3, editorial

Organiser (Periodical), 1965, Karan Singh's Indiscretion, *Organiser* 19(16) December 5, p3, editorial

Organiser (Periodical), 1965, The Sheikh Haj to Cairo, *Organiser* 18(31) March 15, p3, editorial

Organiser (Periodical), 1967, Sheikh Abdullah, *Organiser* 21(7) September 24, p3, editorial

Organiser (Periodical), 1967, Sheikh Saheb, *Organiser* 21(19) December 17, p3, editorial

Organiser (Periodical), 1968, Let Her Redeem the Family Name, *Organiser* 22(10) October 19, p7 +, editorial

Organiser (Periodical), 1981, Well Done Sheikh, *Organiser* 32(44) March 22, p3, editorial

Organiser (Periodical) 1984, Back to Square One, *Organiser* 36(9) July 15, p3, editorial

Padam, Rosha
see Rosha, Padam

Pakistan Times (Newspaper), 1957, Soviet Veto, *Pakistan Times* (Lahore) November 25, editorial

Pakistan Times (Newspaper), 1961, USSR and Kashmir, *Pakistan Times* (Lahore) August 16, editorial

Pakistan Times (Newspaper), 1962, Caution, *Pakistan Times* (Lahore) December 1, editorial

Pakistan Times (Newspaper), 1962, Kashmir and Foreign Policy, *Pakistan Times* (Lohore) May 27, editorial

Pakistan Times (Newspaper), 1962, Kashmir First, *Pakistan Times* (Lahore) November 20, editorial

Pakistan Times (Newspaper), 1963, Mediation Move, *Pakistan Times* (Lahore) May 10, editorial

Pal
see also under full name of the author, i.e., Anandi Pal

Pal, Khagendra Chandra, 1964, A Panchsheel Approach to the Kashmir Problem in the United Nations, *Indian Journal of Political Science* 25(3-4) July-September-December, p136-144

Pal, Pratapaditya, ed, 1989, *Art and Architecture of Ancient Kashmir*, Marg Pub, Bombay

Palit, D.K., 1972, *Jammu and Kashmir Arms: History of the J&K Rifles*, Palit and Dutt, Dehra Dun, xv, 305p, illustrations

Palit, D.K., 1972, *The Lightering Campaign: The Indo-Pak War, 1971*, Salisbury

Palme Dutt, R
see Dutt, R. Palme

Panagariya, B.L., 1994, *Kashmir : Paradise in Turmoil*, National Pub House, Jaipur, 128p

Pande, B.M., 1972, A Neolithic "Tectiform" from Burzahom, District Srinagar, Kashmir, *Journal of Indian Anthropological Society* 7(2) October, p175-177, bibliography, footnotes

Pande, B.M., 1970, The Neolithic in Kashmir : New Discoveries, *Anthropologist* 17(1-2) March-September, p25-41, footnotes

Pandit, B.N., 1973, Monistic Saivite Philosophy of Kashmir, *Cultural Forum* 15(3-4) April-July, p32-35

Pandit, H.N. 1978, Fragments of History: Mountbatten's Role on Kashmir, *Indian Review* 74(6) September, p9-15, footnotes

Pandit, K.N, ed, 1986, *Ladakh: Life and Culture,* University Centre of Central Asian Studies, Srinagar, 138p

Pandit, Ranjit Sitaram, *translator*
see Kalhan

Pangotra, Narendar Nath, 1978, Opinion of Affluent and Poor on School Education and Its Functions, *Progress of Education* 52(9) April, p180-183+, tables

Pant, Kusam, 1987, *The Kashmiri Pandits: Story of Community in Exile in the 19th and 20th Centuries*, Allied, Bombay 1200p

Parakal, Pauly V., 1984, Farooq Ministry Overthrown, *New Age* 32(28) July 8, p1+

Parasuram, T.V., 1962, United States and Kashmir, *Pakistan Times* (Lahore) October 5

Parasuram, T.V., 1963, U.S. Disengagement on Kashmir, *Indian Express*, May 4

Parasuram, T.V., 1965, *Medal for Kashmir*, S.Chand, Delhi, viii, 299p

Parihar, M.C., *jt author*
see Singh, R.S. and Parihar, M.C.

Parihar, R.R., 1967-68, Fourth General Elections in Jammu and Kashmir, *Political Science Review* 6(3-4) - 7(1-2) July-September 1967, April-June 1968, p235-250, tables

Parmoo
see Parmu

Parmu, R.K., 1970, *A History of Muslim Rule in Kashmir, 1320-1819,* People's Publishing House, xiv, 461p

Parmu, R.K., 1977, *History of Sikh Rule in Kashmir, 1819-1846*, Government of Jammu and Kashmir, Srinagar, xvi, 428p

Partridge, Elizabeth, 1956, Indian Neutralism Pays off, *Jerusalem Post*, March 22

Pasricha, Ram Nath, 1965, The Road Never Ends, *Illustrated Weekly of India* 86(10) March 7, p8-11, illustrations

Patel, Vallabhbhai, 1971, *Sardar Patel's Correspondance, 1945-50: New Lights on Kashmir*, ed by Durga Das, Navjivan Publishing House, xciv, 394p

Pathak

see also Pathik

Pathak, K.B., et al, 1994, *Biostatistical Aspects of Health*, BR Publishing Corp, 396p

Pathik, Jyoteeshwar, 1990, *Ghimpses of History of Jammu and Kashmir*, Jay Kay Book House, Jammu Tawi, xii, 160p

Pathik, Jyoteeshwar and Sharma, D.C., 1980, *Cultural Heritage of the Dogras*, Life and Light Pub, New Delhi, vi, 177p

Patriot (Newspaper), 1963, Kashmir "Mediation", *Patriot* August 14, editorial

Patriot (Newspaper), 1963, Mediation, *Patriot* August 8, editorial

Paul, Dharm, 1961, Land of Eternal Beauty, *KT* 5(8) September, p29-30

Peer

see also Pir

Peer Giyasuddin

see Giyasuddin, Peer

People's Democracy (Periodical), 1975, Sheikh Abdullah Takes over, *People's Democracy* 11(8) February 23, p1 +, editorial

People's Democracy (Periodical), 1982, Behind the Raking up of Kashmir Issue, *People's Democracy* 6(10) March 7, p1-2, editorial

People's Democracy (Periodical), 1983, J&K Elections, *People's Democracy* 7(24) June 12, p1-2, editorial

People's Democracy (Periodical), 1984, Jammu Kashmir after a Month, *People's Democracy* 8(32) August 5, p1-2, editorial

Peregrinus (psued), 1956, Inside Pakistan, *Hindustan Times*, December 27

Pineau, M, 1956, M. Pineau Speaks, *Hindustan Standard* March 14

Pir

see also Peer

Pir, S.L., 1971, New Look at Industrial Development, *Mainstream* 9(45) July 10, p37-38

Political and Economic Review (Periodical), 1970, Imbroglio in Kashmir, *Political and Economic Review* 1(3) March 23, p2, editorial

Pompur, Rasool, 1981, Kashmiri Forging ahead towards Survival, *Indian Literature* 24(6) November-December, p84-93

Pompur, Syed Rasool, 1987, Few but Better Publications, *Indian Literature* 30(6) November-December, p93-100

Popov, Y., 1957, Kashmir: Artifical Issues, *New Times* (10) March 7, p9-10

Prabhat Chand, 1967, *Rendezvous with Ichogil*, New Delhi

Prabhu, R.K., 1969, *History of Muslim Rule in Kashmir, 1320-1819*, Peoples Publishing House, Delhi, 560p

Pradeep Kumar, 1978, Demand for State Autonomy: Case Study of West Bengal and Kashmir, *Social Science Research Journal* 3(1) March, p31-45, bibliography

Prakash

see also under full name of the author, e.g., Buddha Prakash

Prakash Chandra, 1985, The National Question in Kashmir, *Social Scientist* 13(6) June, p35-56, footnotes

Prasad, S.N. and Dharam Pal, n.d., *History of Operations in Jammu and Kashmir (1947-48)*, Controller of Publications, Government of India, Delhi, 3vols

Prema Nandkumar

see Nandkumar, Prema

Pringshei, Klaus H., 1965, China's Role in the Indo-Pakistani Conflict, *China Quarterly*, 24, October-December, p423-424

Pulwana, D.R., *jt author*

see Sofi, A.R. and Pulwana, D.R.

Puri, Balraj, 1964, Kashmir Policy: Time for Rethinking, *Economic Weekly* 16(5-7) February, p209-210

Puri, Balraj, 1965, What to do with Sheikh Abdullah, *Economic Weekly* 17(20) May 15, p809-812

Puri, Balraj, 1966, *Jammu: A Clue to Kashmir Tangle*, Balraj Puri, 105p

Puri, Balraj, 1966, State of Kashmir's Finances, *Eastern Economist* 46(25) June 24, p1304-1307

Puri, Balraj, 1967, Politics of the Election in Kashmir, *Economic and Political Weekly* 2(8) February 25, p457-458

Puri, Balraj, 1967, Regional Tension in Kashmir, *Economic and Political Weekly* 2(3-5) February, p149-150

Puri, Balraj, 1970, State People's Convention: An Assessment, *Economic and Political Weekly* 5(37) September 12, p1524-1526

Puri, Balraj, 1970, Trivet of Cultural Heritage, *Cultural Forum* 12(3-4) April-June, p9-19, bibliography

Puri, Balraj, 1971, Bangla Desh and Kashmir, *Janata* 26(37) September 26, p11-12

Puri, Balraj, 1971, Drift in Kashmir, *Economic and Political Weekly* 6(8) February 20, p486-487

Puri, Balraj, 1972, After the Breakthrough in Kashmir, *Janata* 27(26) July 16, p8-9

Puri, Balraj, 1972, Basis for a New Edifice, *Economic and Political Weekly* 7(41) October 7, p2056-2057

Puri, Balraj, 1972, Neglect of Language Policy, *Economic and Political Weekly* 7(48) November 25, p2329-2331

Puri, Balraj, 1973, Competing Claims of Religion, Region and Backwardness-Based Identities, *Economic and Political Weekly* 8(28) July 14, p1223-1224

Puri, Balraj, 1973, Final End of Kashmir Problem? *Economic and Political Weekly* 8(45) November 10, 1991-92

Puri, Balraj, 1973, Must History Repeat Itself? *Economic and Political Weekly* 8(20) May 19, p896-897

Puri, Balraj, 1973, National Experiment of Unity in Diversity, *Cultural Forum* 15(3-4) April-July, p28-31

Puri, Balraj, 1973, Prolonging Dependence, *Economic and Political Weekly* 8(16) April 21, p741-742

Puri, Balraj, 1973, To Prop the Heavy Top, *Economic and Political Weekly* 8(51) December 22, p2252-2253

Puri, Balraj, 1974, The Sheikh's Blind Side, *Economic and Political Weekly* 9(30) July 27, p1181-1182

Puri, Balraj, 1974, Schizophrenia in Jammu? *Economic and Political Weekly* (Annual Number) 9(6-8) February, p185-187

Puri, Balraj, 1975, Students and Politics, *Economic and Political Weekly* 10(28) July 12, p1040

Puri, Balraj, 1975, Timid Economic Start, *Economic and Political Weekly* 10(39) September 27, p1528-1529

Puri, Balraj, 1977, The Article 370 Row : Wasted Years, *Janata* 32(28) August 7, p7-8

Puri, Balraj, 1977, J&K : Another Marriage of Convenience, *Janata* 32(38) November 6, p10-11

Puri, Balraj, 1977, J&K Janata Debacle: Reasons and Repercussions, *Janata* 32(30) August 28, p9-11

Puri, Balraj, 1977, J.P.'s Role in Kashmir, *Janata* 32(43) December

11, p3-4

Puri, Balraj, 1978, August 1953 : An Opinion Survey, *Economic and Political Weekly* 13(27) July 8, p1095-1096, tables

Puri, Balraj, 1978, Collapse of Secessionist Movement in Kashmir, *Janata* 33(5) March 5, p7-9

Puri, Balraj, 1978, The Deluge after the Sheikh? *Janata* 33(35) November 19, p8-9

Puri, Balraj, 1978, Implications of the Kashmir Safety Ordinance, *Janata* 32(49) Janurary 22, p7-9

Puri, Balraj, 1978, Lights and Shades of State Autonomy, *Janata* 33(14) May 21, p11-12

Puri, Balraj, 1978, Political Stalemate, *Economic and Political Weekly* 13(47) November 25, p1925-1927

Puri, Balraj, 1979, J&K State Declining Development Tempo and Rising Central Aid, *Janata* 34(24) July 22, p9-10

Puri, Balraj, 1979, Mass Unrest in Jammu Region: Many Unkept Promises, *Times of India* January 2, p8, col 7-8

Puri, Balraj, 1979, Unresolved Part of Jammu Problem, *Janata* 34(9) April 1, p9-10

Puri, Balraj, 1980, Abdullah vs Congress(I), *Economic and Political Weekly* 15(26) June 28, p1095-1096

Puri, Balraj, 1980, Caste, Charisma and Regionalism, *Economic and Political Weekly* 15(10) March 8, p501-502

Puri, Balraj, 1980, Interplay of Caste, Regional and Secesionist Sentiments through Kashmir Electons, *Janata* 35(9) April 6, p7-8

Puri, Balraj, 1980, Kashmir and the Islam Wave, *Janata* 35(38) November 16, p3-4; 35(39) November 23, p15-16

Puri, Balraj, 1981, 50th Anniversary of Kashmir's Political Movement, *Janata* 36(30) September 20, p7-9

Puri, Balraj, 1981, J&K Indifferent to Sikri Report, *Times of India* Febrary 11, p8, col 7-8

Puri, Balraj, 1981, *Jammu and Kashmir: Triumph and Tragedy of Indian Federalisation*, Sterling, New Delhi, 280p

Puri, Balraj, 1981, Ladakh and National Integration, *Janata* 36(3) March 1, p3-4

Puri, Balraj, 1981, Problems and Prospects of Federalisation: The Case of Jammu and Kashmir, *Economic and Political Weekly* 16(20) May 16, p895-897

Puri, Balraj, 1981, State Stranglehold on Universities, *Economic and Political Weekly* 16(14) April 4, p611-612

Puri, Balraj, 1981, Triumph and Tragedy of Indian Federalism in Jammu and Kashmir, *Janata* 36(28) September 6, p7-8 +

Puri, Balraj, 1981, What is Wrong with Kashmir's Finances, *Economic and Political Weekly* 16(19) May 9, p 845-846

Puri, Balraj, 1982, Battle for the Minds of the People, *Times of India* (Supplement) September 27, p11, col 1-8

Puri, Balraj, 1982, Islam in Kashmir, *Illustrated Weekly of India* 103(35) September 19, p35-37

Puri, Balraj, 1982, Jammu and Kashmir in Framework of Multiple Identities, *Janata* 37(3) February 21, p9-11

Puri, Balraj, 1982, Route of Ladakh's Integration, *Economic and Political Weekly* 17(8) February20, p273-275

Puri, Balraj, 1983, Assertion of Regional Personalities and Emergence of Two Party System, *Economic and Political Weekly* 18(32), August 6, p1378-1379

Puri, Balraj, 1983, The Era of Sheikh Mohammed Abdullah, *Economic and Political Weekly* 18(7) Februray 12, p230-233

Puri, Balraj, 1983, Fall and Decline of BJP in Jammu, *Janata* 38(25) September 18, p11-12

Puri, Balraj, 1983, Kashmir and the Indian Union, *Economic and Political Weekly* 18(40), October 1, p1682, letter to the editor

Puri, Balraj, 1983, Pattern of Kashmir Politics and Elections, *Radical Humanist* 48(7) October, p15-17

Puri, Balraj, 1983, *Simmering Volcano: Study of Jammu's Relations with Kashmir*, Sterling, New Delhi, ix, 144p

Puri, Balraj, 1983, Unpromising Fiscal Start, *Economic and Political Weekly* 18(42), October 15, p1784-1785

Puri, Balraj, 1984, Congress(I)'s Role in J&K, *Janata* 38(39) Januray 8, p7-8

Puri, Balraj, 1984, Driving the People to Extremist Logic of Centre's Policies, *Economic and Political Weekly* 19(35) September 1, p1509-1510

Puri, Balraj, 1984, Grim Forebodings, *Economic and Political Weekly* 19(28) July 4, p1075-1076

Puri, Balraj, 1984, Issues at Stake in J&K : Democracy and Regional Autonomy, *Times of India* October 24, p8, col 3-5

Puri, Balraj, 1984, Jammu's Quest for Identity, *Economic and Political Weekly* 19(41) October 13, 1772-1773p

Puri, Balraj, 1984, On the Wrong Path in Kashmir, *Times of India* Janurary 19, p8, col 7-8

Puri, Balraj, 1984, Kashmir: Who is Playing with National Interest *Janata* 39(5) April 8, p11-13; *Economic and Political Weekly* 19(6) February 11, p235-237

Puri, Balraj, 1985, Consolidation of Kashmir Identity and Fragmentation of Jammu Identity, *Economic and Political Weekly*, 20(3) January 19, p99-100

Puri, Balraj, 1985, Political Implications of Kashmir Poll, *Janata* 40(3) February 24, p5-6

Puri, Balraj, 1986, Autonomy of Jammu and Kashmir State under British Raj, *Punjab Journal of Politics* 10(1) January-June, p55-66, footnotes

Puri, Balraj, 1986, Communal Problem in Jammu, *Times of India* May 12, p6, col 7-8

Puri, Balraj, 1986, Communalism in J&K: Threat to Common Heritage, *Times of India* April 14, p8, col 3-5

Puri, Balraj, 1986, A Policy for Kashmir, *Economic and Political Weekly* 21(6) February 8, p245-247

Puri, Balraj, 1987, Fundamentalism in Kashmir, Fragmentation in Jammu, *Economic and Political Weekly* 22(22) May 30, p835-837

Puri, Balraj, 1987, Stirs in J&K Not at all Communal, *Times of India* November 26, p6, col 7-8

Puri, Balraj, 1989, Implications of One Party System in Kashmir, *Janata* 44(10) May 7, p11-12

Puri, Balraj, 1989, Jammu Riots and after, *Janata* 44(7) April 9, p1-12

Puri, Balraj, 1989, Kashmir Press Bill Bad in Every Way, *Times of India* September 7, p6, col 7-8

Puri, Balraj, 1992, Ominous Portends from Jammu, *Economic and Political Weekly* 27(38) September 19, p2020-2021

Puri, Balraj, 1992, Paralysis in Jammu, *Janata* 47(28) November 15, p3-4

Puri, *Kiran, jt author*
see Bhan, Kiran Sumbali and Puri, Kiran

Purkayastha, K.K., 1968, A New Detente over Kashmir, *Swarajya* 12(32) February 3, p2-3

Pushp, P.N., 1979, Kashmiri Writings, 1978, *Indian Literature* 22(6) November-December, p185-196

Pushp, P.N., 1987, From Slogan to the Symbol and beyond, *Indian Literature* 30(5) September-October, p67-71

Qadir, Abdul
see Abdul Qadir

Qadri, A.S.M, and Wani, Latif Abdul, 1988, Police, Politics and Discretion with Special Reference to Jammu and Kashmir State, *Indian Journal of Criminology*, 16(1) January, p15-20, bibliography

Qaisar Qalandar
see Qalandar, Qaisar

Qalandar, Qaisar, 1976, Music of Kashmir : An Introduction, *Journal of Indian Musicological Society* 7(4) December, p15-22

Qasim, Syed Mir, 1989, Centre Lacks Policy on Kashmir, *Link* 31(37) April 23, p7-8

Qasim, Syed Mir, 1965, *Unwanted Champions*, Publications Division Government of India, Delhi, xi, 40p

Qasim, Syed Mir, 1966, Kashmir's Ties with India, *Illustrated Weekly of India* 87(12) March 20, p26-27

Qasim, Syed Mir, 1969, A Leaf From the History of Kashmir, *AICC Economic Review* (Republic Day) 20(13-14) January 26, p25-28

Qasim, Syed Mir, 1973, People's Participation in Development Programmes, *Thought* 25(5) February 3, p9-10

Qasim, Syed Mir, 1974, J&K: New Dimensions of Progress, *Link* 16(25) January 26, p41-43

Qasim, Syed Mir, *In Sheikh Abdullah's Words Kashmir is India,* New Delhi

Qasim, Syed Mir, n.d., *My Life and Times*

Qureshi, K., *jt editor*
see Sarwar Hasan, K. and Qureshi, K.

Rabbani, G.M., 1981, *Ancient Kashmir: A Historical Perspective*, Gulshan Pub, Srinagar, 263p

Rabbani, G.M, 1986, *Kashmir: Social and Cultural History*, Anmol, Pub, Delhi, p155

Rafiqi, A. Qaiyum, *jt editor*
see Yasin, Mohammad and Rafiqi, A. Qaiyum

Rafique Afzal, M.
see Afzal, M. Rafique

Raghavan, C., 1975, The Kashmir Accord, *Indian and Foreign Review* 12(11) March 15, p18-20

Raghavan, V., 1966, Kashmir in Ancient Times, *Illustrated Weekly of India* 87(12) March 20, p39; 87(13) March 27, p38-39

Raghubir Singh, n.d., *Kashmir: A Garden of the Himalayas*, Perennial Press, Hong Kong, 99p

Raghubir Singh, 1987, *Kashmir*, rev ed, Thames Hudson, 112p, illustrations

Raghunath Ram, 1974, Soviet Policy towards the Kashmir Issue, *Indian Political Science Review* 8(2) July, p186-196, bibliography, footnotes

Rahbar, A.K., 1973, Development of Kashmir Prose, *Indian Literature* 16(1-2) January-June, p107-116

Rahman, Mahfoozur, 1970, Agriculture in Kashmir, *Kurukshetra* 19(6) March, p36

Rahman, Mahfoozur, 1970, Numda Quatity Control and Export Promotion, *Khadi Gramodyog* 17(3) December, p228-232, tables

Rahman, Mahfoozur, 1971, Village Oil Industry in Jammu and Kashmir : A Case Study, *Khadi Gramodyog* 17(12) September 12, p761-765, tables

Rahman, Mahfoozur, 1975, *Cooperative Credit and Agricultural Development*, Sultan Chand, Delhi, xv, 216p

Rahman, Syed Sababuddin Abdur, 1966, Kashmir in Indo-Persian Literature, *Indo-Iranica* 19(2) June, p1-22; 20(1) March, p1-20

Rahmatullah Khan
see Khan, Rahmatullah

Rahul, Ram
see Ram Rahul

Rahul Singh 1985, If Kashmir Sneezes..., *Indian Express*, Januray 20, p8, col 1-5

Raina, A.N., 1963, Observations on Soils and Land Utilisation in Kashmir Valley, *Geographical Review of India* 25(3) p183-199, bibliography, tables

Raina, A.N., 1971, *Geography of Jammu and Kashmir*, National Book Trust, New Delhi, 183p

Raina, Arjan Nath, 1972, Ghani Kashmiri, *Illustrated Weekly of India* 93 (50) December 10, p51

Raina, B.K. 1988, Working of Panchayati Adalats in Jammu and Kashmir with Special Reference to Criminal Jurisdiction : An Empirical Study, *Indian Journal of Public Administration*, 34 (4) October-December, p1073-1094

Raina, B. L; 1987, Vocational Preferences of Secondary School Pupils of Kashmir Valley, *Indian Education Review* 22 (4) October, p39-47, bibliography, tables

Raina, Dina Nath, 1990, *Unhappy Kashmir : The Hidden Story*, Reliance, New Delhi, vi, 210p

Raina, Hriday Nath, 1974, *Theses, Dissertations and Research in*

Progress: A Bibliography of 327 Dissertations and Theses Presented to Kashmir University, University of Kashmir Library, 125p

Raina Jai, 1987, The Bungled "Durbar Move", *Hindustan Times* (Magazine) November 29, p5, col 1-6

Raina, L.N., 1972, Kashmir Makes Steady Progress, *Eastern Economist* 59 (7) August 18, p367-372

Raina, M.K. 1982, The Bhand Pather of Kashmir, *India Magazine* 2 (8) July 82, p36-43

Raina, M.L., n.d., *Kashmir : The Crisis in Perspective*

Raina, N.N., 1982, In the Footsteps of His Masters, *Link* 24 (45) June 20, p14-15

Raina, N.N., 1983, J&K Elections : A Historical Perspective, *Link* 25 (42) May 29, p11-13

Raina, N.N., 1988, *Kashmir Politics and Imperialist Manoeuvres, 1846-1980*, Patriot Pub, New Delhi, xii, 276p

Raina, Roshan, 1982, Special Library Scene of Kashmir, *Herald of Library Science* 21 (1-2), January-April, p51-60, appendix

Raina, S.N., 1968, *Will Abdullah Invite Another Invasion,* S.N. Raina, Calcutta, 32p, illustrations

Raina, Shiv, 1980, Katrah Vaishno Devi, *Haryána Review* 14 (7) July, p33-34

Raina, Triloknath, ed, 1972, *An Anthology of Modern Kashmiri Verse*, N.D.A., 280p

Rais Akhtar
see Akhtar, Rais

Raja Bano
see Bano, Raja

Raja Jai Krishen, 1981, Traditional Theatre of Kashmir : Bhand Pather, *Vidura* 18 (5) October, p321 +

Rajagopalachari, C., 1964, Am I Wrong? *Swarajya* 8 (43) April 25, p1-2

Rajagopalachari, C., 1965, Dr. N.B. Khare's Prophecy, *Swarajya* 10 (19) November 6, p1-2

Rajagopalachari, C., 1965, Suspension of Public Criticism, *Swarajya* 10 (24) December 11, p1-2

Rajagopalachari, C., 1965, To End the Dispute, *Swarajya* 10(13) September 25, p1-2

Rajagopalachari, C., 1965, To Win the World's Opinion, *Swarajya* 10 (20) November 13, p1-2

Rajagopalachari, C., 1966, Raise a Bigger Issue, *Swarajya* 10 (27) January 1, p1-2

Rajagopalachari, C., 1968, Sri Vajpayee's Resolution, *Swarajya* 13 (21) November 23, p1-2

Rajan

see also under full name/surname of the author, e.g., Sundar Rajan, K.R.

Rajbans, Krishen, 1967, *Kashmir and the Conspiracy against Peace*, Peoples Publishing House, New Delhi, 107p

Rajeswara Rao

see Rao, Rajeswara

Rajouri, D.R., 1987, *jt author*

see Kapoor, D.R. and Rajouri, D.R.

Rajpori, G.M., 1965, Kashmir in the Wider Context, *Economic Weekly* 17 (52) December 25, p1893

Rallia Ram, Maya, 1975, Aspects of Social Change in Kashmir, *Mainstream* 13 (30) March 29, p23-24

Ram

see also under full name/surname of the author, e.g., Hari Ram; Rallia Ram, Maya

Ram, 1977, Janata Will Get Majority in Kashmir, *Times of India* July 23, p5, col 3-4

Ram Gopal, 1965, *India-Pakistan War and Peace*, Lucknow

Ram Krishna, H.T., 1969, Status of Jammu and Kashmir, *Swarajya* 13 (27) January 4, p5

Ram Rahul, 1979, Ladhkh Forging ahead in Step with the Rest of India, *Janata* 33 (42) January 7, p9-10 +

Ramachandra Rao, K., 1992, The Indo-Pak Problem, *National Herald* September 13

Ramchandran, G., 1974, Atonement in Kashmir, *Gandhi Marg* 18 (4) October, p209-211, editorial

Ramesh Chandra, 1979, Community Television Viewing in the Kashmir Valley, *Indian Journal of Communication Arts* 4 (9) May, p8-9 +

Ramesh Khazanchi

see Khazanchi, Ramesh

Randhir Singh, 1975, Agricultural Development in Jammu and Kashmir : Problems and Remedies, *Farmer and Parliament* 10 (7) July, p17-18

Rangaswami, K., 1962, Why U.S. Supports Pakistan on Kashmir,

Hindu, June 28

Rangaswami, K., 1964, Ladakh Key to Kashmir Problem, *Hindu*, March 4, p6

Rangaswami, K., 1970, Kashmir's Economic Progress since Independecne, *Indian and Foreign Review* 7 (20) August 1, p11-13+

Rao
see also under full name/surname of the author, e.g., Gururaj Rao, H.S.

Rao, Rajeswara, 1967, Release Sheikh Abdullah: Demands Rajeshwara Rao, *New Age* 15 (43) October 22, p4

Rasheeduddin Khan
see Khan, Rasheeduddin

Rashidov, Sharaf, 1981, *Kashmir Song*, Navyug Pub, Delhi, 72p

Rasook Kochak, Gulam
see Kochak, Gulam Rasook

Rasool Pompur
see Pompur, Rasool

Rose, Leo E., *jt author*
see Sisson, Richard and Rose, Leo E.

Rosenthal, A.M., 1957, Kashmir's Far-Reaching Impact, *Foreign Policy Bulletin* 36 (12) March 1, p93-95

Rastogi, Gaurinath, 1991, *Our Kashmir*, Saruchi Prakashan, New Delhi, 104p

Rau, B.N., 1965, Kashmir in Retrospect, *Illustrated Weekly of India* 86 (45) November 7, p16-17+

Ray, Hemen, 1985, *How Moscow Sees Kashmir*, Jaico, Bombay, 150p

Ray, Sunil Chandra, 1970, *Early History and Culture of Kashmir*, 2nd edn, Munshiram Manoharlal, Delhi, xvi, 288p

Raza, Moonis, et al, 1978, *The Valley of Kashmir : The Land*, Carolina Acad Press, Vikas Pub, New Delhi

Raza Ahmed, 1977, *Kashmir Valley*, Vikas Pub, New Delhi, 125p

Razdan, Prithvi Nath, 1967, Educational Standards : Ganguli Report, *Educational Review* 73 (8) August, p182-186

Razia Bano
see Bano, Razia

Rifaquat, S., 1970, Kashmiri Pandits, *Illustrated Weekly of India* 91 (14) April 5, p6-9

Rizvi, Janet, 1983, *Ladakh : Crossroads of High Asia*, Oxford University Press, New Delhi, 224p

Romesh Chandra, 1964, Bakshi Raj Must End, *New Age* 12 (6) February 9, p4

Romesh Chandra, 1964, Kashmir : Begining of End of Bakshi Raj, *New Age* 12 (10) March 8, p4

Romesh Chandra, 1964, Security Council : Old Stuff, New Wrapping *New Age* 12 (21) April 24, p4

Romesh Chandra, 1964, Security Council again, *New Age* 12 (19) May 10, p4

Romesh Chandra, 1965, US-British Conspiracy Stripped Naked : Bhutto's Dinty Words Echo His Master's Voice, *New Age* 13 (44) October 31, p1

Rosha, Padam, 1989, NC Ducks Challenges of Fundamentalist, *Times of India* September 18, p6, col 7-8

Roy, A.C., 1970, *Second Kashmir War : As Seen from Different Angles*, Lake Pub, Calcutta, ii, 258p

Roy, S.L., 1967, The Two Invasions of Kashmir, *Modern Review* 122 (1) July, p15-18

Roy Chaudhury, Bani, 1972, *Folk Tales of Kashmir*, IBH Educational Trust, Bombay

Rudra, Ashok and Srinivasan, T.N., 1972, Kashmir : A Conspiracy of Silence, *Economic and Political Weekly* 7 (46-47) November 18, p2258-2259

Russell, George, 1984, Show of Force (Government Troops in Jammu and Kashmir), *Time*, 124, July 16, p45, illustrations

Saaz, J.L., 1970, Kathua Project in Jammu and Kashmir, *Kurukshetra* 18 (8) May, p21-25

Saaz, J.L., 1970, Kathua Project in Jammu and Kashmir, *Kurukshetra* 18 (8) May, p21-25Saaz, J.L., 1973, Gabba: The Rug Created out of Rags, *Yojana* 17(10) June 15, p405

Sachar, Gopal, 1987, Farooq's Truncated Darbar Move Order Leaves a Trail of New Tensions in J&K, *Organiser* 39(28) December 20, p8-9

Sachar, Gopal Das, 1967, If Elections Are Free and Fair Congress Will Lose Jammu and Kashmir, *Organiser* 20(24) January 26, p37-38

Sachar, Gopal Das, 1980, Poll-rigging Spree in Jammu and Kashmir, *Organiser* 31(38) February 10, p12

Sadhu, A.N. and Mahajan, R.K., 1980, Key Determinants of Disparity in Farm Income: A Comparative Analysis, *Economic Affairs* 25(11) November, p265-271, bibliography, footnotes

Sadhu, S.L., 1980, Kashmiri: Libraries and Elitist Circles, *Indian Literature* 23(6) November-December, p88-101

Sadhu, S.L, ed, n.d, *Medieval Kashmir*, Atlantic, New Delhi, xiv, 352p

Sadhu, S.L., 1970, Folklore, Tales and Songs, *Cultural Forum* 12(3-4) April-July, p36-46

Sadhu, S.L., 1970, Kashmiri: A Mission of Discovery, *Indian Literature* 13(4) December, p53-60

Sadhu, S.L., 1973, Kashmiri Novel, *Indian Literature* 16(1-2) January-June, p292-300

Sadhu, S.L., 1981, *Folk Tales from Kashmir*, Asia, Bombay, xii, 184p

Sadhu, S.L, 1982, Recalled to Life, *Indian Literature* 25(2) March-April, p74-88

Sadhu, Shyam Lal, 1967, *Tales from the Rajatarangini*, Kapoor Brothers, Srinagar, viii, 198p

Sadiq, Ghulam Mohammad, 1966, Kashmir: From Feudalism to Freedom, *Illustrated Weekly of India* 87(12) March 20, p6-11

Sadiq, Ghulam Mohammad, 1967, Congress and General Elections in Jammu and Kashmir, *AICC Economic Review* 18(13-14) January 26, p105-108

Sadiq, Ghulam Mohammad, 1968, Kashmir's Strength, *Mainstream* (Annual Number) 7(1-3), p20-22

Sadiq, Ghulam Mohammad, 1969, Kashmir's Decisive Role, *Mainstream* 7(42) June 21, p10-11

Sadiq, Ghulam Mohammad, 1971, Kashmir : Bastion of Democracy, *Mainstream* (Annual Number) 10(1-4), p19-20

Sadiq, Ghulam Mohammad, 1971, Pak Action Led to Ban on Front : Sadiq, *Times of India* January 15, p1, col 3-4 +

Sahabuddin Abdur Rahman, Syed
see Rahman, Syed Sahabuddin Abdur

Sahgal
see also Sehgal

Sahgal, Bittu, 1984, Of Himalayan Hearts and Urban Minds, *Indian Express* (Magazine) April 15, p1, col 1-8 +

Sahgal, Nayantara, 1966, Some Recollections, *Illustrated Weekly of India* 87(12) March 20, p16-17

Sahgal, Nayantara, 1967, Kashmir : Heavan and Earth Combined, *Illustrated Weekly of India* 88(25) July 23, p10-18, Illustrations

Sahni, Sat Pal, *jt author*
see Drieberg, Trevor and Sahni, Sat Pal

Saida, Shafi, 1974, Syed Mir Qasim, *Illustrated Weekly of India* 95 (8)

April 21, p 24-27

Saif-ud-din, M., 1969-70, Sources of the History of Kashmir, *Quarterly Review of Historical Studies* 9(1), p17-22

Saif-u-din- Soze
see Soze, Saif-u-din

Saith, Sanjeev, *jt author*
see D'Souza, Marie and Saith, Sanjeev

Sakarikar, D.G., 1965, Indo-Pak Conflict: Western Attitude, *United Asia* 17(5) September-October, p342-348

Saksena
see also Saxena

Saksena, N.S., 1989, Is Kashmir beyond Law of the Land? *Times of India* May 10, p6, col 7-8

Sansar Chand, *jt author*
see Lakshmi Narayan and Sansar Chand

Santhanam, K., 1965, Referendum or Arbitration? *Swarajya* 10(14) October 2, p27-28

Sanyal, Shanta, 1979, *Boats and the Boatmen of Kashmir,* Allied; Sagar, New Delhi, 30p

Sarabhai, Mridula, 1958, *Sheikh-Sadiq Correspondence (Aug-Oct 1956)*, New Delhi, Mridula Sarabhai, iv, 64p

Saraf, D.N., n.d. *Arts and Crafts : Jammu and Kashmir*, Abhinav Pub,New Delhi, 290p

Saraf, Makhanlal, 1978, Kashmiri Theatre: Three Decades: A Survey 1947-1977, *Sangeet Natak*, 50, October-December, p45-51

Saraf, Mulk Raj, 1969, *Jammu and Kashmir Guide 1969,* Universal Pub

Saraf, Suraj, 1965, Development of Jammu and Kashmir State, *Commerce* 111(2827) July 3, p22-23

Saraf, Suraj, 1966, Chhamb-Jaurian Springs to New Life, *Yojana* 10(16) August 21, p14-15

Saraf, Suraj, 1968, Tourist Time in Kashmir, *Illustrated Weekly of India* 89(23) June 9, p18-25, illustrations

Saraf, Suraj, 1969, A New Deal for Kashmiri Handicrafts, *Yojana* 13(21) November 2, p24-25

Saraf, Suraj, 1970, Kudd: The Flok Dance of Jammu Hills, *Times of India* September 27, p9, col 1-4

Saraf, Suraj, 1970, Temples and Tombs of Jammu, *Cultural Forum* 12(3-4) April-July, p33-35

Saraf, Suraj, 1971, The Shrine of Banda Bairagi, *Times of India*

November 28, p11, col 1-4

Saraf, Suraj, 1971, Shrines of Jammu, *Times of India* June 20, p7, col 1-3

Saraf, Suraj, 1975, The Glory That Was Akhnoor, *Times of India* August 10, p9, col 1-8

Saraf, Suraj, 1977, Jammu Youth for Village Welfare, *Social Welfare* 24(3) June, p15-16

Saraf, Suraj, 1985, The J&K You Do Not Know, *Tribune*, October 13, p iv, col 1-8

Saraf, Suraj, 1986, Because of a Dream, *Hindustan Times* (Magazine) March 30, p vi, col 1-8

Sardesai, S.G., 1965, *Defence, Democracy, Secularism and Kashmir*, Communist Party Publication, 54p

Sareen, Rajendra, 1978, Occupied Kashmir Leaders on Confrontation Course, *Times of India* November 18, p6, col 78

Sarkar, Asit Kumar, 1979, Ladakh: The Other World, *Geographical Review of India* 41(4) December, 336-346, bibliography

Sarkar, Bidyut, 1993, Kashmir: India's Bleeding Sore, *Economic Times* November 6, p6, col 3-6

Sarkar, Chanchal, 1965, Kashmir : The War and after, *Illustrated Weekly of India* 86(42) October 17, p13

Sarwar Hasan, K., 1956, Plebiscite in Kashmir : Indian Commitment, *Pakistan Horizon* 9(1), March, p 24-29

Sarwar Hasan, K., 1962, The Kashmir Case, *Dawn* (Pakistan) May 11; May 12

Sarwar Hasan, K. and Qureshi, K., eds, 1966, *China, India, Pakistan*, Pakistan Institute of International Affairs, Karachi, 342 p

Sarwar Hasan, K. and Zubeida Hasan, 1966, *Documents on the Foreign Relations of Pakistan: The Kashmir Question*, Pakistan Institute of Internation Affairs, Karachi, xiv, 484p

Sastri
see also Shastri

Sastri, C.L.R., 1950, Kashmir and Korea, *Modern Review*, 88, August, p116-120

Sastrim C.L.R., 1952, Kashmir once More, *Modern Review* 92 (5) November 1, p 380-386

Sastry, K.R.R., 1964, Sheikh Abdullah's Release, *Swarajya* 8(42) April 18, p13

Satinder Singh, Bawa
see Bawa Satinder Singh

Saxena
see also Saksena

Saxena H.L., 1975, *The Tragedy of Kashmir*, National Publishing House, New Delhi, xv, 580p

Saxena, K.S., 1968, The Ekangas : A Tantrums of Kashmir, *Bharatiya Vidya* 28(1-4), p72-77, bibliography, footnotes

Saxena, K.S., 1973, Role of the Nagaradhyaksha in the Administration of Ancient Kashmir, *Quaterly Journal of Local Self Government Institution* 44(2) October-December, p157-163, bibliography, footnotes

Saxena, K.S., 1974, *Political History of Kashmir (300 BC-AD 1200)*, Upper India Pub xvi, 364p, reprint, 1987, S Chand, New Delhi

Saxena, K.S., 1978, The Deccan Campaign of Lalitaditya of Kashmir, *Bharatiya Vidya* 38(1-4), p66-76, footnotes

Saxena, Krishna Swaroop, 1967, Shahi-Kashmir Relations (AD 700 to 1200), *Bharatiya Vidya* 27(1-4), p86-91, bibliography, footnotes

Sayeed
see also Syed

Sayeed, Mohammed, 1984, Mufti Mohammed Sayeed: The Real Hero of Kashmir, *Link* 26(50) July 15, p25

Sayeed, Mohammed, 1985, Shah on the Way out? *Link* 27(22) January6, 19-20p

Sayeed, Mohammed, 1986, State Unit Backs High Command, *Link* 28(40) May 11, p9-10

Sayeed, Mohammad, 1986, Euthanasia for G.M. Shah Ministry, *Link* 28(32) March 16, p6

Sayeed, Mufti Mohammed
see Mohammed Sayeed, Mufti

Schetter, Margaret and Schetter, Rolf, 1989, *Kashmir, Ladakh and Zamskar : A Travel Survival Kit,* 3rd edn, Lovely Planet, 232p, illustrations

Schelter, Rolf, *jt author*
see Sehelter, Margaret and Sehelter, Rolf

Schuster, Nacy, 1984, Yoga Master Dharmamitra and Clerical Misogyny in Fifty Century Buddhism, *Tibet Journal* 9(4) Winter, p33-46, footnotes

Seervai, M.M., 1989, *Partition of India: Legend or Reality*, Bombay

Sehgal
see also Sahgal

Sehgal, Narender, 1994, *Converted Kashmir: Memorial of Mistakes*, Utpal Publications, Delhi, 474, 2p

Seminar (Periodical), 1974, The Problem, *Seminar*, 174, February, p10-12, editorial

Sen, Anikendra Nath, 1993, Army versus Insurgents: Using Peacetime Methods in a War, *Times of India* May 18, p8, col 3-5

Sen, Chanakya, 1964, De-Internationalising Kashmir, *Mainstream* 2(34) April 25, p6, 20

Sen, L.P., 1969, *Slender Was the Sword: Kashmir Confrontation 1947-48*, Longmans, New Delhi, 308p

Sender, Henrietta M., 1990, *The Kashmiri Pandits: A Study of Cultural Choice in North India*, Oxford University Press, Oxford, 358p, illustrations

Shafi, Mohammad, 1988, Steps towards Progress in Jammu and Kashmir, *Co-operators Bulletin* 31(11), January, p2-4

Shafi Saida
see Saida, Shafi

Shah, B.C, 1986, Sardar's Role in Kashmir : A Dream Unfulfilled, *Journal of Political Studies* 19(1) February, p32-40, footnotes

Shah, G.M., 1984, Cooperation with Centre Must, *Times of India* July 4, p1, col 1-3

Shah, K.K., 1968, Kashmir: Symbol of Secularism, *Link* 10(46) June 23, p27-28

Shah, M.H. and Khan, G.M., 1987, Factors Limiting Oilseed Production in Kashmir Valley, *Indian Farming* 35(5) August, p13-14

Shahabuddin, S., 1982, Five Defects in J&K Permanent Return Act, *Janata* 37(14) May 16, p11

Shahidullah, Khan Mohammed, 1980, Nomads of Jammu and Kashmir, *Social Welfare* 26(10) January, p14-16

Shahwar Alam, Mohammed
see Alam, Mohammed Shahwar

Shali, S.K., 1993, *Kashmir : History and Archaeology through the Ages*, Indus Pub, New Delhi, 289p

Shameem Faizee
see Faizee, Shameem

Shamim, Shamim Ahmed, 1978, Kashmir, *Seminar*, 224, April, p16-20

Shamim, Shamim Ahmed, 1978, Sheikh Abdullah:Then and Now, *Illustrated Weekly of India* 99(43) November 12,p30-31

Shankar
see also under full name/surname name of the author, e.g., Umashankar

Sharaf Rashidov
see Rashidov, Sharaf

Sharif-al Mujahid
see Mujahid, Sharif-al

Sharma, A.K., 1967, Neolithic Human Burials from Burrahom, Kashmir, *Journal of Oriental Institute* 16(3) March, p239-242, bibliography, footnotes, illustrations

Sharma, B.B, 1988, Cooperative Housing Federation Serving the Houseless, *Co-operators Bulletin* 31(1) January, p51-54

Sharma, B.D., *jt editor*
see Khera, M.K., et al, eds

Sharma, B.L., 1967, *The Kashmir Story*, Asia, Bombay, 271p

Sharma, B.L., 1971, *Kashmir Awakes*, Vikas Pub, New Delhi, xiii, 292p,

Sharma, B.L., *jt author*
see Kulshreshtha, Akhilesh and Sharma, B.L

Sharma, B.P., 1985, Maharaja Who Defied Union Jack, *Tribune* September 22, p1, col 1-8 +

Sharma, D.C., *jt author*
see Pathik, Jyoteeshwar and Sharma, D.C.

Sharma, D.C., 1986, *Kashmir Agriculture and Land Revenue System under the Sikh Rule, AD 1819-46* , Rima Pub House, New Delhi, xiv, 160p

Sharma, Dewan Chand, 1983, *Kashmir under the Sikhs*, Seema Pub, Delhi, xv, 334p, plates

Sharma, Dewan Chand, 1984, *Kashmir under Maharaja Ranjit Singh,* Atlantic pub, New Delhi, 128p

Sharma, H.R, 1988, The Jammu Co-operative Super Bazar, *Co-operators Bulletin* 31(1) January, p57-58

Sharma, Indu Bhushan, 1969, Facts about Kashmir, *Janata* 24(39) October 19, p11-12

Sharma, O.P., 1980, *IYC* Reaches Uri, *Social Welfare* 26(11) February, p17

Sharma, O.P., 1980, Nobra: A Maiden Valley, *Rural India* 43(2-3) Februray-March, p48-50

Sharma, O.P., 1986, Marriage: Ladakhi Style, *Social Welfare* 33(7) October, p16-17

Sharma, O.P., 1987, Child Marriage on the Decline in Jammu and Kashmir, *Social Welfare* 34(8) November, p14-15 +

Sharma, O.P., 1987, The Press in Jammu and Kashmir, *Vidura* 24(1) January-February, p38-40

Sharma, P.N., 1965, *Inside Pak Occupied Kashmir*, P.N.Sharma, Delhi, ii, 120p

Sharma, R.C., *jt editor*
see Krishna Rao, D.V.L.N. and Sharma, R.C.

Sharma, R.D., 1975, Action Programme for Kashmir, *Mainstream* 13 (49) August 9, p19-20

Sharma, Ratanlal, 1987, Agriculture in J&K : Wrongs and Remedies, *Co-operators Bulletin* 30 (6) June, p19-21

Sharyal Mujahid
see Mujahid, Sharyal

Shastri
see also Sastri

Shastri, Harabhatta, *jt author*
see Kak, Ram Chandra and Shastri, Harabhatta

Shastri, Shiv Kumar, 1964, Plebiscite : The West Must Say Why? *Indian Express*, April 4, p6

Sheikh Abdullah
see Abdullah, Mohammed Sheikh

Shiva Rao, B., 1964, Indo-Pakistan Relations : Under-currents at Work, *Swarajya* 9 (2) July 11, p11-12

Shiva Rao, B., 1964, Kashmir : Alternative Solutions, *Swarajya* 8 (50) June 13, p9-11

Shiva Rao, B., 1964, Kashmir : Search for a Solution, *Swarajya* 8 (47) May 23, p13-14

Shiva Rao, B., 1964, The Problem of Kashmir, *Swarajya* (Annual Number), p106-107

Shriman Narayan, 1965, Peace with Justice, *AICC Economic Review* 17 (8) October 1, p7 +

Shroff, Phiroze, J., 1965, Our Parliamentary Delegations, *Swarajya* 10 (26) December 25, p4

Shukla, N.S., 1990, *Cultural Trends in Kashmir and Ksemendra*, Nirman Prakashan, xvi, 376p

Siddique, K., 1972, *Conflict, Crisis and War in Pakistan*, London

Siddiqui, Shams, 1962, The Kashmir Problem : The Case for Pakistan, *Far Eastern Economic Review* 37 (8) August, p345-356

Simon, Sheldon W., 1967, Kashmir Dispute in Sino-Soviet

Perspective, *Asian Survey* 7 (3) March, p176-187

Singh

see also under full name of the author, e.g., Jasbir Singh

Singh, H.B., 1966, Flora in and around the Valley, *Illustrated Weekly of India* 87 (13) March 27, p33

Singh, K. Brahma, 1989, *History of the Jammu and Kashmir Rifles, 1820-1956 : The State Force Background,* Lancer, New Delhi, 600p

Singh, Nirmal K., 1991, *Inter-Communal Relations in Jammu and Kashmir, 1846 to 1931*, Jay Kay Book House, Jammu Tawi, xi, 263p

Singh, R.S., 1992, Resource Productivity and Returns to Scale in Dairy on Marginal and Small Farms in Intermediate Zone of Jammu and Kashmir, *Indian Journal of Agricultural Economics* 47 (3) July-September, p537-538

Singh, R.S. and Parihar, M.C., 1992, Scope For Agro-Base Rural Industries in Jammu and Kashmir, *Co-operator's Bulletin* 35 (9) September, p14-16

Singh, Y.B., 1981, Popular Apathy to State's Exploitation in Early Medieval Kashmir : A Study of Its Causes, *Journal of Indian History* 59 (1-3) April-December, p201-206, footnotes

Singh, Y.B., 1982, Copper Coins and Their Minting in Early Medieval Kashmir : A Problem, *Journal of the Numismatics Society of India* 44 (1-2), p180-184

Singh, Y.B., 1984, Legend Diddakshema : A Riddle Explained, *Journal of the Numismatics Society of India* 4 (1-2), p107-110

Sinha, K.K., 1965, New Technique in Kashmir, *Swarajya* 10 (11) September 11, p13-14

Sinha, S.K., 1977, *Operation Rescue : Military Operations in Jammu and Kashmir, 1947-49*, New Delhi

Sisson, Richard and Rose, Leo E, n.d., *Pakistan, India and the Creation of Bangladesh,* Berkeley (California)

Siudmak, John, n.d., Early Stone and Terracotta Sculpture, *Marg* 40 (2), p41-56

Skorupski, *jt author*

see Snellgrove, David L. and Skorupski

Smith, Vincent A., 1981, *The Oxford History of India*, 4th edn, ed by Percival Spear, Oxford University Press

Smith, W.C. n.d., *Modern Islam in India*

Snellgrve, David L. and Skorupske, 1980, *Cultural Heritge of Ladakh*,

Vikas Pub, New Delhi, 144p

Sofi, A.R., and Pulwana, D.R., 1987, Pulwama Cooperatives March ahead, *Co-operators Bulletin* 30 (6) June, p17-18

Sood, Aruna, 1985, Kashmir's Pround Treasure, *National Herald* (Sunday Herald) November 3, p1, col 1-6

Soze, Saif-u-din, 1969, Food Shortage in J&K : Result of Faulty Distribution, Wastage and Hoarding, *Yojana* 13 (5) March 23, p8-9

Spear, Percival, *editor*
see Smith, Vincent A., 1981

Speath, Anthony, 1993, No Peace in the Valley (Kashmir), *Harper's*, 286, April, p81-88, illustrations

Spratt, P., 1965, Portents and Counter-Measures, *Swarajya* 10 (9) August 28, p2-3

Spratt, P., 1965, Shoot Them at Sight, *Swarajya* 10 (10) September 4, p7-8

Spratt, P., 1965, Victory and after, *Swarajya* 10 (14) October 2, p3-4

Spratt, P., 1966, Potti Sriramulu and Kashmir, *Swarajya* 10 (29) January 15, p3

Sridharani, Krishna Lal, 1959, *Smiles from Kashmir*, Vora, Bombay, 74p

Srinivasan, T.N., *jt author*
see Rudra, Ashok and Srinivasan, T.N.

Stacey, Allan, 1988, *Visiting Kashmir*, Hippocrene Books, illustrations

Stein, M.A.
see also Clanson, Gerald L.N., comp, 1912, Catalogue of Stein Collection . . .

Stein, M.A., ed, 1895, *Catalogue of the Sanskrit MSS in the Raghunatha Temple Library of the Maharaja of Kashmir,* Nirnaya Sagar Press, Bombay, 425p

Stein, M.A., *translator*
see Kalhana

Stephens, Ian, 1967, *Pakistan*, 3rd edn, Ernest Benn Ltd, London, 304p, bibliography, map, photos, Nations of the Modern World Series

Streiff, Eric, 1957, The Kashmir Conflict again, *Swiss Review of World Affairs* 6 (12) March, p18-19

Subrahmanyam, K., 1993, Princely State of Jammu and Kashmir, *Economic Times* November 17, p6, col 3-6

Subrahmanyan, *jt author*
see Mohammed Ayoob and Subrahmanyan

Subramaniam, Vasanta, 1964, Prestige or Realism? *Swarajya* 8 (49) June 6, p7

Sufi,G.M.D., 1974, *Kashmir : Being the Comprehensive Political, Social, Economical History of the Kashmir to the Present*, Light and Life Pub, New Delhi, 2 vols

Sufi, G.M.D., 1979, *Islamic Culture in Kashmir*, Light and Life Pub, New Delhi, vii, 383, 14p

Sultan, Mohammed
see Mohammed Sultan

Sumbali Bhan, Kiran
see Bhan, Kiran Sumbali

Sundar Rajan, K.R., 1980, The Sheikh and His Sheikhdom, *Illustrated Weekly of India* 101 (37) September 14, p6-13

Sundar Rajan, K.R., 1982, Brinkmanship in Kashmir, *Illustrated Weekly of India* 103 (27) July 25, p8-13

Sundar Rajan, K.R., 1984, The Kashmir Dilemma, *Illustrated Weekly of India* 105 (31) July 29, p40-41

Sundaram, L., 1951, Anglo-American "Betrayal" in Kashmir, *Commerce and Industry*, 35, February 28, p5

Surendra Mohan, 1986, Somersault in Srinagar, *Janata* 41 (25) November 30, p14-15

Surendra Mohan, 1992, The Gordian Knot in J and K, *Janata* 47 (28) November 15, p9-10

Suresh Chander, 1969, Gajendragadkar Commission Report : Jammu and Kashmir : Then and Now, *Janata* 24 (4) February 16, p7-8 +

Suresh Ram, 1968, A Historic Meeting at Patna, *Sarvodaya* 17 (9) March, p396-400

Suri, J.B., 1992, Jammu Central Cooperative Bank, *Co-operators Bulletin* 35 (6) June, p5-8

Suri, Surindar, 1964, Basic Weaknesses, *Seminar*, 58, June, p16-19

Suri, Vidya Sagar, *translator*
see Ganeshi Lal, 1955, *Sihat-I-Kashmir*

Surjeet, Harkishan Singh, 1955, *Kashmir and Its Future*, People's Publishing House, Delhi

Sujeet, Harkishan Singh, 1974, Kashmir : CPI (M) Stand, *People's Democracy* 10 (30) July 28, p2 +

Surjeet, Harikishen Singh, 1975, What it Means for Kashmir and the

Rest of India, *People's Democracy* 11 (12) March 23, p1 +

Surjeet, Harikishen Singh, 1982, Developments in Kashmir, *People's Democracy* 6 (26) June 27, p1 +

Surjeet, Harikishen Singh, 1984, Murder of Democracy in Kashmir, *People's Democracy* 8 (28) July 8, p1 +

Swaminathan, Mina, 1965, How to Tell Children What We Are Fighting for, *Yojana* 9 (21) October 24, p12-13

Swaraj, N.R.M., 1964, Britain's Attitude Deplorable, *Indian Foreign Affairs* 7 (2) February, p26

Swinrurne, T.R., 1970, *Kashmir : A Holiday in the Happy Valley, with Pen and Pencil*, Lakshmi, New Delhi, x, 348p

Syed
see also Syeed

Syed Mir Qasim
see Qasim, Syed Mir

Syed Mohammad Syeed
see Mohammad Syeed, Syed

Syed Shahabuddin
see Shahabuddin, Syed

Syed Sahabuddin Abdur Rahman
see Rahman, Syed Sahabuddin Abdur

Syed Rasool Pompur
see Pompur, Syed Rasool

Tabasum Ara
see Ara, Tabasum

Tantray, A.M., *jt author*
see Ara, Tabasum and Tantray, A.M., 1988

Tantray, Abdul Majid, 1988, Influence of Farm-Size on the Acceptance of Agricultural Technology, *Co-operator Bulletin* 31 (3) March, p12-15

Talib, Rasheed, 1984, The Valley of Discord, *Illustrated Weekly of India* 105 (8) February 19, 45p

Tariq, A.M., 1966, The Tourist in Kashmir, *Illustrated Weekly of India* 87 (13) March 27, p8-11

Tariq Ali, 1976, *Pakistan : Military Rule or People's Power*, London

Tariq Ali, 1917, Farooq Security Risk, *Times of India* January 29, p1, col 2-5 +

Teng, Mohan Krishan, et al, 1977, *Kashmir : Constitutional History and Documents*, Light and Life Pub, New Delhi, 689p

Teng, Mohan Krishan, 1984, *State Government and Politics : Jammu and Kashmir*, Sterling, New Delhi, 167p

Teng, Mohan Krishan, 1990, *Kashmir : Ariticle Three Hundred Seventy*, Anmol, New Delhi

Thakar Dass, 1988, Jammu Handicrafts Need Attention, *Co-operators Bulletin* 31 (1) January, p60-61

Thakur D.D., 1978, J&K Marches Ahead, *Yojana* 22 (21) November 16, p31-32

Thakur, Sankarshan, 1984, Kashmir : The Sound and the Fury, *Illustrated Weekly of India*, 105 (31) July 29, p20-25

Thapar, Romesh, 1964, Behind the Abdullah Headlines, *Economic Weekly* 16 (22) May 30, p914-915

Thapar, Romesh, 1964, The Corrosion of Secularity, *Economic Weekly* 16 (17-18) May 2, p754-755

Thapar, Romesh, 1964, The Question-Mark over Kashmir, *Economic Weekly* 16 (19) May 9, p804-805

Thapar, Romesh, 1964, Kashmir and the Detente, *Economic and Political Weekly* 10 (8) February 22, p340-341

Tholal, M.N., 1948, British Intrigues for Gilgit, *Organiser*, January, 15, p10

Thomas, Raja G., ed, 1992, *Perspectives on Kashmir : The Roots of Conflict in South Asia*, Segment, New Delhi, 422p

Thomson, Thomas, 1978, *Western Himalayas and Tibet : A Narrative on Ladakh and Mountains of Nothern India*, Cosmo, New Delhi, xii, 501p

Thorp, Robert, 1980, *Kashmir Misgovernment,* ed by F.M. Hassnain, Gulshan Publications, Srinagar, 107p

Thought (Periodical), 1968, Convention That Was a Seminar, *Thought* 20 (42) October 19, p3-4, editorial

Thought (Periodical), 1968, Ensuring Free Elections, *Thought* 20 (11) March 16, p4, editorial

Thought (Periodical), 1968, A Round-Table Conference on Kashmir, *Thought* 20 (9) March 2, p3-4, editorial

Thought (Periodical), 1972, Hope for Kashmir, *Thought* 24 (25) June, 17, p3, editorial

Thought (Periodical), 1972, Kashmir Kaleidoscope, *Thought* 24 (7) February 12, p5-6, editorial

Thought (Periodical), 1972, New Turn in Kashmir, *Thought* 24 (39) September 23, p6 +, editorial

Thought (Periodical), 1973, Curious and Regrettable, *Thought* 25 (46) November 17, p6 +, editorial

Thought (Periodical), 1973, New Turn in Kashmir and beyond, *Thought* 25 (51) December 22, p5-6, editorial

Thought (Periodical), 1973, Sheikh without Prejudice, *Thought* 25 (33) August 18, p4, editorial

Thought (Periodical), 1974, How Not to Lose Sheikh, *Thought* 26 (25) June 29, p3-4, editorial

Thought (Periodical), 1972, India and Kashmir : Any Way out, *Thought* 26 (27) July 13, p4-5, editorial

Thought (Periodical), 1974, Kashmir : Importance of Sheikh Abdullah, *Thought* 26 (38) September 28, p3-4, editorial

Thought (Periodical), 1974, Kashmir : More than a Political Problem, *Thought* 26 (33) August 24, p5-6, editorial

Thought (Periodical), 1975, Bold Initiative in Kashmir, *Thought* 27 (20) May 17, p5-6, editorial

Thought (Periodical), 1975, India's Bangladesh in Offing, *Thought* 27 (7) February 15, p4-5, editorial

Thought (Periodical), 1975, Snags in Kashmir Accord, *Thought* 27 (7) February 15, p5-6, editorial

Thought (Periodical), 1975, What Next in Kashmir? *Thought* 27 (9) March 1, p5, editorial

Tikku

see also Tikoo; Tiku

Tikku, M.K., 1971, Kashmiri Criticism of an Art, *Thought* 23 (48) November 27, p15-16

Tikku, M.K., 1976, Kashmir : Prominence of Translations, *Indian Literature* 19 (1) p65-68

Tikku, M.K., 1984, Kashmir Burns, *Illustrated Weekly of India* 105 (11) March 11, p32-35

Tikoo

see also Tikku; Tiku

Tikoo, Prithvi Nath, 1979, *Story of Kashmir*, Light and Life Pub, New Delhi, xi, 287p

Tiku

see also Tikku; Tikoo

Tiku, J.L., 1981, Migratory Dairy Farming in Jammu and Kashmir, *Indian Farming* 31 (2) May, p15-17

Tiku, P.N., 1967, Birth of Communal Forces in Kashmir, *Organiser* 21 (10) October 15, p6

Times of India (Newspaper), 1956, Desperate Men, *Times of India* November 27, editorial

Times of India (Newspaper), 1962, Hardend Attitudes, *Times of India* December 4, editorial

Times (Newspaper) 1962, Unsettled Border, *Times of India* May 5, editorial

Times of India (Newspaper), 1963, Advisers, *Times of India* March 14, editorial

Times of India (Newspaper), 1963, A Mediator, *Times of India* May 11, editorial

Times of India (Newspaper), 1969, Danger in Kashmir, *Times of India* July 14, p6, col 1-2, editorial

Times of India (Newspaper), 1969, Kashmir Poll, *Times of India* April 9, p8, col 1-2; April 12, p6, col 1-2, editorial

Times of India (Newspaper), 1969, Puppet Regime, *Times of India* January 11, p6, col 2, editorial

Times of India (Newspaper), 1969, Mr. Sadiq's Task, *Times of India* January 28, p6, col 1, editorial

Times of India (Newspaper), 1970, A Compromise, *Times of India* March 26, p6, col 1-2, editorial

Times of India (Newspaper), 1970, New Danger in Kashmir, *Times of India* March 14, p6, col 1, editorial

Times of India (Newspaper), 1970, No Solution, *Times of India* March 24, p6, col 2, editorial

Times of India (Newspaper), 1971, Danger in Kashmir, *Times of India*, January 9, p6, col 2, editorial

Times of India (Newspaper), 1971, Kashmir Patch-up, *Times of India*, October 6, p6, col 2, editorial

Times of India (Newspaper), 1971, Leave it Alone, *Times of India* November 26, p8, col 1-2, editorial

Times of India (Newspaper), 1971, Unlawful Body, *Times of India* June 17, p6, col 1-2, editorial

Times of India (Newspaper), 1972, Health Trends, *Times of India* April 12, p6, col 1-2, editorial

Times of India (Newspaper), 1972, Kashmir Crisis, *Times of India* October 1, p4, col 2, editorial

Times of India (Newspaper), 1972, Kashmir Poll, *Times of India* September 15, p4, col 1, editorial

Times of India (Newspaper), 1973, Kashmir Talks, *Times of India* January 18, p6, col 1-2, editorial

Times of India (Newspaper), 1973, Mr. Bhutto's New Move, *Times of India* December 19, p4, col 1, editorial

Times of India (Newspaper), 1972, No for Complacency, *Times of India* February 2, p4, col 1, editorial

Times of India (Newspaper), 1974, Across the Border, *Times of India* August 30, p4, col 1-2, editorial

Times of India (Newspaper), 1974, Unnecessary Risk, *Times of India* June 12, p4, col 1, editorial

Times of India (Newspaper), 1975, Accord in Kashmir, *Times of India* October 17, p4, col 1, editorial

Times of India (Newspaper), 1975, A New Chapter, *Times of India* February 26, p4, col 2, editorial

Times of India (Newspaper), 1975, New Deal for Kashmir, *Times of India* February 14, p4, col 1-2, editorial

Times of India (Newspaper), 1975, The Only Way, *Times of India* June 9, p4, Col. 1-2, editorial

Times of India (Newspaper), 1975, The Sheikh's Indecision, *Times of India* January 11, p4, col 1-2, editorial

Times of India (Newspaper), 1976, No Cause for Alarm, *Times of India* June 3, p4, col 1-2, editorial

Times of India (Newspaper), 1977, Article 370, *Times of India* June 6, p4, col 1, editorial

Times of India (Newspaper), 1977, The Only Way, *Times of India* March 29, p6, col 1-2, editorial

Times of India (Newspaper), 1977, Sheikh's Victory, *Times of India* July 6, p6, col 2, editorial

Times of India (Newspaper), 1977, Too Sweeping, *Times of India* November, p8, col 1-2, editorial

Times of India (Newspaper), 1977, Unfunny Farce, *Times of India* November 7, p6, col 1-2, editorial

Times of India (Newspaper), 1977, Up in the Air, *Times of India* October 17, p6, col 2, editorial

Times of India (Newspaper), 1978, Highly Odious, *Times of India*, September 26, p6, col 2, editorial

Times of India (Newspaper), 1978, Mattan Outrage, *Times of India* August 3, p6, col 2, editorial

Times of India (Newspaper), 1978, Secret Talks on Kashmir, *Times of India* July 20, p6, col 1, editorial

Times of India (Newspaper), 1978, Strife in Jammu, *Times of India* December 7, p6, col 2, editorial

Times of India (Newspaper), 1979, Deep Trouble, *Times of India* February 8, p6, col 1-2, editorial

Times of India (Newspaper), 1979, Pak-Occupied Kashmir, *Times of India* April 16, p6, col 1, editorial

Times of India (Newspaper), 1979, Playing with Fire, *Times of India* February 16, p6, col 2, editorial

Times of India (Newspaper), 1979, Redressing Imbalances, *Times of India* June 6, p6, col 1-2, editorial

Times of India (Newspaper), 1980, Curb This Menace, *Times of India* August 9, p6, col 1-2, editorial

Times of India (Newspaper), 1980, End of a Wrangle, *Times of India* October 10, p6, col 1-2, editorial

Times of India (Newspaper), 1980, End This Bickering *Times of India* July 26, p6, col 1-2, editorial

Times of India (Newspaper), 1980, Foreign, Money, *Times of India* September 4, p6, col 1-2, editorial

Times of India (Newspaper), 1980, Mischief in Kashmir, *Times of India* July 30, p6, col 1-2, editorial

Times of India (Newspaper), 1980, Strains in Kashmir, *Times of India* July 15, p6, col 1-2, editorial

Times of India (Newspaper), 1980, Unduly Harsh, *Times of India* August 28, p6, col 1-2, editorial

Times of India (Newspaper), 1981, A Momentous Step, *Times of India* July 28, p6, col 1-2, editorial

Times of India (Newspaper), 1981, On a Collision Couse, *Times of India* April 25, p8, col 1-2, editorial

Times of India (Newspaper), 1982, Farooq Shows Mettle, *Times of India* September 14, p6, col 7-8, editorial

Times of India (Newspaper), 1982, A Neat Solution, *Times of India* October 6, col 1-2, editorial

Times of India (Newspaper), 1982, Rift in the Family, *Times of India* August 20, p6, col 1-2, editorial

Times of India (Newspaper), 1983, Farooq under Attack, *Times of India* December 30, p8, col 1-2, editorial

Times of India (Newspaper), 1983, Handle with Care, *Times of India* October 21, p8, col 1-2, editorial

Times of India (Newspaper), 1983, An Historic Election, *Times of India* June 11, p8, col 1-2, editorial

Times of India (Newspaper), Kashmir Dissidence, *Times of India*, September 5, p8, col 1-2, editorial

Times of India (Newspaper), 1983, Risks in Kashmir, *Times of India* April 28, col 1-2, editorial

Times of India (Newspaper), 1983, Violence in the Valley, *Times of India* May 21, p8, col 1-2, editorial
Times of India (Newspaper), 1984, And New Kashmir, *Times of India* July 3, p5, col 1-2, editorial
Times of India (Newspaper), 1984, A Dirty Manoeuvre, *Times of India* August 1, p6, col 1-2, editorial
Times of India (Newspaper), 1984, From Bad to Worse, *Times of India* January 5, p6, col 1-2, editorial
Times of India (Newspaper), 1984, In Her Own Interest, *Times of India* January 28, p8, col 1-2, editorial
Times of India (Newspaper), 1984, Kashmir's Tragedy, *Times of India* January 17, p8, col 1-2, editorial
Times of India (Newspaper), 1984, Nip It in the Bud, *Times of India* May 25, p8, col 1-2, editorial
Times of India (Newspaper), 1984, Striking Unanimity, *Times of India* July 13, p6, col 1-2, editorial
Times of India (Newspaper), 1985, Uncertainty in Kashmir, *Times of India* November 4, p8, col 1-2, editorial
Times of India (Newspaper), 1985, Worse than Futile, *Times of India* January 12, p8, col 1-2, editorial
Times of India (Newspaper), 1986, Choice in Kashmir, *Times of India* March 5, p8, col 1-2, editorial
Times of India (Newspaper), 1986, Elections Are Best, *Times of India* July 31, p8, col 1-2, editorial
Times of India (Newspaper), 1986, Good Riddance, *Times of India* March 8, p8, col 1-2, editorial
Times of India (Newspaper), 1986, Manoeuvres in Kashmir, *Times of India* May 24, p8, col 1-2, editorial
Times of India (Newspaper), 1986, Playing Fair, *Times of India* September 10, p8, col 1-2, editorial
Times of India (Newspaper), 1986, Time for Decision, *Times of India* October 10, p8, col 1-2, editorial
Times of India (Periodical), 1988, Kashmir Portents, *Times of India* November 3, p6, col 1-2, editorial
Times of India (Periodical), 1989, Changes in Kashmir, *Times of India* May 2, p4, col 1-2, editorial
Times of India (Periodical), 1989, Dangerous Drift, *Times of India* August 17, p4, col 1-2, editorial
Times of India (Periodical), 1989, Kashmir again, *Times of India* April 7, p6, col 1-2, editorial

Times of India (Periodical), 1989, Offensive Measure, *Times of India* August 25, p6, col 1-2, editorial

Times of India (Periodical), 1989, Satanic Intent, *Times of India*, February 15, p6, col 1-2, editorial

Times of India (Periodical), 1989, Warning from Jammu, *Times of India* January 17, p6, col 1-2, ediotrial

Times of India (Newspaper), 1993, The Army in Kashmir, *Times of India* May 18, p8, col 1-2, editorial

Times of India (Newspaper), 1993, The Battle in Kashmir, *Times of India* July 27, p6, col 1-2; August 17, p10, col 1, editorial

Times of India (Newspaper), 1993, Death in the Valley, *Times of India* April 3, p10, col 1-2, editorial

Times of India (Newspaper), 1993, Glimmer of Hope, *Times of India* May 15, p10, col 1-2, editorial

Times of India (Newspaper), 1993, Guidelines in Kashmir, *Times of India* April 27, p10, col 1-2, editorial

Times of India (Newspaper), 1993, Kashmir's Demography, *Times of India* June 2, p10, col 1-3, editorial

Times of India (Newspaper), 1993, Line on Kashmir, *Times of India* May 1, p10, col 1-2, editorial

Times of India (Newspaper), 1993, Plans for Kashmir, *Times of India* March 12, p8, col 1-2, editorial

Times of India (Newspaper), 1993, Violence in Valley, *Times of India* April 14, p8, col 1-2, editorial

Times of India (Newspaper), 1993, Way out in Kashmir, *Times of India* April 29, p8, col 1-2, editorial

Tomar, D.S., 1974, *Rail Race to Jammu*, Metropolitan, New Delhi

Tripathi, Srinivas, 1988, Kashipur Comes into Limelight, *New Age* 36 (45) November 6, p7

Trivedi, V.R., 1990, *Facts about Kashmir*, Akashdeep, New Delhi, viii, 367p

Tuckerman, Anne Weill
see Weill-Tuckerman, Anne

Tyabji, A.A., 1981, Ladakh : World's Last Shangri-la? *Illustrated Weekly of India* 102 (7) February 22, p36-38

Tyndale-Biscoe, Cesil Earle, 1971, *Kashmir in Sunlight and Shade : A Description of the Beauties of the Country, the Life, Habits, and Humor of Its Inhabitants and an Account of the Gradual but Steady Rebuilding of Once Downtrodden People*, Sagar, New Delhi, 315p, originally printed 1922, Seeley, London

Umashankar, 1971, *Kashmir : Triumph and Tragedy*, IBH, New Delhi, 212p

Upadhyaya, Deendayal, 1964, Kashmir and East Bengal : Things Have Gone too Far, and Gone on Much too Long, *Organiser* 17 (26) February 3, p8

Upadhyaya, Deendayal, 1964, Kashmir in Doldrums, *Organiser* 17 (30) March 2, p3, editorial

Upadhyaya, Deendayal, 1964, No Truck with Abdullah, *Organiser* 17 (39) April 27, p3

Upadhyaya, Deendayal, 1964, Political Diary, *Organiser* 17 (51) July 20, p2; 19 (6) September 19, p3 +

Upadhyaya, Deendayal, 1965, We'd rather Quit U.N. than Quit Kashmir, *Organiser* 19 (7) September 26, p2

Urashima, Y., 1951, Kashmir, *East Europe and Soviet Russia*, 7, April 12, p12-14

Vaishnavi, Ragho Nath, 1992, Kashmir Problem : First Things First, *Other Side*, 101, October, p9-13

Vajpayee, Atal Behari
see also Rajagopalachan, C., 1968, Sri Vajpayee's Resolution

Vajpayee, Atal Behari, 1974, Vajpayee Warns P.M. against Bargaining with Abdullah, *Organiser* 27 (48) July 13, p3 +

Varma
see also Verma

Vas, E.A., *Without Baggage*, Natraj Pub, Dehradun, 173p

Vasisth, Satish, 1968, *Sheikh Abdullah : Then and Now*, Manlik Sahitya Prakashan, Delhi, 234p

Ved Kumari, 1975, Csemendra's View's about Education, *Vishveshvaranand Indological Journal* 13 (1-2) March-September, p411-414, footnotes

Venkateswaran, A.L., 1986, Pakistan Has No Locus Stand in Kashmir, *Organiser* 38 (16) August 31, p8-10

Verghese, B.G., 1965, *India Answers Pakistan*, Bombay

Verghese, B.G., 1965, No Second Partition, *United Asia* 17 (5) September-October, p332-337

Verma, Ganeshi Lal, 1984, Conversion of Hindu Temples in Kashmir, *Organiser* (Deepawali Number) 36 (26-27), p38-39 +

Verma, Ramesh, 1985, Education under Dogra Rule (1846-1947), *Educational Review* 91 (5-6) May-June, 86-87p

Vidya Bhushan, 1985, Permanent Residents of Jammu and Kashmir State and Their Fundamental Rights, *Indian Journal of Political*

Studies December, p86-94, bibliography

Vijay Kumar, 1954, *Anglo-American Plot against Kashmir*, People's Publishing House, Bombay, 216p

Vijay Kumari, 1974, (Book Review), *Journal of Indian History* 52 (2-3) August-December, p505-506
Review of the Book : Kaul, G.L., 1972, *Kashmir Then and Now : A Historical Survey*, Chronicle Pub, 311p

Virendra Narain, 1969, Kashmir and Major Powers : Study of Motives in Retrospect, *Political Science Review* 8 (3-4) July-December, p418-449, bibliography, footnotes

Vohra, S.G., 1981, Zanskar in Ladakh Badly Neglected, *Times of India* January 8, p6, col 7-8

von Hugel, Charles, 1984, Kashmir under Maharaja Ranjit Singh, Atlantic Pub, New Delhi, 128p

Wakefield, W., 1975, *History of Kashmir and the Kashmiris; The Happy Valley*, Seema Pub, Delhi, xii, 300

Wakhlu, Khem Lata and Wakhlu, O.N., 1993, *Kashmir, 1972 to 1991: Behind the White Curtain*, Konark Pub, New Delhi

Wakhlu, Khem Lata and Wakhlu, O.N., 1993, *Kidnapped : Forty Five Days with Militants in Kashmir*, Konark Pub, New Delhi

Wakhlu, O.N., *jt author*
see Wakhlu, Khem Lata and Wakhlu, O.N.

Waklu
see Wakhlu

Wani, G.M., 1981, Livestock Potential of Jammu and Kashmir, *Yojana* 24 (24) January 1, p26-29

Wani, Latif Abdul, *jt author*
see Qadri, A.S.M. and Wani, Latif Abdul

Wariar, A. Madhava
see Madhava Wariar, A.

Warikoo, K., 1989, *Central Asia and Kashmir : A Study in Conflict of Anglo-Russian Rivalry*, Gian Pub, New Delhi, 270p

Warikoo, Kulbushan, n.d., *Jammu and Kashmir and Ladakh : A Classified and Comprehensive Bibliography*, Sterling, New Delhi

Weekend Review (Periodical), 1968, Towards a Dialogue, *Weekend Review* 2 (15) March 16, p3, editorial

Weill-Tuckerman, Anne, 1965, Kashmir: The U.N.'s Perilous Change, *Nation* 201 (9) September 27, p151-153

Whakhlu
see Wakhlu

William, L.F.R., 1956,Contrasts in Kashmir, *Spectator* 196 (6669) April 20, p521-522

Wilson, H.H., 1958, *Hindu History of Kashmir*, Sushil Gupta, Calcutta

Wint, Guy, 1965, The Indo-Pakistan Conflict: British Feelings, *Listener* 74 (1903) September 16, p400

Yasin, Madhvi, 1969-70, Sources of the History of Kashmir, *Quarterly Review of Historical Studies* 9 (1), p33-40, bibliography

Yasin, Madhvi, 1970, Kalhana and His Rajatarangini, *Cultural Forum* 12 (3-4) April July, p47-51

Yasin, Madhvi, 1985, Trade and Commerce in Ladakh during the First Half of the Nineteenth Century, *India Past and Present* 2 (1), p21-31, footnotes

Yasin, Mohammad, 1972, *Raugabal and Other Mysteries of Kashmir*, Kesar Pub, Srinagar, 38p

Yasin, Mohammad and Rafiqi, A. Quiyum, eds, 1980, *History of the Freedom Struggle in Jammu and Kashmir*, Light and Life Pub, New Delhi, 256p

Yesshov, T., 1948, The Truth about Kashmir, *New Times* March 3, p24-29

Yojana (Periodical), 1973, Land Reform : Laws and Implementation, *Yojana* 17 (8) May 15, p325-326, editorial

Young-Husband, Francis Edward, 1970, *Kashmir*, Sagar Pub, New Delhi, xvi, 282p

Young-Husband, Francis Edward, 1973, *Northern Frontier of Kashmir*, Oriental Pub, Delhi, various pagination

Young-Husband, Francis Edward, 1986, *The Heart of a Continent*, Oxford Univeristy Press, Oxford

Zafar Ali (Begum)
see Ali, Begum Zafar

Zakaria, Fatma, R., 1983, From Sheikhdom to Indian State, *Times of India* (Sunday Review) July 10, p1, col 1-8

Zia-ul-Islam, 1948, Revolution in *Kashmir*, Pakistan Publications, Karachi, 141p

Zinkin, Taya, 1968, How Not to Solve the Kashmir Problem, *Asian Review* 2 (1) October, p41-44

Zubeida Hasan, *jt author*
see Sarwar Hasan, K. and Zubeida Hasan

Zutshi, Bupinder, 1987, Service Centres and Their Impact on Surrounding Hinter Lands : A Study of Kashmir Valley, *Annals of the National Association of Geographers, India* 7 (1) June, p37-50

Zutshi, U.K., 1986, *Emergence of Political Awakening in Kashmir*, Manohar Pub, New Delhi, 252p

Index

CICIL LIST

CONCEPTS IN COMMUNICATION, INFORMATICS & LIBRARIANSHIP

(CICIL)

General Editor: **S.P. AGRAWAL**

CICIL-1 Development of Library Services in India: Social Science Information
S.P. Agrawal Rs. 150

CICIL-2 Development of Documentation in India: Social Science Information
S.P. Agrawal Rs. 250

CICIL-3 UNESCO and Social Sciences: Retrospect and Prospect
S.P. Agrawal and **J.C. Aggarwal** Rs. 250

CICIL-4 INDIANA : A Bibliography of Bibliographical Sources
M.K. Jain Rs. 200

CICIL-5 Dimensions of Library and Information Science: Kaula Festschrift
V. Venkatappaiah (Eds.) Rs. 600

CICIL-6 Book Numbers: Some Indian Methods
M.P. Satija and **S.P. Agrawal** Rs. 100

CICIL-7 National Policy for University Libraries in India: Problems and Perspectives
N.B. Inamdar and **L.S. Ramaiah** (Ed.) Rs. 250

CICIL-8 Media Utilisation for the Development of Women and Children
B.S. Thakur and **Binod C. Agrawal** Rs. 150

CICIL-9 Terrorism: An Annotated Bibliography
Susheela Bhan (Ed.) Rs. 275

CICIL-10 Transnational Library Relations: The Indo-American Experience
M.B. Konnur Rs. 175

CICIL-11 Geography of Marketing and Commercial Activities in India (Documentation on Research Information)
R.S. Dixit Rs. 130

CICIL-12 Information India 1988: Global View
S.P. Agrawal and **J.C. Aggarwal** Rs. 200

CICIL-13 Women's Education in India: Historical Review, Present Status and Perspective Plan
S.P. Agrawal and **J.C. Aggarwal** Rs. 360

CICIL-14 Cultural Communication in India: Role and Impact of Phonograms
J.M. Ojha Rs. 220

CICIL-15 Second Historical Survey of Educational Development in India: Select Documents 1985-1989
S.P. Agrawal and **J.C. Aggarwal** Rs. 490

CICIL-16 Documentation Encyclopaedia of UNESCO and Education
J.C. Aggarwal and **S.P. Agrawal** Rs. 800 (set of 2 parts)

CICIL-17 Attitude Towards Information: A Study of Post-Graduate Teachers and Researchers in Social Sciences
N.G. Satish (in press)

CICIL-18 Librarianship and Bureaucratic Organisation: A Study in the Sociology of Library Profession in India
P.K. Jayaswal Rs. 175

CICIL-19 Literature Search
K.A. Isaac Rs. 150

CICIL-20 Child Education in India: Index to Scholarly Writings in Indian Educational Journals and Newspapers since independence
S.P. Agrawal and **Naresh Kanta** Rs. 100

CICIL-21 Lok Sabha and Vidhan Sabha Elections in India 1989 & 1990: Process and Results with Comparative Study of Manifestos
S.P. Agrawal and **J.C. Aggarwal** Rs. 250

CICIL-22 Islamic Studies in India: A Survey of Human, Institutional and Documentary Sources
Mohamed Taher Rs. 180

CICIL-23 Panchayati Raj: An Annotated Bibliography
N.B. Inamdar, N.G. Satish and **Anil Takalkar** 290

CICIL-24 Information India 1989-90: Global View
S.P. Agrawal and **J.C. Aggarwal** Rs. 500

CICIL-25 First Handbook of Psychological and Social Instruments
Udai Pareek and **T. Venkateswara Rao** Rs. 500

CICIL-26 Educational and Social Uplift of Backward Classes: At What Cost and How? Mandal Commission and After
S.P. Agrawal and **J.C. Aggarwal** Rs. 275

CICIL-27 Mass Media and New Horizons: Impact of TV & Video an Urban Milieu
H.R. Trivedi Rs. 180

CICIL-28 Indian Writings on Education : An Indicator to Indian Educational Journals Grouped by Subject Deseriptors 1979 to 1986 (in two parts)
S.P. Agarwal Rs. 900 (per set)

CICIL-29 Nation in Crisis
S.P. Agrawal and **J.C. Aggarwal** Rs. 200

CICIL-30 Information India 1990-91: Global View
S.P. Agrawal and **J.C. Aggarwal** Rs. 500

CICIL-31 Development of University Libraries in India after Independence
O.P. Gupta Rs. 270

CICIL-32 Handbook on Child : With Historical Background
Pramila Pandit Barooah Rs. 320

CICIL-33 Weaker Section in Indian Society : Undiscovered Past, Uncertain Present and Unpredictable Future : Index to Writings in Indian Scholarly Journals and 10 National Newspapers Classi-

fied under 1500 Descriptors 1886-1990
S.P. Agrawal and **Rajeev Kumar Sharma** Rs. 600

CICIL-34 Communication Informatics and Librarianship in India : An Introductory Guide to Publications Based on a Survey of Libraries in Capital City of India
S.P. Agrawal and **Pushpa Rani Sharma** Rs. 720

CICIL-35 Problems of Collection Development in Special Libraries
M.S. Sridhar Rs. 225

CICIL-36 National Information Resources for Social Sciences in India : Mobilisation, Dispersal and International Enhancement
S.P. Agrawal Rs. 225

CICIL-37 Modern History of Punjab : A Look Back into Ancient Peaceful Punjab Focusing Confrontation and Failures Leading to Present Punjab Problem, and a Peep Ahead : Relevant Select Documents
J.C. Aggarwal and **S.P. Agrawal** Rs. 400

CICIL-38 India Information Sources : Economics and Business
Kyllikki Ruokonen and Manohar Lal Rs.

CICIL-39 Educational Planning in India : With a Slant to Educational Financing and Administration, Vol. 1, Reports of Committees and Commissions, Five Year Plans, Statistical Tables
J.C. Aggarwal and **S.P. Agrawal** Rs. 650

CICIL-40 Integrated Library System : Two Case Studies : Latin America and India
Maria Luiza Rigo Pasquarelli, Rosaly Favero Krzyanowski, Ines Maria M. Imperatriz and **S.P. Agrawal** Rs. 160

CICIL-41 Social Science Information in India: Effort towards Bibliographical Control
S.D. Vyas Rs. 300

CICIL-42 Higher Education in India Since Independence: U.G.C. and Its Approach
O.P. Gupta Rs. 360

CICIL-43 Government and Politics in India: A Bibliographical Study of Contemporary Scenario Chronicling Rajiv Gandhi Era
S.P. Agrawal and **Rajeev Kumar Sharma** Rs. 500

CICIL-44 Second Handbook of Psychological and Social Instruments
D.M. Pestonjee Rs. 300

CICIL-45 Development/Digression Diary of India; 3D Companion Volume to Information India: 1990-91
S.P. Agrawal Rs. 200

CICIL-46 Development/Digression Diary of India; 3D Companion Volume to Information India: 1991-92
S.P. Agrawal Rs. 300

CICIL-47 Information India 1991-92: Global View
S.P. Agrawal and **J.C. Aggarwal** Rs. 500

CICIL-48 Committees and Commissions in India 1974, A Concept's Project, Compiled by a team of professionals guided by Virender

Kumar (Vol. 12) Rs. 450

CICIL-49 Committees and Commissions in India 1975, A Concept's Project, Compiled by a team of professionals guided by Virender Kumar (Vol. 13) Rs. 450

CICIL-50 Committees and Commissions in India 1976, A Concept's Project, Compiled by a team of professionals guided Virender Kumar (Vol. 14) Rs. 450

CICIL-51 Committees and Commissions in India 1977, A Concept's Project, Compiled by a team of professionals guided by Virender Kumar (Vol. 15) (in four parts) Rs. 450 each

CICIL-52 Committees and Commissions in India 1978, A Concept's Project, Compiled by a team of professionals guided by Virender Kumar (Vol. 16) (in two parts) Rs. 450 each

CICIL-53 Subject Guide to Communication, Informatics and Librarianship in India (Based on a Survey of Library Holdings in Capital City of India)
S.P. Agrawal and **Pushpa Rani Sharma** Rs. 400

CICIL-54 Restructurring of Library and Information Science Curriculum
A. Tejomurty Rs. 250

CICIL-55 Committees and Commissions in India 1979, A Concept's Project, Compiled by a team of professionals guided by Virender Kumar (Vol. 17) (in two parts) Rs. 450 each

CICIL-56 Committees and Commissions in India 1980, A Concept's Project, Compiled by a team of professionals guided by Virender Kumar (Vol. 18) (in two parts) Rs. 450 each

CICIL-57 Third Historical Survey of Educational Development in India
S.P. Agrawal and **J.C. Aggarwal** Rs. 700

CICIL-58 Model Library Legislation
Velaga Venkatappaiah Rs. 400

CICIL-59 Indian Library and Information Science Literature (1990-91)
Sewa Singh Rs. 525

CICIL-60 Librarianship and Library Science in India
Mohamed Taher and **Donald Gordon Davis, Jr.** Rs. 350

CICIL-61 Comprehensive Glossary for Library & Information Science by
D.P. Gupta Rs.300

CICIL-62 Information India 1992-93:
S.P. Agrawal and **J. C. Aggarwal** Rs. 500

CICIL-63 Automation of Libraries and Information Science
R.K. Shukla Rs. 250

CICIL-64 Modern History of Jammu and Kashmir
J.C. Aggarwal and **S.P. Agrawal** Rs. 1500 (per set of 2 vols.)

CICIL-65 Library and Information Science: Emerging Trends:
Sister M. Esperanza, A. C. Rs. 250

CICIL-66 Mental Retardation in India (A Bibliography)
S. Venkatesan and **V.G.D. Vepuri** Rs. 275

CICIL-67 Information Management in Health Science Libraries in India
R.P. Dixit (*Foreword* **Dr. Uton Muchtar Rafei**) Rs. 550

CICIL-68 Information Behaviour of Scientists and Engineers:
M.S. Sridhar Rs. 500